Working Through Conflict

Working Through Conflict

Strategies for Relationships, Groups, and Organizations

Second Edition

Joseph P. Folger
Temple University

Marshall Scott Poole
University of Minnesota

Randall K. Stutman
Temple University

HarperCollinsCollegePublishers

Aquisitions Editor: Daniel F. Pipp
Project Editor: Thomas R. Farrell
Design Supervisor: Mary Archondes
Cover Design: Heather A. Ziegler
Cover Photo: Kent Miles Photography
Production Manager/Assistant: Willie Lane/Sunaina Sehwani
Compositor: ComCom Division of Haddon Craftsmen, Inc.
Printer and Binder: R. R. Donnelley & Sons Company
Cover Printer: The Lehigh Press, Inc.

Working Through Conflict: Strategies for Relationships, Groups, and Organizations, Second Edition
Copyright © 1993 by HarperCollins College Publishers

Library of Congress Cataloging-in-Publication Data

Folger, Joseph P., (date)–
    Working through conflict : strategies for relationships, groups,
and organizations / Joseph P. Folger, Marshall Scott Poole, Randall
K. Stutman. — 2nd ed.
        p.   cm.
    Includes bibliographical references and index.
    ISBN 0-06-500658-5
    1. Social conflict.   2. Conflict (Psychology)   3. Conflict
management.   4. Social interaction.   5. Interpersonal conflict.
I. Poole, Marshall Scott, (date)–   . II. Stutman, Randall K., (date)–
. III. Title.
HM136.F56   1993   92-20474
303.S—dc20   CIP

95 9 8 7 6 5

To our parents:
Ed and Virginia, Ed and Helen, Bernie and Marge

Contents

List of Cases   xiii
Preface   xv

Introduction   Conflict and Interaction   1

The Potential of Conflict Interaction   1
  Case I.1: The Women's Hotline Case   2
Definition of Conflict   4
Arenas of Conflict Interaction   6
Productive and Destructive Conflict
    Interaction   8
Conflict as Interactive Behavior   10

Chapter 1   Traditional Perspectives on Conflict   12

Introduction   12
The Psychodynamic Perspective   13
Field Theory and the Concept of
    Climate   18
Experimental Gaming Research   21
The Human Relations Perspective and
    Conflict Styles   31
Intergroup Conflict Research   33
Conclusion   38

Chapter 2 Explaining Conflict Processes   40

Perspectivism and Conflict   40
The Role of Theories   43
  Case 2.1: Are Conflict Theories Just Common
    Sense?   44
Contemporary Perspectives   45
  The Cognitive Perspective   46
  The Interactional Perspective   47
  Cognitive and Interactional Theories   48
Contemporary Theories of Conflict   48
  Case 2.2: The Parking Lot Scuffle   49
  Verbal Aggressiveness Theory   50
  Case 2.3: Verbal Aggressiveness Theory and the
    Parking Lot Scuffle   51
  Attribution Theory   52
  Case 2.4: Attribution Theory and the Parking Lot
    Scuffle   53
  Social Influence Theory   54
  Case 2.5: Social Influence Theory and the Parking
    Lot Scuffle   55
  The Coordinated Management of Meaning   56
  Case 2.6: The Coordinated Management of
    Meaning and the Parking Lot Scuffle   58
  Confrontation Episodes Theory   59
  Case 2.7: Confrontation Episodes Theory and the
    Parking Lot Scuffle   63
  Reciprocity Theory   63
  Case 2.8: Reciprocity Theory and the Parking Lot
    Scuffle   65
Conclusion   65

Chapter 3 The Role of Communication in Conflict   68

Property 1: Moves and Countermoves/
  Power   69
Property 2: Self-Perpetuating Patterns   70
  Working Habits, Trained Incapacities, and Conflict
    72
  Goal-Emphasis   74
  Case 3.1: The Food Cooperative Newsletter   76
  Objective Standards   77
  Procedures   78
  Case 3.2: The Work Stoppage Decision   79

Property 3: Interaction Sequences   80
  Moving Through Differentiation and Integration
    82
  Differentiation and Escalation   83
  Differentiation and Avoidance   84
  Differentiation and Rigidity of Behavior   85
  Other Phase Models of Conflict   86
Property 4: The Direction of Conflict   89
  Case 3.3: The Columnist's Brown Bag   90
Property 5: Conflict Interaction and
  Relationships   92
Conclusion   93

Chapter 4   Power: The Architecture of Conflict   95

Power and the Emergence of Conflict   95
  Case 4.1: Budget Cuts in Academia   96
A Relational View of Power   99
  Case 4.2: The Eccentric Professor   103
Power and Conflict Interaction   106
  Case 4.3: The Creativity Development Committee
    106
The Use of Power in Conflict Tactics   111
The Balance of Power in Conflict   117
  The Dilemmas of Strength   118
  Case 4.4: The Copywriters Committee   119
  Case 4.5: Unbalanced Intimacy   121
  Case 4.6: Job Resignation at the Social Service
    Agency   122
  The Dangers of Weakness   123
Conclusion   125

Chapter 5   Face-Saving   127

The Dimensions of Face   128
Face-Loss   129
Face-Saving: A Threat to Flexibility in
  Conflict Interaction   130
  Case 5.1: The Professor's Decision   131
  Case 5.2: The Outspoken Member   132
  Case 5.3: The Controversial Member   133

Conflict Interaction as an Arena for
Face-Saving   136
Forms of Face-Saving in Conflict
Interaction   143
Resisting Unjust Intimidation   143
Refusing to Step Back from a Position   145
Suppressing Conflict Issues   147
Face-Giving   148
Conclusion   152

Chapter 6   Climate and Conflict Interaction   153

What Is Climate? A Definition   155
Case 6.1: Riverdale Halfway House   155
Climate Themes   159
Case 6.2: The Breakup at the Bakery   161
Climate and Conflict Interaction   163
The Effects of Climate on Conflict Interaction
163
The Effects of Interaction on Climate   165
Case 6.3: The Psychological Evaluation Unit   166
Case 6.3: The Psychological Evaluation Unit
Continued   167
Identifying Climates   174
Creating Constructive Climates   177
Conclusion   179

Chapter 7   Doing Conflict: Styles, Strategies, and Tactics   181

Conflict Styles   182
Describing Styles   182
The Meaning of Conflict Styles   184
Variations on Conflict Styles   186
Shifting Styles During Conflict Episodes   192
Case 7.1: College Roommates   192
Selecting Conflict Styles   195
Evidence on the Effectiveness of Conflict Styles
196
A Model for Selecting Conflict Styles   198
Conflict Tactics   202

Threats and Promises   215
Toughness   217
Tit for Tat   217
Coalition Formation   218
Issue Definition   221
Metacommunication   222
Integrative Tactics   223
Styles and Tactics in Practice   225
Case 7.2: The Would-Be Borrower   225
Conclusion   228

Chapter 8   Changing Conflict Dynamics   229

Self-Regulation of Conflict   230
Working with Power   231
Fostering Shared Power in Group and
Organizational Conflicts   233
Working with Trained Incapacities   237
Reframing Issues   240
Reframing Interaction   245
Working with Face-Saving Issues   246
Case 8.1: The Productivity/Performance Report
248
Working with Climate   249
Case 8.2: The Consulting Agency   250
Case 8.3: The Expanding Printing Company   250
Relations Among the Forces   252
Conclusion   253

Chapter 9   Third Party Intervention   254

Property 1: Moves and Countermoves/
Power   255
Third Party Mandate   256
Responsiveness to Emerging Interaction   260
Case 9.1: The Food Distribution Company   262
Case 9.2: The Radio Station   263
Property 2: Self-Perpetuating Patterns   267
Property 3: Interaction Sequences   270
Third Parties, Differentiation, and Integration
273
Property 4: The Direction of Conflict   278

Property 5: Conflict Interaction and
   Relationships   281
Conclusion   283
Post Script: The Technological Future   284
   Case 9.3: The Negotiation Support System   284

References   291
Credits   310
Index   311

List of Cases

I.1   The Women's Hotline Case   2

2.1   Are Conflict Theories Just Common
      Sense?   44
2.2   The Parking Lot Scuffle   49
2.3   Verbal Agressiveness Theory and the
      Parking Lot Scuffle   51
2.4   Attribution Theory and the Parking Lot
      Scuffle   53
2.5   Social Influence Theory and the Parking
      Lot Scuffle   55
2.6   The Coordinated Management of
      Meaning and the Parking Lot
      Scuffle   58
2.7   Confrontation Episodes Theory and the
      Parking Lot Scuffle   63
2.8   Reciprocity Theory and the Parking Lot
      Scuffle   65

3.1   The Food Cooperative Newsletter   76
3.2   The Work Stoppage Decision   79
3.3   The Columnist's Brown Bag   90

4.1   Budget Cuts in Academia   96
4.2   The Eccentric Professor   103
4.3   The Creativity Development
      Committee   106

4.4   The Copywriters Committee   119
4.5   Unbalanced Intimacy   121
4.6   Job Resignation at the Social Service
      Agency   122

5.1   The Professor's Decision   131
5.2   The Outspoken Member   132
5.3   The Controversial Member   133

6.1   Riverdale Halfway House   155
6.2   The Breakup at the Bakery   161
6.3   The Psychological Evaluation
      Unit   166
6.3   The Psychological Evaluation Unit
      Continued   167

7.1   College Roommates   192
7.2   The Would-Be Borrower   225

8.1   The Productivity/Performance
      Report   248
8.2   The Consulting Agency   250
8.3   The Expanding Printing
      Company   250

9.1   The Food Distribution Company   262
9.2   The Radio Station   263
9.3   The Negotiation Support System   284

Preface

CONFLICT AS A COMMUNICATION PHENOMENON

Interest in conflict as a communication-based phenomenon has increased markedly in the years since the first edition of *Working Through Conflict*. Developments in research and practice have contributed to this wave of interest. In research, more and more work starts from the premise that conflict *is* communication. This has meant an increased focus on process, language use, and the structure of discourse. Studies of how people argue, produce message strategies, or intervene in conflict have all contributed to our understanding of how conflict unfolds. Insights from this work have illustrated the importance of understanding conflict as a communication phenomenon. Increasingly, conflict is seen not as something parties **enter** but as something they **create**—as a series of interdependent communicative contributions.

ALTERNATIVE DISPUTE RESOLUTION MANAGEMENT

In practice, those who encounter conflicts daily in hospitals, neighborhoods, courtrooms, playgrounds, organizations, and decision-making groups are becoming increasingly familiar with a range of intervention options—a range that has widened considerably over the last decade. Patient and client representatives, mediators, facilitators, conciliators, and ombudspersons have been introduced in a diverse set of conflict settings, giving further impetus to what has become known as the alternative dispute resolution movement. These attempts to use third parties to manage conflict through nonadversarial means heighten an awareness of communication processes. As different forms of conflict intervention are tried, the malleability of conflict **interaction** becomes increasingly apparent. Things go differently when different intervention methods are tried. People see how sensitive conflicts are to forces such as working habits, power, climate, face-saving, and reframing—forces known to alter communication in friendships, families, groups, and organizations.

GOAL AND STRUCTURE OF SECOND EDITION

Our goal in this second edition of *Working Through Conflict* is to strengthen the framework we constructed initially, a framework that allows us to capture recent thinking in research and practice about conflict as a process of social interaction. To get there, we have expanded the book considerably. We have broadened the theoretical purview by contrasting traditional perspectives on conflict with current communication-oriented perspectives (Chapters 1 and 2). We have developed the key properties of conflict interaction, making these properties the sole focus of Chapter 3 and adding a property that describes the episodic structure of conflict. We have moved coverage of strategies and tactics to a separate chapter (Chapter 7) and broadened the discussions of face (Chapter 5) and self-regulation (Chapter 8). Finally, we have added a new chapter devoted to third party intervention (9). This chapter uses the key properties of conflict interaction introduced in Chapter 3 to show how a communication perspective furthers our understanding of third party work.

We have also broadened the scope of the book. We give equal weight to conflicts occurring in a wide range of arenas, from intimate relationships and friendships to group, intergroup, organizational, and negotiation settings. This added breadth makes the book suitable as a primary text for courses in conflict and conflict management, as well as a useful supplement to courses that devote substantial attention to conflict or third party work.

We have kept the case examples central throughout the chapters. These cases illustrate the theoretical material. They also demonstrate the complexity of real-life conflicts and stimulate discussion of nuances, alternatives, and ethics. Often these cases raise as many questions as they answer. We find them most useful when they spark discussion of ideas not written about on these pages.

The title of the book is an intentional double entendre. Since its major emphasis is on communication patterns people use when attempting to manage conflict, we hope that the book helps people successfully **work through** difficult conflicts. The book is also built on the assumption that people can complete successful work **through the emergence of conflict**. We hope this book encourages and assists people to confront their conflicts and to work through them creatively, rather than suppressing or "resolving" conflicts.

ACKNOWLEDGMENTS

Thanks are still due to those who helped make the first edition possible. We owe our greatest debt to our colleagues at the Center for Conflict Resolution in Madison, Wisconsin. We are very grateful to Lonnie Weiss for her insight and help with our analyses. We also thank Syd Bernard, Jim Carrilon, Jay Herman, Jan Shubert, Rick Sloan, Dennis Smith, and Kathy Zoppi for reacting to parts or all of the manuscript. In addition, we turned to Betsy Densmore, Robert Everett, and Tommy Vines for an evaluation of the manuscript from a managerial perspective. For extremely helpful manuscript reviews of the first edition, we thank Wayne Beach, Robert J. Doolittle, Dennis Gouran, Thomas Harris, Linda Putnam, Gale Richards, Michael Sunnafrank, and Paul Yelsma. We also thank Linda Klug, Jean Kebis, and Wayne Beach for supplying the transcript of interaction in Chapter 6.

This revised edition is the product of many valuable comments and contributions from students and instructors. We are grateful to the students in our classes who became enthusiastic about documenting and analyzing real-life conflicts. They contributed several detailed cases included in this edition. We are also indebted to those who provided feedback and suggestions for revisions, including Tom Biesecker, University of Kansas; Bruce Gronbeck, University of Iowa; David A. Frank, University of Oregon; Dale Hample, Western Illinois University; Sara E. Newell, West Chester University; Stella Ting-Toomey, Arizona State University; and Hal R. Witteman, The Pennsylvania State University. We are particularly grateful to Charles R. Conrad, Texas A&M University; Tricia Jones, Temple University; Cynthia Stohl, Purdue University; and Shirley A. Van Hoeven, Western Michigan University, who offered insightful commentary on earlier drafts of this edition. Janet Yeddes and Cathie Given provided valuable assistance in preparing the manuscript. The excellent editorial and production staff at HarperCollins has made the technical work on this book almost painless. Special thanks to Melissa Rosati, Dan Pipp, Judith Anderson, and Thomas Farrell, who brought the manuscript through production.

JOSEPH P. FOLGER
MARSHALL SCOTT POOLE
RANDALL K. STUTMAN

Introduction

Conflict and Interaction

THE POTENTIAL OF CONFLICT INTERACTION

It is often said that conflict can be beneficial. Trainers, counselors, consultants, and authors of conflict textbooks point to the potential positive functions of conflict: conflicts allow important issues to be aired; they produce new and creative ideas; they release built-up tension; they can strengthen relationships; they can cause groups and organizations to reevaluate and clarify goals and missions; they can also stimulate social change to eliminate inequities and injustice. These advantages, and others, are raised in order to justify conflict as a normal, healthy occurrence and to stress the importance of understanding and handling it properly.

But why must such an argument be made? Everyone has been in conflicts, and almost everyone would readily acknowledge at least some benefits. Why then do social scientists, popular authors, and consultants persist in attempting to persuade us of something we already know? Perhaps the answer can be found by studying an actual conflict. The twists and turns of a specific case often reveal why negative views of conflict persist. Consider the fairly typical case study of a conflict in a small work group in Case I.1.

Case I.1   # The Women's Hotline Case

Women's Hotline is a rape and domestic crisis center in a medium-sized city; the center employs seven full- and part-time workers. The workers, all women, formed a cohesive unit and made all important decisions as a group; there were no formal supervisors. The Hotline had started as a voluntary organization and had grown by capturing local and federal funds. The group remained proud of its roots in a democratic, feminist tradition.

The atmosphere at the Hotline was rather informal. The staff saw each other as friends, but there was an implicit understanding that people should not have to take responsibility for each other's cases. Since the Hotline's work was draining, having to handle each other's worries could create an unbearable strain. This norm encouraged workers to work on their own and keep problems to themselves.

The conflict arose when Diane, a new counselor who had only six months' experience, was involved in a very disturbing incident. One of her clients was killed by a man who had previously raped her. Diane had trouble dealing with this incident. She felt guilty about it; she questioned her own ability and asked herself whether she might have been able to prevent this tragedy. In the months following, Diane had increasing difficulty in coping with her feelings and began to feel that her co-workers were not giving her the support she needed. Diane had no supervisor to turn to, and, although her friends outside the Hotline were helpful, she did not believe they could understand the pressure as well as her co-workers.

Since the murder, Diane had not been able to work to full capacity, and she began to notice some resentment from the other counselors. She felt the other staff were more concerned about whether she was adding to their work loads than whether she was recovering from the traumatic incident. Although Diane did not realize it at the time, most of the staff felt she had been slow to take on responsibilities even before her client was killed. They thought Diane had generally asked for more help than other staff members and that these requests were adding to their own responsibilities. No one was willing to tell Diane about these feelings after the incident, because they realized she was very disturbed. After six months, Diane believed she could no longer continue to work effectively. She felt pressure from the other women at the center, and she was still shaken by the tragedy. She requested two weeks off with pay in order to get away from the work situation for a while, reduce the stress she felt, and come back with renewed energy. The staff, feeling that Diane was slacking off, denied this request. They responded by outlining, in print, what they saw as the responsibilities of a full-time staff worker. Diane was angry when she realized her request had been denied, and she decided to file a formal work grievance.

Diane and the staff felt bad about having to resort to such a formal, adversarial procedure. No staff member had ever filed a work grievance, and the group was embarrassed by its inability to deal with the problem on a more informal basis. This added to tension between Diane and the staff. The staff committee who received Diane's grievance suggested that they could handle the problem in a less formal way if both Diane and the staff were willing to call in a neutral third party mediator. Everyone agreed that this suggestion had promise, and a third party was invited to a meeting where the entire staff would address the issue.

At this meeting, the group faced a difficult task. Each member offered reactions they had been unwilling to express previously. The staff made several pointed criticisms of Diane's overall performance. Diane expressed doubts about the staff's willingness to help new workers or to give support when it was requested. Although this discussion was often tense, it was well directed. At the outset of the meeting, Diane withdrew her formal complaint. This changed the definition of the problem from the immediate work grievance to the question of what levels of support were required for various people to work effectively in this difficult and emotionally draining setting. Staff members shared doubts and fears about their own inadequacies as counselors and agreed that something less than perfection was acceptable. The group recognized that a collective inertia had developed and that they had consistently avoided giving others the support they needed to deal with difficult rape cases. They acknowledged, however, the constraints on each woman's time; each worker could handle only a limited amount of stress. The group recognized that some level of mutual support was essential and felt they had fallen below that level over the past year and a half. One member suggested that any staff person should be able to ask for a "debriefing contract" whenever they felt they needed help or support. These contracts would allow someone to ask for ten minutes of another person's time to hear about a particularly disturbing issue or case. The group members adopted this suggestion because they saw it could allow members to seek help without overburdening each other. The person who was asked to listen could assist and give needed support without feeling that she had to "fix" another worker's problem. Diane continued to work at the center and found that her abilities and confidence increased as the group provided the support she needed.

This is a "textbook" case in effective conflict management because it resulted in a solution that all parties accepted. It does, however, exhibit several features in common with even the most destructive conflicts and could easily have turned in a destructive direction. First, the situation was **tense** and **threatening**. The weeks during which the incident evolved were an extremely difficult time for the workers. Even for "old hands" at negotiation, conflicts are often unpleasant and frightening. Second, participants experienced a great deal of **uncertainty**. They were unable to understand many aspects of the conflict and how their behavior affected it. Conflicts are confusing; our actions can have consequences quite different from those we intend because the situation is more complicated than we assume. Diane did **not** know her co-workers thought she was slacking. So when she asked for time off, she was surprised at their refusal, and her own angry reaction nearly started a major battle. Third, the situation was extremely **fragile**. If even one worker had acted differently at several crucial points, the conflict might have gone differently. If, for example, the staff had chosen to fire Diane, the conflict might have been squelched, or it might have festered and undermined relationships among the remaining members. If, on the other hand, Diane had won allies, the staff might have split over the issue and ultimately dissolved the Hotline.

The members of this group were walking a tightrope throughout the conflict. Luckily, they managed to avoid a fall. The tension, unpleasantness, uncertainty, and fragility of conflict situations make them hard to face. Because these problems make it difficult to deal with issues in a constructive way, conflicts are often terminated by force, by uncomfortable suppression of the issues, or by exhaustion after a prolonged fight—all outcomes that leave at least one party dissatisfied. Entering a conflict is often like making a bet against the odds: you can win big if it turns out well, but so many things can go wrong that few people are willing to chance it. It is no wonder then that many writers feel a need to reassure us. They feel compelled to remind us of the positive outcomes of conflict because all too often the destructive results are all that people remember.

We believe that the key to working through conflict is not to minimize its disadvantages, or even to emphasize its positive functions, but to accept both and to try to understand **how** conflicts move in destructive or productive directions. Such an understanding requires a conception of conflict that calls for a careful **analysis of both the specific behaviors and interaction patterns involved in conflict and the forces that influence these patterns**. Moreover, we can only grasp the fragility of conflicts and the effects that tension and misunderstandings have in their development if we work at the level at which conflicts unfold—specific interactions among the parties.

DEFINITION OF CONFLICT

Conflict is **the interaction of interdependent people who perceive incompatible goals and interference from each other in achieving those goals** (Hocker & Wilmot, 1985). This definition has the advantage of providing a much clearer focus than definitions that view conflict simply as disagreement, as competition, or as the presence of incompatible interests (Fink, 1968). The most important feature of conflict is that it is based in **interaction**. Conflicts are constituted and sustained by the behaviors of the parties involved and their reactions to one another. Conflict interaction takes many forms and each form presents special problems and requires special handling. The most familiar type of conflict interaction is marked by shouting matches or open competition where each party tries to defeat the other. But conflicts can also be more subtle. Often people react to conflict by suppressing it. They interact in ways that allow them to avoid confrontation, either because they are afraid of possible changes the conflict may bring about or because the issue "isn't worth fighting over." This response is as much a part of the conflict process as the open struggles most of us associate with conflict. This book deals with the whole range of responses to conflict and how those responses affect the development of conflicts. We believe conflicts can best be understood and managed by concentrating on specific behavioral patterns and the forces shaping them.

People in conflict perceive that they have incompatible goals or interests and that others are a source of interference in achieving their goals. The key word here is "perceive." Regardless of whether goals are actually incompatible or if the parties believe them to be incompatible, conditions are ripe for conflict. Regardless of whether an employee really stands in the way of a co-worker or if the co-worker interprets the employee's behavior as interference, the co-worker may move against her or feel compelled to skirt certain issues. Thus the parties' interpretations and beliefs play a key role in conflicts. This does not mean that goals are always conscious as conflict develops. People can act without a clear sense of what their goals or interests are (Coser, 1961). Sometimes people find themselves in strained interactions but are unsure why. They realize afterward what their implicit goals were and how their goals were incompatible with those held by others (Hawes & Smith, 1973). Communication looms large because of its importance in shaping and maintaining the perceptions that guide conflict behavior.

Indeed, communication problems are sometimes the cause of conflicts. Tension or irritation can result from misunderstandings that occur when people interact with very different communication styles (Tannen, 1986; Grimshaw, 1990). One person's inquisitive style may be seen by someone else as intrusive and rude. One person's attempt to avoid stepping on another's toes may be seen by someone else as distant and cold. Style differences create difficult problems that are often related to differences in cultural backgrounds (Kochman, 1981). We do not, however, agree with the old adage "most conflicts are actually communication problems." The vast majority of conflicts would not exist without some real difference of interest. This difference may be hard to uncover, it may be redefined over time, and occasionally it may be trivial, but it is there nonetheless. Communication processes constitute conflicts and can easily exacerbate them, but they are rarely the sole source of the difficulty.

Conflict interaction is colored by the **interdependence** of the parties. For a conflict to arise, the behavior of one or both parties must have consequences for the other. So, by definition, the parties involved in conflict are interdependent. The conflict at the Hotline would not have occurred if Diane's behavior had not irritated the other workers and if their response had not threatened Diane's position. Furthermore, any action taken in response to the conflict affects both sides. The decision to institute a "debriefing contract" required considerable change by everyone. If Diane had been fired, that too would have affected the other workers; they would have had to "cover" Diane's cases and come to terms with themselves as co-workers who could be accused of being unresponsive or insensitive.

But interdependence implies more than this: when parties are interdependent they can potentially aid or interfere with each other. For this reason, conflicts are always characterized by a mixture of incentives to cooperate and to compete. Any comment during conflict interaction can be seen either as an attempt to advance the speaker's own interest or as an attempt to promote a good outcome for all involved. A party may believe that having their own point accepted is more important, at least for the moment, than proposing a mutually beneficial outcome. When Diane asked for two weeks off, she was probably thinking not of the group's best interest but of her own needs. In other cases, a participant may advance a proposal designed to benefit everyone, as when the staff member suggested the "debriefing contract." In still other instances, a participant may offer a comment with a cooperative intent, but others may interpret it as one that advances individual interests. Regardless of whether the competitive motive is intended by the speaker or assigned by other members, the interaction unfolds from that point under the assumption that the speaker may value only his/her own interests. Subsequent interaction is further likely to undermine incentives to cooperate and is also likely to weaken members' recognition of their own interdependence. The balance of incentives to compete or cooperate is important in determining the direction the conflict interaction takes.

ARENAS OF CONFLICT INTERACTION

Conflict occurs in almost all social settings. Most of us learn at a very young age that conflicts arise in families, playgrounds, classrooms, Little League fields, ballet centers, scout troops, and cheerleading teams. As we enter more complex relationships and become involved in more diverse and public settings, we often find that conflicts remain remarkably similar to those in our early lives. (Indeed, some argue that our early experiences shape our involvement in conflict throughout our lives.) As adults, we find conflict as we enter casual work relationships or emotionally intense, intimate relationships. We find it in close friendships or in political rivalries. We encounter it as we interact in decision-making groups, small businesses, large corporations, church organizations, and doctors' offices. Given the diversity of conflicts we typically encounter, what often is of most concern is how much is at stake in any conflict. We assess whether conflicts are pedestrian or profound, whether their effects on our lives will be trivial or tremendous, whether they are major or minor maelstroms. Our estimate of the significance of any conflict often influences the time and effort we invest in strategizing or in developing safeguards or fallbacks.

We examine a broad range of conflicts in this book. Our analysis is aimed at clarifying how conflicts emerge and unfold in three general settings. Throughout the chapters, we will examine conflicts that emerge in **interpersonal** contexts, that is, conflicts that occur between people who have some ongoing relationship and are interdependent in some sense (Putnam & Poole, 1987; Roloff, 1987a). Included in this arena are conflicts that occur between husbands and wives, or among siblings, friends, roommates, or co-workers, as well as between landlords and tenants, or supervisors and employees. These conflicts tell us a great deal about styles of conflict interaction, emotional and irrational impulses, and the diversity of resources people exchange in close or long-term relationships.

We will also analyze conflicts that occur among **groups** of people who share long-term interdependence, such as families. This arena includes work groups, small businesses, classes, clubs, juries, and even therapy or consciousness raising groups. Since much work is done in groups, this arena has been studied extensively and offers a wide range of conflict situations for analysis. These conflicts offer insights about decision-making procedures, group cohesion, the influence of climates, coalitions, working habits, and the distribution of power.

Finally, we will focus on conflicts that occur in **intergroup** settings. The focus here is on aggregates or collections of people, rather than individuals (Putnam & Poole, 1987). This arena includes conflicts among different units of an organization, political action groups, or ethnic and cultural groups. In these conflicts, issues of group identity, stereotyping, and ideologies often come to the fore.

These arenas differ in several ways. One obvious difference is in the number of people typically involved in a conflict. **Interpersonal** conflicts are characterized by face-to-face exchanges among a small number of people. The parties may belong to a larger group or organization (e.g., siblings are part of the same family), but the divisive issues are ones that the parties view as centrally their own. The conflict is played out between them and not in the group as a whole. **Group** conflicts involve a number of people who are members of some larger unit. The parties know each other, have interacted with each other in meetings or work settings, and attempt to reach decisions as a group. The divisive issues in these conflicts are central to the group as a whole. **Intergroup** conflicts often involve two or more large groups of people who represent some political or ideological stance or who are members of cultural, community, action, or neighborhood groups.

As the number of people involved in a conflict increases, important features of the conflict interaction change as well. For example, in interpersonal conflicts, people usually speak for themselves. In group or intergroup conflicts, spokespersons, representatives, or various counselors (such as attorneys, union representatives, presidents of organizations) are more likely to speak for the collective. In addition, we will see how the group or organizational climate also becomes important as the number of people in a conflict increases.

These arenas of conflict also differ in the type of **interdependence** that typically exists among the parties. The resources parties hold, which make each necessary for the other, shift across these contexts. In **interpersonal** relationships, parties depend on each other for a wide range of emotional, psychological, and material resources (Levinger, 1979; Roloff, 1981). Among the resources exchanged in interpersonal relationships are: emotional support; images one holds of oneself as a talented, generous, loving, sensuous, or loyal person; financial security; and ability to meet physical needs. These resources are at stake when conflicts emerge in interpersonal relationships. In **group** and **intergroup** conflicts, the range of interdependence is generally narrower. In task-oriented groups, people are dependent on each other for achieving the goals the group has set for itself, for financial security (if the group provides income for members), and for a person's professional or public identity (e.g., images parties hold of themselves as competent, fair-minded, cooperative, etc.). In intergroup relationships, members are dependent on each other for the environment, or the division of a particular product market, or for group identity (e.g., the sense of self one has as a "Christian," a "liberal," a "Republican"). The different types of resources important in each arena make the use of power different in each, as we will see.

Although these arenas differ in important ways, they are similar in one important sense: **interaction is central to conflicts that occur across these settings**. Regardless of the number of parties involved or the type of interdependence among them, conflict unfolds as a series of moves and reactions that are premised on people's perceptions, expectations, and strategies. Because of this fundamental similarity, many of the principles of conflict that we will examine apply across these arenas. As Putnam and Folger (1988, p. 350) have put it: "Theoretical principles apply across (conflict) contexts because interaction processes form the foundation of conflict management. Fundamental to all conflicts are the series of actions and reactions, moves and countermoves, planning of communication strategies, perceptions, and interpretations of messages that directly affect substantive outcomes."

Because interaction is the key feature of conflict across arenas, many of the theoretical principles we examine in this book do not apply to one particular conflict setting. For example, various **forms** of conflict interaction emerge in all three settings. Forms of interaction are patterns of actions and reactions or moves and counter-moves that parties engage in during a conflict. **Violent exchanges** are a form of interaction that can occur in interpersonal, intragroup, or intergroup conflicts. Similarly, **negotiation** is a form of interaction in which parties engage in any of these settings. **Negotiation** (sometimes referred to as **bargaining**) occurs when parties agree to explicit or implicit rules for exchanging proposals or concessions in order to reach a mutual agreement (Putnam & Poole, 1987). People often think of negotiation as a separate arena because labor–management negotiations are the most prominent example of negotiations in most people's minds. However, negotiations can occur in any of the arenas. Husbands and wives can negotiate their divorce agreements, a professor and student can negotiate a grade, environmental groups can negotiate a land-use policy, or neighborhood groups can negotiate historical preservation standards.

There are other insights, besides those centering on forms of interaction, that cross arenas of conflict covered in this book. We will see, for example, how most conflicts are concerned with power because power is integral to all forms of interdependence among people. We will also see how, across arenas, conflict influences relationships and climate is central to the way conflict unfolds.

PRODUCTIVE AND DESTRUCTIVE CONFLICT INTERACTION

As we have noted, people often associate conflict with negative outcomes. However, there are times when conflicts must be addressed regardless of the apprehension they create. When differences exist and the issues are important, suppression of conflict is often more dangerous than facing it. The psychologist Irving Janis points to a number of famous political disasters, such as the Bay of Pigs invasion and the failure to anticipate the Japanese attack on Pearl Harbor, where poor decisions can be traced to the repression of conflict by key decision-making groups (Janis, 1972). The critical question is: what forms of conflict interaction will yield the obvious benefits without tearing a relationship, a group, or an organization apart?

Years ago the sociologist Lewis Coser (1956) distinguished **realistic** from **nonrealistic** conflicts. **Realistic** conflicts are conflicts based in disagreements over the means to an end or over the ends themselves. In realistic conflicts, the interaction focuses on the substantive issues the participants must address in order to resolve their underlying incompatibilities. **Nonrealistic** conflicts are expressions of aggression in which the sole end is to defeat or hurt the other. Participants in nonrealistic conflicts serve their own interests by undercutting those of the other party. Coser argues that because nonrealistic conflicts are oriented toward the expression of aggression, force and coercion are the means for resolving these disputes. Realistic conflicts, on the other hand, foster a wide range of resolution techniques—force, negotiation, persuasion, even voting—because they are oriented toward the resolution of some substantive problem. Although Coser's analysis oversimplifies things somewhat, it is insightful and suggests important contrasts between productive and destructive conflict interaction (Deutsch, 1973). What criteria could one use to evaluate whether a conflict is productive? In large part, productive conflict interaction depends on flexibility. In constructive conflicts, members engage in a wide variety of behaviors ranging from coercion and threat to negotiation, joking, and relaxation in order to reach an acceptable solution. In contrast, parties in destructive conflicts are likely to be much less flexible because their goal is more narrowly defined: they are trying to defeat each other. Destructive conflict interaction is likely to have protracted, uncontrolled escalation cycles or prolonged attempts to avoid issues. In productive conflict, on the other hand, the interaction in the group will change direction often. Short cycles of escalation, de-escalation, avoidance, and constructive work on the issue are likely to occur as the participants attempt to manage the conflict.

Consider the Hotline case. The group exhibited a wide range of interaction styles, from the threat of a grievance to the cooperative attempt to reach a mutually satisfactory solution. Even though Diane and the members engaged in hostile or threatening interaction, they did not persist in this mode, and when the conflict threatened to escalate, they called in a third party. The conflict showed all the hallmarks of productive interaction. In a destructive conflict the members might have responded to Diane's grievance by suspending her, and Diane might have retaliated by suing or by attempting to discredit the center in the local newspaper. Her retaliation would have hardened others' positions and they might have fired her, leading to further retaliation. Alternatively, the Hotline conflict might have ended in destructive avoidance. Diane might have hidden her problem and the other members might have consciously or unconsciously abetted her by changing the subject when the murder came up or by avoiding talking to her at all. Diane's problem would probably have grown worse, and she might have had to quit. The center would then revert back to "normal" until the same problem surfaced again. While the damage done by destructive avoidance is much less serious in this case than that done by destructive escalation, it is still considerable: the Hotline loses a good worker, and the seeds of future losses remain. In both cases, it is not the behaviors themselves that are destructive—neither avoidance nor hostile arguments are harmful in themselves—but rather the **inflexibility** of the parties that locks them into escalation or avoidance cycles.

In productive conflicts, interaction is guided by the belief that all factions can attain important goals (Deutsch, 1973). The interaction reflects a sustained effort to bridge the apparent incompatibility of positions. This is in marked contrast to destructive conflicts where the interaction is premised on participants' belief that one side must win and the other must lose. Productive conflict interaction results in a solution satisfactory to all and produces a general feeling that the parties have gained something (e.g., a new idea, greater clarity of others' positions, a stronger sense of solidarity). In some cases, the win–lose orientation of destructive conflict stems from fear of losing. People attempt to defeat alternative proposals because they believe that if their positions are not accepted they will lose resources, self-esteem, or the respect of others. In other cases, win–lose interaction is sparked, not by competitive motives, but by the parties' fear of **working through** a difficult conflict. Groups that rely on voting to reach decisions often call for a vote when discussion becomes heated and the members do not see any other immediate way out of a hostile and threatening situation. Any further attempt to discuss the alternatives or to pursue the reasons behind people's positions seems risky. A vote can put a quick end to threatening interaction, but it also induces a win–lose orientation that can easily trigger destructive cycles. Members whose proposal is rejected must resist a natural tendency to be less committed to the chosen solution and may try to "even the score" in future conflicts. Productive conflict interaction is sometimes competitive; both parties must stand up for their own positions if a representative outcome is to be attained. A great deal of tension and hostility may result as people struggle with the conflict. Although parties in productive conflicts hold to their positions strongly, they are also open to movement when convinced that such movement will result in the best decision. The need to preserve power, save face, or make the opponent look bad does not stand in the way of change. In destructive conflict, parties often become polarized, and the defense of a nonnegotiable position becomes more important than working out a viable solution. This description of productive and destructive conflict interaction is obviously an idealization. We rarely observe a conflict that exhibits all the constructive or destructive qualities just mentioned; indeed, many conflicts exhibit both productive and destructive interaction. We maintain, however, that better conflict management will result if parties can sustain productive conflict interaction patterns.

CONFLICT AS INTERACTIVE BEHAVIOR

Conflict is, by nature, interactive. It is never wholly under one person's control (Kriesberg, 1973). The other party's reactions and the person's anticipation of the other's response are extremely important. Any comment made during a conflict is made with some awareness or prediction about the likely response it will elicit. This predictive basis for any move in interaction creates a strong tendency for conflict interaction to become cyclic or repetitive. Suppose Robert criticizes Susan, an employee under his supervision, for her decreasing productivity. Susan may accept the criticism and explain why her production is down, thus reducing the conflict and moving toward a solution. Susan may also shout back and sulk, inviting escalation, or she may choose to say nothing and avoid the conflict, resulting in no improvement in the situation. Once Robert has spoken to Susan and she has responded, the situation is no longer totally under Robert's control: his next behavior will be a response to Susan's reaction. Robert's behavior, and its subsequent meaning to Susan, is dependent on the interchange between them. A behavioral cycle of initiation–response–counterresponse results from the conflict interchange. This cycle cannot be understood by breaking it into its parts, into the individual behaviors of Robert and Susan. It is more complex than the individual behaviors and, in a real sense, has a "life" of its own. The cycle can be self-reinforcing, if, for example, Susan shouts back at Robert, Robert tries to discipline her, Susan becomes more recalcitrant, and so on, in an escalating spiral. The cycle could also limit itself if Robert responds to Susan's shouting with an attempt to calm her and listen to her side of the story. Conflict interaction cycles acquire a momentum of their own. They tend in a definite direction—toward escalation, toward avoidance and suppression, or toward productive work on the conflict. The situation becomes even more complex when we remember that Robert formulated his criticism on the basis of his previous experience with Susan. That is, Robert's move is based on his perception of Susan's likely response. In the same way, Susan's response is based not only on Robert's criticism, but on her estimate of Robert's likely reaction to her response. Usually such estimations are "intuitive"—that is, they are not conscious—but sometimes parties plot them out ("If I shout at Robert, he'll back down and maybe I won't have to deal with this"). They are always based on the parties' perceptions of each other, on whatever theories or beliefs each holds about the other's reactions. Because these estimates are only intuitive predictions, they may be wrong to some extent. They will be revised as the conflict unfolds, and this revision will largely determine what direction the conflict takes. The most striking thing about this predictive process is the extraordinary difficulties it poses for attempts to understand the parties' thinking. When Susan responds to Robert on the basis of her prediction of Robert's answer, from the outside we see *Susan* making an estimate of *Robert's* estimate of what she means by her response. If Robert reflects on Susan's intention before answering, we observe *Robert's* estimate of *Susan's* estimate of *his* estimate of what *Susan* meant. This string of estimates can increase without bounds if we try to pin down the originating point, and after a while the prospect is just as dizzying as a hall of mirrors.

Several studies of arms races (Richardson, 1960; North, Brody, & Holsti, 1963) and of marital relations (Watzlawick, Beavin, & Jackson, 1967; Rubin, 1983; Scarf, 1987) and employee–supervisor interactions (Brown, 1983) have shown how this spiral of predictions poses a critical problem in conflicts. If the parties do not take the spiral into account, they run the risk of miscalculation. However, it is beyond the capacities of any of us to calculate all the possibilities. At best, people have extremely limited knowledge of the implications their actions hold for others, and their ability to manage conflicts is therefore severely curtailed. Not only are parties' behaviors inherently interwoven in conflicts, but their thinking and anticipations are as well. The key question this book addresses is: **how does conflict interaction develop destructive patterns—radical escalation, prolonged or inappropriate avoidance of conflict issues, inflexibility—rather than constructive patterns leading to productive conflict management?** Conflict interaction is always poised on a precipice: one push can send it in a negative direction while another can send it in a positive direction. This book considers several major forces that direct conflicts and examines the problems people encounter in trying to control these forces in order to regulate their own conflict interaction. There are a wide array of forces that can influence conflicts. To sort out the forces that are most influential in leading conflicts in destructive or constructive directions, we will turn to the major theoretical perspectives on conflict that have been advanced in a number of different disciplines. In Chapter 1 we review several **traditional perspectives** in the study of conflict. We point to the major contributions of each perspective and note where they have fallen short of offering a satisfactory explanation of conflict interaction. In Chapter 2, we describe **communication perspectives** on conflict, including cognitive and interactional theories. Building on this review of perspectives, we offer five **properties** of conflict interaction in Chapter 3. We indicate how these properties make conflict interaction vulnerable to forces that can influence the route conflict takes. These forces (**working habits, power, reframing, face-saving, climate, strategies and tactics**) are discussed in detail throughout the book. In the last two chapters, we examine what implications the issues raise throughout the book for **self-regulation** and **third party intervention** in conflicts.

Chapter
1

Traditional Perspectives on Conflict

INTRODUCTION

Conflict is one of the most dramatic—and sometimes traumatic—events in life. Conflict and related subjects, such as bargaining, negotiation, decision-making, aggression, and social influence, have been the subject of more than a thousand studies. The large body of conflict research is an advantage, because it provides a vast knowledge base to build on. It is also a disadvantage, however, for two reasons. First, out of the mass of available research, few theories cover the conflict process as a whole. Research has instead tended to focus on specialized contexts (e.g., games) and on only a few variables at a time. As a result, the "big picture" is often missing. There are dozens of separate explanations and findings, yet it is difficult to integrate them into a whole.

A second disadvantage of previous research is that it has surprisingly little to say about interaction **per se**. Most research has focused either on the psychology of people in conflict or on the solutions they arrive at, rather than on the processes people use to get to solutions. The results of this research are certainly useful, but it reveals little about the essence of conflict: interaction and the moves and counter-moves that constitute it.

As a result, we have several theoretical perspectives and a mass of interesting findings, but no way to link them together. The various perspectives and lines of research operate on quite different levels and are therefore especially hard to reconcile. This book proposes to integrate them by focusing specifically on conflict interaction. It operates on the assumption that conflict is interaction; it assumes that perspectives that ultimately prove important and informative are those that carry insights on how people interact in conflicts.

This chapter and Chapter 2 lay the groundwork for the rest of the book by considering research traditions that have generated important insights into conflict. In this chapter, we consider perspectives that, for the most part, fall outside the field of communication, namely, **the psychodynamic perspective, field theory, experimental gaming research, the human relations perspective, and intergroup conflict research**. We emphasize the insights they provide into conflict interaction, as well as the advantages and disadvantages of each approach for the study of conflict. In the next chapter, we examine contemporary perspectives on conflict from the field of communication. This book attempts to capitalize on the strengths of diverse perspectives without succumbing to their weaknesses or to a fragmented view of conflict.

Since the traditional perspectives discussed in this chapter have spawned a great deal of research, it would be impossible to summarize these perspectives fully. Instead, we focus on the basic assumptions of each view as they relate to conflict. We attempt to evoke the spirit of each position and present its key ideas on conflict. We will return to these basic ideas throughout the book as we examine the major forces that influence interaction in conflicts.

THE PSYCHODYNAMIC PERSPECTIVE

Landmark advances in art and science often elicit as much criticism as praise. At the turn of the century, Freud's psychoanalytic theory altered people's vision of themselves as much as French impressionist art had altered people's view of the world. Yet both Freud and the Impressionists became at different times the target of significant criticism, and even ridicule. Freud and his followers (Freud, 1900/1953, 1925, 1923/1947, 1949; Adler, 1927; Sullivan, 1953; Rapaport, 1951; Erikson, 1950) studied the dynamics of the human mind. They tried to explain how intrapersonal states and mental activities give rise to behavior in social contexts.

The psychodynamic perspective is as controversial as it is ambitious. It has been attacked and ridiculed many times over the years. The crazy psychiatrist in movies and sitcoms is just one example of the harsh reception Freudian ideas have often received. It is certainly true that many psychoanalytic ideas defy common sense. Also, many writers have used them in unjustifiable ways. However, at its core, the psychodynamic perspective provides many insights that have become part of our day-to-day thinking, concepts like the unconscious, the ego, and the id, and processes like repression and wish fulfillment. Several ideas from psychodynamics are fundamental to an understanding of conflict (Coser, 1956).

To understand the contributions of the psychodynamic perspective to conflict research, we must first consider some of its basic assumptions. (The account given here is directed to our concerns, but readers may turn to other sources for a fuller description: Deutsch & Krauss, 1965; Hall & Lindzey, 1970; Hall, 1979). A key premise of the psychodynamic perspective is its "hydraulic" model of human motivation. Freud and his followers portray the human mind as a reservoir of psychic energy that is channeled into various activities. This energy is the impulse behind all human activity and can be channeled into any number of different behaviors, ranging from positive pursuits such as work or raising a family to destructive impulses such as vandalism. But however it is channeled, this energy must be released. If it is not released through one channel, energy builds up pressure to be released through another—hence the analogy to a system of hydraulic pipes, in which turning off one outlet creates pressure on the others. Psychodynamic theorists attempt to describe the mechanisms in the human mind that constrain and channel psychic energy. Their basic model has three components: (1) the id, the source of energy; (2) the superego, the value system designed to constrain this energy; and (3) the ego, the executive function that relates the id and superego to actual behavior.

The **id** is "the primary source of psychic energy and the seat of the instincts" (Hall, 1979, p. 26). It is governed by the **pleasure principle**, which aims to reduce the amount of tension through the discharge of psychic energy. Tension is created by two forces, the basic human drives or instincts, and the frustrations the person encounters in attempting to satisfy these instincts. The basic instincts include the drive for self-preservation, needs for love and social support, and the controversial instincts toward aggression and self-destruction. For the id all ways of discharging energy are equivalent, so it is indifferent as to whether energy is used for positive or destructive tendencies. Energy will tend to flow through whichever channel offers the least resistance. Because needs and drives must be dealt with in social contexts where others may block their satisfaction, they often go unfulfilled. In such cases the energy originally focused on the drive may refocus on the frustrating person or object, especially if no alternative channels are available. This explanation has been given for vandalism in schools. Frustrated children with no other outlets take out their anger on the institution that constrains them.

People are not just willful, impulsive creatures, however. They often have a great deal of self-control and very high moral standards, which route their energy into socially acceptable outlets. Freud called this moral and judicial branch of our personality the **superego**. It consists of two parts, the ego ideal and the conscience. The ego ideal is a person's internalization of who he or she would like to be. It is the person's model for behavior and is usually patterned after his or her parent or some other admired person. The conscience corresponds to what the person believes is morally bad; it is, in essence, a "negative" ego ideal, something the person tries to avoid. The superego is like a parent: it regulates behavior by punishing one for disapproved activities and rewarding him or her for approved activities. These punishments and rewards are usually psychological—feelings of guilt and inferiority if a person has done something bad and feelings of pride and accomplishment for good behavior. However, sometimes the superego's control can be physical, as when someone becomes sick from guilt.

Both the id and superego are forceful influences. The id wants to discharge energy, no matter how or what, and the superego wants to constrain behavior to acceptable paths regardless of the consequences. The **ego** mediates between the two and relates them to real-world concerns. According to Freud, the ego is governed by the **reality principle**; its aim is "to postpone the discharge of energy until the actual object that will satisfy the need has been discovered or produced" (Hall, 1979, p. 28). This "actual object" is defined by the limitations of the social situation and by the superego. For example, a member of a decision-making group may be frustrated by the group's slow pace. One avenue for releasing this tension might be to lash out at other members. However, the member's superego might define "ideal" behavior as kind and self-controlled and therefore tend to suppress tension release through attacking others. The member's ego would mediate between the id and superego to find a suitable means of releasing energy, yet maintain a kind, self-controlled demeanor. The member might, for example, work on solving the group's problems in order to speed it up. If this is successful, the member's tension would be diverted. However, the ego can postpone discharge only for so long. If the group's problems are not soluble and no other outlet is found, the energy will eventually either erupt in a tongue-lashing of other members or be turned back on itself and suppressed. Neither result is good for the member. In the former case the member will feel guilty because he or she has violated an ideal, and in the latter the member will feel more tension from suppressing his or her energy. The ego tries to mediate the superego and id, while avoiding these unpleasant alternatives. To do this it must guide the person into successful and effective channels of activity.

However, as we noted in the Introduction, conflict occurs in situations where people perceive incompatible goals and interference from others, that is, **situations in which people fear they will not be able to act successfully**. As a result, the ego is faced with the problem of managing the id and superego when acceptable, effective behavior channels may not be available. The frustrations and uncertainties involved in conflict generate two powerful impulses that the ego must manage—the **aggressive impulse** and **anxiety**. The various ways in which these energies are channeled play a critical role in conflict interaction, because they determine how members react to conflict.

Freud emphasized that the **aggressive impulse** can be directed toward oneself or others. Energy for this tendency may arise from guilt or from frustrations resulting from unfulfilled needs or thwarted desires. Often this aggression is directed at the actual object of guilt or frustration, either back at oneself in the form of self-hate or in attacks on the frustrating other. However, self-hate is very destructive and aggression toward some people is discouraged, either by moral codes or by the negative consequences of attacking them. As a result, individuals develop strategies for redirecting aggression.

One strategy is to attempt to suppress aggressive drives. This is often done simply by not acknowledging them and undertaking a substitute activity. For example, an employee who is angry at his boss for denying him a promotion may simply suppress his anger and rechannel it into working even harder. The psychodynamic perspective stresses the benefits of suppression, because it leads to less anxiety, guilt, or pain than attempting to fulfill a destructive or impossible need. If drives are recognized explicitly, people must make some conscious response to them, and this can increase anxiety or frustration if they go unsatisfied. On the other hand, if a need is never acknowledged, it can be treated as if it were nonexistent, and the energy associated with the need can be diverted into other channels.

Despite its benefits, suppression can also be a double-edged sword. Suppressing a need is frustrating and if no acceptable substitute is found, frustration can fester and erupt more violently later on. Also, when goals are suppressed, people may still be driven by the need without realizing it. Actions may be guided by unconscious drives or needs, and these may direct behavior in destructive ways. Thus the employee might take out his anger unconsciously by missing the deadline for an important report his boss must give to her superiors. By making his boss look bad, he is getting back at her and assuaging his anger without admitting it; this may have bad consequences for him too, because he might lose his job if his boss believes him to be incompetent or vindictive. Facing up to his anger directly might have been unpleasant for both the employee and his boss, but in this case it would have been less unpleasant than the consequences of suppression.

A second strategy for dealing with aggression is to direct it toward more vulnerable or acceptable targets than the actual source of frustration. This process, **displacement**, is more likely when the true source of frustration is powerful or valued by the individual. Rather than suffering the consequences of an attack on the true source, people attribute their frustration to other parties so that their impulses can be legitimized. They look for distinctions between themselves and others so that "enemy lines" can be drawn and targets are then available for their aggressive urges. In his insightful book *The Functions of Social Conflict*, Coser (1956) notes that the scapegoating of a few group members may be due to displaced aggression. When members of a group face failure or a crisis, they are often reluctant to direct their anger toward the whole group, because they fear rejection. In order to avoid losing the benefits of belonging to the group, they attack a weak member or an outsider. This process can be very destructive for the scapegoat, but it serves to keep the group together because it allows members to vent aggressive energy. Kenwyn Smith (1989) argues that organizational conflicts are often redirected to other issues and people than those who provoke the initial reaction.

In addition to aggressive impulses, **anxiety** is also a by-product of conflicts. Anxiety is an internal state of tension that arises when someone perceives impending danger. It arises when people believe their drives or needs will be thwarted. Since people in conflicts anticipate interference from others, anxiety is likely to exist until they have some hope that all parties are trying to reach an agreement that meets each person's needs. If there is little hope or if members suspect that other parties do not see their needs as legitimate, then anxiety is likely to increase throughout the conflict.

The psychodynamic perspective also points to two other sources of anxiety. First, it suggests that anxiety may result from people's fears of their own impulses. As we have noted, many drives are self-destructive or counterproductive. When people suspect they may be acting on one of these deep-rooted impulses, they become anxious. They may be unsure about the limits of their own behavior and try to determine those limits and prove themselves by testing how far they will go with risky or self-endangering behavior. For example, a receptionist in a law office inadvertently overheard an insulting remark one of the lawyers made about her. She was very angry and began to berate the lawyer with insulting jokes in retaliation. Despite the possibility that the lawyer might fire her, she continued joking for several days. When a friend in the office asked her why she took the chance, she commented that she **was** really afraid the lawyer would fire her. However, she had to prove to herself that she was not a "mouse," so she continued her counterattack. Persisting in and strengthening counterproductive responses is one way of reassuring oneself that they are permissible.

Anxiety also results from the judgments people make about themselves. People have strong behavioral tendencies based on inner needs and impulses, but the superego gives them a capacity to make judgments about their behavior. Anxiety ensues when people are uncomfortable with their actions and realize that they would not ordinarily act this way. Even if they disapprove of their behavior, people may continue with their actions, because at the time there seems to be some legitimate or important reason. They may, for instance, be trying to save face, or they may see themselves using a questionable means to achieve a worthwhile end. The anxiety people experience from engaging in disapproved behaviors may decrease the chances that they will stop these behaviors: anxiety can cloud thinking and prevent people from understanding their own ambivalence.

Anxiety influences conflict interaction by causing members to be excessively rigid and inflexible. Hilgard and Bower (1966) draw on psychodynamic principles to help explain compulsive or repetitive tendencies that can take hold of people's actions, despite the fact that they carry destructive consequences. The mere repetition of unpleasant behaviors is often rewarding because it allows people to achieve a sense of mastery over some activity. Mastery in itself is rewarding, and hence behaviors continue even if they eventually prove to be destructive. Hilgard and Bower note that this sense of mastery, and the compulsive behaviors it promotes, may reduce anxiety. It allows people to cope with a trying situation and it leads to overlearned behaviors that are highly resistant to change. Although this account aims to explain neurotic forms of individual behavior, it can also explain the nature of interaction cycles. Counterproductive interaction patterns can persist because they provide a way to deal with the anxiety that conflict produces. As we will see in Chapter 3, these cycles, fed by members' rigidity, can be very threatening.

The psychodynamic perspective has generated several important insights into conflict interaction. Most important is its explanation of the role of impulses, particularly aggression and anxiety, in conflicts. The idea that these impulses build up and can be redirected into other activities, including attacks on a third person, is crucial to most conflict theories. The psychodynamic perspective recognizes the importance of substitute activities, displacement, scapegoating, and inflexibility in conflicts. It allows us to take many subtle processes into account. The idea of unconscious or subconscious motivation is also very important. People do not always understand what is driving their conflict behavior. Unconscious motivation underscores the importance of helping members gain insight into their behavior. Once members understand what is driving conflicts, they can begin to control them.

In addition to these strengths, two shortcomings of the psychodynamic approach must be registered. First, although the psychodynamic perspective has important implications for the study of interaction, it is not aimed at the study of interaction per se. Psychodynamic analyses focus primarily on **internal psychological processes** and not on **social** behavior. Since the psychodynamic perspective places such heavy emphasis on mental states and the internal motivations, it often fails to recognize that social behavior is always a response to previous actions of others. In interaction, actions are prompted or shaped as much by previous moves of others as they are by the internal states of the person. In order to get a complete picture, we must incorporate others into our explanation and avoid focusing only on internal processes.

The second caveat relates to the first: the psychodynamic perspective by itself is insufficient to explain the rechanneling of psychic energy toward different people or activities (Billig, 1976). The psychodynamic perspective argues that psychic impulses are often rerouted. Without question, this is a major insight. However, the psychodynamic approach provides no way to predict or explain in any meaningful way **what substitute person or activity will be chosen**. The psychodynamic analysis merely shows that rechanneling does occur and gives vague explanations of how substitutes are chosen. For example, psychodynamic explanations have been advanced for the transfer of frustrations into aggression against the Jewish community in prewar Germany. However, they do not account for why the Jews, in particular, were chosen rather than other minorities or non-Germanic nations. In order to predict which substitutes are chosen—and why—it is necessary to consider social factors outside the realm of psychodynamics. In the case of scapegoating, for example, factors such as the person's power relative to others, the person's habitual style of conflict behavior, the degree to which the expression of anger is socially acceptable, and the characteristics of available weaker parties must be taken into account. As powerful and interesting as they are, psychodynamic notions by themselves offer only a partial picture of conflict interaction.

Many of the social scientific perspectives discussed later in this book have rejected psychodynamic approaches. However, despite their explicit rejection of psychodynamics, they often incorporate many of its insights. Few analyses of conflict could function without ideas derived from psychodynamic concepts such as rechanneling or the subconscious. The psychodynamic perspective is a little like an offensive but rich uncle: family members benefit from the relationship, but no one wants to admit it.

FIELD THEORY AND THE CONCEPT OF CLIMATE

Kurt Lewin's field theory, developed in the 1950s, gave the concept of climate an important place in the study of conflict (Lewin, 1951; Deutsch & Krauss, 1965, Chap. 3; Neel, 1977). Lewin represented human behavior as movement through a "life-space" under the influence of various fields of force. The life-space consists of the person's conception of important goals and the barriers and requirements necessary to attain them. Figure 1.1 shows an illustrative space for a worker who wants to become chair of a union committee. To reach this goal she must pass through or around four regions of the space, each of which corresponds to a requirement or barrier: region *a* representing the actions necessary to be elected to the committee; region *b* representing serving on the committee and becoming prominent; region *c* corresponding to opposition expected from Hank, a power-hungry member of the committee; and region *d* representing the "politicking" needed to be elected to the committee. The dotted line represents one path the worker could take in order to achieve the chair. It includes cutting around Hank's opposition and therefore avoid-

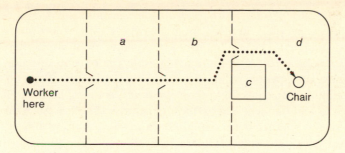

Figure 1.1 A sample life-space.

ing his field of force. This might be done by studiously avoiding Hank's challenges and instead concentrating on other members or issues.

A critical feature of the life-space is that it is determined by how the individual sees the world at a given time; the life-space is not determined objectively, but rather *psychologically*. Lewin and his co-workers identified a number of properties of life-spaces and of the forces that shape them. For the study of conflict, one of the most important properties is the overall character of the social field. As Lewin (1951, p. 241) puts it:

> To characterize properly the psychological field, one has to take into account such specific items as particular goals, stimuli, needs, social relations, as well as . . . more general characteristics of the field [such] as the *atmosphere* (for instance, the friendly, tense, or hostile atmosphere) or the amount of freedom. These characteristics of the field as a whole are as important in psychology as, for instance, the field of gravity for the explanation of events in classical physics. Psychological atmospheres are empirical realities and are scientifically describable facts.

Climate is a quality of the field "as a whole." As such it pervades all thought and action in the situation; it gives a "flavor"—for example, of warmth, safety, fear, or distrust—to everything that happens.

Perhaps the best analysis of the role of climate in conflict was provided by Morton Deutsch (1973), one of Lewin's students. In the opening pages of his discussion, Deutsch notes that "the processes of conflict resolution that are likely to be displayed will be strongly influenced by the context within which the conflict occurs" (p. 10). Deutsch argues that the critical contextual feature of conflict situations—the one that makes the difference between cooperative resolution and potentially destructive competition—is the **type** of interdependence established between the persons involved. For Deutsch, climates are defined by interdependence.

Deutsch defined two basic types of interdependence: (1) **promotive**, where the persons involved in the conflict perceive that gains by either one will promote gains by the other, while losses will promote losses; and (2) **contrient**, where everyone perceives that one's gain will be the other's loss. Perceptions of promotive interdependence, Deutsch argues, tend to promote cooperative interaction, whereas perceptions of contrient interdependence tend to produce competition.

Deutsch identifies several further consequences of interaction occurring under promotive and contrient interdependence. Under promotive interdependence (cooperative climates), people will stress mutual interests and coordinated division of labor, exhibit trusting and friendly attitudes, perceive similarity in their beliefs and goals, and communicate more openly and honestly. Under contrient interdependence (competitive climate), people will focus on antagonistic interests and on constraining each other, exhibit suspicious and hostile attitudes, overemphasize differences, and communicate in a misleading and restrained manner. Studies by Deutsch and later researchers largely confirm these hypotheses and show that eventually these consequences "feed back" to influence interaction, thereby strengthening the dominant tendency in the conflict: "cooperation breeds cooperation, while competition breeds competition" (Deutsch, 1973, p. 367).

Other research enlarges on Deutsch's analysis by suggesting additional climates that arise from and ultimately guide interaction in conflict. White and Lippitt (1968), for example, describe an **individualistic** orientation where members do not believe they are dependent on each other at all; it is characterized by a lack of common motives, autonomous behavior, rather indifferent attitudes toward others, and selfish preoccupation with one's own affairs. As a second alternative, Janis and Mann (1977) warn that overly cooperative orientations can lead to unthinking agreement among members, resulting in poor, unreflective group decisions. They propose instead a **vigilant** attitude, in which members are aware of common interests and trust and respect one another but are wary of each other's ideas (see also Gouran, 1982). Rather than easy cooperation, there may be sharp conflicts in vigilant groups, as members push each other toward the best decision through criticism and debate.

Deutsch's analysis is built on two assumptions particularly useful in understanding the general direction and underlying coherence of conflict interaction. First, as described earlier, Deutsch stresses that the pervasive climate of a situation influences parties' conflict behavior. According to Deutsch, this generalized quality or force emerges as shared perceptions of interdependence develop. Perceptions of interdependence are generalized through parties' assumptions about their common interests, their level of trust, their friendly or hostile attitudes toward each other, their perceptions of similarity or difference in positions, and their communication. These perceptions constitute an overarching climate, a sense of the situation that shapes how parties calculate their moves and perceive each other.

Second, Deutsch points to the cyclical relationship between perceptions of interdependence and interaction. Deutsch suggests that generalized perceptions of interdependence arise from interaction, and once established, they in turn guide interaction. In other words, he assumes that interaction, cooperative or competitive, creates the climates just mentioned and, in turn, that parties' trust, attitudes, beliefs, and so on rebound to influence interaction and reinforce themselves. This cycle is common in groups and organizations. For example, a manager and an employee with a bad work record are likely to come into a performance appraisal interview with the expectation that it will be an unpleasant, competitive situation, where the boss rebukes the employee and the employee tries to evade responsibility. It is this contrient, suspicious climate that causes both to interact mistrustfully and competitively in order to "protect themselves"; this reinforces the climate—which reinforces the interaction, and so on in a deadly spiral. Similar spirals also work for cooperative, trusting climates, as we will see in Chapter 6.

Deutsch's two basic assumptions provide a strong footing for understanding the general direction that conflict interaction takes. However, we must also consider certain limitations of his analysis. Deutsch isolates one feature of conflict situations, interdependence, and derives his entire analysis of cooperative and competitive processes from this feature. Although this has the advantage of permitting a simple, orderly description of cooperation and competition, it carries the disadvantage of an overly narrow focus. Other features of group situations, such as dominance or emotional relationships, are underemphasized in Deutsch's discussion. These omissions can lead to serious misdiagnoses of conflicts. Several features of climates discussed in Chapter 6, including dominance relations, supportiveness, group identity, and goal interdependence, are crucial aspects of group experience that are not directly accounted for in Deutsch's analysis.

A second limitation of Deutsch's analysis stems from his overemphasis on perceptions. Deutsch views participants' perceptions as the immediate cause of cooperative or competitive behavior. Although he recognizes that interdependence is exhibited in the interaction between people, he chooses to emphasize participants' **perceptions** of interdependence as the primary "cause" of conflict behavior. This leads to two problems. By focusing on perceptions of individuals, the analysis shifts away from a focus on a **quality** of the situation. This makes it very difficult to explain behavior in cases where individuals' perceptions disagree. Deutsch explicitly states that his analysis holds only for cases where both persons' perceptions are the same; where individuals differ, it is not possible to predict their behavior. This assumption may rule out a considerable number of important cases, because individuals often have very different perceptions of what drives the group's interaction. Deutsch's focus also has the disadvantage of diverting attention away from behavior and toward individual psychology, thereby making it less likely that we will recognize forces that shape conflict as they are produced in interaction.

Bearing these limitations in mind, we can take away several critical insights from Deutsch's work and field theory, including the importance of **interdependence**, the role of **climates** in conflict, and the **cyclical flow between climate and interaction**.

EXPERIMENTAL GAMING RESEARCH

The social exchange perspective and experimental gaming are two separate, but closely related approaches to the study of conflict. Each has spawned a huge body of research in its own right, with over a thousand experimental game studies alone (Pruitt & Kimmel, 1977) and literally dozens of books summarizing social exchange research (e.g., Thibaut & Kelley, 1959; Homans, 1961; Blau, 1964; Roloff, 1981). Despite the fact that researchers in either approach often seem unaware of studies conducted in the other, the two approaches are based on similar assumptions and lead to complementary conclusions. In this section we discuss the two approaches together. Because of the size and importance of these research traditions, this section is longer and more complex than the others.

Both approaches are based on a recognition of two important facts about conflict: (1) conflicts involve people who are **interdependent**, and (2) conflict behavior involves **rewards and costs** for participants. They attempt to explain conflict behavior (and, indeed, all behavior) in terms of the individual's calculations of the potential rewards and costs associated with different actions. Both perspectives assume that people prefer those behaviors that promise rewards and avoid those for which costs are greater than benefits. Interdependence is critical because (as we noted in the Introduction) how others act and respond determines, in large part, an individual's rewards and costs. Both approaches define interdependence as the degree to which two people can influence each others' rewards or costs. In order to show the relationship between the two approaches, we first discuss the assumptions of the social exchange perspective and then show how they translate into those of Game Research.

The **social exchange perspective** is built on two basic assumptions. First, it assumes that the guiding force behind behavior is **self-interest**. It presumes people monitor their rewards and costs during interaction and strive to achieve a relationship that meets their needs in terms of outcomes. Outcomes are defined as rewards minus costs. There are various ways to define what "meets people's needs." The most obvious way is to assume that people attempt to maximize their profits regardless of the other's loss (cf. Lewin's individualistic climate). However, social exchange occurs in the context of interpersonal relationships, and few relationships could survive for long in this dog-eat-dog situation. Instead, individuals often seem to seek outcomes that are fair in relation to the other's outcomes. This rule of fairness, which has also been called distributive justice (Homans, 1961) and equity (Walster, Walster, & Berscheid, 1978), states that rewards should be proportionate to costs or contributions made to the relationship. Whether people seek to maximize their outcomes or to achieve fair distributions of outcomes, they are assumed to alter their own behavior and to attempt to alter others' behavior so as to achieve desired outcomes. The social exchange perspective does not assume that rewards or costs can always be absolutely or objectively defined. People may be unaware of or mistaken about the consequences of their behavior. Rather, it is the parties' **perceptions** of benefits and costs that guide their behavior.

Second, the social exchange perspective assumes that rewards and costs stem from **exchanges of resources** among participants during interaction. Roloff (1981, p. 21) defines social exchange as "the voluntary transference of some object or activity from one person to another in return for other objects or activities." A wide range of social resources may be exchanged in interaction, including liking, love, status, information, help, approval, respect, and authority. The exchange perspective assumes that people exchange or deny resources every time they interact. When Sherry compliments Herb on his new tie, she gives him approval; when Herb smiles back at Sherry, he gives her liking. In the same vein, when Sherry yells at Herb to pick up his socks she gives him disapproval; when Herb refuses, he denies Sherry his cooperation.

A corollary to the two assumptions is that parties exchange resources in order to influence others to behave in ways that produce acceptable outcomes. Thus Sherry might compliment Herb so that he will wear his tie again; this will make him look attractive and be more pleasant for Sherry to be with. In the same way, Herb might refuse to pick up his socks in order to frustrate Sherry and show her that shouting will not work; if she stops yelling and asks him politely, Herb's outcomes will be better. From a social exchange perspective, interaction is a complex transaction in which individuals calculate present and desired outcomes and act in a manner that will maintain or improve these outcomes. It applies an economic metaphor to interaction.

This analysis suggests that conflict will emerge when one person (1) feels his or her outcomes are too low and (2) perceives or anticipates resistance from another when attempts are made to improve those outcomes (Roloff, 1981, Chap. 4). Outcomes may be too low because the person did not receive an expected reward, or incurred an unexpected cost, or because the person perceives inequity between his/her rewards and those of others. Conflict is triggered when the individual comes to believe that the other is responsible for unsatisfactory outcomes or that the other stands in the way of future improvements. As we will see below, both individuals can take several alternative paths in dealing with this conflict.

Because the social exchange perspective is based on an economic metaphor, it dovetails nicely with **experimental gaming research,** which is based on theories originally developed in economics (Von Neumann & Morgenstern, 1947; Shubik, 1987). The Thibaut and Kelley version of social exchange (1959; Kelley & Thibaut, 1978) is strongly influenced by the economic theory of games and is often used in game experiments. Basically, the experimental gaming approach likens interaction, particularly conflicts, to games of strategy (e.g., chess), in which the results of each player's moves depend on the other player's moves. In its most basic form the experimental gaming perspective makes the following assumptions:

1. The structure of a game is composed of choices (options) available to players and the rewards or costs (payoffs) they receive from selecting a given choice.
2. The choices available to players are limited in number, and players know what these choices are.
3. The payoffs associated with a given move depend not only on the player's choice but also on the choice made by the other.
4. Players know the payoffs associated with each combination of choices and these payoffs are interesting and meaningful to them.
5. A player's choice is determined by calculation of payoffs (rewards and costs). Rational game behavior consists of the selection of choices that yield favorable outcomes, either the maximization of gain or the attainment of a beneficial norm, such as distributive justice.

Based on these assumptions the motivational structure of any conflict can be represented as a payoff matrix like that in Figure 1.2. The particular game portrayed in Figure 1.2 is sometimes called **Prisoner's Dilemma,** after a well-known situation. Consider two criminals who have been apprehended by the police. They are put in separate rooms and kept incommunicado. The police instruct each that they have two choices: confess or keep silent. If only one confesses, he or she can turn state's evidence and go free, with a reward for nailing the culprit; the other prisoner will "take the rap" and receive a heavy sentence. If both confess they both go to prison with lighter sentences. If both remain silent, they go free because the police cannot make a case without a witness. Figure 1.2(a) represents a payoff matrix for this game, and Figure 1.2(b) expresses the payoffs in verbal terms. Note that within this struc-

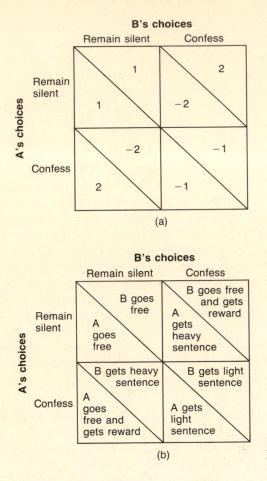

Figure 1.2 Outcome matrices for Prisoner's Dilemma.

ture there are incentives for each to betray the other and a lesser reward for remaining faithful.

The numbers in matrix 1.2(a) represent the values of outcomes for the prisoners for each pair of choices. In each cell of the matrix, the number in the upper corner is prisoner B's outcome and that in the lower corner is prisoner A's. To determine the outcomes associated with each combination of A's and B's choices, locate A's choice on the left side of the matrix and B's choice on the top of the matrix and then find the cell corresponding to the two choices. For example, if A confesses and B remains silent, the cell for this choice is the one in the lower left-hand corner of Figure 1.2(a). (The entries in this cell are A's and B's outcomes.) So the possible outcomes are shown as follows:

1. If A remains silent **and** B remains silent, then A's outcome is $+1$ and B's outcome is $+1$.
2. If A remains silent **and** B confesses, then A's outcome is -2 and B's outcome is $+2$.

3. If A confesses **and** B remains silent, then A's outcome is $+2$ and B's outcome is -2.

4. If A confesses **and** B confesses, then both have outcomes of -1.

All payoff matrices for experimental games can be understood in this fashion.

As this discussion shows, because the two prisoners are interdependent they also face a dilemma. If one confesses and the other does not, the first goes free. If both confess they both go to prison. Can each trust the other to stand fast and not be a traitor? Misplaced trust may result in a severe penalty. The prisoners are thus in a situation where there are incentives both to cooperate and to compete—a **mixed-motive** situation in the terminology of game research. Because, as we have noted, almost all conflicts have incentives for both cooperation and competition, mixed-motive games provide a good experimental model for conflict situations. Although the game is called the "Prisoner's Dilemma," it applies to many other situations than the two prisoners. It applies in almost any situation where each side has incentives both to take advantage of the other and to cooperate.

There are several ways in which the prisoners can attempt to resolve their dilemma, and the particular strategies they choose for doing so are the real interest of experimental game research. If each is only allowed one move, they could attempt to predict or infer what the other would most likely do and base their strategy on that prediction. However, in most experimental games, as in most conflicts, the parties are permitted to make more than one move. Hence they can use the other's previous moves as information for predicting their next move. They can also use their own response to the other (competitive or cooperative) to tell the other what his or her choice should be: if, for example, A always confesses and B wants A to change, B can also consistently confess, which gives A **two** outcomes and an incentive to move toward cooperation. If the two sides are allowed to communicate with each other, they also have other strategies available for maximizing their outcomes. For example, one might persuade the other to remain silent and then betray him or her. The numerous resolution strategies available to parties make it evident that a great many of the processes involved in conflicts—**prediction, persuasion, interchanges of moves, bargaining**—can be simulated with experimental games.

The versatility of games becomes even more apparent when we consider other variations. For one thing, many incentive structures other than the Prisoner's Dilemma can be built into the matrix. Figure 1.3 shows two other structures. Matrix 1.3(a) shows a situation where cooperative matching is encouraged. Individuals receive rewards when they select the same choice and penalties when they make different choices. An example of this situation would be a couple very much in love who are considering whether to move to a different city or stay where they are. If one moves without the other, they both suffer, the mover somewhat more than the stayer. Matrix 1.3(b) shows a game called **chicken**, in which one party can win big if he/she can bluff the other, but loses big if the other calls the bluff. This matrix is illustrated by the game of "chicken," in which players drive their cars toward each other at high speeds. If one swerves and the other does not, the first is "chicken" and the other wins admiration for being brave. If both swerve, they lose face, but at least escape unharmed. If both do not swerve they collide. This game also has parallels to

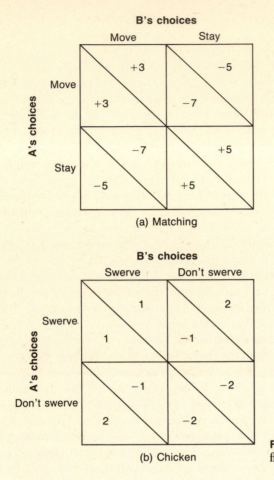

(a) Matching

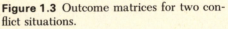

(b) Chicken

Figure 1.3 Outcome matrices for two conflict situations.

the thinking behind nuclear deterrence. Each nation must put itself in danger of annihilation in order to threaten the other. If the threat convinces the opponent to back down, the nation scores a great gain. If, however, the opponent responds in kind, the consequences for both are unthinkable. Many other matrices expressing almost any kind of incentive structure are possible (Kelley & Thibaut, 1978). Game research assumes that all types of interdependence can be translated into these terms.

It is also possible to relax the assumption that members know all options or outcomes equally well. As Kelley and Thibaut (1978) point out, many behaviors can be interpreted as attempts to "explore" the outcome matrices. People ask others what they think of alternatives, observe them interacting with other people, and tentatively test out certain alternatives in order to find out more about the outcomes they are likely to receive from interacting with the other. It is also possible to expand the available alternatives to include mutually rewarding options. Just as people sometimes narrow the options available to others with "either–or" type statements

("Either we go to that movie or I'm staying home!"), so too they can widen the range of alternatives ("Why don't we try?"). As long as we can get a reasonably small set of options, the game approach is workable.

Finally, games do not have to be confined to the matrix format outlined above. As Pruitt and Kimmel (1977) note, there are three main types of experimental games: (1) **matrix games**, like those we have just discussed; (2) **negotiation games**, which simulate formal negotiations over some issue like an award in a legal case or the price of a used car (points are awarded on the basis of the final agreement); and (3) **coalition games**, in which more than two subjects play a game or bargain and subjects can form coalitions to defeat others (the coalition is awarded points and members then bargain to split their rewards). Although these games have different formats, for all practical purposes they are equivalent: their outcomes are determined by numerical assignments, the choices available to players are limited, and multiple trials are run.

The similarities of the experimental game approach and the social exchange perspective are evident. As Thibaut and Kelley (1959) observe, game matrices can be regarded as explicit, numerical formulations of exchange principles. The advantage of games lies in the fact that the numerically specified outcomes allow easy control over experimental situations. This advantage has generated an immense amount of research on conflict and negotiation.

Experimental games have been used to study the effectiveness of various strategies in inducing cooperation between parties. For example, one strategy a player might apply is called **tit for tat** or **matching**. The player matches each of the opponent's moves. If the opponent competes, the player competes; if the opponent cooperates, the player cooperates. The player might adopt this strategy in order to show the opponent that cooperation will be rewarded and competition punished. It turns out that this strategy is amazingly effective in inducing the other to cooperate, as we will see in Chapter 7. A complex study of various game strategies by Axelrod demonstrated that matching could potentially stimulate cooperation, even in situations when there were many competing parties.

Games have also been used to study the effects of variables such as gender or time pressure on conflict behavior. A number of studies have compared the behavior of men and women playing a series of rounds of experimental games. The results of these studies generally seem to indicate that men and women take different approaches to conflicts (Rubin & Brown, 1975). The obvious hypothesis that men would be more competitive than women is **not** supported by these studies. Instead, women seem to vary a great deal in the competitiveness, compared to men. In some studies women have been more competitive than men and in others they have been less competitive. Women's strategies also vary more across different types of opponents than do men's strategies. Rubin and Brown (1975) conjectured that men respond primarily on the basis of the task at hand, that is, the incentive structure of the game itself. So when a game encouraged cooperation, men tended to cooperate, and when another game encouraged competition, men tended to compete. Women, on the other hand, paid more attention to their partners and responded based on their partners' moves. Hence they were more flexible in their responses and had more variation in strategies. Gaming research continues to study the impact of gender differences as well as other variables such as the effects of different payoff structures, time pressure, nationality of the parties, and whether the parties are bargaining for themselves or representing another party.

Experimental gaming research and the social exchange perspective provide several important insights into conflict interaction.

(1) Both approaches focus on the role of **strategic calculation** in conflicts. They recognize that people usually play an active, controlling part in conflict interaction, as opposed to the passive, reactive role assigned to them by psychodynamic analyses. Moreover, the two approaches attempt to specify the principles governing people's choices, in this case the attainment of positive outcomes. These perspectives make it possible to identify factors that may predict others' behavior in conflict situations.

(2) The two approaches also emphasize the importance of **interdependence** in conflicts. They underscore the fact that conflicts almost never occur in wholly competitive or wholly cooperative situations. There is almost always a mixture of incentives to compete and incentives to cooperate. If parties focus on the former, they may be drawn into an ever-escalating spiral; if they recognize the latter, they have grounds for a productive resolution.

(3) The two approaches also give a good picture of conflict as an exchange of moves and countermoves. They show how later moves are shaped and constrained by earlier ones and how each party's power—in the form of control over the other's rewards and costs—determines the moves he or she can make.

(4) Finally, the game and exchange approaches recognize that the rewards and costs associated with moves depend not only on the direct, instrumental gains they yield (e.g., a raise in salary), but also on the effects the moves have on the relationship between the two parties. The social exchange perspective recognizes that resources obtained from relationships—such as love, liking, and self-esteem—are critically important sources of rewards and costs. People's calculations are based not just on gain, but on **consequences for their relationships** as well.

Clearly, game research and the social exchange perspective offer a powerful and useful analysis of conflict. Like all scientific approaches, however, they also have limitations. In effect, both approaches argue that conflict interaction can be reduced to a series of exchanges governed by participants' calculations of potential outcomes. This implies that other aspects of interaction may be interesting, but they are important only insofar as they influence the outcome structure or participants' practical reasoning. This is quite a claim. Can it be sustained?

At least three problems revolve around the issue of human rationality. Both game and exchange perspectives assume people (1) know their options, (2) know the outcomes associated with them, and (3) perform calculations of gains and losses. Consider these three assumptions in turn. As Wilmot and Wilmot (1978) observe, one shortcoming of the gaming approach is that it does not take into account the extremely wide variety of choices people face in real life. Games usually assume there is a relatively small set of options that remain stable over time. Consider the case of John and Steve, who own a business together. Steve, who keeps the books, has let another check bounce because he doesn't keep up with deposits and balancing the account. The bank has just called John, and he is very angry about it. Here are just a few of his choices:

1. Ignore the problem.
2. Leave in disgust and go have a drink.
3. Shout at Steve.
4. Leave Steve a note so Steve won't see how angry he is.
5. Tell a mutual friend so he can let Steve know that John is angry.
6. Call a financial consultant to help straighten out the books.
7. Dissolve the partnership.

These are just some of John's choices. Depending on how Steve reacts to his move, John may face a totally different set of options later. John may, for example, choose response number 4 in the hope that things will cool off. But Steve may feel a note is impersonal and get angry. In the face of Steve's counteraccusation of his coldness, John faces a whole new array of problems. Real-world conflicts often are not fought out of small, well-defined game matrices. The "option" problem becomes even thornier when we consider that parties often create entirely new options as they interact. The structure of options changes constantly as the conflict interaction unfolds.

Second, these perspectives assume that parties know the consequences and outcomes associated with each option and make choices on the basis of expected outcomes. However, this is a much more complex process than it seems at first. Most resources or behaviors are neither totally rewarding nor totally noxious; instead, they have complex sets of properties, some of which are rewarding and some of which entail costs. For example, threatening to break up their partnership may be rewarding to John because he would be free of Steve's sloppiness, he could get out of a business that has become boring, he has the satisfaction of having shown Steve how he feels, and he would have more time to spend with his kids. At the same time this threat may be costly, because John would miss Steve if Steve agreed to the breakup and because bad feelings might arise even if they didn't break up the partnership. If John could consider all these possible consequences prior to acting, he would probably have trouble assigning positive or negative values to them. Is the reward of freedom from Steve's sloppiness greater than the cost of missing his friendship? How much greater? It is one thing to numerically rate rewards on a questionnaire concerning a hypothetical conflict; it is quite another to place values on possible consequences in the flux of an ongoing, highly emotional conflict. People simply do not know what they want sometimes.

Third, these perspectives assume that behavioral choice is based on calculations of gains and losses. However, consider John's situation. If he considers three or four positive and negative consequences for each option, as well as the probability that the option will yield each consequence, he faces a formidable calculating task. This task, as Simon (1955) notes, is far beyond the available capacities of the human brain. It is simply impossible to weigh thirty to forty items of information for every act we undertake.

There is an easy answer to the first three objections. It can be argued that people do not consider a wide range of confusingly similar options, consequences, and outcomes. Instead, they focus on just those few elements that they find salient in the given situation; they simplify issues to fit what they are capable of doing, and if they select a given outcome it is because it is rewarding given their limited perceptions of the situation. This explanation, however, opens the door to the problem of circularity (Skidmore, 1979).

When we see someone doing something, we can conclude that it must be because he or she expects rewards from doing it. We can then identify the rewards or functions of this behavior for them. However, this is circular. Why is Bob doing X? Because it's rewarding to him. Then how do we know it really is rewarding to him? Because he's doing it. According to this logic **any** behavior is rewarding by definition. Skidmore (1979, pp. 105–06) summarizes the implications of this:

> "Reward" and "value" are indeed used as explanatory terms [in exchange theories]; but in every case they are used to explain something that has already happened, and they are used *ad hoc*. That is, we might observe a man doing something and, to explain his doing it, suggest that it might have been rewarding to him or else he would not have done it. Knowing nothing about the man's values or his previous state of reward or punishment, adding the concept of reward is really to add nothing. We could say, "He did it; I saw him." What more do we know, or what more can we predict, when we add, "It must have been rewarding to him"? Whatever he might do, the explanation remains the same. There is no way to prove the theory wrong, if it is.

Thus we can either try to define options and consequences in the full sense, which entails an impossible calculative task, or we can assume people "narrow their fields," which opens us to the charge of circular reasoning when we try to determine how rewards motivate them. If the theory is accepted and we assume that people act because they feel rewarded by something, rewards can always be identified. Either way, however, we are faced with a thorny dilemma if we operate only from this point of view.

A final problem with the experimental game and social exchange perspectives is their oversimplification of complex issues. According to these approaches, options and outcomes are the critical explanatory factors in conflicts. Other variables like power, climate, and the previous history of the conflict are assumed to influence conflict interaction through their effects on rewards and costs associated with options, that is, through their effects on the outcome matrix for the conflict. But this seems to be an oversimplification. As we will see below, climate does influence the rewards and costs associated with various moves: for example, in an open, trusting climate, being honest about one's feelings is not as likely to evoke ridicule as it would in an "ordinary business climate." But climate also has other effects on interaction. It influences group members' perceptions of one another and their predictions of what others will do, as well as their attitudes toward the group. To focus exclusively on members' choices and not on other aspects of the situation seems too narrow and simplistic. This narrow focus filters our perceptions too much and causes us to ignore or trivialize a number of important aspects of conflict interaction.

We have discussed the limitations of the social exchange perspective and game research in great length. We have not done this to refute these approaches. On the contrary, the two approaches provide what are probably the most important set of findings we have regarding conflict. We believe it is important to consider the limitations of these approaches because they are so often accepted "whole cloth" as the correct way to look at conflict. Like the other perspectives considered in this chapter, exchange and game research provide a suggestive, but incomplete, view of conflict. It is important to see their limitations and attempt to build on their strengths.

Given their limitations, what is the ultimate value of experimental gaming research and the social exchange perspective? First, they provide a **metaphorical** analysis of conflict. Even if they are not accurate in all particulars, the game and exchange metaphors bring out the important characteristics of conflict listed above— conflict as a **sequence of moves and countermoves**, the active role of parties in the development of conflicts, interdependence, and the **relational consequences** of conflicts. We will return to these points throughout this book.

In addition, there are cases where these perspectives are directly applicable, that is, cases where options are well-defined, outcomes fairly clear, and parties capable of calculating gains and losses. Conflicts in fairly advanced stages, after the parties have clarified their positions and have developed a "working relationship," are probably the most important case for which these approaches apply. For example, late stages of labor–management negotiations, where only a few options or proposals remain, can be modeled as games. So can conflicts in personal relationships once issues are heading toward a "moment of truth"—for example, to split up or stay together. A second case is when one party narrows the other's options with a statement such as "either you move to California with me or I'm leaving you!" This can happen very early in an interchange, but it has the function of projecting alternatives into a few choices and pressuring parties to focus on them exclusively. Whenever choices are simplified or narrowed, game and social exchange approaches are applicable.

THE HUMAN RELATIONS PERSPECTIVE AND CONFLICT STYLES

The human relations movement, developed in the 1940s and 1950s, has had a lasting impact on the study of organizations and on the field of organizational communication. This perspective assumes that the nature and quality of interpersonal relations in the workplace play a large role in determining employee motivation, satisfaction derived from work, level of absenteeism and resignations, management–employee relations, and, ultimately, the productivity and success of the organization (Perrow, 1986). Human relations research focused in particular on the work group, the site where most relationships develop and play out, and on the superior–subordinate relationship, probably the single most important work relationship.

With this emphasis on human relationships, it is no surprise that conflict was a major concern of the human relations researchers. From this concern came systems to identify recognizable styles or strategies people use in conflict and to determine how effective these styles are in different situations. The concept of style originated with Blake and Mouton (1964) and Jay Hall (1969). These researchers identified five distinct types of conflict behavior. Their classification is based on two independent components of conflict behavior (Ruble & Thomas, 1976): (1) **assertiveness**, defined as behaviors intended to satisfy one's own concerns; and (2) **cooperativeness**, defined as behaviors intended to satisfy the other individual's concerns. These components combine to specify five styles, shown in Figure 1.4.

(1)   A **competing** style is high in assertiveness and low in cooperativeness: the party places great emphasis on his or her own concerns and ignores those of others. This orientation represents a desire to defeat the other and has also been called the **forcing** or **dominant** style.

(2)   An **accommodating** style is unassertive and cooperative: the person gives in to the other at the cost of his or her own concerns. This orientation has also been called **appeasement** or **smoothing** and those who follow it attempt to avoid conflict for the sake of maintaining the relationship. It is a self-sacrificing approach but may also be viewed as weak and retracting.

(3)   An **avoiding** style is unassertive and uncooperative: the person simply withdraws and refuses to deal with the conflict. In this orientation the person is indifferent to the outcome of the conflict and can be described as apathetic, isolated, or evasive. This style has also been called **flight.**

(4)   A **collaborating** style is high in both assertiveness and cooperation: the person works to attain a solution that will meet the needs of both people. This orientation seeks full satisfaction for all and has also been called **problem-solving** and the **integrative** style.

(5)   A **compromising** style is intermediate in both assertiveness and cooperativeness: both people give up some and "split the difference" in order to reach an agreement. In this orientation both are expected to give up something and keep something. It has also been called **sharing** or **horse trading**.

The five styles have been an enormously useful tool for understanding conflict. They provide a common vocabulary and almost every major writer on interpersonal or organizational conflict has used the styles extensively (e.g., Blake & Mouton, 1964; Filley, 1975; Thomas, 1975; Wilmot & Wilmot, 1978). In addition, this classification is grounded in experience: Blake and Mouton developed it from their own experience with organizational conflicts, and later research has supported the existence of the two dimensions and five styles (Filley, 1975; Cosier & Ruble, 1981). As we will see in Chapter 7, numerous variants on styles can be identified.

One labor mediator recently observed that during negotiations he is most confi-

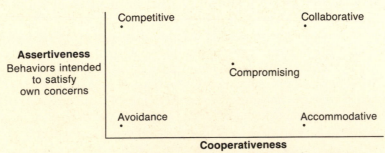

Figure 1.4 Five conflict styles and their relationships. From Ruble and Thomas (1976).

dent that the parties will find a settlement when they have lost any basis for predicting each other's behavior. Although the implications of this statement are intriguing in many ways, one point in particular has long captured the attention of conflict researchers. The mediator's observation implies that people enter disputes or negotiation sessions with set expectations about how others will react. Based on their past experiences, they assume that others will adopt predictable styles to deal with conflict. This is quite useful insofar as it encourages parties to focus on conflict interaction. However, as we will see in Chapter 7, this is a somewhat oversimplified view of how people in conflict behave. It also does not take interaction into account, because styles refer only to a single person's behavior.

The human relations perspective has also been criticized because it emphasizes the resolution and elimination of conflict. This seems like a paradox at first sight, because human relations theorists openly acknowledge conflict as a common occurrence and stress that it must be used productively. However, as Perrow (1986) notes, human relations theorists emphasized managing relationships so that cooperation resulted. Conflict was regarded as an inevitable part of human relationships, but an unnatural one that must be "managed" or "resolved" for the organization to run efficiently in its "natural" cooperative state. Human relations theorists did not entertain the possibility that conflict might be a basic building block of organizations, impossible to remove completely, a positive and innovative force in its own right. As we will see in Chapter 4, low-power groups or minorities sometimes must foment conflict to make society more responsive to them. In this case, sustaining conflict is positive for these groups.

Moreover, the human relations perspective also makes a value judgment about which methods of resolving conflicts are best. Note the labels attached to the various styles: collaborating is clearly the preferred mode of resolving conflicts, with compromising holding second place; the labels given to competing ("forcing"), accommodating ("appeasement"), and avoiding ("apathetic," "isolated," "evasive") styles indicate that they are not regarded as equally valuable. We will argue in Chapter 7 that each of the five styles and their variants are useful under different circumstances. We need make no value judgments that suggest there is one "right" way to work with conflict.

INTERGROUP CONFLICT RESEARCH

That conflict often arises between people of different nationalities, religions, races, ethnic groups, genders, or ages is not news. In Germany the Nazis persecuted the Jews on the grounds that they were inferior to "Aryans"; in Yugoslavia the Serbs and Croats have fought savagely trying to settle "age old" scores; in the United States whites persecuted black people because of their skin; in some large corporations, women are cut out of management by the "old boys" who control the front office and respond with legal charges of discrimination. The list goes on and on. In all these cases, "differences" between these social groups are the alleged cause of conflict. The conflict is presumed to lie in characteristics of the groups, which make it inevitable. The groups are seen as "natural" or "traditional" enemies.

There are at least two problems with this explanation of intergroup conflict. In most cases one or both groups have economic or political interests in the conflict; one or both stand to gain from the other's defeat (Billig, 1976; Tajfel, 1978). Intergroup differences may be used by parties to justify the conflict, but they are certainly not its ultimate or original cause. Second, usually there are several other groups "different" from the conflicting groups, which are not drawn into the conflict. The theories of "natural differences" have no explanation for why **these particular groups** are in conflict and the others are not drawn in (Billig, 1976). To explain this it is necessary to go beyond group differences and to consider intergroup interaction.

While they may not be the ultimate or original cause of conflicts, intergroup differences often contribute to the persistence, intensity, and violence of conflicts. There are few things as troubling as a persistent conflict that feeds on group prejudices. Small wonder that sociologists and social psychologists have devoted a great deal of time to the study of intergroup conflict. In the United States the study of intergroup relations can be traced back to the late 19th century, when the sociologists Robert Park and W. I. Thomas were concerned with the problem of how to integrate multiethnic immigrants into the American "melting pot." One of the most famous works in this tradition is Gordon Allport's (1954) study, *The Nature of Prejudice*. In Europe, similar ethnic tensions and the horrors of the first 50 years of the 20th century inspired social psychologists like Henry Tajfel and Serge Moscovici to investigate the roots of group differences. This research yields some important insights for the study of conflict.

The roots of intergroup conflict lie in the basic human need for identity. European researchers have explored the process of **social categorization**, a basic social process whereby people define themselves by identifying the groups they and others belong to (Doise, 1978; Tajfel & Turner, 1979). Starting in early childhood and continuing throughout adult life, a major factor in the definition of personal identity is the individual's perceptions of the social groups or categories he or she belongs to ("I am an American"; "I am a Minnesotan"; "I am a lawyer"). Moreover, identity is defined not only by the groups to which a person belongs, but the groups to which they do **not** belong. For example, many Americans define themselves both as being Americans and as **not** being Mexicans or Japanese or some other nationality. Members of management can draw their identity as much from being opposed to the union as from being a manager. Every organization and society can be described as a network of complementary and opposing groups. For example, in a typical American factory there might be groups divided between labor and management, line workers and staff, male and female, white collar and blue collar, to name just a few. Each group is defined not only in its own terms, but also with reference to its complementary or opposite group. Social categorization is the process by which people determine to what groups they and others belong. It creates identification and oppositions among people.

The social categories forming the dividing points of organizations and societies differ from case to case and through history. Although men and women have always been important social categories in the United States, the nature of the category "women" and the relationship between the categories "men" and "women" have changed radically. And the men–women differentiation is quite different in Japan, the United States, and Ghana. The importance of social categories also changes through history. In the 1920s, whether one was in favor of or against the legal prohibition of alcohol was an important distinction. Today, it is not even an issue. There is no one set of universal social divisions. They are socially defined and negotiated in each culture and subculture.

Communication plays an important role in social categorization. It is the medium through which people are taught categories. When children hear talk about the general categories "boys" and "girls" or "blacks" and "whites," they are being taught social categories (Doise, 1978). For adults such categorization is second nature, and they learn and create additional categories. With each social category comes a characterization of what people in the category are like, their wants and needs, how they will act, and so on. Of course, the characterization of each category differs depending on who is describing the category. A member of the social group "women" is likely to describe the characteristics of "men" differently than a "man" would. However, there are often communication barriers that prevent people in different social categories from comparing notes, preventing them from recognizing these differences. Blacks and whites, for instance, sometimes keep their theories about the other group to themselves and only discuss them with other blacks and whites. The process of group differentiation, discussed later, adds additional communication barriers that keep people from refuting social characterizations.

In addition, a person's style of communicating often serves as a marker of the social group to which he or she belongs. Giles and Powesland (1975) summarize a good deal of evidence that characteristics of speech such as dialect or accent are used as indicators of the social category to which a person belongs. In World War II, U.S. citizens with German accents were often branded as potential collaborators with the Nazis and kept under surveillance, despite the fact that they were loyal to the Allies.

When people accept social categories, they are likely to act toward those in other groups on the basis of these attributions. This sets up a self-reinforcing cycle that preserves theories about other social groups (Cooper & Fazio, 1979). For example, if people in group A (which generally is politically unconcerned) are taught that people in group B are politically conservative, those in group A may never raise the subject of politics in discussions with members of group B. By so doing, they never give the people in group B a chance to show their true political beliefs. In turn, people in group B (who are actually somewhat centrist in their political beliefs) might think that people in A are "close-mouthed" and manipulative in their political agenda. That members of group A never talk about politics might confirm this suspicion for many group B members. Thomas Scheff (1967) calls this state of affairs "pluralistic ignorance"—each side is mistaken about the other, but neither is aware that it is mistaken. So both sides act on their "true" beliefs and invite behavior that confirms their views.

Intergroup conflict stems from a second process that builds on social categorization, **group differentiation**. By itself social categorization only creates neutral divisions that enable people to situate themselves in society. Group differentiation refers to the polarization between groups and the attendant stereotyping of other groups that trigger conflicts. A wide range of events—including economic and political problems, natural disasters, wars, and population movements—may create conflicts of interest between groups. Conflicts may also arise due to the structure of society, as groups are put into opposition by historical traditions, the structure of economic opportunity, the nature of the political system, changing demographics, long-term shifts in economic fortunes, and other large currents. When this happens, groups tend to attribute responsibility for their problems to other groups and to unite against them.

This "we–they" polarization is produced by several communication dynamics (Sherif, Harvey, White, Hood, & Sherif, 1961; Blake, Shepard, & Mouton, 1964). When groups are put into competition there tends to be an increase in members' expressions of loyalty and commitment to the group. This can be seen in rival street gangs, who trumpet their "groupness" with colors, graffiti, secret signs, and steadfast obedience to their leaders' demands. It is equally evident in the fierce loyalty expressed by employees of competing firms, who will work long hours and devote themselves whole-heartedly to creating the best product or the winning bid. In-group messages also slant positions in favor of the group and demean the claims and validity of the other group. The American news coverage of the Iraq–United Nations war, for example, generally presented the United Nations' side of the issues as reasonable common sense; the Iraqi view was generally presented as illogical, arbitrary, and without merit. The one-sided nature of the coverage served to reinforce American perceptions of the correctness of their stance and to invalidate the Iraqi position. This slanting of positions in favor of the in-group generally prevents reflection on the merits of the other group's claims. The other group may be perceived as the embodiment of evil, with no legitimate claims at all.

These internal communication processes move the in-group toward a narrow, oversimplified view of the other group. It contributes to the development of **stereotypes**, highly simplified beliefs about characteristics of other groups. Examples of stereotypes include "Japanese people all work hard and have no fun"; "men do not care about feelings"; and "gays are promiscuous." In each case all members of the other group are assumed to have the same threatening or undesirable characteristic. People who hold the stereotype may use it to interpret the behavior of a member of another group. During the desegregation crisis that occurred in the Boston public schools during the late 1970s, newspapers reported the following incident (adapted from Cooper & Fazio, 1979, p. 153):

> A white girl who wanted to make a change in her program was using the wrong entrance to the high school, when a young black man touched her arm to get her attention.
>
> She screamed.
>
> The school's headmaster, Boston's title for a high school principal, was nearby and stepped in immediately, averting what he thought might have become a major incident.
>
> "He grabbed me," the girl said.
>
> "I was just trying to help her and tell her to use the front door so she wouldn't get into trouble," the boy said.

Stereotypical interpretations such as the girl's may promote strong reactions, heightening tensions between the groups. Ironically, the stereotyper's expectations may be confirmed by the response his or her interpretations provoke from the other. Had the headmaster not stepped in, a violent confrontation between whites and blacks might have occurred. Whites would have come away with the conclusion that the black student had attacked the white student, and black stereotypes about whites would have been reinforced as well.

Other communication processes heighten perceived disagreements between groups and separate their positions. Discussions in the in-group minimize similarities between the in-group and other groups and exaggerate differences between the groups' positions. In the Iraq–United Nations conflict, news items explaining the "Islamic" way of thinking emphasized its divergence from Western thought. In a study of conflicts between line workers and office staff, Dalton (1959) found that the two groups heightened perceptions of differences between them by emphasizing differences in education level, social skills, and dress. It is evident that the claims serve to differentiate the groups and emphasize the chasm between them. Polarization is heightened by suppression of disagreement in the in-group. In-group messages minimize disagreements between members of the group and present a common front. Members who venture the opinion that the other group may have some valid claims or a legitimate position are often charged with disloyalty (Janis, 1972). This prevents members of the in-group from exploring possible common ground with other groups and preserves stereotypes.

These communication processes result in one group becoming strongly united against the other. As we noted in the discussion of the psychodynamic perspective, Lewis Coser (1956) observed that this "we–they" relationship has useful functions for the in-group. It creates high levels of cohesion and turns attention away from conflicts or dissatisfactions within the group. However, these dynamics may also create self-reinforcing cycles of polarization and hostility between the groups. If members believe the other group is responsible for their problems, hear only bad things about the other group, and are not permitted to test these perceptions and beliefs, there is no way to improve intergroup relations. Members of the in-group, expecting the worst from the other group, are likely to act in a defensive or hostile manner toward members of the other group. In effect, the in-group creates a self-fulfilling prophecy whereby its worst fears about the hostility of the other group seem to be confirmed, justifying further polarizing communication (Cooper & Fazio, 1979).

Once two groups have been in conflict for a time, they develop **intergroup ideologies** to justify their positions. These intergroup ideologies are organized belief systems that describe the differences between groups in terms that present the in-group in a favorable light and explain the conflict from the in-group's perspective. For example, in the long-standing Israeli–Palestinian conflict, both sides have developed elaborate explanations of why they have legitimate claims and the other has wronged them. These explanations provide a ready stock of justifications for aggression toward the other side and for unwillingness to make concessions.

Gouldner (1954) describes a similar case in a gypsum plant facing a strike. A history of confrontation between union and management led management to conclude that the union was simply trying to control everything that occurred in the plant. As a result of this belief, management saw no need to consider the legitimacy of any issues raised by the union, because managers thought that under all of them was the hidden agenda of control. Management's lack of response to worker concerns contributed to a wildcat strike, which might have been averted if the managers had considered the issues on their merits. Intergroup ideologies solidify the conflict between groups because they are taken as unquestionable truth. New members and children are taught these beliefs with the result that they can see the other group only in the terms of the ideology.

Together, the processes of social categorization, group differentiation, and intergroup ideology development define social reality so that members transfer general beliefs about other groups and their differences into conflict situations. These beliefs can funnel interpretations and actions to produce longer and more intense conflicts.

Differences in culture, history, and experience between groups also may create misunderstandings that heighten divisions. It has been said that there are such fundamental differences between black, white, and Hispanic cultures in the United States that it is difficult for members to really understand each other. Shenkar and Ronen (1987, p. 268) discuss possible problems that may occur in negotiations between Chinese and U.S. citizens:

> The Chinese preference for restrained, moderate behavior suggests that one should avoid overtly aggressive behavior. The American task-oriented approach, which allows for the admission of differences in the positions of the parties to a negotiation so as to promote "honest confrontation," is viewed by the Chinese as aggressive, and therefore as an unacceptable mode of behavior. . . . The Chinese tend to prefer to make decisions behind the scenes . . . and this contributes greatly to American anxiety as to where they stand as discussions progress.

These differences in cultural preference can cause serious misunderstandings that contribute to escalation of conflicts.

The intergroup conflict perspective is useful because it reminds us that conflicts cannot be reduced to interpersonal terms. Larger social relations and the history of intergroup relations play an important role in many conflicts. Group identification is an important part of every person's identity, so it is inevitable that intergroup differences will be pulled into interpersonal conflicts. Indeed, sometimes people can be "forced" into a conflict by the structure of intergroup relations. In a community with racial problems, for example, it is difficult for people from different racial backgrounds to have an interpersonal conflict that is not in some way influenced by racial differences. Billig (1976) argues that the only way to prevent such conflicts is to change relationships between groups—a task that is often quite difficult to achieve.

CONCLUSION

The perspectives discussed in this chapter introduce a number of important concepts and ideas about conflict. The psychodynamic perspective probes the basis of conflict in unconscious human needs and psychological dynamics. Field theory, too, is a psychologically oriented approach, but it attempts to portray the field of action perceived by parties as they confront conflicts. It emphasizes parties' perception of the general situation confronting them and the reactions that result from various situational climates. The social exchange perspective and experimental gaming start from the assumption that parties are rational creatures who attempt to maximize their gains and minimize losses in conflicts. This perspective, more socially oriented than the first two, is concerned with how members choose among alternative conflict behaviors, when the outcomes of their choices depend on how others respond. The human relations perspective focuses on the various conflict styles a party might enact. This perspective is quite socially oriented, because styles are defined in relation to the other party. Finally, intergroup conflict research focuses not on individual psychological or interpersonal processes, but on entire social groups and how they become predisposed to conflict with each other. As we move from the psychodynamic perspective to the intergroup conflict perspective, we move progressively from perspectives concerned with internal psychological processes to those concerned with external social processes.

In the following chapters, we weave a tapestry that incorporates the ideas and concepts introduced by these perspectives into a view of conflict as a communication process. As we have noted, one of the major shortcomings of these five perspectives is their lack of attention to conflict interaction. Discussing psychological and social influences apart from the communication processes inherent in conflict is a little like showing someone a blueprint of an airplane—how the airplane is constructed—but not showing him or her the plane in flight. One would see the structure of the aircraft and could imagine the plane's potential, but never see the movement, the dynamics of flight. To more fully capture the dynamics of conflict, Chapter 2 examines contemporary communication perspectives on conflict. Then Chapter 3 discusses five key properties of conflict interaction, offered as a basic model of communication in conflict. When we study conflict as **interaction,** we come to see the inner workings of the process—its movement, direction, and development.

Chapter
2

Explaining Conflict Processes

Truth is a river that is always splitting up into arms that reunite. Islanded between the arms, the inhabitants argue for a lifetime as to which is the main river.

Cyril Connolly

PERSPECTIVISM AND CONFLICT

We can view conflict from many different angles, from many different perspectives. In the last chapter, we explored the traditional perspectives used by scholars to examine conflict. Before discussing more contemporary ideas, we must first explore the nature of perspective-taking itself.

This book is guided by an idea commonly called **perspectivism**. Perspectivism posits that we can know no fact without interpretation, hold no claim of reality independent of belief. Perspectivism also holds that there are many ways of viewing a phenomenon, many angles that offer promise to the viewer. There is no right perspective, only a field of choices from which to select. A perspective colors one's world, guiding the search for answers, determining what questions are worth asking, what data are worth collecting.

Taking a perspective on conflict or any social phenomenon is much like adopting a style of painting. Through the years, painters have represented objects in very different styles of visual representation. Sometimes the same object—the Eiffel Tower, London Bridge, a garden, a bowl of fruit—has been painted in realistic, impressionistic, or cubist styles. These different styles reveal different features and aspects of these objects, much like perspectives reveal different aspects of the same social phenomenon.

Perspectivism maintains that one cannot view a phenomenon without relying on a catalog of assumptions that influence that view. Selecting a perspective, however, is not an irrevocable decision. Perspectivism also means believing in the value of multiple perspectives. After exhausting the potential of a particular perspective, it can be temporarily abandoned for another, allowing one to see dynamics and dimensions that were previously hidden. Although the choice of one's perspective is highly consequential, the standard of judgment is one of utility—of usefulness—not of right or wrong. A good perspective is one that enables the viewer to explain the product or process in question and act on that explanation. We can illuminate perspectivism with an applied example.

Imagine that your interest in conflict processes was brought to the attention of a powerful friend who operates a midsize pharmaceutical company. After hearing you expostulate on the nature and dynamics of conflict processes, she requests that you assist with a problem in her organization that involves conflict. She explains that her company of 4000 employees develops and markets drugs related to heart disease. The company has turned a profit for several years largely because of an aggressive promotion department and sales force. Until recently these two functions were housed in separate divisions, but last quarter promotion and sales were merged, creating a single unit. Since the integration of the divisions, conflict has been the order of the day. It seems every time she turns around she is asked to settle a dispute in the new "marketing" division. She characterizes the situation as involving open hostility and suspicion. This animosity is most apparent between managers but also occurs with frequency between managers and subordinates. She could understand the situation more easily if the split existed along former division lines (promotion versus sales), but in her view the conflict does not discriminate. Given your interest and expertise, she asks that you assess the conflict and offer recommendations as to how it should be managed or resolved.

Granted, this is a complex problem, one that requires more background and context for intelligent study. But for the purposes of our discussion, let us say you work with the facts at hand. Obviously, you cannot intervene until you accurately assess the situation and understand the reasons for the conflict. In addition to determining the root causes of or contributors to the conflict, discerning the effects of the struggle is also paramount. After all, the conflict may be producing productive as well as destructive outcomes. So where do you start? Where do you search for reasons and outcomes? A series of choices is apparent.

Would you look to the history of the company as told by top managers for clues? Or would you interview workers in the division and collect their views and perceptions about the conflict? Would you examine interpersonal or group interaction between division workers? Or would you ask them to report about their feelings, thoughts, and emotions during such encounters? Would you collect recent messages, such as office memos, reports, letters? Or would you collect artifacts of the organizational culture, such as employment contracts, bylaws, policy statements? If you choose to talk to division employees, would you seek to uncover their values, beliefs, and attitudes? Or would their stories, myths, and metaphors be more attractive to you? The choices you make will reflect the premises you hold.

Making a reasonable assessment of a conflict is a rational task, one that requires a series of conscious decisions. The choice of what data are to be included in the analysis and what will be ignored or deemed impractical for study is called "punctuating the conflict." Conflict is like a flowing river. One cannot enter or exit the river at more than a single location at any one time. What counts as the source of the river and its delta depends on the perspective and/or theory one uses. The only sure bet is that the punctuation decision of when to begin and end the assessment cannot be avoided. One must enter and exit the river—begin and end the analysis—in order to make an assessment. Because we draw conclusions based on what we observe or learn, how we punctuate a conflict is highly consequential, shaping our conclusions much more than we readily admit. By making this choice an active and conscious decision, the observer can avoid missing relevant data or feeding the urge to continually collect more and more data before an assessment can be drawn. As we have noted, **any assessment or explanation of conflict requires punctuation, and one's perspective guides this choice.** As an example of punctuation, consider the historical confrontation on the campus of Kent State University in 1970.

The facts are well known. On the night of Friday, May 1, 1970, students outraged by President Richard Nixon's invasion of Cambodia gathered at a string of bars on a street several blocks from campus and created a minor disturbance. City police responded forcefully, and a riot developed, causing damage to the drinking establishments. A curfew was imposed by police. On Saturday night students convened in mass on campus and burned down the Reserve Officers' Training Corps (ROTC) building. Students refused to allow city firemen to fight the blaze. A detachment of more than 400 Ohio National Guardsmen soon arrived in town to restore order. On Sunday, a picnic atmosphere prevailed, and university officials judged the crisis to be past. But on Monday, May 4, about 2000 students gathered on the campus. The commanding officer of the guardsmen believed the assembly violated a campus order. The riot act was read repeatedly, and students were told to disperse. The students ignored this demand. The commanding officer then ordered his troops to clear the campus. At just before the noon hour guardsmen wearing gas masks and armed with high-powered rifles confronted students on a university football field. After an initial exchange of tear gas and rocks, the guardsmen began to retreat. Students interpreted the retreat as victory, and some pursued the soldiers, hurling rocks and yelling obscenities. At 12:24 P.M. on that fateful day, the guardsmen inexplicably turned back to the area and fired their weapons, discharging more than 60 rounds into the crowd. Thirteen students were struck by bullets, four of whom died. As a result of the conflict, a new page of American history was written.

Suppose you were asked to examine the Kent State conflict and present an explanation about its causes. In the course of collecting data, how would you punctuate the conflict? Would you examine Monday's events exclusively, or would you paint the picture, as we have, of the days and hours leading up to the tragic confrontation? Perhaps you might consider expanding your assessment to include the weeks of war protests that occurred throughout the nation surrounding May 4. Would you examine the lives of the protesting students during those weeks, the lives of the Ohio guardsmen, or both? Would university officials seem important to include in your analysis? Or perhaps you would cast an even larger net by examining the entire lives of the students who were shot and the guardsmen who fired, analyzing their thoughts and experiences that preceded that fateful day. As many scholars of rhetoric might suggest, perhaps the American culture would require scrutiny in your analysis. But would you assess the culture during that year or for several years prior to the event?

Your choice of where to begin and where to end an assessment of this conflict constitutes your punctuation. Although theories and perspectives guide our choices, this decision is left largely to discretion. There are no right or wrong ways of punctuating this or any other conflict. Yet the punctuation choices we make shape what we will see and not see.

In sum, the assumptions you privilege and the premises you prefer form your perspective, form the lens through which you will view conflict. As the metaphor suggests, this lens will color your vision, framing what you will and will not see. Your perspective provides focus. It brings conflict processes into sharp relief, revealing what is relevant for study. All scholars and practitioners who study conflict processes must make similar choices. The substantive assumptions or premises from which one views conflict constitute that perspective.

THE ROLE OF THEORIES

If perspectives are the lenses through which we view conflict, then what are theories? Simply stated, **a theory is an explanation of the relationship between elements or variables**. Theories explain the workings of a phenomenon by operating within the confines of a perspective or common set of assumptions. Metaphorically speaking, a perspective is the larger and more general category, an umbrella of premises and assumptions under which a theory operates. Protected from the precipitation of competing viewpoints, a theory capitalizes on the clarity afforded by the perspective, further clarifying the social phenomenon of interest. By explaining the relationship between a particular set of elements the perspective has shown to be important, a theory enhances our understanding.

For example, it is commonly asserted in the conflict styles literature that the nature of the relationship between parties in conflict influences the conflict styles those parties employ. In essence the claim is that people select conflict styles based on the nature of the relationship involved. In particular, researchers have found that subordinates in organizations use more nonconfrontational strategies and less competing styles than do superiors (e.g., Putnam & Wilson, 1982; Rahim, 1983). So far all we have is a stated relationship: that one variable (conflict style) is influenced by a second variable (relationship type). The theoretical question we might ask here is: why? One such explanation focuses on the subordinate in work relationships.

According to one theory (Musser, 1982), subordinates actively select conflict styles based on the perceived likelihood that the style will invite reprisals from superiors. Subordinates consciously evaluate such risks and then select a style less likely to result in retribution. Although the ultimate reprisal is dismissal from the organization, other sanctions also weigh heavily in the decision, such as being verbally abused or ignored by the boss. Musser suggests that subordinates will consider how protected they are from arbitrary actions by their superiors. Perceived congruence between the subordinate's and superiors' attitudes and beliefs strengthens this protection. When subordinates perceive little protection, they are expected to choose more accommodating styles, whereas more assertive strategies should be selected when the subordinate perceives high protection. The heart of the explanation rests on what it suggests about conflict styles. Conflict styles, as explained by the theory, are consciously and actively selected on the basis of perceptions regarding possible sanctions from the superior. Change the perceptions or the nature of the relationship and one can expect changes in conflict styles. Not surprisingly, several other theories have been offered to explain conflict styles used by subordinates.

As explanations, theories, like perspectives, are rarely right or wrong. Rather, they are best judged by their utility. Good theories are useful theories. They explain relationships so that we might describe them more fully, predict their recurring features, and control their dependent outcomes. Theories are the engine of inquiry and must stand the test of moving us forward, propelling us to see things we have not seen before. A common question that misses this point is: what is the best perspective or theory for examining conflict? This is analogous to a novice chess player asking a grand master, "What is the best chess move?" The grand master would shake her head and explain that it would depend entirely on the game. "Show me the board, my opponent's positions and style, and I will suggest a 'good' move." There is no best chess move, just as there is no best conflict perspective or theory. Instead, we find ourselves with many options from which to choose. We make our selections based on our preferences, prejudices, and goals.

In Chapter 1, we outlined several traditional perspectives that are helpful in understanding conflict. Although some of the research reviewed in Chapter 1 was conducted by communication researchers, for the most part these perspectives developed in other fields, including psychology, sociology, political science, economics, and management. Therefore they focus less on interaction and conflict processes than is ideal for our purposes. In this chapter we review six theories of conflict that have been pursued by communication scholars. These theories differ from and complement the perspectives in Chapter 1 by focusing on the communication variables and processes that constitute conflicts. Together, the perspectives discussed in Chapter 1 and the six theories discussed in this chapter form a backdrop for the analysis of conflict processes developed in Chapters 3 through 9.

In this chapter, we first seek to distinguish between and illustrate two popular contemporary perspectives in the communication field: the Cognitive Perspective and the Interactional Perspective. Then six theories, three from the Cognitive Perspective and three from the Interactional Perspective, will be used to explain the same conflict case (Case 2.2). As the chapter unfolds, we will focus our attention on how theories within these perspectives may complement and inform each other or how they may compete, sometimes operating from contradictory assumptions or frameworks.

Case 2.1   **Are Conflict Theories Just Common Sense?**

A student conversing with his professor expressed his chagrin over an encounter he had with his employer. He approached his employer and explained the benefits of a particular conflict theory and how their broadcasting company might profit from it. However, his employer replied that such an approach was simply "common sense." Frustrated by this response, the student confronted his professor and asked how she would respond to this criticism. "After all," he said, "it is common sense, isn't it?"

Rather than arguing that good theory has a duty to seem commonsensical once it is explained and that this parsimony is at the heart of science, the professor instead attempted an analogy between art and science. "Imagine the most beautiful painting you have ever seen," she instructed him. "Do you have one in your mind?" After a moment the student nodded and offered a painting by the French Impressionist Renoir, *Two Women Sitting,* as his choice. "What makes this painting so beautiful?" she asked probingly. The student gave an arresting answer.

"I'm not sure, really. The gentle colors. The expression and mood the artist captured. The lines and composition. Everything really. It's just beautiful."

The professor replied: "Now when you look at such a beautiful work what do you think? In other words, why are you so astonished?"

The student thought long and hard and then looked up. "I think 'Of course.' Why couldn't I see this before the painting. All the lines and colors work perfectly, yet simply."

"Exactly!" cried the professor. "Renoir's painting, like any artistic endeavor that works, is common sense. Yet it took Renoir to show us. Even though less talented persons can copy this work, without Renoir and his painting that simplicity remains hidden, unarticulated. The same is true for theory. Good theory is deceptively beautiful theory. It seems simplicity itself once explained. The challenge for researchers is to create explanations that capture the complexity of human behavior while working from simple premises. Once articulated it is then the charge of the creative practitioner to extend this explanation to practice. Anyone can say "Why, that's common sense," just like anyone can trace a painting, but industrious minds either labor over better explanations or use existing theories to their own advantage."

CONTEMPORARY PERSPECTIVES

Among the permanent questions posed by scholars, the twists and turns of human conflict are perhaps the most pervasive, the most consequential for everyday life. Understanding what gives rise to conflict, how conflict shapes personal and social thought, and why conflict can solidify or stifle relational harmony have consumed serious thinkers for centuries. Contemporary approaches to the study of conflict cross traditional boundaries, and today the scholarly landscape of conflict studies is replete with investigators from numerous fields who operate from a variety of perspectives. Despite wide disagreement as to the causes and consequences of conflict, many have come to believe that the study of conflict is as much the province of communication as it is of psychology, as much an inquiry into the nature of interaction as it is an examination of the psyche. Although this book contains a host of theories from which to understand conflict, they can be roughly divided into two schools of thought: the

Cognitive Perspective and the Interactional Perspective. We will explore these viewpoints in depth.

The Cognitive Perspective

Several of the traditional perspectives displayed in Chapter 1 emphasized the psychological origins of studies of conflict. By history and definition, psychology accentuates the workings of the mind and its influence on behavior. In the area of conflict, researchers generally accept the premise that how and what people think are more impactful than other dimensions of the psychological spectrum. To escape the numerous trappings associated with "psychology" and to stay in step with contemporary approaches, we use the term "cognitive" to refer to those conflict theories that hold thoughts and perceptions as supreme in determining communication behavior.

The Cognitive Perspective is not unconcerned with behavior and interaction but places a far greater emphasis on what goes on in the mind. Theorists working from this perspective privilege perceptions and the characteristics of people over the social construction of meanings and the features of messages in interaction.

According to the Cognitive Perspective, humans are fundamentally goal-oriented beings whose capacities to use information to accomplish personal and social objectives drive their existence. The quest is to understand what goals people seek, in what situations, and why.

The Cognitive Perspective also contends that because people are unique, they interpret and produce messages in unique ways. Therefore the personal characteristics of communicators play a central role in understanding conflict. For the most part, analyzing communication in conflict requires that researchers investigate individual variations in message production and interpretation.

Since the Cognitive Perspective assumes communication does not exist outside the human mind, relevant inquiry into communicator differences examines the mental processes of senders and receivers. Psychological mechanisms characterized by such terms as encoding, decoding, planning, strategizing, remembering, and imagining are the building blocks of the Cognitive Perspective. Cognitive constructs and representations revealed by these mechanisms, such as beliefs, schemata, attitudes, values, perceptions, and attributions, serve to cement the blocks.

Three research questions dominate the Cognitive Perspective: (1) How do individuals and groups differ in their approach to conflict? For example, are males more aggressive than females? Do conservatives use more hard-line bargaining tactics than liberals? Are people high in dogmatism more likely to perceive incompatible goals than people low in dogmatism? (2) What traits best predict communication in conflict? The search for personality traits and enduring beliefs has produced a long list of predispositions to behave, including domineeringness, verbal aggressiveness, assertiveness, locus of control, dogmatism, authoritarianism, and many others. (3) How do perceptions influence communication in conflict? For example, what are deemed socially appropriate strategies for handling conflict? Which strategies are viewed as most effective? What perceptions escalate or mitigate conflict?

The Interactional Perspective

The Interactional Perspective contends that behavior is the place to dig for meaning. Whereas the Cognitive Perspective focuses on the mental processes and perceptions that influence conflict behavior, the Interactional Perspective focuses on the behavior itself. According to the Interactional Perspective, actions or behaviors are a series of interconnected events. Interpretation is established through the patterns of those interlocked events. As an example, consider the pointed question "How about sex?" Between an intimate couple on a late Friday night after holding hands and disclosing secrets, such a question probably stands as an invitation. On a survey questionnaire, following a long set of yes–no questions, such a query undoubtedly serves as a request to respond with an appropriate category. After a painful physical examination and a long look of concern from a physician, the question probably means: "What should I know in order to treat you?" The point is simple. Meaning cannot be discerned independent of context. Messages and behaviors are interpreted in the contexts within which they are embedded. What counts as context, according to the Interactional View, is the general pattern of behavior. Cognitive conceptions of context (such as restaurant, crowd, quarrel) are not as important as the behavioral patterns that define the context. In other words, that one perceives a setting to be a doctor's office is secondary to the behaviors comprising that experience. Action does not occur in isolation. Within the stream of behaviors, meaning becomes apparent.

The Cognitive Perspective defines a given situation as the knowledge structure or schema people hold in their heads. As such, situations are firm, stable entities or activities with fixed labels, such as dining room, party, baseball game, conversation. Actors determine the situation by what they perceive. Perceptions of the situation then influence behavior and strategic choices made by actors. For example, someone may choose to defer to others when in a courtroom and dominate others when playing basketball.

The Interactional Perspective, on the other hand, regards situation as largely emergent. Although perceptions are important, the focus is on behavior. In this light, perceptions constrain but do not define situations. According to the Interactional Perspective, situations are negotiated by actors through the behaviors they enact. Situation is seen as far more fluid than fixed. Although certainly people create the situations they perceive, what they perceive is also influenced by what they do. For instance, imagine a common sales encounter in a retail outlet. The service provider approaches the shopper and offers the standard opening, "Hello, may I help you?" As language is a creatively ambiguous code, the customer looks up and says in a highly suggestive tone, "You sure can help me. What are you doing Friday night?" What situation are these people sharing? Are they involved in what is typically called a customer–service encounter? Or is the situation more one of prospective dating? The Interactional View suggests that it depends how the conversation continues to unfold. The behavior, not the mental category, will define the situation. Just as important, that definition will change when other behaviors are introduced.

Consistent with this position, the Interactional Perspective also embraces the idea of mutual influence. Communication is not so much a product that is produced as it is a process that is enacted. As an ongoing process any given behavior is influenced more by preceding behaviors than by personality or situational constraints. Concepts of importance to conflict scholars—relationships, power, climate, dominance, and the like—are defined not by a single move or by a single actor but through interaction. In this sense, realities and meanings between people emerge and are negotiated through the moves and countermoves of discourse. To be sure, how a particular interaction is accomplished will have an effect on the patterning of future interactions, but the golden rule is that what an interaction is about, its purpose and outcomes, are open to continuous negotiation by the participants.

Three questions dominate the Interactional Perspective: (1) What rules or structures do people use to make interpretations and construct social meanings in conflict situations? (2) What interactional patterns exist in conflict? (3) How do people use messages to accomplish multiple goals in conflicts?

Cognitive and Interactional Theories

As we suggested earlier, theories are framed by the perspectives we employ. In general, theories either attempt to predict or describe relationships. Therefore we often label theories either predictive or descriptive. **Predictive theories answer the *why* behind relationships**. For example, a predictive theory might attempt to explain the connection between verbally aggressive remarks and conflict escalation. Both the remarks and the escalation that occur in conflict vary widely. To say that verbally aggressive remarks lead to conflict escalation is to state that a relationship exists between these two variables. The question that a predictive theory addresses is why. The explanation offered by such a theory will enable researchers and practitioners to predict degrees of conflict escalation. **Descriptive theories**, on the other hand, uncover **how** people do what they do. Although they sometimes have predictive utility, their main focus is to address changes in behavior over time. This is another way of saying that descriptive theories explain the interaction process. Using the same example above, a descriptive theory would attempt to uncover how people engage in verbally aggressive behavior or escalation. What form do the remarks commonly take? How is escalation performed by the parties? What social rules apparently guide such interactions? How does one escalation tactic affect another tactic? These are common questions answered in such descriptive inquiry.

Although they often overlap, theories operating from the Cognitive Perspective generally attempt to predict conflict outcomes whereas theories working from the Interactional Perspective attempt to describe interaction processes.

CONTEMPORARY THEORIES OF CONFLICT

To further illustrate the differences inherent in the Cognitive and Interactional Perspectives, we briefly explore six communication-oriented theories of conflict, three that operate from the Cognitive View and three that privilege the Interactional View. Among the dozens of contemporary theories of conflict in the scholarly pool, the theories in this chapter were chosen for their ability to exemplify the Cognitive and Interactional Perspectives. After first discussing the nuts and bolts of each theory, we then examine how the theory would explain Case 2.2, entitled the "Parking Lot Scuffle." Our aim is to illustrate how different theories and perspectives require that we see markedly different pictures of conflict. In the argot of Madison Avenue, the exposure of several useful conflict theories is a "value-added" feature.

Before diving into the first theory, we review a conflict between two relative strangers as it was captured by an observer. This is the actual talk recorded between the parties. Only key phrases some readers might find offensive were changed in the case study text. We should also note that throughout the remainder of this text we will rely on case studies to illustrate key points and concepts. The first case study offered below is somewhat different as it will serve as a reference tool to highlight the premises of the different theories that follow it.

Case 2.2   The Parking Lot Scuffle

Jay drove to work alone every weekday. On this particular Monday morning, he arrived in his office parking lot a few minutes before 9 o'clock. He had several thoughts on his mind and was not ready for a small moped parked in his reserved spot. In fact, because the moped was set back deep in the spot and between cars, he could not see it until he made the turn into the space. Jay slammed on the breaks but failed to stop before hitting the scooter. The moped wobbled and then fell to the ground. Jay backed up his car and then placed the gear in park. Engine running, he got out of his car and moved quickly to examine the results. He was surveying the damage done to his own bumper when a person (Tim) whom he recognized but could not name approached him on the run. The following conversation then ensued:

01 T: What's your problem? What the hell did you do to my Honda? I said, what did you do?

02 J: I drove into my spot and didn't see your bike. What was it doing parked there?

03 T: Look, my tire's flat. I can't move the wheel. Crushed in and doesn't move.

04 J: I didn't see it until I was on top of it.

05 T: You are going to have to pay for this. I can't afford this.

06 J: What was it doing in a parking space?

07 T: What's your problem? It was parked. Look at the wheel. You came around pretty good.

08 J: Listen, this is my spot. I didn't see it, and it shouldn't have been there. You're lucky I stopped when I did. Look at my bumper. What was it doing there?

09 T: You ass. Who cares whose spot? Some jerk like you drives over my Honda and says, "This is my spot." I don't care who you are, you will fix my Honda.

10 J: You are the one with a problem. Do you work here?

11 T: What does that have to do with anything? Stop looking at your bumper, it looks fine. I want your driver's license and insurance.

12 J: Who in the hell do you think you are? (Starts walking away.)

13 T: You are not going anywhere. (Grabs J's arm.)

14 J: Let go of me. You are screwed. I'm calling the police. (Turns to move toward the office.)

15 T slugs J from behind. The two scuffle for a few moments until others arrive to break them apart.

With the acknowledgment that the punctuation used in Case 2.2 favors the Interactional View, we now demonstrate how several of the contemporary theories of conflict focus on a diverse set of elements in this exchange and draw grossly different conclusions in the process.

Verbal Aggressiveness Theory

In an attempt to explain verbal attacks in interpersonal communication, Infante and his associates (Infante & Wigley, 1986; Infante, 1987) have proposed a theory of verbal aggressiveness. The theory views aggression as a personality trait possessed by people. But unlike traditional concepts of personality that view traits as fixed and stable human properties, Infante sees the aggressiveness trait as a learned predisposition to act. The trait is aroused in situations by cues reminiscent of the learning context. Whether the aggressiveness trait energizes behavior depends on its interaction with factors in the particular situation.

The theory distinguishes between verbal attacks made against ideas or positions and verbal attacks made against self-concept. Argument involves presenting and defending positions on issues while attacking positions held by others. Verbal aggression, on the other hand, includes attacks on another's self-concept. The aggressiveness trait is a predisposition to use personalized attacks in interpersonal communication.

For Infante, verbal aggressiveness is yoked to a trait he labels "argumentativeness." The theory maintains that to understand aggression, we must first embrace the concept of argumentativeness. A person's level of argumentativeness is created by two competing motivational tendencies: the motivation to approach argumentative situations and the motivation to avoid such situations. Highly argumentative people perceive arguing as exciting and intellectually challenging, and experience feelings of invigoration and satisfaction after engaging in argument. People who are low in argumentativeness find arguments uncomfortable and unpleasant. They often associate argument with personal suffering. Not surprisingly, these individuals attempt to avoid arguments or keep them from occurring. In the aftermath of arguments, they often feel anxious and unsettled.

As a result of approaching or avoiding argumentative situations, people develop or fail to develop the social skills needed to succeed in the situation. Highly argumentative persons tend to be more skilled at stating controversies in propositional forms, determining the major issues of contention, discovering arguments to support the position, and delivering arguments effectively. Among the many factors promoting aggressive behavior, it is skill proficiency that weds the traits of argumentativeness and verbal aggressiveness.

In a series of studies, Infante and his colleagues have demonstrated that people low in argumentativeness are more likely to resort to attacks against the self-concept of the other party. In other words, low argumentatives are high in verbal aggressiveness. In a manner of speaking, the two traits represent the opposite poles of a single skill continuum. Because individuals who avoid argumentative situations are often frustrated and lack the skills to succeed in such situations, they turn to aggressive forms of verbal behavior.

Argumentative behavior is a positive trait that is distinct from verbally aggressive behavior. The advantages of argumentativeness are numerous. Research has shown that argumentative behavior is positively related to career satisfaction, career achievement, superior–subordinate satisfaction, and other organizational outcomes (Infante & Gorden, 1985).

Verbal aggressiveness is a negative trait that can produce a variety of effects in interpersonal communication, including conflict escalation, long-lasting damage to self-concepts, and deterioration of relationships. Infante believes that teaching people to value argument and providing them with the skills to succeed in argumentative situations will increase productivity in society and reduce the amount of verbally aggressive acts in interpersonal conflicts.

Case 2.3 Verbal Aggressiveness Theory and the Parking Lot Scuffle

In light of Infante's work, the Parking Lot Scuffle is a clear example of verbally aggressive behavior between two parties. What is at issue here is unclear. The parties jockey back and forth without clarifying the major issues of contention or making any arguments in support of a position. Instead, what transpires, from the view of verbal aggressiveness theory, is an exchange of highly personalized attacks, a volley of verbally aggressive remarks. Tim initiates the conflict with an attack by immediately accusing Jay of aberrant behavior. Although the accusations are couched as questions, their intent is to point a finger at Jay and to put him on the defensive. Jay responds defensively but continues to walk a fine line between seeking information and making a counteraccusation. Finally, by line 10, after absorbing a nonstop barrage, Jay responds with a clearly aggressive remark. The result is an escalation of the conflict from verbal to physical aggression.

While Tim is clearly more aggressive in this encounter, to be fair, both parties personalize the exchange throughout the conflict by using the imperative "you," which has the potential, according to the theory, to count as aggressive. Jay's line 14 cannot be taken as anything less than a personalized attack.

Presumably, the factors in this situation, such as damage to the bike, possible status differences, and the workplace setting promoted the aggressiveness trait in Tim, energizing his verbal behavior into attacks against Jay's self-concept. Given the number of aggressive remarks Tim makes, the theory would presuppose that this actor lacks the skills to argue. As a direct result of this deficiency and the unknown factors that serve as learning cues in the situation, Tim resorts to verbal aggression to resolve this dispute.

Attribution Theory

In a number of studies, Sillars (1980a–c) and his associates (Sillars & Parry, 1982) have applied attribution theory to the study of interpersonal conflict processes. Before describing how this theory has been applied in the conflict arena, we must first review the nature of attribution processes.

At the heart of attribution processes are two premises. First, people interpret behavior in terms of its causes. People naturally attribute characteristics, intentions, and attitudes to the people they encounter. Through this linking process, people attempt to organize and understand the world around them. Second, these causal explanations affect reactions to the judged behavior. Attributions enable actors to behave appropriately toward others in varying contexts.

When trying to make sense of others' behavior we scrutinize the environment, the setting, and people's actions in an attempt to search for reasons behind their actions. Upon discovering a plausible reason or cause, we attribute the other's behavior to this rationale. These reasons fall into two categories: (1) **situational** factors or (2) **dispositional** factors. For example, ability, mood, effort, and knowledge are dispositional causes arising from the individual, whereas task difficulty, interference, and luck are causes considered to be situational in nature stemming from external sources. All factors internal to the individual are considered dispositional, and all factors external to the individual are deemed situational. Two critical biases influence the attributions that actors make.

First, individuals commonly attribute others' behavior to dispositional factors and their own behavior to situational factors (Jones & Nisbett, 1971; Ross, 1977). This is especially true when they believe another's behavior is intentional and goal-directed (Heider, 1958). For example, when searching for reasons for our own behavior, such as nervousness in speaking situations, we commonly attribute our unease to the situation, but when confronted with a nervous speaker we are more apt to attribute his unease as a permanent feature of his character. The tendency for attributors to underestimate the influence of situational factors and overestimate dispositional factors in attributing others' behavior is remarkably strong. Research confirms that attributors infer attitudes from behaviors even when they know the behavior has been severely constrained (Snyder & Jones, 1974; Miller, 1976). This tendency even occurs when observers are told of this bias.

Second, to maintain and enhance self-esteem individuals often defensively attribute actions resulting in negative consequences to external forces and attribute positive consequences of the action to themselves (Bradley, 1978; Zuckerman, 1979). This is especially true in situations involving success and failure. One educational study nicely illustrates this tendency. Based on test scores, math teachers either believed that a student improved in math or regressed in math skill (Beckman, 1970). When asked to explain this difference, the teachers consistently attributed student improvement to their own teaching prowess and performance descent to factors related to the students. Predictably, students reached the opposite conclusion, attributing their success to internal factors and their failure to their teachers.

We can now turn our attention to the attribution in the conflict setting. In several studies, Sillars and his associates investigated three types of conflict management strategies: integrative, avoidance, and distributive. Integrative strategies are messages designed to manage conflict openly through discussion while refraining from negative evaluations of the partner. These benevolent strategies place a premium on collaboration and joint problem-solving. Avoidance strategies are attempts to avoid direct discussion and management of the conflict. These strategies include statements that deny the presence of conflicts, shift the focus of conversations, and sidestep discussions about conflict through indirect or ambiguous talk. Distributive strategies include attempts to resolve the conflict in a zero-sum manner in which one party wins at the others' expense. Distributive messages often include negative evaluations of the partner, such as insults and direct criticism. Sillars has made a strong case that the use of these strategies is mediated by the party's attribution for the conflict. Due to attributional biases, people are more likely to attribute the negative effects of conflict to partners rather than to self. Moreover, people more often see themselves as employing integrative strategies and others as using distributive tactics (Thomas & Pondy, 1977). This bias has important effects on strategy selection. When actors attribute conflict responsibility to their partners, they perceive no threat to escalate the conflict. Hence they turn to distributive and passive-indirect strategies. Conversely, those who attribute responsibility for the conflict to themselves are likely to desire sensible resolution through integrative strategies.

Just as conflict is not static, the attributions we make do not remain constant. As a conflict unfolds, attributions may change, thereby promoting different strategy use. In this sense, the strategies a person employs are part of an emergent process mediated by ongoing reevaluation and attribution. Sillars and Parry (1982) found that as stress levels in conflict situations increase, other-directed blame also rises. Spontaneous verbal statements that provide integrative understandings decrease as stress increases.

On the whole, the research and theory in this area can be summarized by three propositions. First, people choose conflict resolution strategies based on the attributions they make regarding the cause of the conflict. Second, biases in the attribution process tend to encourage noncooperative modes of conflict. Third, the choice of conflict strategies influences the likelihood of conflict resolution and the degree of satisfaction in the relationship.

Case 2.4 **Attribution Theory and the Parking Lot Scuffle**

The Parking Lot exchange is characterized by conflict strategies that promote negative outcomes. Attribution theory describes Tim as employing distributive tactics, including accusations, negative evaluations, insults, and physical aggression. Jay, on the other hand, is attempting to find answers to the dilemma, thereby engaging in a more integrative approach. Whether Jay's line 2 stands as a question or an accusation is open to debate. But given the context of Jay's justification in line 4, he deserves the benefit of the doubt.

If we presume the attributional biases outlined in the theory, then we can surmise that Tim attributes both the accident and the escalating conflict that follows to Jay. While we cannot say for sure, presumably Tim attributes these negative events to Jay's qualities as a person. This dispositional attribution casts Jay as generally uncaring of others' property and unwilling to accept responsibility. From this vantage, Jay is seen by Tim as the aggressor, one who deserves distributive tactics and violence.

According to the theory, Jay is undoubtedly guilty of the same attributional biases and probably is confused early in the encounter about why Tim takes such an aggressive posture. Toward the end of the episode, however, Jay may have concluded that Tim is generally an aggressive person and deserves the hostility expressed in line 14.

Without the perceptions of the parties, we can only surmise as to the attributions made. But attribution theory suggests that Tim's choice of distributive tactics, including the concluding violence, is a direct result of the attributions he made. Given Tim's distributive tactics, it is hard to imagine that a more positive outcome was possible in this conflict.

Social Influence Theory

Our culture frowns on aggression. We learn in stories, in classrooms, and in the workplace that aggression is socially unacceptable, harmful to all parties, and rarely without serious consequences. Social influence theory suggests that people avoid aggressive acts due to the corresponding judgments associated with such a stamp, such as blame, lowered attraction, avoidance by others, fear, legal sanctions, and other forms of retribution. But despite the social norms and pressures against aggressive acts, people all too often resort to verbal and physical abuse to resolve conflicts. The question is—why? Tedeschi and his associates (Tedeschi, Schlenker, & Bonoma, 1973; Tedeschi, 1983) have puzzled over this social paradox and offer an explanation of aggression that attempts to distinguish between actions and perceptions. For Tedeschi, coercion and aggression are terms that, though intertwined, are distinctly different.

According to the theory, coercive power exists when actors employ any of the various forms of threats and punishments. Punishment is defined as any stimulus a person will seek to avoid and do nothing to attain, ranging from noxious stimulation (physical pain) to social punishments such as insults and rejection, from the deprivation of existing resources, such as attention, money, or information, to the denial of promised rewards. Tedeschi defines threats as any message that includes a demand and a statement that punishment will follow noncompliance. People engage in coercive power anytime they punish another or make a threat.

Aggression, on the other hand, is a matter of perception and moral judgment. Aggression is the negative label used in our culture to describe the antisocial motives behind coercive power. At the heart of this theory lies the premise that not all coercive actions are perceived as aggressive. Coercion is perceived as aggression only when it is not legitimized by social norms and values. A parent disciplining a child, a firefighter knocking down a door with an ax, a lifeguard immobilizing a thrashing swimmer all involve some form of coercion, but none would be labeled aggressive. The key determinants of perceived aggression are the judgments made by the observer that the intent to do harm exists and that there is no reasonable explanation for the action to justify it (Tedeschi, Smith, & Brown, 1974). Under certain conditions, coercion is warranted and the actor averts the indictment of aggression. The theory contends that people use coercive power when they believe such acts will not be viewed as aggression by observers.

For example, when people do not believe they can successfully gain interpersonal objectives by using benevolent modes of influence, such as reasoning or rewards, they may choose to use coercive power to gain their way with others. The theory suggests that people are motivated to employ coercive tactics because they are highly effective, but they refrain from using such tactics to avoid the stigma of the aggression label. To avoid perceptions of aggression, social influence theory submits that people search for justifications for the use of coercion. Justifications are explanations or reasons for behavior that accept responsibility for the outcomes but assert that positive motives or values led to the behavior. Essentially, justifications attempt to reverse or neutralize initial negative impressions formed by others.

Explaining the use of coercive behaviors boils down to the conditions surrounding observer and actor perceptions. When someone believes that a justification exists, then coercive behavior is likely. Stated more simply, **justifications encourage the use of coercion**. Although the grounds for coercion are often situation- and person-specific, certain factors increase the availability of potential justifications in the person's mind. In particular, social injustice, violation of social rules and norms, and unprovoked threats serve to justify or legitimize coercive acts. A series of studies have enabled Tedeschi to conclude that the availability of justifications for the use of coercion in a given situation is directly related to the frequency of coercive acts.

Case 2.5 **Social Influence Theory and the Parking Lot Scuffle**

The use of coercive power, as conceptualized by social influence theory, abounds in the case. Tim begins the series of threats in line 5 when he suggests that Jay will be punished for his mistake. Specifically, this turn threatens to extract money from Jay to pay for the damages. In line 9, Tim again issues a threat. He implies that, regardless of Jay's status, he is responsible to repair the damages. In line 13, Tim's demand not to move is coordinated by his physical grabbing of Jay. Essentially, Tim threatens that further physical punishment will follow a retreat. Jay responds to this last threat with a coercive statement of his own. He threatens Tim's freedom by suggesting that he will be punished by the authorities once they are informed of the events. Tim follows this threat with physical punishment, hitting Jay from behind.

This analysis leaves little room to doubt that coercive power is employed by both parties in this conflict. Social influence theory offers an explanation for the reasons why. According to the theory, in order to avoid the label of aggression the parties will engage in coercive acts only when available justifications exist. Presumably, Tim believes that

the damage done to the moped supports the use of coercion. A possible status difference between the two parties may promote the feeling of injustice. That Jay did not
immediately apologize might also have served to justify his actions.

  Jay, on the other hand, has a host of possible justifications that might lead him
to use the threat in line 14, including self-defense, Tim's unusual behavior, unprovoked
threats, and the fact the moped was wrongly parked and hidden in his parking space.

The Coordinated Management of Meaning

The coordinated management of meaning (CMM) is the first of the interactional
theories we will consider. The theory focuses on how individuals organize, manage,
and coordinate their meanings and actions with one another (Pearce, 1976; Pearce
& Cronen, 1980). Basically, the theory proposes that the interpretation of the meaning of a conversation or message will be shaped by the context or nature of the
relationship between the interactants as well as the self-concept and culture of each
individual. Because each individual inevitably brings unique experiences and meanings to any conversation, meaning will always be to some degree idiosyncratic or
unique. The more individuals share similar or complementary world views, self-
concepts, and understandings of their relationship, the more likely they will arrive at
similar interpretations of conversations and messages. The theory provides a framework for explaining both how an individual attributes meaning to a message, conversation, or relationship and how interactants then come to coordinate both their
meanings and actions in the course of a conversation. Meanings are important
because they lead to decisions about what action to take and what action to avoid.

  The theory proposes that individuals organize meanings hierarchically, and use
one level of meaning in order to determine meaning on another level (Figure 2.1).
The seven levels of meaning described by the theory range from the broad and
abstract to the concrete and specific. The hierarchy can be viewed as an inverted
pyramid or triangle. At the bottom of the triangle is a specific message within a

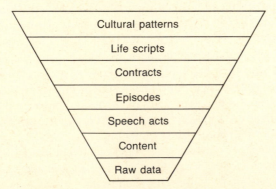

Figure 2.1 Coordinated management of
meaning: hierarchy.

conversation. The hierarchy demonstrates the many layers of meaning that we coordinate and use to create coherence in interpreting specific messages and actions. Starting from the top, the first two levels of meaning are broad-based, cumulative ways of viewing the world and one's self. **Cultural patterns** refer to a socially shaped framework for viewing the world and one's roles and actions within it. This broadest context acknowledges the influence of one's particular cultural experience and how it shapes, how all experience is viewed and interpreted. The second level, **life scripts**, specifically encompasses the individual's self-concept and expectations for what can and should happen to him/her. The next level of meaning concerns the specific individual or individuals with whom one is interacting at a particular point in time. **Contracts** define and specify expectations of the particular relationship based on the kinds of episodes that occur within the relationship. The next level of meaning focuses on the particular interaction taking place at a particular point in time. **Episodes** define the kind of activity that is occurring between individuals based on the kinds and sequencing of messages being exchanged. More specifically, the next three levels focus on a particular message that a speaker has produced in the flow of interaction. **Speech acts** identify the intent of the speaker ("What is the speaker trying to do by saying this to me?"), while **content** is the decoding of the substance of the message, and **raw sensory data** concern the audio and visual signals that reach the brain.

An individual coordinates meaning by using one level in the hierarchy to aid in the interpretation of meaning at another level. For example, if the intent of the speaker is unclear (speech act) then the receiver relies on the nature of the episode, the kind of relationship, and his/her life script and culture to help identify the likely intent. This logical relationship between levels produces **constitutive rules** for determining meaning. Constitutive rules stipulate how meanings at one level determine meanings at another level. For example, if an individual tells you "you're looking good" you would rely on the nature of the relationship (e.g., doctor–patient versus male–female strangers versus romantic partners), your self-concept (healthy, attractive), and the nature of the interaction between you (physical exam, chance encounter on a street, romantic interlude) to determine what this message "counts as." This interpretation then becomes a basis for action. Relying on **regulative rules** formed by one's culture, self-concept, relationship, type of episode, and speaker's intention, one determines an appropriate response. Regulative rules specify what is appropriate action given the nature of the relationship, the episode, and what the other person has said. Do you respond with relief to an indication that you are healthy? Or do you give the stranger an icy stare? Or do you return the compliment to your romantic partner? So constitutive rules are means for identifying the meanings of relationships, messages, and so on, while regulative rules identify what action to take given these meanings. In this way, we determine both meaning and action.

An individual's meanings and actions become coordinated with one another as their rules become intermeshed. However, it is important to note that "coordinated" does not necessarily mean that individuals agree on the meaning of what is going on. Rules can be shared in common as individuals share meanings on a variety of levels. But rules may also differ yet yield coordinated action. Consider the young college student who complains that he hates going home on the weekend because as soon as he enters the house his father starts interrogating him about his personal life at college. The son feels that he is independent, that he no longer needs to report to his father. The father, he believes, should respect his privacy. When his father asks him questions he feels that he is treating him as a child and does not trust him. If the father were asked for his interpretation of these visits home he would explain that he wants to be a good father and maintain a close and caring relationship with his son; therefore he tries to show his interest and caring by asking about his son's life at school. The more his son withdraws, the more he feels he must persist because he does not want their relationship to deteriorate and become distant. And, of course, the more he persists, the more the son withdraws. The result is a very well-coordinated conversation, one in which the participants do not even suspect that the event has a different meaning for the other. The coordinated management of meaning provides a basis for identifying and understanding how the same event can have different meanings for the parties involved and how these meanings affect their actions.

The theory explains why participants sometimes seem vulnerable to escalating moves in interaction. According to CMM, people act according to the interpretive rules they use. Through interaction, participants create an interlocking rule system. The system is considered interlocked because the rule-guided behavior of each party is interpreted and responded to by the rules of the other. In other words, each action becomes the condition of the next rule-guided interpretation. Since the type of interaction participants produce is a function of the rule system they create, certain patterns can be self-sustaining. Although most episodes vary widely, in some cases, people become so enmeshed in an episode as to be "out of control" (Cronen, Pearce, & Snavely, 1980). In these situations, the rule system created by the participants produces unwanted repetitive patterns (URPs). The same patterns emerge again and again as participants interpret and respond to each other's actions in the same way. Such repetitive patterns are difficult to recognize for participants and are hard to break.

Case 2.6   **The Coordinated Management of Meaning and the Parking Lot Scuffle**

According to CMM, each individual inevitably brings unique experiences and meanings to any conversation; hence meaning will always be to some degree idiosyncratic. The more individuals share similar or complementary world views, self-concepts, and understandings of their relationship, the more likely they will arrive at similar interpretations of conversations and messages. The lack of a common context in the Parking Lot Scuffle portends that interpretations of utterances will be especially problematic.

In this case we do not have data concerning the individuals involved and their perceptions, so we must infer from their actions how they might see the situation. Furthermore, the individuals are strangers and so are more likely to see the situation differently and to not understand one another's perspective.

Tim aggressively confronts Jay over the accident. This strong opening may reflect a life script that includes a self-concept of standing up for himself, to avoid being pushed around by others. In addition, as strangers Tim's and Jay's relational contract is one totally defined by the situation of the accident and each must use extraneous information to predict how the other might act. Given that Tim tells us that he cannot afford to have a moped fixed and that we know Jay has a parking place while Tim does not, it is possible that Tim perceives Jay as a higher status person who may treat him poorly. These conclusions may produce the regulative rule that if one is in a threatening situation with a higher status person then one must stand up for oneself so that advantages will not be taken. Note how Tim continues to focus on the damage done to his bike and how Jay must pay for it.

What counts as appropriate behavior in this situation is up to the participants. Because the nature of the relationship and the episode is relatively unfamiliar, other regulative rules specifying appropriate action are also unclear. Constitutive rules are also contested. Both Jay and Tim struggle over how to interpret their speech acts, as displayed in lines 10 and 11, when Tim impugns Jay to explain what employment has to do with the accident. Only general cultural patterns help the actors interpret many of the remarks and questions they receive. In fact, it appears as if Jay may be slow on the uptake, taking questions in lines 1 and 8 on face value, rather than as challenges.

We might speculate that the participants have created a rule system that encourages the use of escalating tactics. The redundancy of tactics in the episode supports this conclusion. Tim repeatedly threatens Jay, using a wide variety of speech acts to do so. Jay, on the other hand, who seems always to be on the defensive in the episode, repeatedly resorts to questions and justifications. Almost as if the episode is written to music, each accusation or threat by Tim increases in intensity, while each question by Jay responds with rising force. This may suggest that Tim and Jay have created a repetitive pattern of caustic actions. From this vantage, we can see the same patterns emerge line after line as participants respond to each other's actions in the same way. In any case, the theory would suggest that the Parking Lot Scuffle is more a conflict over how to coordinate necessarily ambiguous meanings than it is a conflict about the moped accident.

Confrontation Episodes Theory

Newell and Stutman (1988, 1991) offer a descriptive theory of social confrontation episodes. Their description of confrontation episodes is based on a view of communication as an activity performed cooperatively between two or more parties. According to the theory, an interaction is not simply talk about some topic but a purposeful event that participants co-create.

Social confrontation episodes involve conflict over conduct and rules of conduct. The confrontation episode is initiated when one participant signals the other participant that his/her behavior has violated (or is violating) a rule or expectation for appropriate conduct within the relationship or situation. The function of a social confrontation may generally be described as working through disagreement over behaviors and thus negotiating expectations for future conduct. The episode is recognizable as a sequence of behaviors moving from initiation to resolution.

The function of the episode appears to be to produce typical issues and sequences of interaction. Before the problematic issue can be explored in the episode, the participants must first agree to the social or relational legitimacy of the rule. Once this critical issue is settled, the behavior in question can be assessed with respect to the rule. For example, a person may confront a spouse over spending money for clothing beyond a budget limit. Once the confrontee acknowledges the legitimacy of this relational rule (budget), questions concerning the act of spending too much for clothing in relation to this rule can be explored. For example, did the confrontee perform the behavior in question? Does the behavior constitute a violation of this rule? Is there a superseding rule that takes precedence? Is the confrontee responsible for his/her behavior? The episode is then concluded with solutions ranging from remedy to legislation of a new rule.

Newell and Stutman (1988) provide a model of the social confrontation episode, which displays the various ways the episode may develop depending on the issues between the parties (Figure 2.2).

The purpose of this model is to define the confrontation episode and to illustrate how confrontation episodes may differ from one another in their lines of development. While action moves from initiation through development toward some sort of closure or resolution to the problem, the pattern of interaction may vary greatly. Although the confronter may perceive that the confrontee has behaved in a rule-breaking manner, how the problem ultimately comes to be defined and resolved depends on the interaction between the participants. Confrontation episodes are **issue driven**. In other words, the development of the episode emerges from the points of controversy between the participants. The model then illustrates the major variations in how the problem is defined and resolved through interaction.

Constructed as an issue tree, the model displays the various issues likely to occur within confrontation (designated A–F), and the track or the line of development (designated 1–6) that any particular episode might take depending on the points of disagreement between the participants. The point of controversy determines the variation of a particular confrontation episode (tracks 1–6). The model serves as a visual display of the logical relationship between central issues that may emerge in any particular confrontation. As such, it illustrates ways in which the episode may develop depending on the interaction between the participants.

The major split between tracks occurs over whether the confronter's expectations are explicitly or implicitly granted legitimacy by the confrontee, or whether the confrontee challenges the legitimacy of the expectations. The conversation moves along track 1, **nonlegitimacy**, if the confrontee challenges the legitimacy of the confronter's expectations, in essence arguing that the implied rule is not mutually acceptable or agreed upon. If the confrontee does not challenge the legitimacy of the rule, a number of other lines of argument remain. On track 2, **justification**, the episode revolves around whether or not this is a "special" situation for which the confrontee invokes a superseding rule for the extenuating circumstances. This rule is also open to challenges of legitimacy, but this time by the confronter rather than the confrontee. On track 3, **deny behavior**, the question concerns whether or not

A. Is the implied rule mutually accepted as legitimate?
B. Is this a special situation?
C. If invoked, is the superseding rule mutually accepted as legitimate?
D. Did the confrontee actually perform the behavior in question?
E. Does the behavior constitute a violation of the rule?
F. Does the confrontee accept responsibility for the behavior?

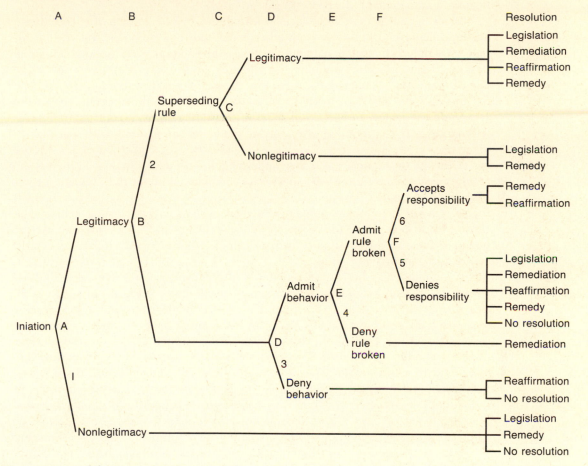

Figure 2.2 An elaborate model of social confrontation. Adapted from Newell and Stutman (1988). Copyright by the Speech Communication Association; reprinted by permission of the publisher.

the confrontee actually performed the behavior in question. On track 4, **deny rule broken**, the issue is one of interpretation as to what constitutes a violation of the rule. On track 5, **deny responsibility**, the issue revolves around the excuse offered by the confrontee in order to deny responsibility for the behavior. Confrontations that develop along the lines of track 6 stand out from the others because of the lack of controversy in defining the problem. On track 6, **accepts responsibility**, the confrontee accepts responsibility for his/her behavior and moves to reaffirm the rule or remedy the situation. The response of the "accused" to the confrontation determines the track the episode will take. Once on a particular line of development, the confronter is primarily left the job of evaluating the confrontee's response. The confronter's evaluation may either "hold" the interactants to a particular issue or may allow them to move toward resolution. Resolution requires interactants to negotiate an acceptable response to the problem.

According to the theory, the social confrontation episode has a particular pattern, an imprint, which stands out from other communication episodes. Yet within this pattern is diversity; each enactment of social confrontation may display the uniqueness of a fingerprint. In particular, the initiating act serves to identify or define the episode that is to be enacted. Furthermore, the manner of the initiation sets the tone for the episode. The key for a social confrontation episode to occur lies in the receiver's willingness to honor the speaker's initiating act as a confrontation. This willingness may be described as conferring the act of complaining with social legitimacy.

Although the expectation or rule underlying the complaint may be arguable, the receiver accepts the right of the speaker to complain. Without this element a complaint may be ignored, a complainer requested to go away, or the message responded to as if it were some other complaining activity such as nagging or bellyaching. The receiver may even refuse (or be unable) to hear the message as a complaint. Actors negotiate the episodes they enact by first dealing with problematic initiatives in such a way as to satisfy their goals.

A complaint may be "heard" naively or strategically and receive a multitude of responses. For an example of the range of possibilities, let's consider the fairly straightforward statement, "You're late." A receiver might directly acknowledge this as a complaint, signifying a confrontation over rule infringement by responding: "I'm sorry. I forgot to set my alarm clock. I won't let it happen again." Or the receiver might respond in a manner that suggests the statement may simply be an assertion of a fact without a necessarily negative connotation. By asking, "Did I miss anything important?" the receiver at least opens up the conversation for confrontation should the sender decide to persist. Other responses simply add additional comment on this "fact": "Everyone says I'll be late for my own funeral." "This is early for me." Alternately, responses may cast the statement as a complaint, but one requiring sympathy or commiseration: "Isn't it terrible? You just can't count on anyone anymore." "I know just how you feel. I hate waiting for people." Of course, the receiver may directly or indirectly challenge the sender's right to complain about the receiver's behavior: "You're not my keeper." "Your watch is keeping good time." Finally, the statement may be cast as an insult deserving reciprocation: "Not late enough to miss you."

The possible range of responses pinpoints the problematic nature of initiation. The receiver is always able to respond to the initial act in a manner inconsistent with its intent. Unwittingly interpreting a complaint as an insult or some other speech act is a common occurrence that forces the confronter to meet the resistance if confrontation is to occur. Such naive responses on the part of the receiver are not necessarily an issue of communication competence, but rather a function of the unique nature of communication episodes. To recast an episode is not a simple matter of reinitiation but one of gaining the cooperation of the other so that a confrontation will proceed. No one move can meet these conditions. Meaning is therefore negotiated by both parties even at the point of initiation.

Case 2.7 **Confrontation Episodes Theory and the Parking Lot Scuffle**

From the view of confrontation episodes theory, the Parking Lot Scuffle could be subtitled "Who Broke What Rule?" Tim and Jay each frame the problem and thus the responsibility for the problem differently. Ultimately their failure to agree on the root problem leads to escalation and a physical fight. Tim focuses on the implicit rule that one should not hit a parked vehicle. Meanwhile, Jay focuses on the implied rule that one should not park in someone else's parking space. This rule provides backing to Jay's excuse that he did not see the moped in time to stop. Inevitably what unfolds is competition over who gets to be the confronter in this episode. Each is trying to establish that he has been harmed by the behavior of the other. Tim claims he was harmed by Jay running into his parked bike. Jay claims that his car was damaged because Tim parked where he should not have. Their inability to negotiate the episode in terms of what is the relevant rule and who is the confronter and confrontee leads to a breakdown of conversation and resorting to physical violence. Each party lays down different tracks for the conversation, riding a train right past the other.

If we look at each of Tim's turns in the conversation, we see that his points are coherent with one another. He begins by confronting Jay for hitting his bike, then lists damage done, and seeks a remedy: "You're going to pay." Meanwhile, Jay only fleetingly follows Tim's lead by offering an excuse for his violation of the rule invoked by Tim: he could not see the bike in time to stop. But Jay immediately moves to shift to a different confrontation by counterconfronting Tim for parking in his space. Tim repeatedly denies the relevancy of Jay's counterconfrontation and returns to the damage done, seeking a remedy. When Jay attempts to shift the conversation by asking Tim if he works there and then to end it by walking away, Tim makes verbal and physical moves to continue the episode.

Reciprocity Theory

Conversations unfold as each person takes a turn at talk. With each turn the person makes a "move"—performs a behavior that has strategic significance. Any particular interaction is created through a particular sequence of moves as each participant takes a turn in response to the other's turn. Each move influences the next move, which in turn influences the following move and so on. Within the Interactional View, this is known as mutual influence.

Perhaps the strongest feature of mutual influence is the norm of reciprocity. According to several theorists, reciprocity is a social norm that undergirds all social exchange processes (Roloff & Campion, 1985). Gouldner (1960) suggests that the norm prescribes two things: "people should help those who have helped them, and people should not injure those who have helped them." As Roloff (1987b, p. 12) puts it, "a recipient of a benefit is morally obligated to return a benefit in kind."

More specifically, **reciprocity** is defined as the process of behavioral adaptation where one party responds in a similar direction to another party's behaviors with behaviors of comparable functional value (Street & Cappella, 1985; Burgoon, Dillman, & Stern, 1991). The key to reciprocity is function. Because the same behavior may serve different purposes, reciprocity is often more complex than matching. For example, a joke may serve to reduce anxiety, establish rapport, or point out an imperfection in a nonthreatening way. If party A tells a joke to defuse tensions, party B is said to have reciprocated if she engages in a behavior that also serves that function. Party B need not tell a joke to reciprocate.

Compensation is the corresponding process of behavioral adaptation where one responds to a partner's behaviors with opposite behaviors of comparable functional value. For example, suppose party A initially uses dominant gestures and remarks in a conflict situation, while party B employs more conventional messages. If party A then reduces dominance in response to B, reciprocity is said to have occurred. The same would be true if party B increases dominance in response to A. Reciprocity also occurs in the example of mutual convergence where party A decreases dominance while at the same time party B increases it. But when one or both parties change in opposite directions, then they have compensated rather than reciprocated. This would be the case if party B became submissive in response to the dominance of party A.

Reciprocity and compensation are highly evident in conflict interaction. Research clearly shows that threats are often followed by counterthreats (Deutsch & Krauss, 1960), while concessions offered in bargaining situations are frequently followed in kind (Putnam & Jones, 1982a, b). In an analysis of oppositional interchanges in 52 different families during routine family dinners, Vuchinich (1984, 1990) found strong evidence of a symmetrical matching of conversational behaviors. His analysis showed that the best determinant of any given move was the immediately preceding turn.

Reciprocity theory maintains that escalation and de-escalation patterns in conflict interaction are often a result of reciprocity and compensation. Any move is likely to establish a new and powerful sequence in a conflict encounter. Initial moves and patterns set the tone in brief episodes, such as confrontations, while more protracted conflicts move through stages of reciprocal patterns. For example, Gottman (1979) observed that in distressed relationships wives often match their husbands' initial moves and engage in one-upmanship, creating a highly charged and bitter interaction. Putnam and Jones (1982a, b) found that bargainers generally engage in an attack–defend style of conflict but uphold the norm of positive reciprocity when cooperative gestures are offered.

Case 2.8 **Reciprocity Theory and the Parking Lot Scuffle**

The parties in the Parking Lot Scuffle demonstrate the reciprocal nature of conflict interaction. In this exchange, the parties reciprocate behaviors that functionally serve to threaten, insult, and blame one another.

Let's track the sequence of turns by the functions they serve. In line 1, Tim makes an accusation cast as a question. Jay reciprocates by matching Tim's accusation with a negative question of his own. Tim ignores the question and challenges Jay with a commentary about the damage to the moped. Jay compensates by offering an excuse in line 4, but Tim does not follow suit. In line 5, Tim makes a clear threat. This move is functionally reciprocated with an accusing question. Jay matches this accusation with a question that serves the same purpose. Tim continues to reciprocate and then follows with a description of damage. Jay compensates for the accusation in line 8 by offering a justification, matches Tim's damage description with one of his own, and then adds an accusatory question. Tim reciprocates with an insult and threat. Jay holds firm in line 10 and reciprocates with a veiled counterthreat. Tim defends in line 11 and counters with a demand, which is disconfirmed by Jay in line 12. Tim escalates the conflict in line 13 by reciprocating with a threat. Jay raises the stakes with a counterthreat. Tim resorts to violence.

While a number of the interpretations made are open to debate, the point is clear. The unfolding interaction can be seen as enormously influenced by norms of reciprocity. From this view, reciprocity of the accusations and threats offered by both parties escalates the conflict into a destructive situation.

CONCLUSION

In our effort to understand some of the contemporary perspectives on conflict, two questions have received less attention than they deserve: What is a theory of conflict? and Why are theories important? Through the six theories presented, we have demonstrated that different explanations point to entirely disparate features and issues of conflict. Differing treatments also lead to distinctive claims and conclusions. Whereas one theory pointed at the perceptions held by the actors, another theory ignored perceptions and focused instead on the interpretive rules used by conflict participants. Where one theory makes predictions about the causes of aggression, another describes how conflict episodes are negotiated. Without question, theories frame what we see. They allow us to explain conflict processes.

So what is to be learned from this exercise? At least three points are worth noting. First, different theories can complement, inform, or compete with each other. In many instances, theories serve to distinguish different issues in a conflict, thereby offering unique strengths and weaknesses. Depending on the premises they embrace, these multiple images will furnish us with a well-rounded view of a conflict. Occasionally, however, the premises found in theories will compete, forcing us to choose one vantage or another. For example, verbal aggressiveness theory informs us that aggression is largely a matter of situational learning and argumentation skill deficiency. In contrast, attribution theory suggests that aggression occurs as a result of perceptions, not traits or skills. We are likely to engage in aggression when we attribute incompatibility to the other party. On one level these two theories appear compatible. They are, after all, both concerned with the verbal tactics participants employ and consequences that result from their use. But the reason why a person behaves aggressively is markedly different for these theories. So much so, that conflict intervention (an area for discussion in Chapters 8 and 9) is an entirely different matter depending on the explanation one prefers. Where one theory suggests teaching people how to argue, the other theory implicitly recommends changing participant perceptions.

The first impulse for many of us is to select one and reject the other on the basis of what rings true. Just remember that ringing true and being true are different matters. As we suggested earlier, theories are rarely right or wrong. We would suggest that explanations will make more sense in some situations than in others. Do not accept one theory and reject another. Instead, collect them voraciously and use them as you would a hammer, wrench, or saw, selecting them when the right project comes along.

Second, the practitioner must make a series of choices when attempting to assess and study conflict processes. Of greatest consequence is theory selection. Although this need not be a permanent choice, the practitioner must guard against two traps. First, we must remain true to the theory, allowing it to expose the concepts and relationships of importance. This can occur only if we use one explanation at a time and develop our analysis fully before looking through another lens. Mixing and matching theories will often result in distortion. The metaphor of theories as colored lenses is particularly pertinent. If a red theory will have us see red, and a green colored lens will make conflict appear green, then will we see more if we combine them? The answer is usually no. The natural inclination is to combine theories to acquire the most powerful lens possible. But because many of the premises inherent in the explanations compete or are contradictory, we see less, not more. By combining the colors, we are left with a glass so dark that it is opaque. Second, we must guard against an interpretation of theory that is so rigid as to render it useless in a specific case. A theory is a broad explanation, one that may not account for the intricacies and nuances of a particular case. To apply theories to cases with success, we must be creative, allowing the explanations to point the way, to frame our inquiries, but not to complete them. The urge to use theories to create formulas or cookbooks for assessing and managing conflict misses the mark entirely. If the complexities of conflict interaction could be boiled down to a few steps or how-to rules, there would be a great deal less destructive conflict in society and a great deal more optimism. Unfortunately, matters are not that simple. We are not likely to solve the riddle of human behavior anytime soon. Instead, the best we can do is apply theories we believe are useful and manage conflict as these theories suggest.

Finally, theories should be evaluated on the basis of utility. As you read through this book, certain concepts and theories will speak to you and others will not. Some theories will confirm your already existing prejudices; others will stretch your thinking and supply you with new insights and avenues for conflict management. The ideas and theories presented in this book have stood the first test of utility. Scholars and researchers have turned them over time and again, looking for flaws and searching for benefits. While no consensus exists regarding the ideas presented in these pages, the very fact that they receive continued scrutiny suggests they may hold promise. The real test, however, is for practitioners to employ these ideas in the marketplace of everyday life. The best theories and concepts are the ones that allow you to understand and manage the conflicts in your relationships, in your family, in your organization, in your life. No other measure of a theory can compete with that crucial test.

Chapter
3

The Role of Communication in Conflict

Some perspectives on conflict are concerned more directly with explaining the role of communication in conflict than others. As we noted in Chapter 2, communication perspectives start with certain assumptions about and emphasize certain features of conflict. Although cognitive and interactional theories highlight different elements of conflict behavior, taken as a whole they suggest some important properties of communication.

We will discuss five key properties of conflict interaction that help to explain the thrust and direction of conflict. These five properties of conflict interaction are:

1. Conflict interaction is sustained by the moves and countermoves of participants; moves and countermoves are based on the power that parties exert.
2. Patterns of behavior in conflicts tend to perpetuate themselves.
3. Conflict moves are embedded in larger interaction sequences.
4. As senseless and chaotic as conflict interaction may appear, it has a general direction that can be understood.
5. Conflict interaction affects the relationships between participants.

There are two main reasons why these properties in particular emerge as central principles. First, these five properties map a fairly comprehensive and unified approach to understanding how conflicts are pushed in constructive or destructive directions. The first property concerns the mechanics of interaction itself; it demonstrates how behaviors in sequence, moves and countermoves, are the means through which conflicts unfold. The second property deals with the momentum of conflict behavior; it recognizes the tendency for conflicts to build their own thrust as they progress. The third describes how sequences of conflict moves group into larger units. These units carry meaningful interpretations for parties in conflict. The fourth property points to the underlying coherence of conflict interaction and thus helps to explain its direction. The final property focuses on the interplay between conflict interaction and the relationships between participants; it emphasizes the consequences that result when conflicts head in either constructive or destructive directions.

There is a second reason why these five properties of conflict interaction emerge as keys for understanding conflict. Each property suggests a place where conflict interaction is vulnerable to constructive and destructive influences; each points to a force that influences the route conflict interaction takes. We describe these forces in more detail below. One force, working habits, is discussed in detail in this chapter. The other four forces (power, reframing, climate, and face-saving) are discussed in depth in later chapters.

We will overview each of the five properties, noting how communication is central to each.

PROPERTY 1   *Conflict interaction is sustained by the moves and countermoves of participants; moves and countermoves are based on the power that participants exert.*

Conflicts emerge as a series of actions and reactions. All of us have heard someone using the "He did X and then she said Y and then he said Z and then . . ." formula to explain a quarrel. When incompatibility arises people try to cope with it; the way in which their actions mesh plays an important role in the direction the conflict takes. Moves and countermoves in conflict are often based on the participants' ability and willingness to exert power. **Power** can be defined as the **capacity to act effectively**. Power sometimes takes the form of outward strength, status, money, or allies, but these are only the most obvious sources of power. There are many others (like time, attractiveness, persuasive ability) that operate in a much more subtle fashion.

In the Women's Hotline (Case I.1), for example, Diane might have used the other workers' guilt to try to get her way, and the workers did use their seniority and familiarity with their jobs to pass judgment on her by drafting a list of worker responsibilities. In both cases, power is used much more subtly than is commonly assumed. More generally, a person is powerful when he or she has the **resources** to act and to influence others and the **skills** to do this effectively (Deutsch, 1973). The third party in the Hotline case provides a good example of the effective use of power: she had certain resources to influence the group—experience with other conflicts and knowledge about how to work with groups—and made skillful use of them to move both sides toward a solution.

Power exerts an important influence over conflict interaction; people's attempts to mobilize and apply power can drastically shift the direction conflict takes. As possible solutions to the conflict are considered, the parties learn how much power each is willing to employ to encourage or prevent the adoption of various alternatives. This is critical in the definition of conflict issues and solutions, because it signals how important the issue is.

The balance of power often tips the scale in a productive or destructive direction. If he or she perceives that he or she can dominate others, there is little incentive to compromise; a dominant party can get whatever he/she wants (at least in the short run), and negotiation only invites others to cut into the parties' solution. In the same vein, feeling powerless can sap parties' resolve and cause them to appease more powerful individuals. Of course, this method often encourages powerful people to be more demanding. Only when **all participants have at least some power** is the conflict likely to move in a productive direction. At the Women's Hotline (Case I.1), the third party was only called in after both sides, Diane and the workers, had played their first "trumps"—the workers by informing Diane of her responsibilities, and Diane by filing a grievance. The use of power could have prompted further moves and countermoves: rather than calling in a third party, both sides could have continued to try to force each other to yield, and the conflict could have continued escalating. However, in this case the two sides perceived each other's power and, because they wanted the Hotline to survive, backed off. As risky as this process of balancing power is, many social scientists have come to the conclusion that it is a necessary condition for constructive conflict resolution (Deutsch, 1973; Folberg & Taylor, 1984; Pruitt & Rubin, 1986).

Power often begets power. Those who have resources and the skills to use them wisely can employ them so their power increases and reinforces itself. Those with little power find it hard to assert themselves and build a stronger base for the future. Yet, as we have noted, for conflicts to maintain a constructive direction there should be a **balance of power**. This requires members to **reverse the usual flow**: the weaker parties must build their power; the stronger ones must share theirs or at least not use it to force or dominate the weaker ones. As we will see in Chapter 4, managing this reversal is both tricky and risky. It is tricky because power is hard to identify and sharing power may run against members' natural inclinations. It is risky because the process of increasing some parties' power and decreasing or suspending others' is a sensitive operation and can precipitate even sharper conflicts.

Regardless of how unpleasant or risky it may be to deal with power, power is a fact of life in conflicts. Ignoring it or pretending power differences do not exist is a sure formula for failure, because power is operating and will direct the moves and countermoves in the conflict. Power is one of the strongest influences on conflict. We will examine power as a force that influences conflict moves and conflict interaction in detail in Chapters 4 and 7.

PROPERTY 2   *Patterns of behavior in conflicts tend to perpetuate themselves.*

Almost inevitably, conflict interaction gains a momentum or life of its own. It tends toward repetitive cycles. In part, this tendency is present in any type of human interaction—conflict or otherwise. Any message is based on some perhaps only barely conscious assumption about how it will be received. Each assumption or prediction about the reaction is based on an estimate, a best guess, about the other person or group as a whole. The choice of message anticipates and reflects the response it seeks and thus promotes the reaction included in its construction. A predictable sequence of act–response–counterresponse gets established quickly in conflict interaction because each message in the sequence helps to elicit the response it receives.

This tendency toward self-perpetuation is encouraged and reinforced by its own usefulness. People in conflict find it useful to "know what to expect." Any basis of predictability is more assuring than not knowing what the group will do next. One can prepare counterresponses and strategies during a conflict if one can predict reactions to one's own statements. For this reason, people are often willing to make assumptions about the way others will act before any move is made (Kriesberg, 1973; Sillars, 1980b). They therefore run the risk of eliciting the response they assume will occur. As we discussed earlier, anticipating that someone will react with a certain style, like a tough battler, can encourage a battling response. It becomes the appropriate response, given the previous comment. Since all parties can find this predictability useful in preparing their own responses, the cycle feeds on itself. In some cases a cycle may be helpful: cycles can be productive if they include a periodic check for possible inflexibility or if they lead to success on "easy" issues, which then carries over in more difficult disputes (Karrass, 1970). In many other cases, however, the cycles become the basis for inflexibility and lead to uncontrolled destructive interaction.

Research in diverse contexts suggests that conflict interaction is self-perpetuating. Studies comparing distressed and nondistressed intimate couples, for example, have found differences in how repetitive the communication patterns are for these couples (Gottman, 1979; Ting-Toomey, 1983). Couples in more distressed conflictive relationships tend to interact in highly structured ways—their interaction tends to be built on more repetitive cycles and exchanges. This repetition is symptomatic of self-perpetuating interaction where one party's move elicits a highly predictable response which in turn produces a predictable counterresponse. In addition, these studies also reveal the nature of these repetitive cycles. In distressed intimate couples, parties tend to exchange hostile and confrontive remarks so that common exchanges include one person complaining or confronting while the other defends (Ting-Toomey, 1983; Gaelick, Bodenhausen, & Wyer, 1985). In family conflict, there is a tendency for opposition statements to continue across speakers in successive turns at talk (Vuchinich, 1984, 1986). Studies of children's conflicts suggest that an opposition move made by one child is likely to elicit a sequence of oppositional moves (Eisenberg & Garvey, 1981; Goodwin, 1982). These repetitive cycles of hostile or negative actions and responses have also been found to characterize labor–management negotiations (Putnam & Jones, 1982b).

In both intimate and labor–management contexts, cycles of positive responses (e.g., supportive statements, agreements) have also been found to occur, usually when the conflict has taken a fundamental turn in a constructive direction (Donohue, Diez, & Hamilton, 1984; Gaelick et al., 1985).

The self-perpetuating nature of conflict suggests that when conflict interaction is examined closely, on a turn-by-turn basis, it is often not resolved in any real sense (Vuchinich, 1984). Conflict often unfolds in waves of somewhat repetitive interaction sequences and moves that start and stop in a variety of ways. Repetitive sequences can end, for example, with topic switches, withdrawals, and standoffs, and may resurface later and end differently the next time the repetitive sequence occurs (Vuchinich, 1990).

The self-perpetuating nature of conflict interaction makes conflict highly sensitive to any force that prevents parties from stopping or reversing a conflict cycle. For this reason, the working habits that people adopt can be influential in moving conflict interaction in either destructive or constructive directions. In the next section we will consider working habits in detail, examining the blinding force they can become in conflict when they emerge as trained incapacities.

Working Habits, Trained Incapacities, and Conflict

> But, Wally, don't you see that comfort can be dangerous? I mean, you like to be comfortable, and I like to be comfortable too, but don't you see that comfort can lull you into a dangerous tranquillity? I mean, my mother knew a woman, Lady Hatfield, who was one of the richest women in the world, but she died of starvation because all she would eat was chicken. I mean, she just liked chicken, Wally, and that was all she would eat, and actually her body was starving, but she didn't know it, because she was quite happy eating her chicken, and so she finally died. . . .
>
> Roc used to practice certain exercises, like, for instance, if he were right-handed, all today he would do everything with his left hand. All day—writing, eating, everything—opening doors—in order to break the habits of living, because the great danger for him, he felt, was to fall into a trance, out of habit.
>
> Wallace Shawn and Andre Gregory, *My Dinner with Andre*

Working habits are the habitual interaction strategies people use to accomplish tasks or solve problems. For example, decision procedures such as voting, leadership styles normally employed in a group, or the practice of frequently joking during meetings in order to vent the frustrations of work are all examples of working habits. Sometimes these are formally and consciously adopted, but more often people are not conscious of their habits or their effects. People employ them without thinking. These habits are a critical force in conflicts because they establish a framework for group interaction. As habits, they encourage interaction cycles to continue once they start despite changing events or circumstances that may call for new approaches. They establish expectations about how people will obtain ideas for consideration and how alternatives will be evaluated as the conflict is addressed. Working habits may be beneficial or harmful depending on the situation. The most troublesome habits are those that normally yield benefits but backfire when the conflict situation changes and people fail to take these changes into account.

Understanding the role of **habits** in group behavior helps to explain why conflicts get out of hand, why in many cases people cannot see that their behavior is becoming destructive and change it. It is true that people sometimes choose to use force to defeat their opponent, and in these cases a destructive conflict can be stemmed only by altering the motives or power of the participants. However, in many cases, conflicts move in negative directions because people are **incapable** of diagnosing the conflict and altering their behavior. Once people are in a conflict cycle, they may be trapped by their own interaction patterns.

In the Hotline case we described in the Introduction the workers had a "standard operating procedure" that discouraged workers from taking problems with their cases to each other. When Diane asked for time off, the other workers disregarded her problem as irrelevant and evaluated her request only on the basis of its implications for work loads at the center. As a result, the staff concluded that she was slacking off and responded by defining "worker responsibilities," hoping they could get her back in line with "normal" procedures. It was only when Diane escalated the conflict further that the workers were jolted out of their "task-centered" frame of mind and forced to address the issue at hand. In another group where work habits were more firmly entrenched, Diane's grievance may not have broken the habitual interpretation of her behavior, and she might have been fired.

When confronted with conflict, parties often fall back on behaviors that have proved effective in other contexts. However, behaviors effective in some circumstances may actually worsen conflicts. For example, the common practice of openly evaluating ideas or proposals in an attempt to reach a decision can deepen parties' feelings of anger or competition in conflicts, resulting in escalating hostilities. These behaviors hold a "catch"—because they seem ordinary and have proved useful so often that people may be blinded to problems they create. The social critic Kenneth Burke (1935) has termed this "catch" a trained incapacity. He argues that we become so well trained in our strategies that they begin to serve as blinders. We think we know what to expect, so we ignore signs that something is wrong. These incapacities are particularly pernicious because people may assume they are doing the right thing when actually they are worsening the situation.

Burke offered two simple and somewhat outlandish examples as illustrations of this concept: a chicken can be taught to repeatedly come to a specific place to receive food when it hears a certain pitch of a bell. On one occasion, however, the chicken responds to the bell as it always has by coming to the same place in search of food. This time the chicken finds not food, but the threatening axe of its owner. In Burke's second example, a trout that has had a near miss with a fishhook on its way upstream avoids all food sources that even remotely resemble the color of the bait that nearly caught it. In both cases the animals' past training causes them to misjudge their present situation; their training has incapacitated them.

Certain **working habits** are adaptive and beneficial in the contexts in which they are learned; however, as conditions change and as conflicts deepen, they become maladaptive, harmful, and irrational. These behaviors are injurious, because they shape thinking and perception and therefore can prevent recognition of changed circumstances. When this happens, people continue to do "what has always worked," resulting either in no change or in an actual deterioration of the situation.

Trained incapacities play a crucial role in conflict sequences. Confronted with a real or imagined conflict, parties tend toward habitual responses. As we have noted, the stress of differentiation can decrease individuals' ability to think clearly. Several researchers (Beier, 1951; Holsti, 1971; Dill, 1968; Janis & Mann, 1977; Smart & Vertinsky, 1977; Zillman, 1990) provide evidence that people under stress screen out essential environmental cues, distort incoming information, and are less flexible and creative problem solvers. Habitual, preprogrammed responses provide excellent ways to cope under such circumstances; indeed, they are often all a person can think of in the heat of a crisis.

Because of cultural tendencies to repress and avoid conflict if at all possible, many people have not had much experience with conflict situations; fewer still have reflected at length on how to deal with conflicts. As a result, conflicts are novel, uncertain, and often threatening situations for most people. Faced with such situations, individuals cling to habitual responses.

Some habitual patterns facilitate conflict management. Others may immediately seem to improve the situation, but actually cause it to deteriorate over the long run. These patterns blind people to the negative consequences of their behaviors and may prevent them from altering the direction of the conflict when harmful escalation or avoidance cycles begin. People are locked in destructive cycles because they cannot recognize that behaviors that were once beneficial are now counterproductive.

Conflicts are, in effect, problems that people must attempt to solve. Therefore the trained incapacities most likely to worsen conflicts are those arising from work habits that facilitate decision-making and problem-solving. Work habits become second nature; people come to rely on them as heuristics to guide work efficiently and solve problems.

Since the major task in resolving conflict is to construct an acceptable and workable decision, people's working habits usually come into play as they confront conflict issues. These working habits may be adaptive and beneficial, because they tend to facilitate decision-making. However, they can also have corrosive effects on parties' ability to manage and contain conflict if parties come to rely on them in situations where they should be disregarded. **The benefits of these habits enhance their potential for harm precisely because it is so difficult to determine when the negative consequences begin to overwhelm the positive ones.** By the time the participants recognize they are in trouble, their interaction may have become so tangled that it is difficult for them to detect or to correct their destructive tendencies. The parties' working habits have become trained incapacities.

As illustrations of these destructive and often unseen tendencies, we briefly describe three trained incapacities: goal-emphasis, objective standards, and the use of procedures.

Goal-Emphasis

A good deal of our behavior in everyday life leads toward achieving some goal or plan. As Miller, Galanter, and Pribram (1960) argue in *Plans and the Structure of Behavior*, our activities are frequently organized in a sequence of moves that have some desired end point. Plans generate and control the sequence of behaviors we carry out. In everyday life, these goals range in type and in the number of behaviors required for their execution. Obviously, having plans or goals serves people well in a number of ways. Most importantly, they allow for the completion of critical activities and make it possible to direct and evaluate our actions, because each action can be assessed by determining whether it contributes to successful completion of the plan.

In conflict and decision-making situations, one set of goals is the solutions or outcomes parties would like to see adopted. They are individuals' estimates of the best decision or course of action. Entering a discussion with a solution to a problem or conflict in mind is natural and in some respects useful. It is natural because people often have explicit needs, which they believe can only be met by the adoption of a particular solution. Having a solution in mind can also be useful because it provides clear guidance about the type of communicative behavior parties should engage in during conflict interaction. The goal or solution can dictate the type of information each should contribute and the arguments that should be made in support of a position. Each person can build a case for the solution he or she wants adopted. If parties start the discussion of an issue by arguing for alternative solutions, the information and arguments in favor of each solution will be aired and points of difference can be clarified. People need to hear the pros and cons of suggested solutions in order to evaluate and choose choice among them.

Goal-emphasis becomes an incapacity, however, when (1) it prevents parties from conducting an adequate assessment of the problem underlying the conflict (in other words, when it undercuts the group's attempt to orient itself to the problem), or (2) it becomes a way to quickly make a decision without a complete analysis of the chosen solution (in other words, when it prevents the group from establishing criteria for solutions or examining a solution in light of established criteria).

The tendency to be goal-centered may encourage people to begin discussion of an issue with an evaluation of alternative solutions. There is, however, persuasive evidence to suggest that the group's attempt to define the problem (asking "what is wrong here?") should be separated from the search for solutions (asking "what should be done to alleviate the problem?") (Maier, 1967). Time should be divided between analysis of the problem and evaluation of solutions. Thorough analysis of the symptoms and causes of the problem is likely to yield the best solution—the one that comes closest to meeting all parties' needs or all causes of the problem. However, if parties make statements about solutions they would like to see adopted at the outset, conflict cannot unfold in a "problem analysis–solution evaluation" sequence. Of course, all solutions are founded on some conception of the problem, but this may never be articulated if the solution is proposed first.

The experience of a 12-person food distribution cooperative illustrates how excessive emphasis on goals can prevent members from making an adequate assessment of the problem (Case 3.1). The conflict in question concerned whether or not to continue publishing the cooperative's newsletter.

Case 3.1   ## The Food Cooperative Newsletter

An umbrella organization that handled the advertising and some financial decisions for a number of food cooperatives had recently lost a member who published the cooperative's monthly newsletter. The former member had journalism experience and was able to publish a successful periodical that reflected the values and sentiments of the cooperative movement while maintaining professional publication standards. When this member left, no one in the group had the experience or motivation to publish a periodical of similar quality. The group was faced with the issue of what to do about the dying newsletter.

The group had one discussion of the issue at a meeting, but no agreement was reached. The meeting became very tense because the newsletter was related to a number of unresolved issues. A third party, who was providing the group with a series of training sessions on meeting and decision-making skills, was called in to facilitate the meeting at which the newsletter was to be discussed. When this agenda item arose, members almost immediately made statements about **what should be done about the newsletter.**

One solution was to let the newsletter die because there was no one in the group who could successfully publish it. Another member soon responded by suggesting that the group as a whole try to publish the periodical. A third member suggested that the group hire a part-time worker. The discussion began with little direct attention to the underlying nature of the problem the group faced. Instead, the members entered the discussion with set ideas about what the solution should be. These solutions were debated before the group adequately assessed what functions the newsletter served, what needs prompted its publication, or what were the possible consequences of not publishing it. An examination of these issues would have given the members a clearer understanding of the problem they were trying to solve. Since these issues were not clarified, no criteria for what a good solution might look like emerged. Tension and hostile comments began to infect the second discussion of the issue, and a stalemate seemed likely.

After the third party prodded the group toward a discussion of the problems it was clear that there were two different problem definitions underlying the suggested solutions. One doubted the ability of an outsider, as editor, to remain responsive to the group and to reflect the group's values in the newsletter. There was a fear that the tone and character of the paper would change radically if it were handed over to a professional journalist who was not a member of the group. The other problem definition emphasized the critical need for communication with the member stores. This view emphasized that the newsletter served an important function in getting information about prices, staffing, and so on to people who needed these updates periodically. Once these conceptions were clarified the group could view them as criteria that a satisfactory solution to the problem must meet. It allowed the group to assess any suggested solution by determining how well it would meet these two needs. Would the solution continue to get needed information to the stores? Would the solution remain true to the co-op's philosophy and image? Unearthing the implicit conceptions of the problem was critical in avoiding further impasses.

Objective Standards

Moscovici's (1976) analysis of social influence processes points to another trained incapacity. Moscovici focuses on the **social norms** that determine the basis on which people make judgments and reach consensus. These norms serve as criteria people employ to assess their own judgments and decisions. Parties also employ these criteria to persuade others to adopt new positions.

The **objectivity norm** often emerges in conflict and decision-making situations. This norm "concerns the need to test opinions and judgments according to the criterion of objective accuracy, so that decisions can be made on whether they may be universally accepted" (Moscovici, 1976, p. 153). When parties adopt this norm as a basis for judgment, they believe that there are definite correct choices or responses for each issue in the conflict. The objectivity norm dictates that "in the course of social interaction, every person thinks and behaves with reference to the public reality—that reality which is open to inspection by all, which is the same for all and which is easily interpreted by all who have eyes to see and ears to hear" (Moscovici, 1976, p. 155). The objectivity norm stands in contrast to the preference norm, where judgment is anchored in personal tastes; it presumes that differences of opinion can exist. It also differs from an originality norm, which assesses alternatives both by their degree of novelty and by their promise of practical innovation.

People must rely on some criterion or social norm to make judgments. If the decision is one that **can** be evaluated by **some objective standard**, then it is in the best interest of the parties to measure alternatives against that criterion. The use of objective criteria depersonalizes the conflict by allowing it to be decided on the basis of standards external to any party's preferences or prejudices. Objective standards are possible for such decisions as determining the amount of space needed for an organization, deciding on what type of training members may need to handle financial operations, or determining how many people are needed to complete a project. For these types of decisions, lengthy arguments can be costly and frustrating and are, for all practical purposes, counterproductive because objective standards can be used to determine them. They can be prevented by a clearer articulation of the standard and careful assessment of the possible solutions. Some bargaining texts also argue that negotiators should try to link their offers to objective standards in order to reinforce their legitimacy (Fisher & Ury, 1981).

There are, however, other types of decision where there is no clear, objective standard for judging alternatives. The preferences of the parties themselves determine the set of possible alternatives. These decisions might include: reorganization of work space (Katz, 1979); assessing how much time, money, and energy members of a consulting firm should invest in a particular project; or deciding whether to increase the membership of a voluntary organization.

The interaction is the same for both types of decision; opinions and suggestions are stated, viewpoints are criticized and discussed, points of dissimilarity are clarified. It is the assumption parties make about whether the decision can or cannot be assessed according to some objective standard that is critical. **The trap is set, however, because the conflict can encourage members to presume the existence of an objective standard in cases where there is none**. The assumption that some objective standard underlies one's position is a useful justification for arguing vehemently for a position, regardless of the nature of the decision itself. Consequently, parties can easily lose sight of the preferential nature of the decision before them—they mistakenly search for the **one right solution**. Moreover, anxiety about how the conflict will turn out may incline parties to jump at "objective standards" when they are really grasping at straws.

In the Food Cooperative Newsletter (Case 3.1), the discussion of solutions was premised on the existence of an objective standard. There was a strong sense underlying the discussion that there would be only one right choice. As long as this norm prevailed, there was no consideration of provisional means to implement solutions. If the group decided to hire an outsider to publish the newsletter, for example, this solution could have been enacted on a one-month trial basis with a further stipulation that the editor give the final draft of any issue to some co-op member or committee for review before publication. As obvious as these modifications are, they were never discussed as long as the group held to its belief in the viability of only **one** solution.

Procedures

One of the primary characteristics of organizations and groups is their tendency to use **structured procedures** to help complete their tasks (Hall, 1972). Although rules are often adopted formally, many procedures evolve without being explicitly acknowledged. A procedure that works becomes institutionalized through repetitive use. For example, when a group often spends the first 15 minutes of its meetings socializing, it may eventually expect to do so at every session. Procedures become traditions. Members come to assume things should be done in a certain way and the organization's identity often becomes tied to its procedures (e.g., "This is a democratic group—we vote on all major decisions").

Standardized procedures hold several advantages (Poole, 1991). If procedures are set **before** a decision is made, members have **sufficient knowledge about the process to participate and contribute.** They know, for example, when votes will be taken, how long they have to suggest alternative proposals, and who will end discussion of a topic. Chaotic or ill-defined decision-making procedures discourage participation and may result in an inferior decision because some members feel lost during the meeting. Knowledge of set procedures like parliamentary procedure reduces members' uncertainty about how to behave in the group and may therefore reduce stress for some members.

Procedural rules can also serve as **standards for deciding disputes** in the group. For example, a disagreement over whether a decision was made fairly might be settled by checking the rules on voting procedures. Since procedural rules are used and accepted by the group before the dispute, they may have a degree of legitimacy in the eyes of all, which allows the disagreement to be settled without arousing personal antipathies.

Finally, set procedures can often **equalize power among group members**. In the Nominal Group Technique, a structured decision-making method developed by Delbecq, Van de Ven, and Gustafsen (1975), preliminary ideas are elicited by going around the group in order and having each member give one idea. This process is repeated until all members' ideas have been contributed. The Nominal Group Technique ensures that everyone contributes; it gives those members who are usually quiet or hesitant a formal opportunity to participate without being interrupted by more talkative or powerful members.

Procedures can become **incapacities**, however, when (1) they structure interaction so that confrontation and escalation are inevitable, or (2) they are used to suppress or avoid conflict. Procedures that institutionalize controversy and opposition, such as the use of Robert's Rules of Order in meetings, serve a useful function for a group because they ensure that all sides of an issue are heard and they force members to make a definite choice among alternatives. The orderly, sharp debate of a well-run meeting under Robert's Rules often illustrates the benefits of parliamentary-type methods. However, since the discussion of a motion begins with the expectation that a vote is inevitable if a serious conflict develops, parliamentary procedure may polarize opposing factions and cause competition and rifts among members.

Case 3.2 **The Work Stoppage Decision**

In one labor union that used Robert's Rules, a major conflict erupted over whether or not to call a work stoppage in response to a grievance against plant administration. As debate proceeded, it became clear that over two-thirds of the membership did not favor the stoppage, although a large minority remained very much in favor of the move. The minority, however, was able to advocate its position long after it was evident the union would vote down the work stoppage by using parliamentary rules as tactics. Some members, for example, attempted to add the work stoppage as an amendment to an unrelated proposal generally favored by the union. These tactics resulted in a polarization of union members: many of those opposed to the work stoppage were outraged at the minority's persistence; the longer members of the minority argued for the stoppage, the more convinced they became of their positions. The end result was a major rift in the union. The minority—voted down—felt cut off from the rest of the membership, left the union, and attempted to form their own organization. In this case the easily manipulated rules of parliamentary procedure contributed to the problem. Just as important was the general climate that parliamentary methods can create in groups: an adversarial atmosphere that encourages stubborn adherence to one's own position in the face of opposition. Such a climate can be more conducive to factionalism than to common ownership of the problem and a united pursuit of a workable solution.

Procedures can also stifle differentiation by discouraging a direct assault on the issues. Voting on proposals is often used to avoid difficult situations (Hall & Watson, 1970). If two sides appear to be forming, the chairperson calls for a vote and assumes that once the vote is taken the issue is decided and the problem solved. This reasoning is flawed, however, because only the winning side gets what it wants in this case. The members who lose the vote may be dissatisfied and withdraw from the group or be much less committed to the decision. Disagreement can also be stifled by informal or implicit rules such as "let's get through our agenda as fast as possible." Such an attitude can make members feel they are imposing on the group by raising or complicating issues. As Janis (1972) has noted, decision-making groups often do not realize they have suppressed contributions or criticism and may even think they are doing an excellent job of decision-making.

There are many other trained incapacities besides the three—goal-emphasis, objective standards, and procedures—that we have examined here. Even the most constructive behaviors can undermine interaction if members blindly cling to them. Because they are deeply ingrained habits, trained incapacities mold members' perceptions of the situation so that their negative consequences are not easily discovered. As a result, trained incapacities promote interaction patterns that head toward escalation or avoidance of conflicts.

PROPERTY 3   *Conflict moves are embedded in larger interaction sequences.*

The moves and responses that comprise any conflict interaction can be viewed as a series of isolated acts that parties take as they address or avoid issues. Interaction, in this sense, can be looked at as a sequence of individual moves, moves that parties design by taking prior actions and possible long-term strategies into account. Our first property of conflict interaction—moves and countermoves are sustained by the power that parties exert—is built on this view of how conflict interaction unfolds. Although this view is accurate and insightful in its own right, it is limited. Viewing the interaction through only this lens is like watching a dance as a series of individual steps. The larger patterns and movements in sequence are missed. Conflict interaction needs to be considered from a larger sequential perspective as well.

Conflict interaction, like other forms of interaction, falls into larger units, sometimes called **episodes**, which are comprised of **a series of moves and responses** (Harre & Secord, 1972). As conflict interaction unfolds, a series of actions and reactions emerge as identifiable and meaningful units in themselves. These episodes can reveal what the parties are "up to" at any time in the conflict. For instance, a married couple may "test the waters" when they first talk to each other about a potentially explosive issue they have tried to avoid. In testing the waters, they are doing something recognizable at that point in the conflict. They see themselves in the episode, understand what consequences the episode might have for the development of the conflict, and notice when the episode has ended.

Each episode in a conflict is **meaningful** in that it can guide people's interpretations and shape future actions. Parties may realize that they are engaged in an episode and can use this realization to act strategically or appropriately. It is through episodes—identifiable sequences of moves and countermoves—that "participants enact and reveal their purpose in the pattern of interaction" (Newell & Stutman, 1991). When people are engaged in an episode, they share an understanding of the situation they are creating through their interaction. By creating situations, episodes allow people to reach goals, to accomplish certain objectives. For this reason, episodes offer useful insights into how parties coordinate their actions to accomplish their individual goals.

This episodic characterization of interaction recognizes that parties construct their own patterns of interaction through the moves they make. Moreover, they can interpret these patterns and use their interpretations to understand messages and shape future moves. The study of episodes as sequences of actions places the focus squarely on communication as it occurs naturally in conflicts. The study of **sequences** of episodes over time in a relationship can lead to a further understanding of how past interactions form a **context** for present and future interactions, and how relationships evolve through patterns of interaction.

Episodes vary greatly in breadth. Some may be comprised of only one move by each party, such as an attack–defend exchange. Other episodes may be much longer and be comprised of multiple acts, responses, and counterresponses. For example, in Ingmar Bergman's realistic film about intimate relations, "Scenes from a Marriage," a rather lengthy segment of interaction between a married couple is labeled "Sweeping It Under the Rug." This segment is a series of interactions in which the couple masks discussions of threatening issues in mundane talk. The couple is, in a real sense, creating an episode of "sweeping things under the rug" by making certain types of comments and not others and by interpreting comments in the most innocuous way possible.

The range of possible episodes is great, from giving and receiving accounts for one's behavior (McLaughlin, Cody, & Rosenstein, 1983), to resolving issues, "blowing off steam," apologizing (Edmondson, 1981; Fraser, 1981), and confronting (Newell & Stutman, 1988, 1991). These are only a few of the many possible episodes through which conflict interaction might pass. An episodic view of conflict leads one to look at conflict in broader developmental terms.

To capture the development of conflicts, some researchers have tried to describe the **phases** or stages through which conflicts tend to pass. The identification of stages or phases is consistent with an episodic view of conflict interaction. Researchers identify larger meaningful units by describing the characteristic sequence of moves and responses—the pattern of interaction—that constitutes the stage. The identification of a sequence of stages is then used to map the trajectory of typical conflicts.

Some phase analyses (Kriesberg, 1973; Rummel, 1976) are based on studies of social conflicts and wars, while others are drawn from studies of organizations (Pondy, 1967; Walton, 1969), bargaining and negotiation (Douglas, 1962; Morley & Stephenson, 1977; Gulliver, 1979; Holmes, 1992), and small group processes (Ellis & Fisher, 1975; Sambamurthy & Poole, 1991). Although there are some differences in the phases described by each account, all suggest that **conflicts can be broken down** into recognizable, sequential periods marked by different behaviors and sequences of behaviors. Because an understanding of conflict episodes is so important in understanding the development of conflict, we examine a number of phase analyses of conflict in detail and discuss how they are useful in understanding the route conflict interaction takes.

Phase models are built on close analyses of interaction and are, by definition, concerned with the sequences of moves as conflicts unfold. They attempt to outline meaningful segments of interaction based on analyses of actions and reactions. One model views conflict in terms of two broad phases, a **differentiation** phase followed by an **integration** phase (Walton, 1969). In differentiation, parties raise the conflict issues and spend sufficient time and energy clarifying positions, pursuing the reasons behind those positions, and acknowledging the severity of their differences. At the point at which further escalation seems fruitless, an integration phase begins. Parties begin to acknowledge common ground, explore possible options, and move toward some solution—sometimes one that meets everyone's needs but sometimes simply one that they can live with. If integration is not completely successful, the conflict may cycle back through a new differentiation phase.

Although this two-phase model of conflict is elementary in one sense, it is highly suggestive because it indicates what parties must cope with to move successfully through a conflict. How or whether conflict interaction moves from differentiation through integration is complicated; we will consider in further detail some of the dynamics of this two-phase analysis of conflict.

Moving Through Differentiation and Integration

People rightly fear and often retreat from the process of differentiation, because it is here that conflict is most vulnerable to uncontrolled, hostile escalation. There is always the possibility that the interaction will not be able to move from differentiation to **integration**, to that phase of conflict in which "parties appreciate their similarities, acknowledge their common goals, own up to positive aspects of their ambivalences, express warmth and respect and/or engage in other positive actions to manage their conflict" (Walton, 1969, p. 105). The **simultaneous need for and fear of differentiation** poses a difficult dilemma for parties who want to work through important conflicts. A closer examination of this dilemma reveals how it becomes the basis for people's inability to redirect their own destructive interaction.

Adequate differentiation is a critical prerequisite to constructive conflict resolution. Without a clear statement of each party's position, finding a problem-solving solution—one in which "the participants all are satisfied with their outcomes and feel they have gained as a result of the conflict"—is a hit-or-miss venture (Deutsch, 1973, p. 17). Without an appreciation of the severity of the differences and the consequences of leaving the conflict unaddressed, even a hit-or-miss attempt at resolution may not be made. Parties may not be sufficiently motivated to deal with the problem.

Differentiation initially **personalizes** the conflict as individuals clarify their stands and people are identified with positions; however, it is not until these positions are articulated that the conflict can finally be depersonalized. Once individual positions are clarified, the groundwork has been laid for members to realize that the conflict lies in the **incompatibility** of positions and not in the needs or sentiments of one person or faction. Through differentiation people can gain a depersonalized view of the conflict that sets it apart from any one person. If people can clarify the issues and air diverse positions without losing control (a difficult problem in its own right), they can recast the conflict as an external obstacle that all must overcome together. Once achieved, this depersonalized view provides a basis for commonality. It often marks the beginning of an integrative phase, but by no means signifies the end of the conflict process. The parties must still generate ideas and choose a solution that, as Simmel (1955, p. 14) puts it, "resolves the tension between contrasts" in the group. From this point, however, the group can build on the accomplishments of differentiation.

Differentiation and Escalation

While differentiation is necessary for constructive conflict resolution, it can also nourish destructive tendencies. During differentiation, disagreements that parties were previously afraid of, or unmotivated to deal with, take hold. The stakes seem higher because an unsuccessful attempt to resolve the issue means that members must live with a keener awareness of differences and a more vivid understanding of the negative consequences of leaving the issue unresolved.

Research from several areas points to several strains and pitfalls likely to ignite the process of differentiation into a spiraling escalation of "malevolent cycling"—highly personalized conflict that is turned away from issues and threatens interpersonal relationships (Walton, 1969).

(1) Research on **balance theory** (Swensen, 1973) suggests that relationships will become strained when group members disagree over important issues. Balance theory assumes people attempt to maintain consistency among their beliefs and feelings; for example, people tend to like people they agree with and dislike people with whom they do not agree. When a person finds out that someone he or she likes disagrees on an important issue, the inconsistency creates an uncomfortable strain in the person's thinking. Balance theorists argue that this strain is usually resolved either by a change in the person's beliefs about the issue or by a change in the person's liking for the other. These changes are assumed to follow the path of least resistance: feelings about whichever is less important—the issue or the person—will change most. Hence the longer two people who like each other hold to opposing positions, and the more crucial these positions seem to them, the greater pressure they are under to feel hostility and lose respect for each other.

(2) Leary's (1957) classic research on **interpersonal reflexes** also points to likely sources of emotional escalation during this process. If a comment is made that is perceived as hostile, Leary's analysis predicts that it is likely to elicit further hostile responses. Similarly, Gibb's (1961) analysis of defensiveness indicates that **evaluative comments** (e.g., "I don't think that proposal is any good because . . .") can easily elicit defensive responses because they seem threatening to the listener. Since differentiation calls for evaluation, defensiveness is likely.

(3) Research on the nature of **commitment** (Kiesler, 1971; Janis & Mann, 1977) suggests that making a position public or restating it several times can increase one's commitment to the position or behavior. When commitment to a position is high and

that position is called into question by new information or arguments, people often intensify their stands in an effort to preserve their "good name" and self-image. Comments that attack others' positions run the risk of increasing polarization even further because parties may respond by taking more extreme stands than they originally held. Apfelbaum (1974) summarizes a number of experimental studies that indicate that once one side in conflict openly signals commitment to a position (and thus indicates they will be competitive rather than cooperative), the other side becomes more inflexible as well. Thus the positions people take and their styles of interaction can become rigidified when members commit themselves to some position in front of the group. Since differentiation calls for statements of positions, the risk of escalation runs high during this phase of the conflict process.

Taken together, balance, interpersonal reflexes, and commitment generate potent forces toward destructive cycling. To break this cycling some means of counteracting these effects must be found.

Differentiation and avoidance

Although people in conflict sometimes fall prey to the dangers of differentiation, they can also fall victim to an overly zealous attempt to avoid these dangers. When parties try hard to avoid divisive issues, they may never realize their own potential for finding creative solutions to important problems (Pruitt & Lewis, 1977). Indeed, the early acceptance of a solution about which most parties feel lukewarm and dissatisfied, often signals a group's retreat from the pressures of differentiation. The Guetzkow and Gyr (1954) study of 72 decision-making conferences illustrates this.

Guetzkow and Gyr compared interaction in groups with high levels of **substantive conflict** (conflict that is focused on the issues and on disagreements about possible solutions) to interaction in groups with high levels of **affective conflict** (interpersonal conflict characterized by extreme frustration—according to an outsider's observations). They were interested in the difference between substantive and affective conflicts because affective conflicts are more likely to exhibit spiraling escalation. Affective conflict is highly correlated with how critical and punishing members are to each other and how unpleasant the emotional atmosphere in the group is. In essence, affective conflict is a sign of differentiation gone awry. The objective of Guetzkow and Gyr was to determine what conditions allowed both types of group to reach consensus about the issue they were attempting to resolve.

These researchers found very different behaviors contributing to each group's ability to reach consensus. Groups that were high in substantive conflict and were able to reach consensus sought three times as much factual information and relied on that information more heavily in reaching a decision than groups not able to reach consensus. In other words, substantive conflict was resolved by a determined pursuit of the issue.

In contrast, groups high in affective conflict engaged mostly in flight or avoidance in order to reach consensus. Members withdrew from the problem by addressing simpler and less controversial agenda items, showed less interest in the discussion overall, and talked to only a few members of the group. When consensus was achieved in the affective conflict groups, it was most often the result of ignoring the critical problem at hand and finding an issue on which members could **comfortably** reach agreement. If the group's or organization's goal is to reduce tension and discomfort at any cost, then these flight behaviors serve it well. When members cannot easily ignore an issue, however, destructive tension can result from their inability to pursue the conflict.

Differentiation and Rigidity of Behavior

Avoidance of an issue is one possible outcome of an unsuccessful attempt to deal with the demands of differentiation. Spiraling, hostile escalation is another possible outcome of an inability to differentiate. The anxiety-producing nature of differentiation gives rise to a set of possible **intermediary** behaviors, which can lead to either avoidance or radical escalation. **The most direct link between the stress of differentiation and either avoidance or escalation is the tendency for people to cling inflexibly to patterns of interaction that occur during differentiation.**

Figure 3.1 summarizes the relationship among differentiation, inflexibility, and possible conflict resolution outcomes. The source of members' inflexibility can be found in the psychodynamic theories discussed in Chapter 1. These developmental theories of maladaptive repetitive behavior (behavior that persists despite its destructive outcomes) trace the origin of these behaviors to a threatening or anxiety-inducing environment. The psychoanalyst Alfred Adler, for example, maintains that running through a normal person's life is a consistent pattern of responses, a way of reacting to the world. This orientation gives rise to the person's character and a set of guiding principles that are used to make decisions, to deal with people, and, in general, to give meaning to the events of one's life. There are points in life, however, when a person's orientations clash with events in the world, when a guiding principle appears false. Adler offers an explanation for why, in some cases, individuals fasten onto their orientations despite severe clashes with reality.

> The relatively normal person, when he [sic] realizes that his scheme is seriously in conflict with reality, is adaptable and modifies his orientation, abandoning what is patently false. But there are certain situations which work against flexibility and adaptability and favor rigid adherence to the guiding fictions. These are conditions in which the individual experiences exaggerated feelings of inferiority and psychological uncertainty, conditions that spell anxiety to him since anxiety is the sensation accompanying a strong uncompensated inferiority feeling. Under such conditions even a normal person may

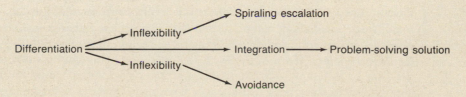

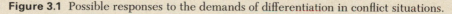

Figure 3.1 Possible responses to the demands of differentiation in conflict situations.

cling to his guiding fictions despite their conflict with reality. There are some individuals who live quite constantly under such anxiety-inducing conditions; and so rigidly do they adhere to their guiding fictions that these become accentuated and create a rigid, hardened lifestyle or character, an orientation out of tune with reality but nonetheless dogmatically maintained. (Luchins & Luchins, 1959, p. 19)

In much the same way, parties in conflict are faced with anxiety-inducing conditions that work against flexibility and adaptability. These conditions are the result of the inherent demands of differentiation. The conditions that produce anxiety for people are those **pressures that work toward radical escalation**: (1) an initial personalization of the conflict, (2) the stress of acknowledging opposing stands, (3) hostile and emotional statements, (4) uncertainty about the outcomes of the conflict, and (5) heightened awareness of the consequences of not reaching a resolution (Holsti, 1971; Smart & Vertinsky, 1977).

Differentiation is a necessary but anxiety-provoking process that people face in any conflict. If parties pursue issues and work through the demands of differentiation without rigidly adhering to counterproductive interaction patterns, there is a clear promise of innovation and of finding an integrative solution to the conflict. The pressures toward escalation are formidable, however, and the anxiety of differentiation can promote rigidity of behavior, resulting in either spiraling conflict or flight from the issue.

Other Phase Models of Conflict

There are many other phase descriptions of conflict that go beyond two-phase analyses and rely on a multiple stage characterization of how conflict develops. These phase descriptions are often developed from diverse conflict contexts, from broad societal and international models of conflict to much narrower accounts of small group decisions and intimate conflicts.

Based on a study of international conflicts, Rummel (1976) suggests that conflicts pass through five sequential phases. In the earliest stage, Rummel says, conflict is **latent**. In other words, individuals hold different dispositions or attitudes that carry the potential for conflict. Differences in values, objectives, and outlooks are present and lay the groundwork for future behavior. During the **initiation** phase, some "triggering event" causes the individuals to act. At this point, the potential differences become the basis for interaction. After the conflict has been initiated, the interaction turns toward an attempt at balancing **power**. In this third phase, individuals assess each other's capabilities and willingness to use force, threats, rewards, and so on, and they actually confront the issue as they try to reach some accommodation or settlement. The accommodation leads to a **balance of power** phase, in which the participants come to understand the consequences of the resolution and learn to live with the outcomes. This phase is characterized by the "set expectations" of individuals and may last for some time until significant changes in circumstances, attitudes, or goals arise. Such evolving changes lead to a **disruption** stage where parties realize that circumstances are ripe once again for the emergence of potential conflict and eventual confrontation. This model implies a continual cycle from latency to initiation to balancing power to a balance of power to a disruption back to a new latency, and so on, until the issue is ultimately resolved.

In the organizational context, Pondy (1967) developed a somewhat similar phase analysis of the emergence and development of conflict. Pondy suggests that conflict passes through five stages. Conflict is first **latent** in that some set of conditions such as insufficient resources or divergent goals comes to exist but is not yet perceived or acted on. Then the conflict is **perceived** when the latent issues reach awareness. Pondy notes that conflict can be perceived when no latent conflict exists. This happens when parties misunderstand each other's positions. Parties then enter a stage of **felt** conflict in which the conflict changes one party's feelings for or effect on the other. It is here that the conflict becomes charged emotionally as parties feel anxiety, mistrust, or hostility toward a perceived opponent. **Manifest** conflict occurs when parties act on the perceived and felt differences. In this stage, behaviors are said to be conflictural if one or both parties perceive them as thwarting the attainment of goals. Finally, conflict enters an **aftermath** stage in which new relationships and arrangements are formed and assessments are made of outcomes. All through the stages, the development of conflict can be influenced not only by the moves of the parties but by changing environmental conditions in the organization.

Analyses of formal negotiations suggest that the negotiation process unfolds in identifiable phases as well (Douglas, 1962; Morley & Stephenson, 1977; Putnam & Jones, 1982b; Putnam, Wilson, Waltman, & Turner, 1986). One ground-breaking study of the interaction that occurs in union–management negotiations found that a three-phase framework described conflict development in this context (Morley & Stephenson, 1977). In the first phase, called **distributive bargaining**, the parties test the feasibility of possible demands, establish criteria for appropriate settlements, assess the power of each side, and evaluate the strength of the cases being made. Here the parties see themselves fulfilling their role as representatives of a "side" in the negotiations, building planned cases for constituents. In the second phase, **problem-solving**, the parties explore a range of solutions that might satisfy the criteria established at the outset. There is some tactical maneuvering but by and large the focus is on establishing a working relationship by proposing and evaluating solutions to identified problems. In the final **decision-making** phase, the parties come to agreement on some terms and explore the implications of their decision. The focus is on reality-checking, assessing the feasibility and implementation of terms that both sides support.

All phase analyses of conflict are built on an episodic conception of how conflict interaction unfolds. Although somewhat different sequences of episodes are posited for different conflict contexts, the basic premise that conflicts travel through meaningful segments of interaction is common to all the models. Phase theories offer several important insights about the nature of conflict interaction.

(1)   Phase research suggests that conflicts have a definite **pattern** or rhythm. The pattern often seems to depend on participants' expectations about likely directions conflicts will take. These expectations seem to be governed by an underlying logic of progressions that conflicts go through and serve to make even apparently confusing interaction understandable over the long run. Looking back and forward

simultaneously, parties can see an ambiguous situation of latent conflict growing into a test of power and can anticipate the need to de-escalate the conflict by compromise or at least by "backing off." Phase models imply that an understanding of the direction and pattern of conflict behaviors can only be gained if conflicts are looked at broadly with an eye toward the sequence of behaviors that occur over time. Phase models lead to a conception of conflict that includes not only confrontation and discussion of differences between parties, but also intermittent periods of equilibrium and calm when the parties "settle into" new arrangements resulting from the conflict.

(2)   The same patterns or forms of interaction can serve **different functions** in different conflict phases. Each phase provides the broader, meaningful context that makes behavior understandable in light of what is going on at any particular stage of the conflict. Ellis and Fisher (1975) argue, for example, that ambiguous comments occur in both the beginning and end phases of decision-making conflict in small groups. At the beginning of a conflict, these comments reflect the ambiguity of indecision; people are unsure about their attitudes and are trying to orient themselves to the issue before the group. In the final phase, however, the ambiguous comments reflect members' moves from one position to another. Members are changing their minds so that agreement can be reached in the group and a decision can be made. So an understanding of the general phase guides interpretation of more specific comments or sequences of acts occurring at any moment in the conflict.

(3)   Phase research also suggests that certain **events can ignite confrontation**, not because they are particularly important in themselves, but because they occur at a critical point in the conflict interaction. As a conflict ripens and people feel pressure to face up to the issues, seemingly common and inconsequential events can trigger rapid escalation. A misplaced criticism, teasing, or even a casual reference to a touchy subject can be tinder in a dry forest that is soon to ignite. Any of these comments can force parties to address an issue or act on previously unacknowledged differences. While latent differences may influence interaction in subtle and destructive ways, the issues themselves are often hazy or ill-defined until the triggering event brings them out in the open.

(4)   Conflict often includes a **testing period** before any direct confrontation occurs. This testing period allows parties to reduce their uncertainty about what others will do if they make certain moves. For example, in the face of an impending conflict one person may want to cooperate but fears being taken advantage of. By making certain subtle cooperative overtures the individual can assess likely responses without taking big risks. By "testing the waters" parties gain knowledge of the likely consequences of moves they might make. This knowledge enables people to develop broad strategies and to choose specific tactics as the conflict unfolds. Phase models suggest that these testing periods can play a critical role in determining the direction conflicts take; they offer a chance for people to flirt with various approaches without overly exposing themselves.

The main weakness in phase models of conflict is that they are too simplistic. Recent research suggests that phasic analyses may sometimes overemphasize the role of a "logical" step-by-step sequence in the development of conflicts. Poole (1981; Poole and Roth, 1989), for example, found that the assumption of a set sequence of phases was often not correct for decision-making groups. Instead of a single set of phases applicable to all decisions, he found numerous different sequences, depending on how the group chose to attack its problem.

Sambamurthy and Poole (1991) found that conflicts, too, develop in several different sequences. In a study of 40 groups, they found four general patterns of response to differences. The first pattern was characterized by low confrontation on conflict issues. Instead of confronting, the group spent most of its time in phases of cooperative, "focused" work broken by "integration" phases consisting of tangential discussions or joking. Conflicts simply never surfaced in this first pattern. A second pattern was characterized by phases of focused work alternating with phases of "critical work," in which members raised alternative points of view but did not openly acknowledge opposition. In critical work phases, differences were aired in a low-key manner. This often proved to be an effective method of working out differences between members. In some cases, groups passed through three or four cycles of focused work phases, alternating with phases of critical work.

Neither of the first two patterns confronted conflict directly. A third pattern consisted of phases of focused work and critical work followed by a phase of open opposition, in which the conflict surfaced. Once the opposition was expressed, members resolved the conflict **either** by dropping the subject and reentering a phase of focused work **or** when one party gave in to the other. The first method of resolving the opposition corresponds to conflict avoidance, while the second method corresponds to a win–lose conflict resolution. A final pattern had phases of focused and critical work followed by opposition. In this case, however, the opposition was resolved by problem-solving or compromising. This final pattern corresponds to the entire differentiation–integration sequence discussed above. Interestingly, Sambamurthy and Poole found that this fourth sequence resulted in better outcomes for their groups than did the first three sequences, consistent with predictions in the differentiation–integration model.

Phase theories point to the ways in which members' behaviors tend to perpetuate conflict cycles and illustrate how conflicts develop a momentum that leads interaction in constructive or destructive directions. The episodic view of conflict interaction, including any phase analyses, suggests that conflict interaction is vulnerable to any force that can cause a redefinition of what the parties see themselves doing at any point in the conflict. When a disputant or a third party intervenor changes perceptions of what the parties see themselves doing, he or she can create changes in the moves and responses that follow. Disputants, in other words, will act in accordance with (or in defiance of) the episodic structure of the conflict as it is perceived. There are a series of techniques, often referred to under the general name "reframing," that can create changes in perceptions of conflict episodes. We will examine these reframing techniques as a set of forces that can influence conflict interaction in Chapter 8.

PROPERTY 4 *As senseless and chaotic as conflict interaction may appear, it has a general direction that can be understood.*

Although shouting matches or heated discussions are often the first images that come to mind when we think of conflict, our conception argues for a more broadly based understanding of conflict interaction. Active suppression of issues, an exchange over who is an authority on some issue, a round of comments explaining positions to a third party, a discussion of the decision-making procedures the group should adopt, or a series of comments that back the group away from a stand so that one member is allowed to "win" a point are all forms of conflict interaction as well. **Conflict interaction is any exchange of messages that represents an attempt by participants to address some incompatibility of positions.**

Although conflicts can emerge and be played out in many forms, they are not chaotic or anarchic. As confused and irrational as the conflict situation may seem to participants and observers, nearly every conflict exhibits definite themes that lend coherence to the exchanges and make certain forms of interaction more likely to emerge than others. Even in a brutal, cutting free-for-all, a competitive coherence can be discerned. We noted in Chapter 1 that these **themes**, the generalized character of the situation, have traditionally been termed the situation's climate (Lewin, 1951; Tagiuri, 1968).

Climate emerges from the enduring and momentary pursuits of people in relationships; it is a **generalized composite of properties that arise from and guide people's interaction**. The climate provides important information to the parties about how conflict is likely to be handled; more specifically, it sets expectations about what participants can safely say, establishes the emotional tenor of the interaction, influences how much tolerance for disagreement seems possible, and determines whether the emergence of any conflict will be an immediate threat to the personal relationships. A change in climate most often means a noticeable difference in the way the parties interact. Consider the illustration of a shift in climate and its influence on interaction (Case 3.3).

Case 3.3   **The Columnist's Brown Bag**

An editorial columnist from *The New York Times* was asked to participate in one of a series of brown-bag discussions that a university's department of journalism hosted over the course of a semester. Faculty, students, and journalists from the community attended these noon-hour seminars. While some speakers in this series of talks gave formal presentations and then left a few minutes for questions afterward, this columnist said, at the outset of his talk, that although he had prepared comments on a number of different topics he would rather spend the entire hour responding to questions.

Within a few minutes after the session began, a climate of open interaction was established in this group of 12 people. The speaker responded to a wide range of questions. People asked about national economic policy, press coverage of news events, politically based indictments of the press, and the use and misuse of the term "the media." Despite the potentially controversial nature of many of these issues, there was an expectation set in the group that the questions would seek information or opinions from the columnist, who had over 30 years of experience on the prestigious newspaper. In his first answers, the speaker told amusing anecdotes, gave background information about recent news events, and offered unmuted commentary on key issues. The atmosphere was relaxed, almost reverent, and the speaker himself continued to eat his brown-bag lunch as he spoke.

In the last ten minutes of the question-and-answer discussion, there was a sudden shift in climate that brought about a remarkable change in interaction. A student sitting in the back of the room sat up and leaned forward in his chair. Speaking more loudly than anyone else during the previous 45 minutes, he said he had a question about editorial responsibility. He said that the *Times* ran a story about atrocities in an African tribe but the paper made no editorial comment on the killings until three years after they occurred. He wanted to know if the paper had the editorial responsibility to comment on this event at the time it happened. It soon became clear that both the student asking the question and the columnist knew, as the question was asked, that American arms had been used in the killings. The student did not, however, explicitly mention this as he asked the question.

With the student's question and the first response it received, the previously established climate in the group changed. The expectation that questions would seek information or a desired opinion from the speaker was overturned by the student's entry into the exchange. The question sought a defense of the paper's policy and assumed that the speaker would take a stand supporting the paper.

The group resented the attempt to change the tone of the interaction. Almost immediately, a journalism professor, who had introduced the speaker and was instrumental in getting him to visit the campus, defended the paper's policy before the guest speaker had a chance to respond. Neither this professor nor anyone else in the group had previously interrupted the "question–answer–question" format that the group had adopted; no one had previously made a comment in response to any other person's question. The professor was visibly upset by the student's question, said he had worked on the paper himself at the time the story broke, and contended that the editorial decision was justified because insufficient information was available about the incident for quite some time. The student responded with a pointed declaration of mistrust in the paper. The columnist then took the floor and commented that, although the paper had made several editorial blunders in the years he worked at the paper, he could not accept the accusation that editorial comments were withheld because U.S. arms were involved. There were, he said, too many editorials to the contrary in the paper.

The whole climate for the presentation clearly shifted as this exchange occurred. People sitting in the room turned to look back at the person who was asking the questions, some side comments were made, and a few people smiled uncomfortably at each other. A second professor interrupted the columnist and said, in a somewhat self-conscious tone of voice, that "we had better leave the seminar room because another class had to meet in it soon."

The climate of this discussion shifted in midstream, with profound effects on the interaction. In order to understand how conflict interaction unfolds, it is necessary to explore how climates are created and changed and the effect this has on the direction of conflicts. We will examine climate as a force that influences conflict interaction in Chapter 6.

PROPERTY 5 *Conflict interaction affects relationships among parties.*

It is very easy to focus only on the substantive issues in a conflict, on the problem and its proposed solutions. In fact, centering only on issues and ignoring the other, "emotional" aspects of a conflict has sometimes been recommended as the best way to deal with conflicts. However, focusing on the "bare facts" of the case can cause one to overlook the important effects that conflict has. Conflicts are often emotionally laden and tense. This is in part because participants are concerned about getting (or not getting) what they want, but it also stems from the implications the conflict has for their present and future relationship to the other party. The conflict in the Hotline case had the potential to drastically alter the relationships in the group. Until the staff openly challenged Diane for not living up to her responsibilities, she believed she was doing adequate work and was regarded as an equal by the other workers. The reprimand called her competence and responsibility into question and told her that others felt she was not on an equal footing. It challenged her attitudes and assumptions about her relationship with the other workers and caused her a great deal of self-doubt and soul-searching, as well as stimulating her angry retaliation against the center. The workers' judgment of Diane also affected their attitudes and assumptions about her. Coming to the conclusion that Diane was slacking off generated distrust for her in the minds of the other staff members. It also made her an object of anger, and some members admitted a tendency to want to "gunnysack," that is, pile up a long list of problems with Diane and then attack her with it. Luckily this never happened and the third party was able to restore some trust and encourage a more open and understanding approach among the parties.

This case illustrates two levels operating in all communication: every message conveys not only substantive content but also **information about the relationship of the speaker to the hearer** (Bateson, 1958; Watzlawick et al., 1967). If Diane angrily says, "I don't deserve this reprimand, I'm filing a grievance!" to her co-workers, her statements convey two levels of meaning. First, and most obvious, is the information that she is angry and is filing a grievance to challenge the reprimand, a countermove in the conflict. But second, Diane's message also carries the information that she believes her relationship with the workers has deteriorated to the point that she must file a formal grievance: it redefines the relationship between Diane and her co-workers. Even in formal negotiation contexts, verbal and nonverbal cues carry relational information that has significant impact on the relationship between negotiating parties (Donohue, Diez, & Stahle, 1983).

This relational aspect of communication is critical because it affects both present and future interaction. It affects present interaction because people often respond to relational messages immediately and emotionally. If someone insults us, we may become angry and want to retaliate. If someone implies that our friendship is in jeopardy because of an argument, we may back down and become conciliatory. However, relational communication has its most profound effects through influencing future interaction. How people interact in conflicts is colored by their assessments of others, judgments about such things as others' trustworthiness, intentions (good or bad), and determination to win. These assessments bear directly on the relational aspects of communication and, because of this, people often try to project a certain image in order to shape others' assumptions about their relationship. For example, one person may act very defiant and angry to project an image of cold determination that tells the other, "Our relationship is not that important to me, as long as I get what I want." If this projection is successful, the second person may back down, believing the first person has no regard for him/her and will go to any lengths to win. Of course, this tactic could also backfire and make the second person resentful and defiant, because the first seems cold and ruthless. Attempts at managing image and relationships prompt many moves and countermoves in conflict.

As important as relational management is in conflicts, it is not surprising that it plays a critical role in generating the direction conflicts take. **Face-saving**, people's attempts to protect or repair their images to others, has great potential to send conflicts into destructive spirals. One particularly dangerous form of face-saving stems from people's **fear of losing ground in an exchange** (Brown, 1977). Parties in conflict often believe that if they move from a stated position or back away from a set of demands, they will appear weak or vulnerable in the eyes of the group. This concern for face—a concern for how one appears to others during the conflict interaction and the effects this will have on future relationships—can encourage people to keep arguing for a position even though they no longer believe in it or they recognize it is not contributing to a workable resolution to the conflict.

A second form of face-saving can prompt groups **to continually ignore or avoid an important conflict issue**. In relationships that have had a history of resolving conflicts in a friendly and cooperative manner, a concern for face may prevent parties from raising an issue that is far more threatening than any conflict the parties have previously addressed. People may believe that if they raise the issue others will see them as a person who is trying to destroy the friendly relationships that have been cautiously protected and valued. This concern for face may prevent parties from calling in a third party when intervention is needed because they are reluctant to admit that they cannot resolve an issue on their own.

People's ability to define and maintain positive working relationships during conflict interaction depends heavily on how much concern they have for saving face as they approach the issue, take stands, and try to construct a resolution. For this reason, it is important to understand how people create pressures or incentives that heighten or lessen concern for saving face during conflict interaction. We will examine face as a force in conflict interaction in Chapter 5.

CONCLUSION

From our review of the major theoretical approaches to conflict and our belief in the importance of the communication process in conflict, we have distilled five properties of conflict interaction. These properties allow us to draw a complex net of ideas, which we will explore in the remainder of this book. Throughout, we will constantly return to the point that conflict interaction, deceptively simple on the surface, is incredibly complex and can only be understood by analyzing its flows and the forces that shape them. Conflict, like any other form of behavior, can only be understood at the level of concrete interaction **where moves and countermoves take many forms and unfold in diverse episodes yet maintain some level of coherence, where interaction patterns tend to perpetuate themselves in destructive and constructive cycles, and where messages define and alter relationships among people**.

We have examined **working habits** as a force that shapes conflict interaction. Conflict interaction is particularly vulnerable to this influence because of the self-perpetuating nature of conflict interaction. Each of the other properties of conflict interaction we have described point to a potent force that shapes and directs conflict. These forces are the use of **power**, the concern for **saving face**, the **climate** that is established, the **strategies and tactics** that parties employ, and the ability to **reframe** conflict. In the following chapters we will explore these forces and the practical implications they hold for conflict management.

These chapters are, of course, concerned with conflict, but they are also concerned with **change**. Because conflicts are rooted in differences and incompatible interests, conflict always confronts participants with the possibility of change. Indeed, that differences arise at all is a flag indicating a need for adjustment of the group in response to members' difficulties or to an external problem. Once a conflict emerges, resolution of differences may require redefinition of policies or goals, reassignment of responsibilities, shifts in expectations for individual members, or even changes in the group's power and status structures. Members' recognition of these possible changes guides the forms that conflict interaction takes. The active suppression of issues, the positive or negative evaluation of possible solutions, and the clarification of differences between members are all forms of conflict interaction, which can be motivated and shaped by the participants' awareness of imminent change. In a very real sense, as a group manages its conflicts, so too does it deal with the need to change in response to its environment or members' needs. Some wise sage in the 1960s said that "not to change is to die." The same can almost be said for failure to work through conflict.

Chapter
4

Power: The Architecture of Conflict

POWER AND THE EMERGENCE OF CONFLICT

The first principle of conflict interaction we discussed in Chapter 3 noted that **conflict is sustained by the moves and countermoves of the participants and that moves are dependent on the power that people exert**. Those who have power in a conflict have the resources to act and influence others and the skill to use these resources effectively. In order to understand how power functions in conflict, it is necessary to examine the emergence of conflict interaction—the turn conflict takes from a latent awareness of differences to actions and reactions that shape the direction and outcomes of conflict interaction.

It is rarely a surprise when conflict emerges. In any setting where people work together or are in some way dependent on one another, people usually become aware of important differences before any conflict-related interaction occurs. We noted in Chapter 3 that Rummel and Pondy identified a series of steps in the emergence of conflicts. They found that before any observable conflict surfaces, there is usually a "latent conflict phase" in which participants become aware of opposing viewpoints, attitudes, or goals. A "consciousness of opposition" precedes conflict interaction and lays the groundwork for it. During this latent conflict phase, parties may become aware of differences that actually exist among them, or they may incorrectly **assume** there are differences when none exist. In this phase, however, parties do not attempt to achieve their objectives or to interfere with each other's behavior. There is an awareness of differences, but no stimulus to react to it.

Knowledge of real or assumed differences stems largely from parties' **experience** of each other. In relationships with a history, parties know the stands others have taken on various issues and the alternatives they supported during previous discussions or decisions. They come to expect some people to push for cautious or conservative choices and others to suggest or encourage major innovations. They know which people are allies and which enemies. Each person's stand provides a general sense of where he or she would like to see the conflict head. In assessing and planning their own stands, people try to forecast likely positions and anticipate where support or opposition will arise. This creates a consciousness of opposition when individuals foresee disagreement or incompatible goals.

As an illustration of how this consciousness emerges, consider the example of an academic department in a large university (Case 4.1).

Case 4.1 **Budget Cuts in Academia**

Traditionally, faculty members in academic departments have responsibility for decisions about a wide variety of issues. In smaller subcommittees or as a whole group, they discuss and decide issues such as how the yearly budget should be spent, who should be hired when new positions become available, what the curriculum requirements should be, what graduate programs should be offered, which students should be admitted to the graduate programs, and so on. As these issues are discussed, faculty members learn how each of their colleagues would like to shape the department. In most cases, each faculty member covers some "subfield" within the broader discipline the department represents (e.g., in an English department—British literature, American poetry, writing and composition). These subfields may become the basis for the partisan stands that faculty take; they can influence preferences about who should be hired when a position is being filled, where research money or teaching assistants should be allocated within the department, and so on. Faculty members often argue that their subfield is underrepresented within the program and that it needs to be buttressed in order to maintain the department's reputation.

In our case, the university faces severe budget cutbacks and the department's chairperson has told several people informally that he thinks each department may be asked to eliminate two faculty positions for the next academic year. As this information travels through the grapevine, informal discussions occur between faculty members concerning how the department should handle the cutbacks. Some members may state their positions explicitly as they discuss the consequences of eliminating someone from the current faculty. Through these discussions and through recollections of how various faculty members have felt in the past, members may garner sufficient knowledge to anticipate the areas people are likely to suggest for elimination. If preferences differ, an awareness of opposition can mount as the department considers what it would mean to lose two teaching positions. The untenured faculty who may be asked to leave obviously have the greatest stake in the outcome of the decision and are likely to assess how much support they (or their area) have in the department and who are their potential advocates and opponents.

In this hypothetical example, the faculty has a prevailing sense of an issue arising, they recognize likely differences in viewpoints on this issue, and they share an uncertainty about whether these differences will need to be addressed. There is, in other words, **a perception of potential incompatibility of goals or objectives**. However, at this point the conflict remains **latent**, because there is no immediate stimulus for the professors to act on their positions.

What might make the department members act on their expectations? In examining phases of conflict interaction, Rummel (1976), Pondy (1967), Walton (1969), and others have suggested that some critical event activates latent conflict. This **triggering event** turns a "consciousness of opposition" into acknowledged conflict. Obviously there are any number of events that could become triggers in the case described above: the dean could notify each department that two positions must be eliminated; an untenured faculty member who wants to start looking for another position could request an early decision on the issue; or a faculty member could send a formal letter to the chair that argues strongly for the elimination of two specific colleagues if the cutbacks materialize.

Any of these incidents could be triggering events for conflict interaction by stimulating parties who perceive incompatible goals **to move toward obtaining their objectives and to anticipate and elicit countermoves by those who hold opposing stands**. Once parties are acting in behalf of their positions, the conflict interaction can move through cycles of withdrawal, joking, problem-solving, heated arguments, proposals and counterproposals, and so on, in all their many forms. The triggering event signals a transition in the way people think and act about the conflict. **While latent conflict is sustained by perceptions of differences, conflict interaction is sustained by the moves and countermoves of the participants**. In the latent phase, people think in terms of **possibilities**, while conflict interaction confronts them with **real** threats and constraints. Just as a critical incident changes the general tenor of the group's climate, a triggering event alters people's response to differences and shapes the particular form conflict takes.

It is easy to think of triggering events in negative terms, as "the straw that breaks the camel's back." However, a triggering event also carries with it an important **opportunity**. As we noted in Chapter 3, a critical requirement of constructive conflict management is **thorough and successful differentiation of conflicting positions**. Before they can move to an integrative solution, parties must raise the conflict issue and spend sufficient time and energy clarifying positions, pursuing the reasons behind those positions, and acknowledging their differences. By bringing the conflict out, a triggering event sets the stage for constructive resolution. It opens the possibility of clearing away problems and tensions that undermine relationships or group performance. There is, of course, no guarantee that a constructive resolution will happen. As we observed in Chapter 3, uncontrolled escalation and destructive avoidance can also develop during differentiation. **How** the parties handle differentiation is the key to whether it becomes destructive or constructive. In part, how people handle differentiation depends on individuals' **ability to recognize and escape their trained incapacities and to diagnose and alter negative features of the prevailing climate**. It also depends on **specific responses to the triggering event**, which are shaped by parties' access to and use of power.

A letter from a faculty member advocating the elimination of two colleagues could be a triggering event in the latent conflict situation described above. The response it elicits depends on how the move is perceived. In one possible scenario, the faculty might believe that the letter will fall on "deaf ears." They might predict that the chairperson is likely to read the letter, perhaps acknowledge its receipt, and say that it will be kept on hand for later use. In this case the response or countermove to the letter is essentially the chairperson's appeasing comments to its author, accompanied by inaction by other faculty members. In a second scenario, the letter might be sent to a faculty member who is a good friend of two associate deans, has made "end runs" around the chairperson to the dean on previous decisions, and usually carries considerable weight in shaping departmental policy. In response to the letter, those who are concerned about the proposal might ask the chair to call a meeting to discuss the whole array of options for dealing with the potential cutbacks. Some faculty members may write their own letters to put other positions on the matter "on paper." Others may confront the member who wrote the letter and ask why such a proposal was offered when no requests for cutbacks had yet been made. Any of these responses would in turn be likely to elicit further moves.

In both cases, the letter was a move that fractured the latent conflict phase; one person acted in behalf of his or her own goals and others responded to the move. Once the faculty **recognized and acted on the latent issue** the conflict entered a new phase of open engagement. **How** they reacted to this trigger set the stage for how the conflict was played out. In the first scenario, others did not believe the letter presented much of a threat. As a result, it did not elicit a strong reaction and it did not begin a chain of reactions and countermoves aimed at settling the issues. Members recognized an issue had been raised, but there were no drastic countermoves because its consequences were neither immediate nor threatening. The letter "set the agenda" for future discussions. In the second case, the letter began a lengthy series of moves and countermoves that would not only determine how the department would handle the cutbacks but may change the relationships among the faculty members and alter the department's long-term climate.

Once a conflict is triggered, the moves people make depend on the power they can marshall and exert. **Parties' ability and willingness to use power and their skills at employing it determine the moves and countermoves that sustain the conflict.** Available power establishes the set of actions that individuals may employ and sets limits on the effectiveness of others' moves. Each move reveals to others how willing a party is to **use** power and what kinds of power that party has. The response to the move reveals whether the use of power will go unchallenged.

The most important difference between the two scenarios just described is the difference in power held by the faculty members who wrote the letters. In both cases the letter could easily be construed as an attempt to sway attitudes by getting a "jump" on others. Laying out one set of arguments before other positions or proposals are developed or stated could give the writer a great advantage. Despite their common objective, only the second letter was perceived to have the potential to influence the outcome of the cutback decision. The second faculty member was perceived to hold power and had been known to use it on previous occasions: other faculty members knew that this individual had strong persuasive abilities, was a good friend of two deans, and was willing to discuss departmental issues with the deans before raising them with the chair or colleagues in the department. In responding to the letter, other faculty had to rely on their own sources of power (e.g., the right to request a faculty meeting about an issue, the ability to build faculty alliances) to prevent the letter from firmly setting attitudes before a full discussion of the issue occurred.

The shift from latent conflict to the emergence of conflict interaction inevitably confronts the participants with the issue of power. During latent conflict, parties may have a sense of the sources of power people hold and they may make estimates of how likely it will be for others to use power if the conflict surfaces. Once conflict interaction begins, however, each move and countermove confirms or challenges previous assessments of power. Individuals are caught up in an active process of testing and determining the role and limits of power in the conflict. But how, exactly, does this happen? In the next section we will examine the nature of power more closely and point to several defining characteristics that make power a major influence on the direction conflict interaction takes.

A RELATIONAL VIEW OF POWER

The everyday use of the term "power" often clouds or misrepresents its nature (Bachrach & Baratz, 1970; Deutsch, 1973; Janeway, 1980). Expressions like "He holds enormous power" or "The purchasing department's manager has lost the power she once had" imply that power is a possession, something that belongs to an individual, that can be increased or lost and that, by implication, can be carried away from a group or organization. In this view, power is a quality of the strong or dominant, and something the weak lack. This view is dangerously misleading. The social philosopher Hannah Arendt (1969) points to the problem with this view when she states: "power is never the property of an individual; it belongs to a group and remains in existence only so long as the group keeps together" (p. 44).

In Chapter 3 we defined power as the **ability to influence or control events**. What does it mean to say this ability "belongs to the group"? For one thing, it means recognizing that social power stems from relationships among people. Individuals have power when they have access to resources that can be used to persuade or convince others, to change their course of action, or to prevent others from moving toward their goals in conflict situations. These resources (which give power if used effectively) are controlled by individuals; it is easy to assume the resources themselves equal power and that their owner therefore possesses power. However, this conclusion ignores the fact that any resource serving as a basis for power is only effective because others **endorse** this resource (Jewell & Reitz, 1981). The resource only imparts power because it carries some weight in the context of relationships where it is used. The young child who throws a temper tantrum has power over his or her parents only if they are bothered (or touched) by the raucous fits and are willing to appease the child because the behavior is annoying (or heartbreaking). The boss who threatens to fire a worker can only influence a worker who values the job and believes his or her boss will carry out the threat. In both cases the second party must "endorse" the first's resources for them to become a basis for power.

Individuals can employ a broad range of resources to exert power (French & Raven, 1959; Wilmot & Wilmot, 1978; Kipnis, Schmidt, & Wilkerson, 1980). Potential resources include **special skills or abilities, time, expertise about the task at hand, personal attractiveness or likability, control over rewards and/or punishments, formal position in a group or organization, loyal allies, persuasive skills,** and **control over critical group possessions** (e.g., the treasury), to name a few. Anything that enables individuals to move toward their own goals or to interfere with another's actions is a resource that can be used in conflicts. Communication skills like being articulate or being able to construct effective arguments can be power resources in themselves. However, in order for a move to have an impact on others' moves or on the outcome of the conflict, the resources it uses must be given some credence by others: either consciously or unconsciously others must endorse them. In this sense, **power is always conferred on someone by those who endorse the resources**.

At first glance, it would seem that the need for endorsement leaves an easy way out for weaker parties in conflict. Isn't it always possible to undermine the use of power by withholding endorsement of some resource? In principle, weaker parties always have this option. But the claim is misleading, because the tendency to endorse power is deep-seated and based in powerful and pervasive social processes. At the most superficial level, we endorse power because the resources it is based on enable others to grant or deny things that are valuable. As Richard Emerson (1962) states: "[the] power to control or influence the other resides in control over the things he values, which may range all the way from oil resources to ego-support" (p. 11). This is an important, if obvious point, and it leads to a more fundamental issue: **this control is exerted in interaction**. Therefore both the would-be controller and the controlled have a part in playing it out. One person makes a control bid based on real or potential use of resources, and the other accepts or rejects it.

Perhaps the most critical aspect of this process is the second person's acceptance or rejection of the legitimacy or force of the bid; in other words, the second person's endorsement (or lack of endorsement) of the other's resources and his or her ability to use them. This social process of endorsement is what underlies people's perceptions of others' behavior as attempts to influence or control. If someone imitates the shape of a gun with his or her fingers, points them at someone else, and says, "Hand me your wallet," the "target" person may laugh at the joke, but he or she would not see this as a power move. If that same person picks up a gun and does the same thing, nearly everyone would see it as an attempt to influence or control. A person's endorsement of a gun as an instrument of force is a product of years of experience (education, television shows, first-hand encounters), which give him or her an idea of its power and of how someone could handle it.

At the same time, even the power that a gun confers is not inherent in the possession of the gun itself. Because power is relational, the effectiveness of any resource is always negotiated in the interaction. If the person at whom the gun is aimed tells the assailant to "Move out of my way," this is an attempt to withdraw endorsement of the assailant's potential power. The response may or may not succeed—that is the nature of any unfolding negotiation—but as the interaction proceeds the perceptions of power can change. It is interaction then that changes perceptions of resources and the power they can ultimately generate. The influential powers of intangible social resources, such as a good reputation or persuasive abilities, are built in much the same way: people must endorse them if they are to carry any weight. The tendency and willingness to endorse power stem from several sources:

(1) **The social categorization process**, discussed in Chapter 1, creates strong preconceptions about what types of people are usually powerful and what types are generally weak. Erica Apfelbaum (1979) investigated the relation of social categorization to people's sense of their own and others' power. She notes that different resources and the ability to use them are associated with different social categories. Ranking executives, for example, are assumed by society to be wealthy, have connections, and be skillful at negotiation. Welfare mothers, on the other hand, are assumed to be poor and have little ability to get ahead in the world. An aura of competence and power attaches itself to the executive that the welfare mother does not have. So it is with all social categories, Apfelbaum argues: each is associated with a definite degree of power, with certain resources, and with certain abilities to use the resources available to them. These associations set up expectations that work in favor of or against endorsement of power moves by people from various categories: we endorse those we expect to be powerful and do not endorse those we expect to be weak.

These associations have several consequences. For one thing, they make the use of power easier for certain people and more difficult for others. In the 1960s sociologists conducted a number of studies on the effects of members' status outside decision-making groups on member behavior (Wilson, 1978). Consistently, members with higher status in society (doctors, lawyers, university students) were more influential than those with lower status (laborers, high school students), even if both members had exactly the same resources.

For example, a study by Moore (1968) had junior college students work in pairs to estimate the number of rectangles in an optical illusion. The experimenter led the students to believe that their partner was either a Stanford University student or a high school student. There was no difference in the ability of the students to estimate squares, but those who thought they worked with university students changed their estimates significantly more often than those who thought they worked with high school students: in other words, they allowed themselves to be influenced by "university" students and exercised influence over the high school students. The junior college students expected university students to be brighter and therefore to be better at the task. This assumption led the junior college students to endorse the university students' resources; the opposite assumption encouraged them to give less weight to the high school students' attempts to use their own resources. Whenever people from different social categories work together, similar preconceptions about their respective powers will strengthen endorsement for some and weaken it for others.

Expectations about social categories not only shape members' perceptions of others' resources and abilities, but also influence their perceptions of themselves. People who belong to a social category generally expected to be powerful and who regularly receive endorsement for power moves (e.g., corporate executives) will tend to see themselves as powerful and effective. They will be confident when making future moves, and their confidence, in turn, is likely to lead to effective use of power, which reinforces their self-concepts. The same is true for those belonging to "power-less" categories. They expect to be ineffective and therefore give way before the powerful. Janeway (1980) argues that this is one of the major reasons women, minorities, and other low-power groups often take weak roles in conflict situations: they see themselves as having fewer resources than dominant groups, as being spectators rather than actors. Even though these groups have resources, including intelligence, social skills, and even sheer numbers, they do not realize their potential power. They believe they are weak and isolated and have little chance of competing with the "powers that be." In conflict, such people often do not assert themselves, and when they do their efforts are not given the same weight of endorsement that people from powerful categories receive. Once again, there is a self-reinforcing cycle that serves to prove the weak are powerless and further strengthens other people's tendency to refuse endorsement.

Apfelbaum calls the socialization process that creates these perceptions of weakness **degrouping**; she argues that it is the most important mechanism by which the powerful maintain their position. Here also is one of the roots of the common idea of power as a **possession**: if certain social groups are assumed to be consistently powerful, it takes only a small step to assume power is theirs by right; in other words, it is their possession. Since the process of learning social categorizations is very gradual and extends over years, it is easy to lose sight of their flexibility and forget that all social groups are, to a great extent, created by those within and outside them. If the social definition of **who** is powerful changes, patterns of endorsement and therefore of who can exert power effectively can change radically.

Tedeschi's work on social influence and aggression, discussed in Chapter 2, illustrates the need for people to justify coercive actions. Related work suggests that people often perceive another party as a member of a group rather than as an individual because it allows them to act more aggressively (Pruitt & Rubin, 1986). This perceptual preference is called **deindividuation** because it removes the personal and human characteristics normally associated with a party and replaces them with more global features. For example, it is not uncommon for people in conflict to refrain from using another party's name and to refer to him or her according to physical attributes or social roles, such as "that loud-mouthed boss" or that "aggressive lawyer." As the conflict and aggression escalate, so too does the degree of deindividuation. The opposing party may be identified by race or religion, denoting a more impersonal perception and label. Because people are seen as less human, the social inhibition on acting aggressively toward them disappears, or so we believe. Entire nations can get caught up in this pattern of deindividuation as a means to justify and absolve their citizens from being seen as aggressors. In every war in which the United States has been involved during the past century, examples of dein-dividuated names and labels for enemies, including the civilian populations, have surfaced. Such labels as "Krauts" and "Gooks" allow us to act aggressively without regulation or remorse.

(2)   The use of power also carries a **mystique** that reinforces endorsement of moves by powerful members. Janeway (1980) explores the childhood and adolescent experiences through which people learn to use and understand power. The actions of adults are incomprehensible to children and so, Janeway argues, children attribute to adults mysterious, unfathomable powers. As the rich fantasy life of childhood gives way to the mastery of adulthood, people learn how power works, but the aura persists, dimmed, perhaps, but never extinguished.

In addition to childhood experiences, the historical connection between kings and queens and the divine also contributes to power's magical aura, Janeway (1980) observes. As a result, "even today, it seems, the governed are ready to accept the idea that the powerful are different from you and me, and not simply because they have more power. We grant them a different kind of power that contains some element of the supernatural" (p. 77). This mystique functions to reinforce existing power relations: "for the powerful the magic aura offers a validation of dominance over and above the consent of the governed; for the weak, a defensive shield against feelings of inferiority and ineffectiveness" (p. 126). After all, if power is a magical, unattainable possession, the strong must have special qualities and the weak cannot handle it and should not try. Kipnis (1990) notes that the supernatural mystique of power often carries with it reckless license: "throughout history, we find a special divinity is assumed to surround the powerful so that they are excused from gross acts such as murder, theft, terrorism and intimidation"(p. 40).

The magical aura about power inspires a certain awe that facilitates its endorsement. It also tends to perpetuate power and weakness in the same hands over time. In groups, for example, more experienced, "older" members are often granted this aura or mystique. Although they may have more knowledge and information because of their longer stay in the group, the mystique assigned to them by newer members can linger and keep certain members in unwarranted influential positions.

As an illustration of how a sense of mystery can sometimes transform perceptions and create power, consider the following case of a unique and self-styled individual (Case 4.2).

Case 4.2 **The Eccentric Professor**

In one large academic department, a professor became known as an exceptional intellect, a person who possessed unfathomable powers of insight and perspective. As a result of this perception, his colleagues and students often deferred to his judgment and looked to him to provide solutions to complex problems. In time, he came to hold the most powerful position in his college, choosing when he would teach and to whom.

The professor, Harold, was a prolific researcher and talented teacher. But perhaps his most singular trait was that he was fond of the unusual, the offbeat, the uncommon. He surrounded himself with objects and fashion from an earlier era, often wearing knickers, bow ties, and driving caps. He made it clear to anyone who inquired that he liked books and cats more than people. Because of his tastes, he kept to himself, shunning parties and all social gatherings. He maintained this interpersonal distance in his classes, using seat assignments, lecture outlines, and a question period to solidify a formal classroom climate. Not many months after his arrival on campus, he was asked to address the faculty as part of the college's colloquium series. His lecture, on thinking and learning, incorporated NFL training-camp films and analogies from the history of the stock market. In every conversation, from the important to the mundane, colleagues and students learned that Harold approached ideas and problems in unusual ways, from unusual angles. Whereas he was first ridiculed and avoided, he soon became an enigma to understand. And so the stories began.

He spent late evenings in the library and was seen carrying throngs of books. When asked by one bold student what he was after, he supposedly replied that he was committed to having read a portion of every book in the library.

After Harold worked months on a computer algorithm, a colleague supposedly learned that he was to use the program to make all his important decisions, from buying a house to selecting a wife.

After receiving a national award for one of his essays, he chose not to attend the award ceremony, claiming that he would not fly or take a train. When beseeched to attend, he finally agreed and spent a week riding a bus to and from the distant ceremony. Rumors spread that he had made a million dollars in the stock market and that he owned dozens of cats. As the years rolled on, the stories grew and the mystery and power deepened.

Most of the stories became so embellished as to represent anything but the truth. In reality, Harold, though offbeat, was much more similar than dissimilar to his peers. He was a smart man, to be sure. Yet the mystery that enshrouded him led to beliefs that he possessed such an extraordinary intellect that he could perform incredible feats, such as beating the stock market or providing mathematical proofs without effort. Even his fellow professors found themselves caught up in this mystery and made attributions regarding his behavior that were consistent with this powerful image. This image, perpetuated by mystery, allowed Harold to gain considerable influence in his working environment.

(3) **Interaction** in the immediate situation is the primary means through which endorsement is achieved. The response of other parties to a power move has a strong influence on an individual's endorsement. If, for example, the foreman of a painting crew gives an order, and all members of the crew follow it without question, they are reinforcing one another's endorsement of the foreman's authority. Each worker observes the others obeying, and this lends additional weight to his or her own respect for the foreman's authority. Assume, on the other hand, that the foreman has been unfair in the past and that workers have doubts about whether he deserves his authority. If one worker refuses to go along with the foreman's order, it may very

well undermine other workers' endorsement of the foreman's moves. Others see that some do not accept the foreman unquestioningly, and their respect for his authority and ability to use it may subsequently decrease.

The **way** in which someone executes a power move will also influence its endorsement. Power involves the use of resources; **successful** power moves require **skillful** and **appropriate** use of resources. For example, when a leader or supervisor gives feedback and criticism to subordinates, it is more effective when (1) it is done privately rather than in front of co-workers, (2) positive points and improvements are discussed in addition to problems, and (3) raises or compensation increases are not tied to criticisms or the subordinate's attempts to solve his or her problems (Meyer, Kay, & French, 1965; Downs, Smeyak, & Martin, 1980) A supervisor who follows these rules is more likely to elicit cooperation from subordinates, partly because they offer a positive method of giving feedback, but also because they allow the subordinates to save face and do not push them into challenging the supervisor's authority. A boss who berates workers in front of their co-workers is likely to face a challenge or, at least, create resentment that may emerge later on. Exerting power in a socially appropriate manner that follows the path of least resistance is conducive to present and future endorsement by others.

Exactly what constitutes "appropriate and skillful" use of power varies from case to case. Research offers a few general principles, but they are sketchy at best and do not add up to a systematic theory.

(4)   To this point we have emphasized what might be called the "unconscious" bases of endorsement. However, endorsements are often openly discussed and decided on. In these cases, **parties value certain abilities, knowledge, or personal characteristics** and explicitly support the legitimacy of the resource. A group might, for example, pride itself on always having sufficient information before reaching any final decision and compliment those who are most persistent in gathering and evaluating background material. One member could use this knowledge of the group's self-image as a basis for a move in a decision-making conflict. He or she could attempt to stop the group from adopting a solution by making the members feel guilty about not conducting an adequate search for information. In this instance the "powerful" individual uses a resource that the group willingly endorses as a basis for a move. The move may or may not be successful and may or may not be intended for the good of the group, but it appeals to a resource that, as Arendt says, "belongs to the group."

Recognizing the **relational nature of power** forces us to acknowledge the status of resources. Regardless of how tight a hold someone has on any resource, the resource is always **used** in the context of a relationship. It is the **other's view** of the resource that makes it a basis for influence. If this view is altered during the conflict interaction, the bases of power shift, and the possibilities for moves in the interaction are redefined. Because power is inherently relational, it is never entirely under one's control. The **response** to the use of power determines whether the resource that has been employed will remain a source of power as the conflict unfolds. The impact of power in conflict is constantly negotiated as interaction unfolds; it is interaction that changes perceptions of power.

As parties use resources, their moves renew, maintain, or reduce the weight a resource has in the interaction. A clumsy move can weaken endorsement of a resource and confidence in the abilities of the user. A well-executed move can enhance endorsement of a resource. The **skills of the user, the response of other members, and the eventual course that the conflict takes**, all determine whether a resource maintains or loses its endorsement. Even the nature of the resource itself is important, because some resources (e.g., money or favors) can be exhausted and others (e.g., physical force) allow no turning back once employed. The use of resources is an extremely complex process, and we will return to it throughout the rest of this chapter.

POWER AND CONFLICT INTERACTION

The use of power imposes constraints on the other person. A power move usually brings about a reduction of others' options by limiting the forms of interaction the other person can engage in, by eliminating a possible resolution to the conflict, or by restricting the other's ability to employ countervailing power. These constraints influence the direction the conflict takes. They make certain behaviors or styles desirable or, alternatively, impossible. They shape parties' perceptions of each other, kindling hope or desperation, cooperation or competition. As the conflict evolves and changes, so do the constraints under which the participants operate. The other's responses to moves set further constraints, the responses to the countermoves set still further constraints, and so on, until the conflict is no longer wholly controlled by either party but is a collective product. It is greater than—and in a real sense out of the control of—any single person.

To illustrate the relational nature of power, the influence of power on conflict interaction, and the multiplication of constraints, consider the case of a research and development committee in a large corporation (Case 4.3).

Case 4.3   **The Creativity Development Committee**

Tom was manager of three research and development laboratories for a large chemical and materials corporation. He supervised general operations, budgeting, personnel, and proposal development for the labs. Each lab had several projects, and each project team was headed by a project director, who was usually a scientist or an engineer working on the problem. Tom had been a project director for ten years in another of the corporation's labs and had been promoted to Lab Manager four years ago. Although he had to transfer across the country to take this job, he felt he had earned the respect of his subordinates. He had been regarded as an outsider at first, but he worked hard to be accepted and the lab's productivity had gone up over the last two years. Tom's major worry was keeping track of everything. His busy schedule kept him from close supervision over projects.

As in most labs, each project generally went its own way. As long as it produced results, a project enjoyed a high degree of autonomy. Morale was usually high among the research staff. They knew they were on the leading edge of the corporation's success and they enjoyed it. The visibility and importance of research were shown by the fact that project directors were regularly promoted upward. In fact, the presiding officer of the board had once been a project director. Because of this, scientists with an interest in management were drawn to project directorships. Although not necessarily the best researchers, they were the most ambitious. Playing their political cards right was very important for project directors. A negative evaluation from the "man upstairs" could be the kiss of death for their aspirations. At the same time, it was also important to produce. A record of innovative successes was invaluable in gaining promotions.

It was in this milieu that Tom decided to try to increase productivity still further by introducing procedures to enhance research creativity. Research teams often met to discuss ideas and to decide on future directions. In these meetings ideas were often improved, but they could also be killed or cut off. Tom had studied research on decision-making, which indicated that groups often suppress good ideas without a hearing; the research suggested ways of preventing this suppression and enhancing group creativity. Tom hoped to harness these findings to increase productivity. He wanted to develop standard procedures for making decisions in research meetings, procedures that would enhance rather than hinder idea development.

Tom decided to form a committee of some project directors and himself to develop a procedure for the project teams. He asked four project directors if they were willing to review the research and meet regularly over the summer to help formulate appropriate procedures. The four agreed to take on the task and the group began its work enthusiastically.

During the first six weeks of the summer the group met weekly to discuss articles and books that members had read and to hear consultants. The group was able to narrow down a set of about 15 procedures and programs to four prime possibilities. Eventually, two programs emerged as possibilities. However, as the list was narrowed from four to two there was a clear split in how the group felt.

One procedure was strongly favored by three of the project directors. The fourth project director liked the procedure better than the other option but was less vocal in showing her support for it. In general, the project directors felt the procedure they favored was far more consistent with what project teams were currently doing and with the problems faced by the corporation. They believed the second program, which involved a lot of writing and the use of special voting procedures, was too abstract for working research scientists to accept. It would be difficult, they said, to use this procedure because everyone would have to fill out forms and explain ideas in writing before a meeting could be held. Because of already heavy work loads, their people would not go along with the program. Researchers would ridicule the program and be prejudiced against future attempts to stimulate creativity.

Tom argued that the second program was more comprehensive, had a broader conception of problems, and would help develop more creative ideas than the first, which was a fairly conservative "brainstorming" process. Although discussion focused on the substantive nature of each program and its relation to the objective of creativity, the project directors knew that the program Tom favored was one he had been trained in at his former lab. Tom was a good friend of the consultant who had developed it. The project directors talked outside meetings about this friendship and questioned whether it was shaping Tom's attitudes. The climate of the group, which had initially been positive and enthusiastic, grew tense, as issues connected to the power relations between the manager and project directors surfaced.

Although the project directors knew Tom could choose the program he wanted, how the final choice would be made was never clarified at the beginning of the summer. The time that the project directors spent reading and evaluating the programs created an implicit expectation that they would have an equal say in the final choice. At the same time, the project directors had all worked at the lab for at least four years and had experienced firsthand the relative power of managers and project directors. They heard horror stories of project directors who had gotten on the manager's "wrong side" and been denied promotion or fired. When push came to shove, they expected the manager to have greater power and to be willing to use it.

At its final meeting the group discussed the two programs for quite some time, but there seemed to be little movement. The climate became somewhat uncomfortable at the meeting as the group began to wonder how the final choice would be made. Somewhat hesitantly, the manager turned to each project director individually and asked the same question. Tom asked each person, "How upset would you be if I choose the program I prefer?" The project directors gave a number of different responses to the question. One said he was uncomfortable answering. Two indicated that they felt they would have difficulty using the creativity program as it was currently designed. The fourth said she thought she could live with it. After these answers were given, Tom told the project directors he would leave a memo in their mailboxes informing them of the final decision.

Two weeks after this discussion, the project directors were told that the second program, the one the manager preferred, would be ordered. The memo also said that the other program would be used, on an experimental basis, by one of the 18 projects.

The decision caused considerable resentment. The project directors felt "used." They saw little reason to have spent so much time discussing programs if Tom was just going to choose the program he wanted, regardless of their preferences. When the program began in the fall, one of the project directors told his team that the program would be recommended rather than required, and he explained that it might have to be adapted extensively to fit the unit's style. He made this decision without telling the manager. While the move was in clear violation of Tom's authority, he knew Tom could not visit the teams often and was therefore unlikely to find out about it. Another project director instituted the program but commented afterward that he felt he had not integrated it into his unit well. He questioned how much effort he had actually invested in making the program "work."

The incident also caused the manager's stock to fall in the eyes of the project directors. Several commented that they had lost their respect for Tom as a result. They saw Tom as someone who was willing to manipulate people for his own purposes. This opinion filtered to other project directors and scientists through the "grapevine" and caused Tom considerable difficulties in a labor grievance during the following year. In this dispute several researchers banded together and defied the manager, because they believed he would eventually back down. The lack of respect generated in the creativity committee undermined Tom's authority with his subordinates. In addition, the project director who made the program optional for his workers served as a model for similar defiance by others. Once the directors saw that "optional" use of the program would go unpunished, they felt free to do it themselves, and Tom's control was further reduced. Tom eventually transferred to another division of the corporation.

This case is set in a corporate lab, but it could just as easily have occurred in other situations, such as a committee developing an advertising campaign, a team developing new software for a computer company, or a textbook selection committee in a university department. The case offers a clear illustration of the role of power in conflict interaction. During the early meetings members offered their reactions to various programs and tried to move steadily toward a final choice. Although there were differences of opinion about the programs in these early meetings, **expertise and knowledge** (the resources used by members to exert influence and shape attitudes about the programs) were implicitly endorsed by the whole group. Members tried to articulate criteria for assessing the programs and to apply the criteria to the programs being considered. The moves people made to keep a particular program under consideration were arguments based on knowledge and experience they had as researchers. Reasoned argument was the operating norm for the group, and as members worked together to make decisions through rational argument, they were, in effect, reinforcing the group's endorsement of expertise.

Once the list was narrowed to two programs and a consensus did not emerge through reasoned argument, members began to use other resources. In turning to each project director and asking him or her, "How upset would you be if I choose the other program?" the manager gave a strong indication that he might be willing to use his **formal authority** to force selection of the program he preferred. This move was significantly different from any move that participants had made before, and it broadened the scope of the conflict considerably. The assumption that influence would rest on logical argument and expertise was now overturned. The project directors anticipated that Tom might exercise his right to choose the program. Although Tom's question was not the actual exercise of his right, it signaled the potential use of this power base to "resolve" the group's conflict. Tom was testing what impact the move might have if he disregarded the project directors' arguments and chose the program he wanted. In some ways, Tom's move was predictable. Research summarized by Kipnis (1990) suggests that people tend to use reason, logic, and simple requests until resistance occurs. At that point, beliefs about power guide the choice of tactics.

Tom's move marked a turning point in the conflict because it **altered the resources** members used. **Tom moved from the use of expertise and knowledge, resources common to all members, to invoking his formal authority, a resource exclusively his.** The project directors' response to Tom's move also invoked a new resource, their ability not to cooperate with their superior. The ability to run their projects independently was an "ace in the hole" for the project directors. Tom was responsible for productivity in all projects, and if his actions in this committee undermined the project directors' motivation or ability to work effectively, the outcome might reflect poorly on his ability to direct the labs. If projects were not productive, it would undoubtedly reflect on the project directors, but the reputation of the labs in the corporation ultimately rested with Tom. This reputation would be threatened if word got out that several project teams were unproductive and unruly.

In suggesting that he might use his power, the manager **elicited** the threat of a similar use of power by the project directors. The project directors signaled their potential willingness to act on their own power in responding to Tom's move; Tom's move elicited **a reciprocal use of power** in the conflict interaction.

It is instructive to stop for a moment and reflect on what this countermove meant to the project directors. They were well aware of the power their manager could exert, because they had all been in the corporation for many years. They held the manager–project director dichotomy firmly in mind and were well **aware that they had few resources in comparison** to Tom. Moreover, because they themselves aspired to rise in the corporation, greatly admired the intellectual and political prowess of higher officers, and saw Tom's station as well beyond reach for the time being, Tom's acts held a certain **magical aura** for the project directors. The group operated in a fairly egalitarian and congenial manner, and this also reinforced the project directors' endorsement of Tom's moves. Each project director saw the others going along with the process in apparent satisfaction, so there seemed little reason to question Tom's moves. However, when Tom threw over the rational basis of influence and invoked the authority of his position, the project directors were jolted into considering countermeasures. They raised the argument of difficulty in using the program, but implicit in this was the threat that they would undermine it. This threat was probably not consciously planned. Their response was fairly weak because of the considerable endorsement they accorded to Tom's power. However, it carried the germ of an idea, and later, when their respect for Tom had waned even further, at least some of them would act against him.

The question–response exchange between Tom and the project directors illustrates how the use of power (or, in this case, the indication of a willingness to use power) imposes constraints and thereby directs future moves in the conflict. When Tom asked for a response to the unilateral choice he might make, **it reduced the range of appropriate moves his subordinates could make at that point in the interaction**. It would not have been appropriate, for example, for them to comment on the relative academic merits of the two programs in responding to Tom's "How upset would you be . . . ?" question. This question **sought** an indication of how willing the project directors were **to employ the power they had**. If, in response to the question, one of them had said "I think the program we want has the following strengths . . . ," the statement would not have been an appropriate response to the question (although it might have been effective as a strategy to change the subject and avoid the question altogether). The question—along with Tom's direct focus—created a subtle but strong pressure to respond on the manager's grounds.

The question moved the discussion away from a consideration of the relative merits of the two programs; information and expertise were no longer a basis for influence at that point in the exchange. Tom's move **constrained** the project directors' options in the interaction and actually **directed** them toward a reciprocal use of power. Any statement that would have been a conversationally appropriate response to the question (for instance, "I'll walk out of the meeting," "I'll be very angry and notify your supervisor," or "I'd get over it") is a comment about the project directors' ability or willingness to use their own bases of power. Tom's remark interrupted the group's present direction and turned the interaction toward a series of moves based on **alternative resources**: it was a classic triggering event.

Tom's final decision to choose the program he preferred and the response of the project directors to this move illustrate the importance of endorsement. In moving away from a form of influence that the group as a whole endorsed, Tom relied on his right as manager to choose the program he wanted. Although the right was a "given" in the situation, it did not necessarily have to be endorsed or accepted once that power was exercised. A bid for influence may not be successful if other members do not endorse the basis for the move. The project director who decided to recommend rather than require the program and the director who said he did not use the program effectively did not fully endorse Tom's right to decide what program would be used. Although the project directors may or may not have been intentionally challenging Tom's power, in effect their response was based on a belief that they had a greater say in how their projects were run than they had previously assumed. The project directors' decision questioned Tom's authority—his right to enforce the use of a program in the labs.

This does not mean that the project director did not fear reprisals by the manager. If Tom found out about this decision, he would either have to reestablish his power by imposing sanctions on the errant director or have to accept his diminished managerial role. It is likely he would have done the former. The project director was aware of this and gave credence to Tom's power, but he did so to a much lesser extent than he might have. After Tom's move, the project director saw him as unworthy of respect; he saw a way around Tom's power. The project director's original endorsement of Tom began to ebb.

The decline in endorsement of Tom's authority begun by this incident continued through the labor dispute. Other subordinates saw that Tom could be defied successfully and heard disparaging remarks about him. They gossiped about "stupid" things they had seen Tom do and about his lack of respect for other project directors. The firm base of managerial respect was eroded and the project directors became more and more confident of their own resources vis-à-vis their manager. Tom's loss of endorsement clearly points to the dangers of using strength.

THE USE OF POWER IN CONFLICT TACTICS

Several researchers have developed extensive lists or typologies of conflict tactics (Sharp, 1973; Roloff, 1976; Wilmot & Wilmot, 1978; Kipnis et al., 1980). A number of conflict tactics are discussed in Chapter 7. The variety and range of these tactics clearly show the many guises power can take in conflicts. Within this diversity, however, four distinct modes of power can be discerned. (1) Some tactics operate through the **direct** application of power: they are intended to compel the other to respond regardless of what the other wants. These tactics bring physical, economic, and political resources directly to bear in order to force the other to comply. (2) Other tactics involve a **direct and virtual** use of power: they attempt to elicit the others' compliance by communicating the **potential** use of direct force. In direct, virtual uses of power, parties openly display their resources and ability to employ them. Threats and promises are probably the purest examples of this tactic. (3) Third, tactics may employ power in an **indirect** mode: someone may attempt to employ his or her power to shape interaction without ever making the use of power explicit. In the indirect mode, power or the potential use of power remains implicit and tacit. (4) Finally, tactics may constitute a **hidden** use of power: in this mode, tactics use power to hide or suppress potential issues. The actual consequences of power are hidden, because the issue is decided before it even develops or emerges.

Some tactics employ more than one mode of power. The particular mode or modes involved determine how open or explicit the influence attempt can be, the conditions it must meet in order to be effective, and the parties' general orientation and attitudes toward the other. The modes in which a tactic operates indicate several important things about the tactic. First, they determine what skills and styles of behavior are necessary to use the tactic effectively. Making a threat, which involves direct, virtual power, requires a fundamentally different approach than does postponement, which uses the power indirectly. Second, power modes shape the type of resistance the tactic is likely to meet. Different measures are necessary to counteract different modes of power. Finally, each mode has different effects on the endorsement of power underlying the tactic. For example, direct uses of power are much more likely to undermine endorsement than are hidden uses.

We illustrate the fundamental principles and processes involved in the "nondirect" power modes by considering three important and common tactics: **threats and promises** (direct, virtual power), **relational control** (indirect power), and **issue control** (hidden power). For each we outline how the tactic can be used, some conditions governing its effectiveness, and the likely points of resistance it can meet. Because the three tactics are "pure" examples of each category, the principles and problems enumerated here can be generalized to other tactics employing the same power mode.

Threats and Promises   These tactics are discussed in detail in Chapter 7 but are used as illustrations here. In one form or another, threats and promises appear in almost every conflict described in this book. We define a **threat** as **an individual's expressed intention to behave in a way that appears detrimental to the interests of another, if that other does not comply with the individual's request or terms** and a **promise** as **an individual's expressed intention to behave in a way that appears beneficial to another, if the other complies with the individual's request or terms.** Threats and promises then are two sides of the same coin, one negative and the other positive (Kelley, 1965; Deutsch, 1973; Bowers, 1974).

Threats and promises are important not only because they are so common, but also because they are clear examples of the **direct, virtual** use of power to influence interaction. Threats and promises directly link resources—rewards and punishments—with influence attempts and therefore offer a clear illustration of the essential features of the implied use of power. Perhaps because of this, threats and promises have been researched more than any other conflict tactics (Tedeschi, 1970; Bowers, 1974; Rubin & Brown, 1975, pp. 278–288). Although this research is fragmented, sometimes contradictory, and often hard to grasp, it can be put into perspective by considering threats and promises as aspects of power—**as moves involving the skilled application of resources with an impact dependent on the endorsement of the influenced individuals**.

It is obvious that effective promising or threatening depends on one person's control over resources the other person values. A manager in a large corporation can hardly threaten an employee with dismissal if the employee knows the manager has no authority to hire or fire; nor will employees believe the manager's promise of a raise if they know the manager has no clout "upstairs." However, effective influence does not necessarily stem from the person's **actual** control, but rather the other's **perception** that the person controls an important resource. A person's actual control over a resource becomes critical only if he or she has to carry out the threat or deliver the promise. The effectiveness of threats and promises is thus dependent on the individual's skill at convincing others that he or she has the resources and willingness to use them. In Chapter 7 we discuss several factors that determine the effectiveness of threats.

As with all power processes, the very act of threatening or promising can create or dissipate others' endorsement of the resources being used. If a threat or promise is not carried out, it can suggest to others that the person does not have the necessary resources or the will to use them. This may in turn make others less likely to give credence to the person's resources and less likely to respond in the future. This development is particularly true of intangible resources, such as authority. If the manager of a working group cannot carry out his or her promise to get a raise for his or her workers, they may lose respect for the manager and refuse to go along with future attempts to motivate or guide them (Pelz, 1952; Stogdill, 1974).

Carrying out threats or promises also has consequences for their endorsement. As might be expected, actually carrying out threats may cause others to resent that person and may ultimately undermine his or her resources. Promises have a unique advantage over threats in that carrying them out actually enhances others' endorsement of the person's power. The use of promises tends to make the party seem more likable, trustworthy, and considerate in the eyes of others. These perceptions reinforce the very credibility needed to pull off a promise effectively. In an effort to combine the greater compliance created by threats with the credibility reinforcement of promises, Bowers (1974) has suggested that most people use "thromises"—messages that convey both rewards and punishments simultaneously. If a manager says "We really can't take Friday off unless we finish this report today," she is conveying a rewarding offer in language often used for threats. By doing this, she may be able to enhance her employees' liking for her by indirectly offering a reward, yet constrain their behavior effectively. In addition, by indirectly indicating that she wants Friday off, she may increase the workers' identification with her and further strengthen her credibility and their endorsement of her authority.

The basic properties of threats and promises apply for all direct tactics. Most important, they depend on the person's ability to project the potential consequences of a direct move. This requirement makes the person's credibility critical.

Relational Control   During any face-to-face interaction, people constantly **define and redefine their relationships**. In describing how this process occurs, Watzlawick et al. (1967) have noted that every message carries two levels of meaning. Messages have a **report** aspect that conveys the content of the statement (in other words, the meanings people understand because they know the semantics of the language) and a **command** aspect that carries relational messages. A relational message is a verbal expression that indicates how people regard each other, their relationship, or regard themselves within the context of the relationship (Burgoon & Saine, 1978). In effect, a relational message says "I see us as having this type of relationship." Relational messages are always bids. They attempt to define a certain type of relationship but may or may not be successful, depending on the listener's response.

There are as many possible relational messages as there are different types of relationships. These messages can convey implicitly that someone feels inferior or superior to another person, that he or she is irritated, likes someone, or sees the relationship as one where it is all right to discuss very personal feelings. Any of these relational statements sends information about the way the speaker wants the relationship defined. If the listener responds with relational messages that accept the speaker's bids, the speaker controls the definition of the relationship. A group member who continuously refuses to take stands on important issues could be sending a relational message that says, "Don't see me as someone who will share responsibility for decisions made in this group." If other members allow this person to demur, they have accepted the relationship for which the recalcitrant person has bid. Alternatively, people who "guilt-trip" others are also bidding for a certain definition of the relationship. They want to induce a feeling of indebtedness in the other and to establish a relationship where the other will go along because he or she feels obligated to do so.

Having one's definition of the relationship accepted is an indirect use of power that can yield considerable control in a conflict. Relational control is indirect because it sets expectations about what can and cannot be said in future interactions without any **explicit** statements or directives to other people. Relational messages are, by nature, implicit messages. We generally have a good sense of what our relationships with others are like without them having to tell us explicitly. We know whether someone likes or dislikes us, treats us as inferiors, equals, or superiors. Although there are instances when people overtly discuss and define their relationships, even these discussions carry implicit relational messages about what the relationship is like now that the participants have decided to talk about their relationship. A relationship between two close friends, for example, often changes dramatically when they talk about whether they love each other. The mere occurrence of such a discussion, regardless of the actual content of the conversation, says something about what the relationship is currently like. The discussion is a turning point in the relationship because the friends have signaled to each other that these types of discussions are now possible (or impossible) on a relational level.

Relational control is an important form of influence because people often accept previously defined relationships without question. Their understanding of a relationship sets a frame or context that defines what can or cannot be said in a conflict as long as that frame is in place. The parties' relationship may prevent certain moves from being used either because they seem inappropriate or because they are inconceivable, given the nature of the relationship. The relationship itself would have to be renegotiated in order for certain moves to be feasible.

Because relational messages are implicit, they are often problematic. First, **they can easily be denied, misinterpreted, or reinterpreted**. Comments that seem condescending or demeaning to one person may be viewed as helpful or assisting by others. Second, **conflicts that escalate over trivial or inconsequential issues are often fights over the implicit relational messages and definitions that these issues carry**. For instance, fights over who will do a trivial task may reflect an unsettled relationship issue. Typically, the relationship issue centers implicitly around who has the **right** to assign such tasks. As long as the relational issue goes unacknowledged, escalation over such minor problems is likely to continue. Finally, **the implicit nature of relational messages often masks the interactive nature of relational control**. Like any use of power, relational control requires the endorsement of others. A relationship is not established until a relational bid has been accepted. Because relational messages are implicit, people often fail to recognize the ways in which they contribute to the definition of their own relationships.

Like other indirect tactics, relational control requires that the use of power remain undetected. If someone sees that there is an attempt being made to manipulate a relationship, the attempted control can be undermined. Indirect tactics, on the other hand, are often particularly effective as a means of control because they go unnoticed: they gain their advantage before they are seen. Relationships are defined and redefined with every message that speakers send. As a result, relational moves are second nature: we do not reflect on whether we are accepting or rejecting a certain definition of a relationship each time one is offered.

Issue Control   In an effort to clarify several power-related issues, Bachrach and Baratz (1962, 1970) criticized the available sociological and political studies of power. They argued that power researchers were blinded to the most important and insidious use of power by their emphasis on observing the behavior of parties in conflict. This emphasis constrained them to study only direct, virtual, and indirect uses of power to control decisions and prevented them from considering hidden uses of power, which resulted in what they called "nondecisions." A **decision** is a "choice among alternative modes of action" (1970, p. 39); it is arrived at through interaction among the parties and hence is shaped by moves involving the direct, virtual, and indirect use of power. A **nondecision** is suppression or avoidance of a potential issue that might challenge or threaten the values or interests of one of the parties. It is a "nonevent," which never surfaces and results from the hidden use of power by one or more members. **Power is hidden** in this case because there is no opportunity to observe its operation. If an issue never even materializes and nothing happens, it seems as though power has never come into play when in fact it is responsible for the lack of action.

Crenson (1971) illustrates "nondecision-making" in a study of air pollution control in Gary, Indiana. He marshals impressive evidence that U.S. Steel prevented the adoption of air pollution standards not by directly opposing them but by controlling the political agenda of the city. Because U.S. Steel was responsible for Gary's prosperity and had a powerful reputation, the issue simply was not raised for a number of years. When the issue did finally come up the company was evasive. U.S. Steel did not take a strong stand for or against the issue and most of the opposition was managed by community leaders with little connection to the company. As Crenson (1971, pp. 76–77) reports:

> Gary's anti-pollution activists were long unable to get U.S. Steel to take a clear stand. One of them, looking back on the bleak days of the dirty air debate, cited the evasiveness of the town's largest industrial corporation as a decisive factor in frustrating early efforts to enact a pollution control ordinance. The company executives, he said, would just nod sympathetically "and agree that air pollution was terrible, and pat you on the head. But they never **did** anything one way or the other. If only there had been a fight, then something might have been accomplished." What U.S. Steel did not do was probably more important to the career of Gary's air pollution issue than what it did do.

Its reputation for power and for benefiting Gary was sufficient to protect U.S. Steel from having to face the pollution issue for quite some time. Lukes (1974) and Bachrach and Baratz maintain that the hidden use of power is one of the most important and potentially dangerous aspects precisely because it often goes totally undetected.

Issue control frequently occurs in face-to-face interaction. In many families, for example, issues simply are not raised because one or both parents refuse to allow them. In families with domineering fathers, young children may not even try to voice their opinions because they know they will meet strong disapproval. This prevents their concerns from becoming legitimate issues.

Two types of power resources come into play in issue control. First, **parties may make definite moves that direct others' attention away from an issue**. Control over what information people have access to is the most common means for accomplishing this. In his book *Victims of Groupthink* (1972), Janis notes that certain members of Kennedy's cabinet acted as "mindguards" to prevent the emergence of counterarguments against the CIA's plan for the Bay of Pigs invasion. As a result, the CIA's position was never challenged, and it led to the ill-fated attack.

The forms or types of information the parties work with can also limit the issues it raises. A study of university departmental budget allocations illustrates this point (Pfeffer, 1978). Most people would agree that considerations such as quality of teaching, level of scholarship, and general concern with social values are the criteria that should guide decisions about where a university should spend (or cut back) its money. However, with the advent of computerized information systems that provide "hard" numerical data on enrollment levels, number of articles published, and other performance measures, administrators have turned away from "soft" criteria judgments of educational quality, which cannot be numerically quantified. Although sheer number of students served is not nearly as good a criterion as educational quality, it determines decisions because it can be "objectively" measured. As a result, the hard, soul-searching questions about quality (which also may be threatening to some administrators and departments) are seldom raised and rarely dealt with. The form of information that groups utilize has built-in biases that preclude consideration of some issues by omitting them. If the group does not know that problems or alternatives exist, it can't very well raise them or promote open conflict.

The second type of resources involved in issue control function negatively: they suppress conflicts by creating fear of raising issues. One person's power and prominence may keep other people from even broaching a problem. Fear of the unknown—of whether raising an issue will create deep enmities with other members or upset the existing balance of power in the group—can also limit the issues raised. Even if there is no single overpowering person, people may fear an unpredictable collective reaction from the group if they transgress a strongly shared norm. Janis's *Victims of Groupthink* reports numerous cases where prestigious presidential advisors were subjected to ostracism, pressure, and even ridicule for disagreeing with the dominant sentiments of the cabinet.

There is also a **skill factor** in issue control. Because it operates tacitly, skillful issue control requires that the dominant person's power remain hidden. In the Gary pollution control case, U.S. Steel never openly agitated against the ordinance; to have done so would have aroused the community against it. As Pfeffer (1978) notes, this is one reason it is so hard to determine who holds power in organizations: members do not want to divulge their strength because they may become points of opposition for others.

Almost as effective, a dominant party may control issues by **manipulating other issues indirectly related to the threatening issue**. Pfeffer (1978) notes that one of the best means of influencing a decision is to control the criteria by which the decision is made. Since this is generally done very early in the decision-making process, its influence on the final outcome is often not apparent. Group leaders may shape members' evaluations by speaking briefly about what an "effective" decision might look like. These initial suggestions often have a strong influence on final decisions, despite the low-key manner in which they are delivered.

As with all tactics based on hidden power, **how issue control is managed can undermine or strengthen the endorsement** of the controlling person's power. If control is flaunted openly, others may band together to counteract the person's dominance. Hence working quietly and through indirect channels offers the greatest chance to preserve and strengthen endorsement. Issue control tends to perpetuate itself as long as it operates tacitly, because it defines "reality." It restricts people's thought processes and the alternatives considered and therefore rules out challenges to the power base that sustains it.

THE BALANCE OF POWER IN CONFLICT

There is widespread agreement that any significant **imbalance of power** poses a serious threat to constructive conflict resolution (Walton, 1969; Rummel, 1976; Wehr, 1979; Folberg & Taylor, 1984; Pruitt & Rubin, 1986). When one person can exert more influence than others because he or she holds greater power resources, or is more willing to employ his or her resources, the odds against reaching a mutually satisfying solution increase.

In the creativity development committee described above, the group initially acted under an assumption of equal power. The project directors believed the manager was holding his power in abeyance because he had called the group together to read, evaluate, and presumably select a new program for the lab. Interaction in early meetings was premised on the assumption of a balance of power. Members acted and reacted on the basis of their knowledge as researchers. Since every member had experience with research, there was an assumption that all had a say in the outcome. The project directors reported that it never occurred to them to refuse to use the program until after Tom indicated he might make the final choice himself. The shift from a recognized and self-endorsed balance of power to a state of potential imbalance when Tom acted on his managerial rights turned the course of the conflict away from a pursuit of a mutually satisfactory outcome. Tom asserted that he could make a choice that others would have very little control over, and the project directors challenged that assertion.

Originally, Tom may have wanted to find a program on which the whole committee could agree. It is unlikely that he envisioned a split on the final options. Once the split occurred, however, the decision to act on a basis of power not available to project directors elicited their reciprocal use of power and triggered the beginning of potentially destructive interaction. The relationship between Tom and his subordinates was strained, the quality of research could have been jeopardized, and the project directors' careers could have been threatened if Tom chose to retaliate.

When power imbalances exist, acting on those imbalances can easily escalate conflicts and promote the kind of destructive consequences no one in the research and development committee believed were even remotely possible at first. Stronger and weaker parties in conflict are both in precarious positions as they make moves in the conflict interaction. Although the dangers and problems of being the weaker party may seem more apparent at first glance, stronger parties face as many dilemmas as weaker ones in trying to act in a conflict where a significant power imbalance exists.

The Dilemmas of Strength

Power doesn't corrupt people; people corrupt power.

William Gaddis

. . . control of other people's behavior and thoughts encourages the belief that those we control are less worthy than ourselves.

David Kipnis (1990, p.38)

Holding more power than others in a conflict is usually seen as a competitive advantage. However, the use of power in conflict interaction is often far more complex and self-threatening than is commonly assumed. To demonstrate this complexity, we consider three dilemmas that the more powerful party in a conflict typically faces.

First, the moves that a more powerful party makes in a conflict are sometimes self-defeating because **any source of power can erode once it is used**. Since power must be endorsed by others in the group to be a basis for successful influence, using the resources one holds can prompt others to begin **withdrawing** their endorsement of those resources. Bachrach and Baratz have suggested two reasons why this erosion tends to take place. First, they note that the use of power can cause "a radical reordering" of the values in the coerced person and undermine the power relationship (Bachrach & Baratz, 1970, p. 29). The person who is the target of a power move may reshuffle his or her values so that the stronger party becomes less consequential. This clearly happened in the creativity development committee case. The project director who decided not to require the program in his unit made a value decision about the relative importance of his role in the lab. He placed a higher value on his right to work as he thought best than on honoring his manager's right to assign the decision-making procedure. The project director had never considered counteracting his superior's orders before the summer committee met. It was Tom's use of power that prompted the project director to question it. Did Tom actually have the power of his position once he used it? In a real sense, he did not. The basis of his power eroded, in his subordinates' eyes, when he **used** the unique source of power he held in this situation. Tom still held the legitimate authority of his position, but that authority was weakened: the endorsement that gave it force over his subordinates was undermined.

Bachrach and Baratz also suggest that power may be exhausted because the constraint or sanction imposed by a powerful party "may prove in retrospect far less severe than it appeared in prospect. . . ." (p. 29). The threat of power may be more effective than its actual use because **the actual constraint may be more tolerable than was ever expected**. Future attempts to influence the "weaker" party or gain compliance may fail because the power has been used once and the weaker party has "lived through" its consequences (Case 4.4).

Case 4.4 **The Copywriters Committee**

This is illustrated by the case of a new copywriter in an advertising department of a large company. A committee of all the copywriters normally approved ads. In this committee one member, Ruth, often dominated discussions. Ruth was extremely forceful and had a habit of making cutting remarks about others who disagreed with her. Sometimes she shouted them down. This forcefulness initially cowed Jan and she generally went along with Ruth's positions, however unwillingly. Jan finally decided to defy Ruth when Ruth attempted to revise an ad on which Jan had worked for several months. She attempted to refute Ruth's objections and received what she described as "a torrent of abuse" questioning her qualifications, competence, and loyalty to the department. Jan reported that once Ruth's attack started, she realized it wasn't as bad as she thought it would be. She recognized that Ruth was simply trying to manipulate her. Jan stood firm and, after some discussion, managed to work out a compromise in the committee. After this incident Jan was much less fearful of Ruth and became one of Ruth's leading opponents in the group.

Sometimes parties realize that using their power advantage may exhaust it. One tactic in this case is to make **bogus power** moves that only appear to employ power. To protect specific resources, the stronger party follows the "rule of anticipated reactions" (Bachrach & Baratz, 1970): the party anticipates the reactions or preferences of the weaker party and tailors any demands to these anticipated preferences. When this happens, the "weaker" party appears to be influenced by the "stronger," but the stronger party has actually tailored any demands to the behaviors he or she knows the weaker party will accept. When bogus power moves are made, they often reflect the stronger party's fear of exercising power. The use of the power is forestalled but, ironically, the base itself is protected because it has not been put to the test. There is no risk that weaker parties will withdraw their endorsement of the power.

Not only do powerful people face the dilemma of losing power with its use, they also run a second risk, **the risk of making false assumptions about the weaker person's response**. Raven and Kruglanski (1970) suggest, for example, that stronger people often anticipate that those in a less powerful position will resent the power they hold or dislike them personally. This assumption gives rise to an image of the weaker person as unfriendly or hostile. This image, in turn, "convinces" the stronger person that they must take even tougher stands to defend themselves against possible counterattack. The stronger person moves as if the weaker person intends to undermine or challenge his or her power base, regardless of the weaker person's actual intentions or feelings. In conflict situations, this assumption can quickly promote hostile escalation and can remove the possibility that people will act without using force or threats.

False or untested assumptions about a weaker party are also likely when the more powerful party **is successful**. In research on how people explain their ability to influence successfully, high-status individuals who were able to change others' opinions were likely to believe that the change occurred because of **ingratiation** (Jones, Gergen, & Jones, 1963) or because the weaker party is not in charge of his or her own behavior (Kipnis, 1990). Stronger people tend to believe, in other words, that people change their minds because they want to win an influential person's favor or because they are incapable of greater self-determination. Similarly, Walton (1969) suggests that in unbalanced power situations the stronger person's trust in the weaker is undermined, because the more powerful person may assume others act out of a dutiful sense of **compliance** rather than by their own choice (Pruitt and Rubin, 1986). This belief can encourage a stronger person to mistrust the behaviors of less powerful individuals and can prevent powerful people from recognizing instances where others act, not out of a sense of duty, but because they see that the more powerful person is worthy of a receptive response (Case 4.5).

Case 4.5 **Unbalanced Intimacy**

Power imbalances can exist in intimate relationships and undermine the trust of the stronger party in the weaker. A college-aged couple (Tim and Lisa) had been dating for almost two years and, according to both of them, they had a fairly enjoyable relationship. They shared many interests, liked each other's friends and families, and had relatively few disagreements during their relationship. Lisa began to feel, however, that the relationship was imbalanced in a fundamental sense. Tim was an unusually insecure person. He felt that he was unattractive and was just lucky to have Lisa interested in him. He often said that if she ended the relationship, it would be unlikely that he would ever meet anyone again. Lisa enjoyed Tim very much and wanted the relationship to continue but also felt secure enough to think that if this relationship ended, in time she would probably meet someone else. The difficulty for Lisa was that she began to mistrust Tim's expressions of love for her. She said she could never be sure that Tim actually cared for her. She kept thinking that his feelings were simply based on his own insecurities rather than real attraction for her. She ended up leaving the relationship because of these nagging doubts—doubts that ultimately stemmed from the much stronger position she held in the relationship.

A third dilemma of strength stems from the stronger person's ability to set the terms for reaching a settlement. In conflicts with significant differences in power, the stronger individual frequently controls how destructive the conflict interaction becomes (Komorita, 1977). This control may stem not from the stronger person's power moves but from failure to make de-escalation an attractive alternative to the weaker person. A weaker individual may have little motivation to stop destructive interaction cycles and begin searching for some workable solution to the problem, unless the stronger person demonstrates that this approach may be worthwhile. If the weaker person believes that compromising on an issue will **mean** "total loss" because the more powerful person can **obtain** "total gain" once the weaker person begins making concessions, the weaker person has little incentive to begin negotiating. If the more powerful person demands total capitulation, continued fighting or avoidance of the issue may be more attractive to the weaker person than an attempt to resolve the conflict through negotiation or problem-solving.

In many conflict situations, it is easy for the stronger person to lay an implicit or explicit claim to a desired solution to the conflict and to create an impression in the weaker party that nothing short of that outcome will be acceptable. This impression can be enough to dissuade a weaker person from pursuing constructive approaches to the problem. The subtle ways in which a more powerful faction in a group can deter a weaker member from working on a conflict are illustrated in the following case of a three-person office group (Case 4.6).

Case 4.6   # Job Resignation at the Social Service Agency

A small social service agency employed three women to coordinate and plan projects that a large group of volunteers carried out. The agency was a fairly informal, non-hierarchical organization. The women did not have written job descriptions; instead, an informal set of expectations about the agency's objectives guided their day-to-day work routines. All these women assumed they had equal say in the projects that were conducted by the office. None of them held the role of director or boss; all three answered to an agency board.

One of the women, Kathy, was a single parent in her mid-forties who had worked at the office for a little over three years. The other two workers, Lois and Janelle, were in their early twenties, had just graduated from college together, and were good friends when they were hired. They had been at the office for less than a year. The younger women had a great deal of energy to devote to the agency, in part because they had few personal commitments outside work that would direct their time or attention elsewhere and, in part because they had a well-developed and somewhat idealistic view of the path they wanted the agency to follow. Kathy, on the other hand, found it difficult to support and raise a child while working. Also, because she had been working at the agency for three years, she did not have as much enthusiasm for her work as the other two staff people. The job had become more routine for her and was primarily a way of making ends meet.

Over a period of several months, Lois and Janelle became increasingly dissatisfied with Kathy's work at the agency. They felt she did not complete project reports on time or in sufficient detail and, as a result, they tried to complete or revise a considerable amount of her work. They felt that Kathy had a different perspective on what their jobs entailed and what the goals of the agency should be. They were frustrated by the additional work they were forced to do and by their belief that Kathy was not allowing the agency to change and move in new directions.

In a fairly short time, the two younger women became more vocal about their dissatisfaction with Kathy's work. Although they would occasionally give specific criticisms about her performance, the larger issue of how much say they would have in moving the agency in new directions brought them to a quick, defiant stand against Kathy. The issue that "Kathy is not doing her work right" quickly became "we want Kathy out." Kathy was aware of her co-workers' feelings and realized that they had different conceptions about the agency and their roles in it. On a day-to-day basis, however, she tended to avoid confronting the issue as much as possible. When questioned about her work, she would typically respond with a question that mirrored Lois and Janelle's resentment and hostility (e.g., "How could I do all that when I've been trying to deal with a sick child at home all week?"). Kathy felt that the two women had very little understanding of her situation. She knew that the two younger women saw her as a "bad person" and she felt they did not seek the kind of information that would allow them to see why her view of the job and agency differed from theirs.

Lois and Janelle eventually confronted Kathy with the problem by bringing it up to the agency board. They told the board that, in their view, Kathy was not fulfilling her job requirements and that Kathy was resisting efforts to improve the agency. When questioned about the situation, Kathy tried to defend herself, but soon became conciliatory. Feeling enormous pressure from the two other women, Kathy resigned from the agency within a few weeks after the board meeting.

Because this office had little organizational structure and few direct lines of authority to evaluate performance formally, the two newer workers at this agency developed a considerable power base. Their friendship and similar views about what the agency should be doing made the pair a strong coalition, capable of making Kathy's situation unbearable. In taking an early hard-nosed stand and concluding that Kathy had to leave, the women provided no incentive for Kathy to change her behavior. It is surprising that Kathy did so little to change in the face of her co-workers' criticism because, as a self-supporting parent, she needed the job badly. Although the two newer employees may have had valid criticism of Kathy's work, their belief that Kathy had to leave the agency was, in effect, a demand for total capitulation. Kathy became convinced that there was little reason to work through the issue. Even if the board had decided she should stay on, it would have been difficult for her to work closely with the other women. The women had the ability to pressure Kathy out of the office and, by leaving the impression that they indeed wanted this outcome, they discouraged any initiatives to work on the conflict constructively.

The Dangers of Weakness

Conflicts are often analyzed by defining the various needs of the participants and noting where these needs seem to be incompatible. In the social service agency described above, for example, the needs of the two newer staff people were basically twofold: to move the agency in new directions and to have the office run efficiently while maintaining an equal division of labor among the three workers. Kathy's needs centered around the necessity of balancing a difficult home life with a demanding job. This general concern lay behind her need to continue with established programs rather than begin new ones and to work at a slower pace than her co-workers at the office. Although the issue spread fast and became highly personalized, the "problem" underlying this conflict centered around the apparent incompatibility of these two sets of needs. A collaborative or "problem-solving" orientation to this conflict would have set the participants in determined pursuit of a solution that could have met both sets of needs simultaneously. However, problem-solving approaches to conflict are premised on an assumption that participants recognize the legitimacy of each other's needs. When the needs themselves are held in question, there is no reason for the participants to search for some way of satisfying those needs.

In an unbalanced conflict situation, the greatest danger for weaker parties is that **their needs will not be seen as legitimate**, that they will not be taken into account as possible resolutions are sought. When more powerful parties discount others' needs, the solutions they seek (e.g., firing Kathy) are ones that, by definition, are unacceptable or unsatisfying for other parties. This is more than just a case of the stronger person's needs winning out over those of the weaker. The stronger person can often determine what needs are relevant through his or her ability **to define what the conflict is about**, in other words, to exert **issue control**.

The social service case just mentioned provides an excellent example of the effects of issue control on the weaker party. When the issue was brought before the board it was defined as a conflict over whether Kathy would or could hold up her end of the agency's work and adapt to its new directions. This put Kathy in a defensive position. There were several possible alternative definitions that were not proposed: the conflict could be (1) over whether the agency should expand, or (2) over whether fair and reasonable demands were being made of Kathy, or even (3) over what general life-style the work promotes (Kathy claimed it militated against family time and the two new members wanted the work to play a big role in their lives). Each of these definitions implies a different focus for conflict interaction than the definition presented to the board. Definition 1 defines the conflict as a problem common to all three members concerning the agency's goals, while definition 2 questions the behavior of Lois and Janelle, and definition 3 reorients concerns to "external" issues such as members' overall satisfaction and life plans. Clearly it would be easier for Kathy to respond to any of these issues than to the issue presented before the board, but they were not raised. Lois and Janelle used their power and momentum to press their attack before the board and, by "getting the first word in," set an agenda to which Kathy had to reply. Kathy had little choice but to attempt to defend herself, and this response no doubt made her look bad in the eyes of the board and undermined her already shaken confidence.

A danger of weakness is that stronger parties may be able to **define the terms and grounds of the conflict in their own favor** (Bachrach & Baratz, 1962). Even the language a powerful party uses can have a significant impact on the way an issue is perceived or it can be used to legitimize and maintain the status quo (Deetz & Mumby, 1985; Giles & Wiemann, 1987). This type of definition not only puts the weaker member at a disadvantage, but it may also hurt both people by resulting in an ineffective or harmful solution. The more powerful person often only understands one side of the conflict and his/her grasp of the underlying causes may be imperfect. As a result, the definition of the conflict advanced by the stronger person may not state the problem in terms that would lead to an effective solution. For example, in the social service agency, Lois and Janelle defined the conflict as Kathy's lack of cooperation. This definition pressured Kathy to resign. The social service agency lost Kathy's experience and talent and had to pay for hiring and training a replacement.

The outcome might have been different had the conflict been defined as a conflict over whether the agency should expand. This definition recognizes both sides' concerns by emphasizing the agency, not the members. Although the same issues would probably have come out—Kathy's lack of energy, Lois and Janelle's desire to innovate—they would be discussed in terms of a common issue, and much of the pressure would have been off Kathy. Perhaps, if managed correctly, a problem-solving approach could have generated solutions all could live with, while preserving Kathy's talents for the agency.

A second danger of weakness is its **tendency to become self-perpetuating and**

self-defeating. We mentioned above that weak parties tend to perceive themselves as powerless. These perceptions can discourage parties from attempting to resist or make countermoves to a powerful person's moves. The end result is a reinforcement of the powerful person's control and further proof of the weak person's impotence (Janeway, 1980; Kipnis, 1990). This process simply reproduces both parties' positions. Research on dating partners (Roloff & Cloven, 1990) supports this self-perpetuating tendency in unequal power relationships. There can be a "chilling effect" on the expression of conflict when perceived power differences exist between dating partners. When one person feels that his or her partner has superior alternatives to the current relationship (i.e., has more power), the weaker person is less likely to express conflict issues. Weaker parties who are influenced by the chilling effect are reluctant to raise issues because they fear that conflict escalation might damage the relationship further and put it at risk. Similarly, research on marital partners (Kelley, 1979) suggests that the more dependent partner attends more to the care of the relationship than the less dependent partner. The effect of such moves by less powerful parties is to preserve and reinforce existing power structures in relationships.

When someone becomes convinced that he or she has little influence and is threatened with loss of a particularly valued goal or possession, he or she may feel pressure to commit an "act of desperation" in a last-ditch attempt to avoid the loss. As we noted in the previous section, sometimes the weaker person may be convinced that he or she has little to lose by resisting, and a serious attack—one that threatens the existence of the relationship or organization—may appear to be the only course with a chance of success. For example, in a charity fund-raising committee, one man with very low power faced the loss of money necessary for the survival of his "pet" project, a community development loan corporation. If the project fell through, the member stood to lose his job as director of the corporation as well as his position on the committee. Believing the committee was about to veto his project, the member threatened to go to the local newspaper and state that the committee gave no support to the local economy. This would arouse a great deal of controversy around the committee and possibly hurt its major fund-raising drive, which was to begin in two months. The committee ultimately forged a compromise that gave the project partial funding, but considerable anger was caused by the member's move. The committee's cohesion was undermined, and the project was canceled two years later. The desperation of weakness can motivate "absolute" acts with the potential to destroy relationships or groups or lead to worse retributions later on.

CONCLUSION

Power is the architecture of conflict interaction. The moves and countermoves in a conflict are based on parties' ability and willingness to use power. Power moves are based on resources people hold that serve as a successful basis of influence. These resources can range from material goods to time, physical attractiveness, communication skills, and other talents. Power must be viewed as a relational concept because in order for resources to be a basis for influence, the resources must carry the endorsement of others. Power is thus always conferred on people by those who endorse the resources and it is conferred through interaction. At first glance, the relational nature of power seems to suggest that weaker parties in a conflict always have a way out: they can withdraw their endorsement if more powerful parties apply pressure. There are, however, strong social forces that encourage or sustain the endorsement of various forms of power. Whatever the distribution of power may be, its balance is critically important in determining the direction of conflict. When power is imbalanced, the stronger and weaker parties both face dilemmas as they make moves and step through difficult conflict situations. Stronger parties can exhaust their power by its use, they can consciously or inadvertently set terms for a settlement that encourage continued escalation, and they can make faulty assumptions about the likely response of a weaker person. Weaker parties may have to live with a definition of the problem that ignores their real needs because they have no hand in determining what issues get addressed.

Chapter
5

Face-Saving

*I*magine that you are so absorbed in reading a new movie review while walking to class or work that you fail to notice a stairwell in the near-distance. Just when you reach a particularly arresting section in the review, you notice something is not right. You are off-balance, falling on what should be level ground. Thanks to superior coordination skills, you do not go end-over-end down the steps, but jerk and jump down the jagged cement. Your belongings fly into the air, but you make a remarkable recovery, landing on both feet and catching one of your things before it spins into a bush. Just as your nerves and heart settle, you notice that a group of your co-workers is watching you. In fact, it is obvious from the expressions on their faces that they have watched the entire humiliating event. A million thoughts race through your brain. What do you say or do? Do you walk on and ignore them? What about your things? You are struck by a sudden desire to say something intelligent, something that reflects you are not the clumsy boob you appear to be. Instead, you stoop down to pick up your things. You look at the steps and curse them, as if they possessed a human quality that consciously decided to trip you. With a new-found composure, you turn to your colleagues and say, "What are you looking at?" You immediately realize this is a moronic question, so you add, "I was reading, didn't see the steps." They laugh. You turn red. One says, "Hope you didn't break your newspaper." He probably meant it as a joke to ease the moment. Somehow, though, this joke stings.

They turn and walk away. Half-jokingly, you vow to hate these people for the rest of your life. You are amazed at how bitter you feel. Hours later, you wonder what the big deal was. How could you have gotten so flustered and bent out of shape over a simple misstep and comment? The answer lies in what scholars (and now practitioners) commonly refer to as "face."

Face is a central theoretical concept used in a wide array of disciplines and is defined in as many ways. Yet most definitions concur that face is concerned with identity needs. People have identities or public images they want others to share. Although the attributes vary, people want to be seen by those they encounter as possessing certain traits, skills, and qualities. In short, **face is the communicator's claim to be seen as a certain kind of person**. As one central scholar in the area puts it, face is "the positive social value a person effectively claims for himself by the line others assume he has taken during a particular contact" (Goffman, 1955).

The concept of face originated in China as early as the 4th century B.C. The Chinese distinguish between two aspects of face, *lien* and *mien-tzu* (Hu, 1944). *Lien* stands for good moral character. A person does not achieve *lien*, but rather is ascribed this quality unless he or she behaves in a socially unacceptable manner. To have no *lien* means to have no integrity and is perhaps the most severe condemnation that can be made of a person. *Mien-tzu* reflects a person's reputation or social standing. One can increase *mien-tzu* by acquiring social resources, such as wealth and power. To have no *mien-tzu* is simply to have floundered without success, an outcome that bears no social stigma.

THE DIMENSIONS OF FACE

Although scholars generally concur that face is a universal characteristic of being human, there is less agreement as to the common identities or face wants people share. The most popular view is proposed by Brown and Levinson (1978, 1987) in their theory of politeness. Politeness theory conceives of face as something that can be lost, maintained, or enhanced and must constantly be attended to in interaction. Specifically, the authors propose two dimensions of face. **Positive face** refers to a person's desire to acquire the approval of others. **Negative face** is the desire for autonomy or to not be imposed on by others. Conflict may arise because many communicative acts, especially instances of social influence, are face-threatening. For example, a request to "get busy with that report" may interfere with the hearer's negative face wants or the desire for autonomy. According to the theory, the degree to which face is threatened by a request is a function of three factors: the social distance between the parties, the relative power of the parties, and the intrusiveness of the request or act. The greatest potential face threat is found when there is greater social distance between the parties, the hearer has more power than the speaker, and there is a great degree of imposition placed by the communicative request or act. The authors refer to the theory as "politeness" because the degree of face threat is thought to determine how polite a speaker will be. Brown and Levinson propose that people use five general strategies to perform a **face-threatening act (FTA)**, represented in Table 5.1.

Table 5.1   BROWN AND LEVINSON (1987) POLITENESS STRATEGIES

Example: Request to Begin Fixing the Dinner Meal		
Politeness	Strategy	Example
High	Do not perform FTA	No request is made.
	Go off-record	I'm really getting hungry.
	Negative politeness	I know you are busy, but could you start cooking dinner?
	Positive politeness	You are such a good cook, I can't wait until you start on dinner.
Low	Bald on-record	Would you fix dinner?

The strategies and examples in Table 5.1 are presented from most to least polite. The most polite strategy is to avoid the FTA completely. The speaker makes no request. The next strategy is called "going off-record." This is when the FTA is performed in such an ambiguous manner that it could be interpreted as some other act by the hearer. Going off-record is stating a request indirectly or inexplicitly. The third strategy is the use of negative politeness. This strategy attempts to mitigate the threat to the hearer's negative face wants of autonomy. Positive politeness is the fourth strategy. In this strategy, the speaker performs the FTA with attention to positive face needs (the want of approval). The least polite strategy is to perform the FTA "baldly" with no attempt to acknowledge the face wants of the hearer. Politeness theory contends that speakers will employ the strategy that fits the situation. The more serious the FTA, the more polite the speaker will attempt to be.

Lim and Bowers (1991) extend the Brown and Levinson concept of positive face (the want for approval) because it compounds two different human face needs: the need to be included and the need to be respected. The need for inclusion, they maintain, is the need to have one's person and personality approved of, whereas the need for respect is the need to have one's abilities and skills be approved of. As a result, Lim and Bowers distinguish between three types of human face needs: the want to be included or **fellowship face**, the want that one's abilities be respected or **competence face**, and the want not to be imposed on or **autonomy face**.

FACE-LOSS

When face wants are not addressed in interaction, one or both of the parties may experience face-loss. People are said to "lose face" when they are treated in such a way that their identity claims are challenged or ignored. Given the strong need to maintain a favorable image, face-loss can lead to an impasse in interaction and exacerbate or create conflict between parties. Goffman (1955) describes several consequences of face-loss. Face-loss often causes a person to be momentarily incapacitated or confused. The shock that one's identity is facing attack sometimes takes a moment to adjust to. Second, the individual may feel shame or embarrassment. This feeling is often accompanied by a host of common symptoms that reflect this social distress, including blushing, sweating, blinking, fumbling, stuttering, and general nervousness (Sharkey, 1988). Third, the person may feel inferior or less powerful. In sum, face-loss is an unpleasant experience, seen from the eyes of the harmed party as social humiliation. Not surprisingly, research shows that people are willing to retaliate and sacrifice rewards at great costs when they perceive the threat of humiliation (Brown, 1977).

Face-saving behaviors are defensive attempts to reestablish face after threats to face or face-loss. In other words, face-saving is what a person does to regain the image he or she believes has been dismissed. The remainder of the chapter explores the consequences of face-saving strategies for parties in conflict.

FACE-SAVING: A THREAT TO FLEXIBILITY IN CONFLICT INTERACTION

Continued change is often a good sign in conflict. Changes in a person's positions and styles, as well as more general shifts in a group's climate and emotional tenor, indicate that a person or group is successfully resisting tendencies toward rigid perpetuation of conflict interactional patterns. They also decrease the likelihood that the parties will lock into the destructive cycles that trained incapacities often produce. As uncomfortable as it sometimes is, people should be encouraged by change because it usually means that others are still working on the issue and that a breakthrough is possible. Change requires energy; the use of energy to move the conflict interaction in new directions suggests there is still some level of motivation to deal with the unresolved issue. Any signs of stalemate or rigidity can easily paint the first grey shades of discouragement on a colorful, although difficult and emotionally draining, conflict.

The emotional side of conflict is intimately connected with a person's flexibility. As we noted in Chapters 1 and 2, every move in conflict interaction affects relationships, liking (or disliking) for each other, mutual respect or lack of respect, beliefs about each other's competence, and a score of other beliefs and feelings. **Face-saving** is an attempt to protect or repair relational images, in response to threats real or imagined, potential or actual. It can limit a person's flexibility in taking new approaches to the conflict issue. In addition, because of its relational consequences, face-saving often carries an emotional "charge" that can greatly accelerate destructive escalation or avoidance in conflict. Like the effects of trained incapacities, **face-saving** issues often redefine conflicts. Once face-saving becomes a concern, people's perceptions and interaction patterns can lead to a progressive redefinition of the conflict, which changes a potentially resolvable difference over some tangible problem into an unmanageable issue centering on the relationships between the parties and the images people hold of themselves.

Before exploring face-saving in detail—its causes and its consequences—it is useful to consider a few illustrations. Cases 5.1–5.3 show three diverse conflict situations where the ability to be flexible and to change approaches, positions, or interaction styles is in jeopardy. At the heart of each case lies a concern with saving face.

In Case 5.1, a university professor became increasingly concerned about the way students would be likely to see her if she changed her mind about a decision she had recently made.

Case 5.1 The Professor's Decision

An English professor at a Midwestern university was called by the academic appeals referee and told that a student in her introductory writing course filed a grievance about a grade he received last semester. The student was given a "D" in the class because he did not take the final exam in the course. On the day of the exam, the student had left a message with the department secretary saying that he was ill and would not be present for the test. Although the professor received this message, the student did not get back in touch with her until after the grades had to be submitted. When the student did get in touch with the professor, he told her that he had three other final exams scheduled that week and had decided to take those tests to stay on schedule rather than making up the English final immediately. He said he had thought he would be able to contact her again before the grades had to be reported but, as it turned out, he was too slow in doing so. On hearing the student's explanation, the professor decided to stick with her earlier decision to give him the grade he received without any points on the final. The student's grades on the earlier tests and writing assignments were good enough that if he had received a "B" on the final exam, he would have finished with a "B " in the course.

After receiving the call from the appeals referee, the professor began to question her own decision. Originally she had felt justified in taking the tough stand because she had stated a very clear policy about missing tests and assignments early in the term. She began to believe, however, that she might have been somewhat dogmatic in this case and was leaning toward allowing the man to take a make-up exam and using that score in recomputing his final grade. But as she entered the meeting with the appeals referee and student, she became increasingly concerned about changing her mind. She knew that word travels fast among students, and she was worried that soon she would have a reputation for changing grades or class policy when the right pressure was applied. She was also increasingly bothered by the student's decision to register a formal complaint against her in the college.

In Case 5.2, a group had fears that an outspoken, quick-thinking member would have trouble backing off from a position once she took a stand on an issue. To the group's surprise, she had little concern for face and changed stands once a better argument was made by other members.

Case 5.2 The Outspoken Member

A group of 12 leaders and activists in the antipollution movement of an eastern city began meeting to discuss strategies for dealing with an attack on water standards that was currently being made in their area. A local business executive was mounting a campaign that could have jeopardized water and waste treatment standards if it gained sufficient support. The group of 12 met to determine what could be done to counteract the business campaign and to coordinate the efforts of environmentalists who wanted to work on the project. They saw their main task as building an effective alliance of people in town who wanted to work for environmental quality at this crucial time.

The people in the group were from a wide variety of backgrounds and professions: some headed smaller civic organizations, some were students, one worked for a local newspaper, one was an elected city official. One member, Ruth, was a woman in her thirties, an attorney, and a longtime activist in local politics. She was an outspoken person who took the floor several times early in the first meeting and spoke in a loud and confident tone of voice. She came to the meeting with well-developed ideas about what the group should do and she was able to argue her position clearly and forcefully, while other members, on the other hand, still seemed to be thinking about what the current situation was like and calculating what should be done as an immediate plan of action.

When Ruth made a strong case for what the group should do in the first part of the initial meeting, the climate in the group grew uneasy and tense. Several people looked at each other uncomfortably and most people seemed hesitant to speak. The group seemed to be "holding its breath" and anticipating that Ruth would be difficult to work with. Although Ruth was obviously bright and had good reasons supporting her suggestions, members feared that she had set ideas and that she would not budge from the proposal she had just articulated so forcefully. The group thought she would feel as if she had lost face if she moved away from her stated position.

After several people made comments that were not related to Ruth's proposal, one man in the group began pointing to possible complications and problems with Ruth's suggestion. Ruth listened intently and when he was finished speaking, she said that she really had not thought of the points he had raised and that she felt they posed a very serious set of problems. She asked the man if he had an alternative suggestion, listened to it, and then shortly began arguing for it. She made stronger and more well-reasoned arguments for the man's proposal than he himself had made, and she was able to clarify questions other people in the group had about the proposed plan without dominating the interaction or intimidating people further.

The group soon saw Ruth as one of its most valuable members. She could carry a line of thought through for the group, lay out a well-reasoned set of arguments for a stand she was taking, but at the same time, she was not hesitant to turn 180 degrees on an issue if new information or evidence was presented that she had not previously considered.

In Case 5.3, the group felt its face was threatened by one person who "took charge" without the group's endorsement.

Case 5.3   **The Controversial Member**

Four staff members in a personnel office at a large computer corporation were assigned to a rather demanding recruitment project in addition to their regular job of interviewing and placement. They were asked to design and implement an effective program for minority recruitment and placement within the corporation. The project was viewed as one of the top priorities for the department and the workers knew that the success or failure of the project would have a significant impact on their advancement in the organization.

About a month before the project was due, one of the team members asked her immediate supervisor if the group could meet with him. The supervisor agreed, but when the group arrived only three of the four members were present. The group had not asked the fourth member to attend this meeting with the supervisor. The problem the group faced was that the fourth member repeatedly made decisions and completed tasks that the group as a whole had not endorsed. The three staff members **felt that these decisions and actions** were threatening the quality of the entire project.

The fourth member was a man who had been in the personnel office a year longer than the other three people. He felt he had more knowledge and experience than the other staff, and he made this point to the group on several occasions. He also told the group that he did not want this project to interfere with the time he needed to complete his normal work routine, and so he was willing to make certain decisions about the project on his own to move things along faster. Although the staff felt intimidated by their co-worker's outspoken and evaluative style, they felt that he was bright, hardworking, and that he did have some experience that they lacked. In most cases, however, they felt this additional experience was unrelated to the assignment they were currently given. They saw the man's concern about the project taking time away from his normal work assignment as pure arrogance; they all had the same work schedule to complete each week and needed to find time to work on the recruitment project. The group felt particularly insulted because on several occasions, the man did not show up for meetings that had been scheduled. He did not let the group know that he would not be attending nor did he offer any explanations for his absence afterward. He made no attempt to get information that he held to these meetings. Thus the group's work was often delayed. When he was present, meetings **were tense and antagonistic** and the motivation of the whole group had plummeted because of the problem.

When the supervisor asked the group if they had discussed their reactions openly with the "problem" person, they said they had not. They had wrestled with the idea but decided that the issue may just be too emotional to air openly. They were, however, mad at their co-worker, felt intimidated by him, and wanted management in the department to hear about the problem.

In all three cases, some form of face-saving was a central concern and could have undermined the parties' ability to deal successfully with the conflict. In the grade dispute, the professor had taken a stand on an issue and was reluctant to move from that position, because she might be seen as indecisive or unsure of herself. When she reconsidered her decision, she recognized that the student may have had a good case and that she may have been too harsh in enforcing her no make-up policy. As she entered the meeting where the conflict was to be addressed, however, there was a great likelihood that her current beliefs on the problem would not be stated unless something was done to ease her concern about the image she might acquire by following her inclinations. Part of her reluctance to move also stemmed from an already existing threat to face: the image she had of herself as a fair professor had already been called into question publicly by the student's decision to contact the college official.

In the environmental group, the face-saving issue was anticipated by members who heard Ruth make early and forceful arguments. A tense and uneasy climate arose because most members assumed Ruth had made a strong commitment to her position and would be very hard to move. There was a general sense that Ruth would be a "problem" because others assumed a strong public defense of her position meant Ruth's self-image would be at stake if the group challenged her suggestions. The group was surprised and relieved to find that Ruth's intellectual and verbal abilities could provide information and clear reasoning for the group without being tied to Ruth's self-image. If no one in the group had run the risk of questioning Ruth's initial stand because they feared embarrassing her, the group could easily have become dissatisfied with the decision-making process but remained silent, perhaps eventually splintering into pro- and anti-Ruth factions.

For the staff on the personnel project face-saving was at least one of their concerns as they entered the supervisor's office. Although the group feared the emotional strain and potential long-range consequences of raising the issue with their co-worker, they felt this person had treated them unfairly. They were made to feel as if their input on the project was unnecessary or even harmful. At least part of their motivation for contacting the supervisor was to restore face: they did not want to think of themselves as incompetent. Nor did they want to see themselves as people who would accept unfair treatment without resistance. If the supervisor agreed with their accusations and assessment of the situation their face would be restored.

When face-saving becomes an issue, people's ability to remain flexible and shift their modes of conflict interaction is threatened. Face-saving reduces flexibility and the likelihood of change in group and interpersonal conflict situations for two reasons. First, the emergence of a concern with saving face inevitably **adds an issue to the conflict**. The additional problem tends to take precedence because it stands in the way of getting back to the main issue. Energy and attention are drawn away from the central issue and are spent on peripheral matters; work may stop on the issues that count most as people deal with a threat to face. In each of the three cases described above, face-saving added issues to the conflict that diverted attention—and interaction—away from the central concern, or exhausted the parties before an adequate resolution was reached.

In the grade dispute, for example, the main conflict was over the professor's policy on make-up exams and her decision to enforce that policy in the current situation. The professor's reputation as indecisive or soft was really a secondary (although related) issue. In the environmental group, members' attention started to shift from a concern with how the group should go about protecting water standards to how the group was going to deal with a member who appeared to be dogmatic and would likely be threatened by criticism. In the personnel project team the central conflict was over decision-making rights in the group. In allowing the issue to go unaddressed, the three workers added a face-saving concern: they felt unjustly intimidated by the man and spent considerable time trying to feel better about the situation and attempting to decide whether they had somehow helped elicit the man's arrogant behavior. These additional issues can easily displace the group's focus if they remain salient concerns or if the members fail to address a face-saving issue that is influencing the behaviors in the group.

Besides multiplying issues, face-saving **makes inflexibility likely** because face-saving concerns usually entail the real possibility of a future impasse in the conflict. Motives to save face are difficult to alleviate in conflicts and tend to foster interaction that heads toward stalemates and standoffs. After examining face-saving in a variety of formal bargaining settings, Brown (1977, p. 275) notes that issues related to the loss of face are "among the most troublesome kinds of problems that arise in negotiation." Several factors contribute to the tendency for face-saving issues to head toward impasse.

Face-saving issues often remain highly **intangible** and **elusive** because people are reluctant to acknowledge that an image they want to preserve or restore has been threatened. People can sense that something is going wrong and that positions seem to be tightening but the face-saving motive may never be explicitly raised. To acknowledge a threat to one's image is in some ways to make that threat all the more real. One can maintain a desired self-image despite what others think as long as one can somehow deny what others think. To openly state what the threat may be and risk confirmation of the belief is in some cases to remove the possibility of denial. Thus the threat to one's image may be real and may be influencing the conflict interaction but it often lies beneath the surface where it will go unrecognized or unaddressed.

The professor in the grade controversy might, for example, go through the entire meeting with the student and appeals referee without raising the issue of her image or without noting that she felt put off by the student's decision to contact the referee about the matter. Although these concerns may never surface they could prompt her to make strong arguments in favor of her original decision (even though she now doubts its fairness) or make unreasonable demands on the student before moving from her initial stand. An effective third party appeals referee might anticipate these face-saving concerns and make suggestions that alleviate them but do not require that the issue be stated explicitly (Shubert & Folger, 1986). Often the mere presence of a third party allows someone to move from a position without losing face because they can attribute any movement they make to the third party: "I never would have settled for that if the appeals referee hadn't pushed for it" (Pruitt & Johnson, 1970; Brown, 1977).

There is another reason why impasses are likely outcomes of conflicts complicated by face-saving issues: conflict interaction becomes highly vulnerable to an **"all-or-nothing"** approach to resolution when face-saving issues arise. A gambler who loses through an evening at a casino table may feel a need to bet big at the end of the night to restore face with those who have watched him or her struggle for a missed fortune. When an issue becomes heavily steeped in establishing or protecting face it is often easier for the participants to "go for broke" or walk away than to remain in a situation that in an important sense undermines their self-concept or sense of self-worth. Face, in many instances, is seen as an uncompromisable issue. Personal honor and a commitment to oneself can take precedence over any continued involvement with or commitment to the relationship.

The staff who worked on the personnel recruitment project were all too willing to let the one man make decisions for them even though they were insulted and upset with his behavior. They expected further embarrassment if they brought the issue to the man's attention; they thought he would defend himself by pointing to his own experience and chide them for ignoring their daily work tasks to work on this project. Rather than risk this confrontation and a further affront to their self-image, members were willing to walk away from the issue even though it meant continued frustration with the project.

CONFLICT INTERACTION AS AN ARENA FOR FACE-SAVING

Face-saving messages are concerned with an image the speaker is trying to maintain or reestablish in the interaction. Because this image depends on others' reactions, any attempt to save face is an attempt to negotiate the speaker's relationship with other parties in the conflict. Face-saving messages offer information about how the speaker wants and expects to be seen in the exchange. Studies of how communication is used to define interpersonal relationships have noted that this type of "relational comment" (in other words, "This is how I see you seeing me" or "This is how I want you to see me") is carried by any message a speaker sends (Watzlawick et al., 1967). In the case of face-saving messages, however, the relational comment is more salient because it is under dispute; the face-saving message is a defensive response to a perceived threat. The speaker has reason to believe that his or her desired image will not be accepted by other members. As a result the speaker feels a need for assurance or confirmation and engages in various behaviors such as those in our examples to "restore face." Interaction usually cannot proceed without resolution of the "face" problem and will often be dominated by this problem until the speaker feels satisfied that enough has been done to establish the desired image. It is clearly the speaker's perception of how others are taking him or her that determines when the face-saving issue is lifted from the interaction.

If a person rushes into an important meeting 15 minutes late and says, "Back-to-back meetings never seem to work out," the comment carries a face-saving message. It asks the group to see the person as someone so busy that he or she may have to overschedule meetings and end up being late at times. This relational message serves a face-saving function because it supplants a potentially threatening image others could hold; it asks people not to see the speaker as someone who is inconsiderate of others' time or is unconcerned about what may go on at the meeting. Being busy, hardworking, or overtaxed is a positive image; being inconsiderate, slow, or careless about the group is an image the person wants to avoid.

In an insightful analysis of face-saving work in everyday interactions, Goffman (1967) has described how people try to conduct themselves in social encounters to maintain both their own and others' face. Goffman emphasizes that the mutual acceptance of face is "a condition of interaction not its objective" (p. 12). Interaction ordinarily proceeds on the assumption that the faces people want to project are in fact the ones that are accepted as the exchange unfolds. There is a noticeable strain or a recognizable problem when face maintenance becomes the objective rather than a precondition of interaction. Even in nonconflict interaction then, people feel a need to amend the situation when a face-saving issue arises so that the exchange can unfold without the concern.

In group conflict there is a noticeable difference in interaction when face-saving issues arise and become the objective of the interaction. There is a shift away from group-centered and group-directed interaction and toward interaction focused on the experience of the individual group member and his or her relationship to the group. Conflict interaction is **group-centered** when all parties take into account their membership within the group and continuously recognize that any movement made on an issue must be made **with** other parties in the conflict. Individual positions and stands can be argued (and indeed must be, if adequate differentiation is to occur). However, when the interaction remains group-centered, there is a continual recognition that individual positions are being offered and that all comments are geared toward issues that result from differences in needs or goals of the members. Members never lose their identities and concepts of self when interaction is group-focused; the commitment to self and the sense of personal identity become secondary to the awareness that the conflict is a shared experience and that change or movement in the direction of the conflict will be **with** other members.

The emergence of face-saving as an issue undercuts this group-centered focus in conflict interaction. By its very nature, face-saving gives prominence to the individual members and their sense of self in the group. Attention is turned toward the experience of the individual in the group because face inevitably raises a question about the way some member is seen by others in the group.

Face-saving issues always cross the line between group- and individual-centered interaction. This crossing reflects an ambivalence about the role of individuals in groups that has been noted repeatedly in analyses of group experience. Several researchers have observed that the

> individual's fundamental attitudes toward group membership are characterized by ambivalence. . . . The basic antagonism is between the individual's commitment to himself—to his own needs, beliefs and ambitions—and his yearning for psychological submersion in a group, for an obliteration of those qualities that make him unique and thus distinct and separate from others. . . . Submersion brings a measure of security and a sense of connectedness and belonging, but it also undermines individual autonomy . . . and may in other respects demand a sacrifice of individual wishes to those of the group. (Gibbard, Hartman, & Mann, 1974, p. 177)

When a face-saving issue arises, an individual's concern is not placed in a secondary role to group issues or disputes. The commitment to self and, in particular, the commitment to establishing a desirable self-image take precedence over the sense of belonging and cohesion that exists when members "step into" the group more fully.

What is important about the emergence of face-saving concerns is that they produce a **qualitative change** in the nature of the group's conflict interaction. Group-centered interaction is founded on the assumption or precondition that all are acting and responding primarily as **group members**. In this sense, everyone remains at the same level in the interaction because they all take into account their membership in the group and act on that awareness when they speak and respond to others. When interaction becomes individually focused, one person steps into an "official role" that he or she holds as an individual. Obviously, such a role is always present for each member but it can easily remain dormant while members try to sustain group-centered interaction. The role of the **group member as individual** raises concerns about what the person **looks like** to the group, what **impact** that person, in particular, is having on the outcome of a decision, what **place** he or she holds in the group's power structure, and so on. In a sense, the individual adopts an "authority" position; the individual is, and wants to be seen as, the authoritative representative of an image he or she wants to maintain or a role he or she wants to play in the group's process. There is an awareness of someone carving out an individual figure from the composite interaction that the group has molded. This separation lays the groundwork for the inflexibility discussed above.

The following example, which is an actual transcript of a discussion among four graduate students, illustrates a turn from group- to individual-centered interaction. The students in this discussion were given a topic as part of a class assignment. Believe it or not, their task was to clarify Plato's conception of truth. In the interaction just prior to this segment, the students (who were from the same department and knew each other quite well) joked about the seriousness of the topic and were somewhat eager to go off on a tangent before leaping into the task at hand. As this segment of interaction begins, Kathy asks Peggy about her research on sex differences in people's thought patterns. The group recognizes that the question is somewhat off the assigned topic, but they are more than willing to pursue it and delay their discussion of truth. The group eventually ties the issue of sex research back to the main topic, but that part of the exchange is not included here. Watch for the turn the interaction takes toward individual-centered interaction.

KATHY: *(to Peggy)* Are you doing any more work on differences in male–female thinking?

PEGGY: *(answering Kathy)* Uh, hum.

DAVE: I have an article.

PEGGY: Collecting data as a matter of fact.

DAVE: I have an article that is so good. This is off the subject, but let's talk about it for a few minutes.

PEGGY: That's right, let's forget truth. I'd rather talk about males and females than truth.

KATHY: Mhmmm.

GARY: Mhmmm.

DAVE: Candice Pert is into, got into, pharmacology and is now in neuro-science. She is the discoverer of what's called the opiate receptor in the brain. Those are the brain cells which opium have an effect on. The ones they're attracted to.

PEGGY: Hmmmm.

DAVE: And they've, they've gone from opium receptors to ah Valium receptors to any tranquilizer. And she's working now on a marijuana receptor, that the cells hit. And it's so neat . . .

(Some laughter while Dave is talking; Gary mimes something and Kathy makes a comment under her breath and laughs.)

DAVE: *(laughing slightly)* Now wait a minute, wait a minute. This is fascinating.

(General laughter)

GARY: I've already heard it, so I'm spacing off on my own here.

DAVE: She made this discovery when she was a grad student.

KATHY: Then there's hope for me yet.

(General laughter)

PEGGY: *(pointing to the back of her head)* Ah, here are my opiate receptors.

DAVE: She's first author, and her male mentor and advisor and teacher is second author.

PEGGY: Hmmmmm.

DAVE: There was an award given called the . . .

KATHY: *(interrupting)* And he got it, right?

DAVE: *(continuing)* the Lasky award, which is seen as a stepping stone to a, to a Nobel prize, and ah. . .

KATHY: What do opiates have to do with men and women?

DAVE: Now wait a minute.

PEGGY: *(jokingly)* Wait, wait—have patience, have faith.

DAVE: Here's, here's your politics in it to start with.

KATHY: All right.

DAVE: She was first author on this paper when this Lasky award was given; it was given to four men.

KATHY: Mhmmm.

DAVE: And she was invited to the awards ceremony. That's the extent of it. And she talks about it a little bit.

PEGGY: Oh, marvelous.

DAVE: But in the interview she talks about the, you know, I can be known as a scorned woman here, but I've done some other things since then that are really important to me. And she, she uses the analogy of the brain as a computer. And although she doesn't talk about what we would commonly call software, that's what you learn, she really, she's looking at what she calls the hardwiring. The circuitry in the brain. And the differences in male/female circuitry.

PEGGY: And she's found some?

DAVE: She's found some possibilities. Some probable areas. Now there are differences, there are some other differences that are not just male and female. There are differences, say, between what we would consider healthy, normal personalities and, say, schizophrenia.

PEGGY: Mhmm.

(There's a three-second interruption here as someone enters the room, then Dave continues.)

DAVE: Ah, you look at the evolution of language instead of being male-oriented and thinking that men had to learn how to use language so that they could coordinate hunting down a large animal, it was women who were the ones who were staying home.

KATHY: *(sarcastically)* To get them out of the cave.

(General laughter)

PEGGY: To talk to the walls.

DAVE: Yeah, you know talk to walls, talk to the kids.

PEGGY: Well, that's interesting I'd like to read that.

DAVE: And from the beginning. Yeah, it's really fascinating because there are detectable differences in male and female brains.

KATHY: Hmmm *(makes a face)*.

PEGGY: Yeah, I'd like to read that.

DAVE: *(to Kathy)* You act like I'm being chauvinistic.

PEGGY: No.

KATHY: No, I'm just, I'm . . .

DAVE: *(interrupting)* Oh boy, this is terrible.

GARY: She'd act a whole lot worse if you were being chauvinistic.

KATHY: Do I act like you're chauvinistic? Yes.

DAVE: You made a face.

KATHY: *(laughing)* I'm trying to see inside my brain to see if there are any differences. That's all.

DAVE: Differences. What, from mine?

KATHY: Yes.

DAVE: But how can you see mine?

KATHY: Oh, I don't know. I can't see in mine either. Let me be successful here first. No, I was thinking of brains, young Frankenstein you know.

DAVE: *(laughing)* Oh yeah.

KATHY: Twelve years dead, six months dead, freshly dead.

DAVE: Yeah, yeah.

KATHY: Sorry, Dave, I'm just not on that level today.

DAVE: No, no.

PEGGY: Well, I think there are some very definite differences in language use and that would be some clue as to why. I've always talked about it being culture, socialization, and that sort of thing, but, ah . . .

GARY: I wonder if there's a change coming in that with the revolutionary changes in men and women's roles in society—they're now becoming different—and if that will have an effect on this too.

PEGGY: Go back far enough and actually you can see that the species will evolve differently. . . .

Initially, the group's interaction in this exchange consists primarily of offering and evaluating information about research on sex differences. Although Peggy did not elaborate on her research when Kathy asked her about it, Dave's comments about the brain's sensitivity to drugs held the group's interest and prompted continued interaction on this topic. It became the focus of questions and jokes in the group, and it also raised the issue of how sexual politics becomes involved in research. Dave's summary of the article he had read and his commentary about the possible implications it might have for understanding the evolutionary development of male and female language use set the stage for the turn toward individual-centered interaction that took place in this discussion.

After Dave says "Yeah, it's really fascinating because there are detectable differences in male and female brains," the next twenty speaking turns are focused on Dave's image in the group. These comments deal with Dave's relationship to the group rather than with the topic that had surfaced and engaged the group as a whole. Kathy's facial response to Dave's statement made Dave concerned about whether Kathy or the other group members saw him as a chauvinist. Peggy, Gary, and Kathy all attempt to reassure him (although sometimes lightheartedly and perhaps unconvincingly) that he is not seen as a chauvinist because of the way he summarized the article and reacted to it. In the main, the group handles the face-saving concern by joking about the article, becoming somewhat ludicrous (with the references to young Frankenstein's brain) and finally treating one of Dave's major points (about the possible value of an evolutionary explanation for language differences) seriously. When Peggy and Gary make their comments in the last three speaking turns in this segment, the interaction is turned back to a group focus. The interaction is no longer focused on Dave's experience in the group and the way he is seen by others. Dave lets his concern about his image drop and the group continues with an exploration of the merits and problems with research on sex differences.

Since any group is composed of members with self-concepts and concerns about their roles within the group, group interaction, conflict or otherwise, tends to teeter somewhere between group and individual emphases. It is possible to achieve a healthy balance that eases the "basic antagonism" between individuals' commitments to themselves and the need or desire to move the group along as a group. This balance can allow the group to remain a cohesive unit able to settle disputes, yet, at the same time, minimize the threat to individuals and meet individual needs. Needless to say, this balance is difficult to maintain when conflicts occur.

Conflicts provide an arena where the balance of group- and individual-centered interaction is easily tipped toward the concerns of individual group members, making face-saving likely to occur. Several factors, in combination, are likely to lead the group away from group-centered interaction once conflict arises. First, the **process of differentiation** is, as we have noted in Chapter 2, one that temporarily associates individuals in the conflict with "sides" of an issue and reveals the main differences between members. This differentiation is desirable, because it articulates individual stands and creates an understanding of the differences between members. Clarifying individual positions is, however, a powerful thrust toward individual-centered interaction. People hear themselves argue for a position in front of others and may be hesitant to leave their initial positions once they make a public statement.

Second, there is **a tendency for members to point a finger** at others and assign responsibility for the emergence of the conflict to a single individual or faction in the group. Sometimes this arises from displaced aggression as we discussed in Chapters 1 and 2. This tactic ignores the fact that conflicts always lie in some incompatibility of goals or needs among all concerned; it also focuses group attention and interaction on the roles or behaviors of individuals in the conflict. The "accused" are put in the paradoxical position of, on the one hand, having to defend themselves against the charges and thus giving continued prominence to their individuality, while, on the other hand, needing to move the interaction toward a group focus if real progress toward reaching a resolution is to be made.

Third, as we observed in Chapter 4, parties in conflict often turn to **unique sources of power** during conflict interaction. Any move based on unique power sources gives prominence to the characteristics of individuals in the conflict and promotes countermoves that are also based on unique sources of power. These moves work against members' constructing and using group-endorsed bases of power as a means of influence. When people use unique sources of power to try to influence the group, they put an important part of themselves on the line. If the move is not successful, **their image**, not the image of the whole group, is threatened and may need to be redeemed through the use of threats, force, or deception.

Besides the effects of differentiation, the tendency to attribute conflict to individuals, and the use of unique sources of power, interaction in groups can also tip toward an individual focus because of **decision-making procedures that groups employ in conflict settings**. If members know that decisions will be made and conflicts settled by, for example, a voting procedure, a group will often "walk" through conflicts with an expectation that the vote will settle things. Voting **labels** people as "winners" and "losers." Each member knows whether he or she is on a winning or losing side as issues are discussed and solutions chosen by the group. This awareness can heighten members' sense of themselves as allied with, or against, others and promote comments and responses that defend individual positions and self-images. ("I lost out this time, but you can bet it won't happen again soon.")

In sum, conflicts are likely arenas for establishing and defending members' images of themselves. These concerns can easily turn interaction away from constructive work on the conflict issue and toward secondary, but troublesome, issues that stem from the individual's relationship to the group. When these concerns arise, they tend to promote **inflexibility** in interaction and prevent the group from approaching the conflict from new directions.

Although these destructive tendencies are likely, it should be noted that there may be times when a turn toward individual-centered interaction is useful or necessary in a group. Some members may need certain images of themselves confirmed, even though the image may not have been questioned by other people in the group. Someone may, for example, have a strong need to know that his or her contributions are valued by other people in the group. In order to fulfill this need, the group's interaction would have to center on the member's relationship to the group. This turn could serve a useful function, if it provides valuable feedback about a member's performance or an incentive for someone to continue with his or her work and involvement in the group. In most cases, this type of interaction occurs outside conflict situations, so it rarely becomes problematic for the group.

FORMS OF FACE-SAVING IN CONFLICT INTERACTION

Although there are many ways in which concerns for self-image can surface in interaction, **three general forms of face-saving** tend to emerge repeatedly in conflict settings. Each of these forms reflects a different interpretation the person trying to save face might assign to the situation. These interpretations act as "mind-sets" to promote defensive, face-saving behavior. Each type of face-saving has recognizable symptoms that distinguish it from the others and each requires different corrective measures. Two of these forms have been studied by researchers who focused on competitive contexts such as negotiation and bargaining settings. We have alluded to them in the earlier cases, but they deserve more explicit attention because they pose a serious threat to constructive conflict interaction. We will also discuss a third form of face-saving that has not been studied by previous researchers; this form is unique to more informal conflict settings (like most work or group decision-making contexts) where the interaction is premised, at least initially, on the assumption that people will act cooperatively to make decisions and settle differences. Few researchers have studied these noncompetitive contexts.

Resisting Unjust Intimidation

Brown (1977) and others (Deutsch & Krauss, 1962) have suggested that face-saving often results from a need to "resist undeserved intimidation in order to guard against the loss of self-esteem and of social approval that ordinarily results from uncontested acquiescence to such treatment" (Brown, 1977, p. 278). When people feel they are being treated unfairly or pushed in a way that is unjustified, they are likely to make some attempt to resist this treatment. Interaction can turn toward a defense of the individual's self-image as the individual tries to establish that he or she will not accept intimidation without resistance. There is an "I don't have to take this" or "Any fair-minded person wouldn't stand for this" message to the other party.

When this form of face-saving message is sent, it always carries two components. First, there is an **accusation** that others are in fact treating the person in an unfair or intimidating manner. In some cases the other party will recognize (although perhaps not admit) that there may be some grounds for the accusation. The response in this case is likely to be a defense of the behaviors or charges made against the person who is trying to save face. For example, in a local health department, an assistant administrator conducted several surprise inspections that made employees very nervous and defensive and came near to causing a labor dispute. When the supervisor of one unit that had been inspected by the assistant administrator confronted her with this problem and challenged her fairness, she refused to discuss the issue. Her responsibilities, she argued, forced her to "tighten up the ship" and increase work quality by whatever methods she had available.

In other instances, the accusatory face-saving message may take the parties by surprise and may elicit either an initial defensive response ("We never did that to you") or total avoidance because people are unaware or do not believe that the person has grounds for feeling unjustly intimidated. Regardless of the response it receives, this type of face-saving message necessitates a reaction because it carries an accusation. It is the accusatory nature of the message that prevents it from remaining an isolated event in the stream of interaction; rather, it becomes a force that redirects interaction because it necessitates a response. Even active avoidance means that the parties have decided to allow future interaction to be influenced by the unacknowledged but real effects of an issue that they have decided to ignore.

The second important component of this type of face-saving message is the sense of **adamant resistance** it conveys. The speaker suggests, in effect, that "business as usual" cannot continue until the concern has been addressed. This sense of resistance often accompanies messages that are sparked by perceived threat (Gibb, 1961). The major impact this component of the message has on interaction is its potential for **altering the climate** of the relationship or group. Once this type of face-saving message is sent, the other may feel that it is no longer safe to allow the interaction to continue in the present direction or to suggest new questions or issues for discussion. The defensive party has claimed the right to define the immediate topic of conversation and to insist that it remain until he or she is satisfied with the outcome of the exchange. Other people can challenge this claim, but the move would be immediately recognized as a challenge and thus contribute to an air of threat; it would increase the chance that the relationship would be adversely harmed or that the group may splinter. Messages that suggest someone has not been treated fairly (like those sent by the workers in the personnel department who felt unjustly treated by their co-worker) may also imply that people are not committed to one another. It hoists a warning flag signaling problems with trust and responsibility. If this issue is not met head-on, the parties may have difficulty sustaining an image that they are committed to each other.

In groups when one or more members feel a need to resist what they see as undeserved intimidation there are usually **important consequences** for the group. Whether these consequences are ultimately destructive depends on how the group deals with the issue. **When the issue is ignored, destructive consequences often threaten the group**: a woman who had planned on leaving a job in a food distribution company for unrelated personal reasons decided to stay on six months longer to "fight it out." She did not want to leave feeling like she was the cause of some problem that led to her departure. In the personnel staff project discussed above, the three intimidated workers spent considerable time and effort trying to feel better about themselves. This time could have been spent on the project if the issue had been addressed at an earlier point.

When this type of face-saving issue goes unaddressed it is also common for the threatened person to contact an **outside party** for help, hoping that a neutral outsider might understand and perhaps exonerate him or her. Although a third party can help in many instances, when the person who is trying to save face contacts the outsider it may subvert any legitimate effort to mediate the problem. The parties have to recognize the problem and agree on a need for outside help before any intervention is likely to be successful. Finally, if this type of face-saving issue is left unaddressed, people who are trying to save face are left with a need to explain the **causes** behind the unjust or intimidating treatment. Since the other has not supplied any reasons or denied that the threat exists, the party may begin attributing the intimidation to some set of causes that may or may not be true. These unchecked attributions can shape the comments the party makes from that point on and lead to a more serious set of problems that are impenetrable. For example, in the food distribution company mentioned above, three people were involved in the conflict (including the woman who stayed six months extra); all three incorrectly assumed the others hated them and were attacking them for reasons of personal incompatibility. Actually, all three were merely responding to each other's aggressive behavior, and their responses fed on each other, thereby escalating the conflict.

The key to alleviating face-saving concerns that emerge from feelings of unjust intimidation lies in people's ability to give feedback without eliciting further animosity. People who feel they are being unjustly treated or intimidated must be able to state the basis for their feelings in a way that does not prejudge others or discourage them from explaining their behavior. Escalation and standoffs are likely when criticism is handled poorly as a face-saving issue is addressed. Although many prescriptions have been given for constructing feedback, most discussions of constructive criticism stress that feedback must be **timely** (in other words, offered at a point that is both relevant and least disruptive) and centered on **descriptions of the party's own feelings** rather than assumptions about what the other intends (e.g., "When you didn't show up for the dinner I felt put down" rather than "You wanted to teach me a lesson by not showing up for our dinner").

Face-saving concerns that stem from feelings of unjust intimidation can best be managed if the parties have set aside time for **regular evaluations** of the process. Setting aside five or ten minutes at the end of each meeting or day for an evaluation session can allow people to raise issues early before they become impasses and give positive or negative feedback to each other without interfering with work or other obligations. Resentment and hostility are less likely to build and affect other issues if the parties know time has been set aside to address relational issues or concerns about interaction.

Refusing to Step Back from a Position

A second form of face-saving is based on people's fears that they will **compromise** a position or stand they have taken on some issue (Pruitt, 1971; Brown, 1977). People often remain committed to a stand or solution even in light of convincing refutations, not because they still believe it is the best option, but because they believe moving away from that position will harm their image. When this form of face-saving emerges, a party believes that conditions in the situation are such that reversing one's stand or stepping back from a position is unsafe.

There are many reasons why this fear may become real for parties who are involved in a conflict. In their analysis of the forces governing commitment to decisions, Janis and Mann (1977) have suggested that people may remain committed to an undesirable decision because they believe that they will look indecisive, erratic, or unstable if they retract or reverse their choice. "To avoid perceiving himself as weakminded, vacillating, ineffectual and undependable, the person turns his back on pressures to reconsider his decision and sticks firmly with his chosen alternative, even after he has started to suspect that it is a defective choice" (p. 283). For example, Epstein (1962) reports that novice parachutists, fearing loss of face, often go through with their decision to jump, even though as the time draws near, their desire to skip what may seem a dangerous and senseless endeavor increases. Fear of losing face is a stronger motive in this case than their own judgment at the moment. If others place a higher value on **consistency** than accuracy, this fear may prevent people from changing their minds or remaining flexible as new information is given and new proposals are considered during conflict interaction.

Janis and Mann also suggest that there is a certain **momentum** behind reaching a decision or articulating a position in public. This momentum stems from the difficulty of reversing a decision once it is made or retracting a position once it is stated. It simply takes more work and effort to explain why one has changed one's mind than it does to leave a previously stated position on the table. If the person is at all uncertain about the reversal, he or she may not make the effort necessary to feel comfortable reversing a stand.

Goffman (1967) discusses a similar motive for this form of face-saving. He indicates that people's fears of moving from a position can rest on a belief that they will not be taken seriously in the future if they step away from a position they have taken on a current issue. In this case the person believes that **his or her credibility will suffer** if he or she moves on an important issue or decision. Others have established a climate—or at least the person believes that a climate exists—where reversal will be costly in future situations. Ideas or suggestions the person makes will be overlooked or considered less seriously, if the other believes that ideas are not developed fully enough to warrant continued commitment. There is a fear that future suggestions will be seen, in all cases, as potentially problematic so they will be given less weight in the discussion when they are offered.

Finally, Brown (1977) and other researchers (Tjosvold & Huston, 1978) point to a somewhat different motive for this type of face-saving in adversarial contexts, such as bargaining and negotiation sessions. Whenever people make initial settlement offers and then try to negotiate an agreement without losing much ground, they are often reluctant to move from their initial position because they may be seen as weak bargainers. In a negotiation context, people often want to appear tough as long as it is to their advantage. If the opposing side believes they will give in easily, the opposition may hold their ground because they believe they can obtain concessions (Stevens, 1963). When group conflict interaction becomes competitive, and members believe that the outcome will produce **winners and losers**, this belief becomes a possible source of face-saving concerns. If members believe that their goals are inherently incompatible and that they cannot find a solution that meets everyone's needs, then the **appearance of strength or weakness** influences the moves people make in the conflict.

Whatever the motivation, whether people feel comfortable in changing a stated position is ultimately tied to **expectations** they have about how ideas (in other words, suggestions, information, proposals) are treated. The climate tells people how ideas should be proposed and, perhaps more importantly, how they will be taken once they are offered. People have a sense, for example, of whether exploratory questions will be valued or discouraged. In the same vein, others may welcome or discount suggestions that are not fully developed. Ideas that are offered tentatively can be seen either as a waste of time or as a sign that people feel comfortable making comments that may not be complete but could spark ideas. Some parties seek or value "authoritative" statements—statements well supported by reliable evidence or proposals that have known consequences. If the other party expects authoritative statements, the person may feel more closely bound to any position already taken or idea offered. Since the parties work under this shared expectation, once an idea is offered it is easy for people to convince themselves that they would not have offered it unless the idea was worth continued support.

Statements like "I really haven't thought this through but I'd like to suggest . . ." or "I don't know exactly how I feel about this but we could try . . ." may be an indication that people feel they have to apologize for "half-baked" ideas. They may indicate that the other party does not encourage or accept tentative suggestions. At the same time, however, these types of phrases may **promote** a more exploratory climate. In effect, speakers who use these phrases are attempting to establish that it is all right to offer tentative ideas. The statements can provide a frame or context for the interaction, which says, in effect, that the parties are in an exploratory frame of mind. Ideas can be offered and evaluations can be made without committing an individual to any suggestions. A tone can be set that helps preserve flexibility and the possibility of continued change when conflicts arise.

Suppressing Conflict Issues

In situations that assume people should be able to reach agreement without conflict or that people can handle any conflict without seeking outside help, we may strongly discourage each other from admitting that a conflict exists or is beyond our control. If a person attempts to acknowledge the existence of a conflict or raise the possibility that they seek third party assistance, he or she may lose face in the eyes of others. The person may be seen as someone who causes problems or is eager to find fault with the way the other party operates. This threat may deter people from engaging in adequate differentiation, and it may promote prolonged and destructive avoidance of an issue.

If someone decides to raise an issue in such a climate, conflict interaction may unfold on more complicated grounds than necessary. A turn toward inflexibility and stalemate may be imminent if the person feels his or her image must be defended at all costs ("I don't care what you think of me for raising this issue, I think we need to address it"). These complications may mean that the parties cannot differentiate successfully or that integration is unattainable.

Academic appeal referees at colleges and universities are assigned the task of mediating disputes that arise between students and faculty about grades, financial aid, discrimination, enactment of departmental or university policies, and so on. One referee at a large university reports that students there are often reluctant to raise conflict issues and, as a result, conflicts are not addressed until the issues have gotten out of hand. Students are often hesitant to raise their concerns with a third party because they fear loss of face in the eyes of their mentors. In university settings student–faculty relationships are premised on a cooperative assumption: students (especially graduate students) and faculty are expected to work and learn together to advance knowledge in their academic fields. When a conflict arises over such issues as grading or interpretation of departmental policy, students feel that if they take the issue to a third party (even one that the university endorses), they may threaten or destroy their relationship. The student fears that the faculty will see him or her as someone who is unwilling to work through difficulties cooperatively and who may be trying to make the professor look bad in the eyes of a representative of the institution. Third parties who work in this context need to address this threat to face and help restore an atmosphere of cooperation so that the relationship can continue after the specific issue has been resolved.

In these types of conflicts, the threat to face stems from a fear of being seen as someone who is willing to jeopardize a "good" relationship by bringing a conflict out in the open. This fear is almost inevitably founded on a belief that the very emergence of conflict is always harmful or destructive.

FACE-GIVING

Now that we have explored the destructive nature of face-saving, it is time to turn our attention to how people help others avoid taking such extreme measures. In this final section, we examine the dynamics of face-giving.

Face-giving refers to the strategic moves that support the other's image or identity claims. In order to fully grasp how people "give face," we must first examine how people orient to face in everyday interaction.

Goffman (1957) identifies two strands of face-orienting or face-giving strategies: corrective and preventive practices. As the names imply, **corrective practices** are what people do after a face-threatening act or loss of face. Face-saving strategies are corrective practices. In contrast, **preventive practices** are what people do to avoid threats to face. Preventive practices may be either defensive or protective. Defensive strategies involve actions to prevent threats to one's own face. For example, people often ask the hearer to suspend judgment by using disclaimers, such as "Now some of my best friends are professors, but . . ." Protective strategies consist of those actions that prevent or minimize threats to another's face. For example, people often provide normative accounts for others, such as "The traffic must have been horrendous. I'm surprised you got here so fast."

Defensive strategies can be seen as **alignment actions** (Stokes & Hewitt, 1976). Alignment actions are verbal efforts to resolve discrepancies between people's conduct and cultural expectations. Essentially, these actions or messages align a person's behavior with cultural norms. For example, imagine you are late to a very important meeting. Just as you slink into your chair, the group pauses and your colleagues turn to greet you. Feeling that your absence has clearly violated the group's expectations, you say, "I'm really sorry. My car would not start." Such an alignment message demonstrates that you are not eccentric and allows you to manage your social identity in the group.

Researchers have identified several types of alignment actions used in everyday speech. The largest group of alignment actions falls under the rubric of "accounts." **Accounts** are reason-giving descriptions that presume one of the parties has committed an offense. They serve as devices to make failure or inappropriate behavior sound reasonable. In addition to descriptive reasons for behavior, common accounts include excuses, justifications, apologies, and quasi theories. An **apology** expresses regret over an earlier action. Statements such as "I'm sorry," "I will never do that again," and "What can I do to make up for this?" acknowledge responsibility and express remorse. When speakers use apologies they presume that the other recognizes with them that a failed and face-threatening event has occurred. **Quasi theories** are simplistic formulas or adages that are used to explain away complex situations. "Boys will be boys" and "We had a falling out" are examples of quasi theories. The most common accounts are excuses and justifications. These devices attempt to shift the burden of accountability. When people admit that their actions may be wrong or inappropriate but deny responsibility, they are employing an excuse. **Excuses** such as "I didn't feel well," "I couldn't resist," and "The phone was busy" readily acknowledge a mistake but resist responsibility. Researchers classify excuses into three types: (1) statements that deny harmful intent, (2) statements that deny volition and assert lack of bodily control, and (3) statements that deny the party performed the action (Tedeschi & Riess, 1981). Whereas excuses focus on responsibility, justifications focus on the consequences of the actions. **Justifications** are statements where the party admits personal responsibility but denies negative consequences, usually by relating the action to some socially acceptable rule of conduct, such as higher authority, self-defense, company policy, or situational norms. Statements such as "It was necessary in the long run" and "If we had held the meeting, it would have been a disaster" are examples of justifications.

Other types of alignment actions include disclaimers, counterclaims, licenses, and conversational repairs. **Disclaimers** ask the hearer for a suspension of judgment to prevent a negative typification (Hewitt & Stokes, 1975). Statements such as "I realize you might think this is wrong but" and "This is only my opinion but" defeat in advance doubts and unfavorable reactions. **Counterclaims** are devices used to deny unfavorable intentions (Stutman, 1988). People intuitively know that a speaker with persuasive goals is considered less trustworthy by others. When one party may benefit from a persuasive exchange, such as in sales encounters, the hearer naturally becomes more resistant to messages he or she receives. As a result, when people pursue persuasive goals they often deny that intent by stating the opposite. Because they counter the perceived goal of the message that follows them, these devices are called counterclaims. Statements such as "Now I'm not trying to persuade you but," "I don't want to change your mind but," and "This isn't an excuse but" deny unfavorable intentions.

When people make conversational errors, they often attempt to revise what has been said with corrections, restatements, or requests to ignore earlier actions. Statements such as "Oh, I didn't mean that" and "You get the just, eh, gist" serve as **conversational repairs**. Such repairs serve as "detours" and "time-outs" for people to correct an utterance they have employed (McLaughlin, 1984). Interestingly, what gets repaired may not appear wrong or in need of correction. Sometimes only the speaker perceives that a conversational misstep has been made.

A **remedy** is often proposed to make reparations to an offended party. This sometimes occurs even when the offense is unstated or unknown to the hearer. For example, imagine a scenario where at the beginning of a joint assignment, a co-worker mistakenly misplaces a file that may be used in the project. Even though the other has neither requested the file nor knows of its disappearance, the co-worker feels guilty. The co-worker then begins to offer a series of remarks that can be seen as remedies: "I think I should keep a list of all files that move through the office." "My organizational skills are not up to par. I should probably seek training." "It's time I reorganized my desk." Remedies, like other alignment actions, signal that a party is attempting to preserve face.

Grice (1975) maintains that people follow four implicit rules or maxims in conversations. Speakers cooperate with each other by (1) offering accurate or truthful information, (2) maintaining economy in speech by being neither too brief nor too lengthy, (3) offering relevant and topical points, and (4) refraining from overly obscure or ambiguous speech. When speakers anticipate breaking one or more of these rules, they often employ **licenses** to forecast the rule violation (Mura, 1983). Licenses give the hearer notice that a violation will or is occurring but that the infraction is necessary or unusual. For example, a speaker who breaks the rule of speech accuracy may qualify the statement: "I love your new car. I don't know much about cars." Phrases like "in fact," "actually," "really," and "of course" are often used to signal qualification. After being verbose and breaking the rule of speech economy, a speaker may say "I told you everything so that you could decide for yourself." A license used for breaking the rule of relevancy might sound like this: "I went off on a tangent because I need a plan for tomorrow." Breaking the rule of not using ambiguous speech might be followed by: "I know that sounds confusing, but it's really not." As alignment actions, licenses serve to defend the face of the speaker by reframing the rule-breaking event.

The devices used to prevent threat to one's own face may also serve as flags or markers that attention to face wants is desired. At the very minimum, such markers signal that the hearer is experiencing or anticipating a threat to face, and further challenge will result in a face-saving strategy. Protective strategies basically consist of the same alignment actions. The only difference is that we align for the other party. When people preface their statements or evaluations with any of the alignment actions they are essentially protecting the face of the other. Consider the possible ways a superior might protect the face of a subordinate while communicating that an improvement in work quality is needed. One might use an excuse: "You have been working hard the last few weeks, but let's talk about where this effort gets you." One might use a justification: "With all the assignments I throw at you, it's no wonder I have noticed a problem with quality." Or a disclaimer might be used: "Heaven knows quality is impossible to define, but." The options are diverse and plentiful. The key point is that **protective strategies provide the hearer with a means to protect face.**

Goffman (1955) maintains that all interaction is potentially face-threatening. Whenever people interact, they are making identity claims. Tracy (1991) notes that these claims may be quite general as opposed to personalized and specific. For example, in a grocery line we often want to be seen as patient; in a car, that we can drive with skill. Because people care deeply about how they are perceived almost all the time, there is always some potential for face-threat.

Inadvertently, people walk on each other's identity claims. Social situations involve tensions between cooperation and competition, between self's and other's face. Even in situations where it is in the best interest of the speaker to cooperate, people employ messages that are threatening and antagonistic (Craig, Tracy, & Spisak, 1986). The need to protect another's face is ever present. Related research suggests that some people seem to be better at face-giving than others.

A wide body of research in communication has been aimed at understanding how communicators design messages that promote relational harmony and facilitate goodwill between parties. This work can loosely be described as investigating "person-centered" speech. Any communication that is intended to support, comfort, or otherwise confirm the hearer can be considered person-centered. Person-centered speech consists of prosocial behaviors and displays a willingness on the part of the speaker to verbally express his or her thoughts and feelings in a way that takes the other into account.

Essentially, researchers conclude that this message design is driven by an ability and by a desire on the part of the speaker to adapt his or her communication to the hearer in order to achieve one or more strategic goals (Applegate & Delia, 1980). In order to engage in person-centered speech, research demonstrates that the speaker must possess an ability to take on other perspectives. This perspective-taking suggests a skill to adopt the psychological viewpoint of the other and allows the speaker to anticipate the behavior and reactions of others. Perspective-taking presumes that the motivations, intentions, and feelings of any individual are unique. Moreover, it presumes the character of each situation is equally original. Once a speaker understands the psychological viewpoints of others, he or she can then adapt their communication to achieve any of a number of strategic goals, such as task (persuasion, instruction, entertainment, etc.). or identity (credibility, social status, intent, etc.). Of the many strategic goals a speaker might pursue, person-centered speech highlights the importance of relational maintenance. Hence a focus on the unique characteristics of others or the situation to promote the relationship is highly personal or person-centered.

In contrast, many communicators assume the identities of others, and the meaning of their actions can be understood in terms of assigned roles, contexts, and topics. Communicators working from this mode need not understand others' perspectives, nor adapt to other actors. Instead, they focus on the assigned roles of the participants, the authority that inheres in those roles, and the norms surrounding such role relationships. This position-centered speech expresses feelings through nonverbal channels, rather than elaborating them through verbal codes, and often appears to focus on the topic on the floor or the task at hand at the expense of others' feelings. It is not that communicators who use position-centered speech are insensitive to others, but rather that they assume that individual identities, such as image or motivation, can be dispensed with by following fixed rules of social conduct.

Whereas person-centered speech promotes relational harmony and facilitates goodwill between parties, position-centered speech encourages defensiveness and caution. Communicators who employ person-centered speech generally exhibit the following patterns:

1. Speech that is more indirect so as to lessen the degree of imposition placed on the hearer (but not to the point of inhibiting the hearer's understanding).
2. Use of face-sensitive messages (messages that attempt to protect the desired image of the hearer).
3. Ability to align others' behavior to situated norms.
4. Reliance on information-seeking through questions.
5. Refraining from overt evaluations and attacks of others' self-concept.
6. Sensitive use of challenges, directives, and demands.

CONCLUSION

Face-saving concerns are, at base, concerns about relationships. When interaction becomes centered on these concerns during a conflict, people are negotiating how they will see each other; each message and response establishes whether a desired image will be allowed to stand in the eyes of others. Since these images are closely tied to people's self-concepts, face-saving interaction has a strong influence on how comfortable people feel and how successful the parties will be at resolving conflicts constructively.

Groups and dyads often benefit when the role of individuals and their sense of self become the focus of interaction. Relationships can be improved and people can feel better about themselves because others have confirmed a self-image they value. When the need to **save** face emerges, however, interaction can head toward destructive escalation because a person's self-image is under dispute. Uncertain that a desired self-image is accepted by others (or certain that an undesirable image has been established), a person seeks confirmation of a new relational image. If the acceptance of this bid is problematic, moving on from this issue may be difficult. Attempts to redirect the topic or shift back to group-centered or person-centered interaction may be thwarted by feelings of resentment or a preoccupation with the other party's resistance to changing its view. When face-saving issues go unresolved, making any decision or addressing any issue can be a highly volatile task. Unsettled issues about public images can be played out in other more substantive contexts with potentially disastrous effects for the relationship or group.

Chapter
6

Climate and Conflict Interaction

Perhaps because we live in the scientific age, most people prefer well-defined, straightforward explanations for the way things are. Ideally we should be able to isolate the forces that shape conflict and then define, measure, and study these forces to come up with a fairly complete explanation. Unfortunately, however, the world seldom lives up to our ideals. There is simply more there than is dreamed of in this simple scientific philosophy. Conflict behavior cannot be reduced to a small set of well-defined variables. People also act on the basis of their general "feelings" about a situation, feelings that often cannot be precisely defined or boiled down to a simple explanation.

People often speak of "getting the feel of" a situation or "learning the ropes." Managers, labor leaders, and politicians observe an "air of conflict" or "a mood of compromise" among their employees, colleagues, or opponents. Planners and consultants assess the "climate for change" in the organizations or groups they try to influence. These people are responding to the general, global character of the situation, to what has been called the **climate** of the situation. Climate represents the **prevailing temper, attitudes, and outlook** of a dyad, group, or organization. As the meteorological name implies, climate is just as diffuse, but just as pervasive, as the weather.

Climate is important in understanding conflict interaction, because it provides

continuity and coherence to mutual activities. As a general sense of a relationship, group, or organization, climate enables members to ascertain their general direction, what it means to be part of the group, what actions are appropriate, how fellow members are likely to react, and other information necessary to guide members' behavior and help them understand the relationship, group, or organization. In the Columnist's Brown Bag (Case 3.3), the open and relaxed climate encouraged participants to exercise their curiosity and to be receptive to each others' comments. Questions, answers, and discussion flowed freely and spontaneously for most of the session. When the columnist was challenged, the atmosphere grew tense, and members became hesitant and defensive.

The challenge seemed out of place, given the openness of previous discussion; it introduced great uncertainty and some hostility into the proceedings. Members reacted to the challenge as a violation of appropriate behavior, and subsequent interaction was colored by this. Eventually, rather than risk escalation of the challenge and permanent collapse of free, relaxed exchange, group leaders chose to terminate the session. By evoking certain types of behavior and discouraging others, the open climate gave the discussion direction and held it together. It united the diverse styles and concerns of individual members by providing a common ground for acting together and for reacting to a "crisis."

Implicit in any climate is an attitude toward conflict and how it should be handled. Climate constrains and channels conflict behavior; it lends a definite tenor to interchanges that can accelerate destructive cycles or preserve a productive approach. In the brown-bag session the questioner's challenge was hastily cut off because the group was in "guest speaker mode," which implied a respectful and friendly attitude toward the editor. The challenge raised the specter of open and prolonged disagreement and potential embarrassment of the speaker. The group's open, nonevaluative climate made the challenge seem inappropriate; rather than allow disagreement to ripen, those in charge were eager to end the session. Interestingly, the reaction of other members to the challenge contributed to the sudden shift from an open climate to a tense and evaluative one, even though this is the last thing they would have wanted. The interplay of concrete, specific interactions and generalized climate is a critical force determining the direction of conflicts. We will spend a large part of this chapter exploring this relationship.

At first glance, climate is an uncomfortably vague concept. In order to get a handle on it, it is tempting to define a set of variables or properties that "make up" climate and classify different sorts of climates (e.g., cooperative versus competitive climates) on the basis of whether they have various combinations of properties. Most social scientists have tried to do just this (e.g., see Deutsch, 1973; James & Jones, 1974). We believe the utility of this approach is limited. Climates are extremely complex and diffuse. As a result, it is difficult, if not impossible, to isolate a few defining variables that can capture all the varied forms and nuances of climates. More importantly, the concepts we use to explain and understand human behavior should be equivalent to those used by people in the situation. Our explorations of climate should take into account its diffuse, general quality. Therefore, while we will define some properties of climates in order to help people analyze their own groups, we will always operate from the assumption that climate is a holistic, general characteristic. We will emphasize how climates are created and sustained, because we believe climate can best be understood and controlled if we can clarify how it is produced, maintained, and changed by people's actions.

Climate is a characteristic of social units, such as relationships, families, work groups, crowds, and organizations. When not exploring specific examples, we will use the general term "social unit" to indicate that our discussion refers to climates in all types of units.

WHAT IS CLIMATE? A DEFINITION

To get a grasp on this elusive concept it is helpful to consider a specific example of how climate develops and operates in a work group. Case 6.1 was reported by a third party who was called to intervene in a thorny conflict.

Case 6.1   Riverdale Halfway House

Riverdale Halfway House is a correctional institution designed to provide low-level security confinement and counseling for male youth offenders. It houses about 25 second- and third-time offenders and for all practical purposes represents the last stop before prison for its inhabitants. Residents are required to work or look for work and are on restricted hours. Counseling and other life-adjustment services are provided, and counselors' reports on a prisoner can make an important difference in both the length of incarceration and conditions of release. Since the counselors are also authority figures, relationships between staff and prisoners are delicate and touchy. Staff members are subjected to a great deal of stress as the prisoners attempt to manipulate them.

The staff of Riverdale consists of a director who handles funding, general administration, and external relations with other agencies, notably the courts and law enforcement offices; an assistant director who concentrates on external administration of the staff and the halfway house; three counselors; two night caretakers; and an administrative assistant who handles the books and paperwork. The director, George, was the newest staff member at the time of the conflict. The assistant director—who had also applied for the director's slot that George filled—and the three counselors had been at Riverdale for at least a year longer than George. They described George's predecessor as a very "charismatic" person. Prior to George's arrival relations among the staff were cordial. Morale was high and there was a great deal of informal contact among staff members. The staff reported a high level of respect for all workers under the previous director. Workers felt engaged by an important, if difficult, task that all would work on as a team.

With George's arrival the climate at Riverdale changed. Right before George started, the staff changed offices and rearranged furniture, leaving the shoddiest pieces for George. George regarded this as a sign of rejection. He believed the staff had "worked around him" and had tried to undermine his authority by rearranging things without consulting him. He was hurt and angry despite the staff's attempts to explain that no harm was meant. Added to this was George's belief that Carole, the assistant director, resented him and wanted his job. Carole claimed she did not resent George, although she did fear that he might have her fired. She tended to withdraw from George in order to avoid conflict. Her withdrawal was interpreted by George as a sign of further rejection, which reinforced his suspicion of Carole.

The previous director left pretty big shoes for George to fill, and this showed especially in George's working relationship with the staff. The staff felt he was not open with them, and that he quizzed them about their work in a manipulative fashion. Several staff members, including Carole, complained that George swore at them and ordered them around; they considered this behavior an affront to their professionalism. George's attempts to assert his authority also angered the staff. In one case, George investigated a disciplinary problem with two staff members without consulting Carole, who was ordinarily in charge of such matters. George's investigation did not reveal any problems, but it embarrassed the two staff members (who had been manipulated by prisoners) and made Carole feel George did not respect her. George admitted his mistake and hoped the incident would blow over.

Ten months after George arrived at Riverdale, the climate had changed drastically. Whereas Riverdale had been a supportive, cohesive work group, now it was filled with tension. Interaction between George and the staff, particularly Carole, was formal and distant. The staff had to some degree pulled together in response to George, but its cohesiveness was gone. Informal communication was down, and staff members received much less support from each other. As the third party mediator observed, "the staff members expected disrespect from each other." They felt stuck with their problems and believed there was no way out of their dilemma. There was no trust and no sense of safety in the group. Members believed they had to change others to improve the situation and did not consider changing themselves or living with others' quirks. The staff wanted George to become less authoritarian and more open to them. George wanted the staff to let him blow up and shout and then forget about it. There was little flexibility or willingness to negotiate. As Carole observed, each contact between herself and George just seemed to make things worse, "so what point was there in trying to talk things out?" The consultant noted that members seemed to be unable to forget previous fights. They interpreted what others said as continuations of old conflicts and assumed a hostile attitude even when one was not present.

The third party tried to get the group to meet and iron out its problems, but the group wanted to avoid confrontation—on several occasions, scheduled meetings were postponed because of other "pressing" problems. Finally, George found another job and left Riverdale, as did one of the counselors. Since then, the staff reports that conditions have improved considerably.

We offer the following definition: **climate is the relatively enduring quality of group situation that (1) is experienced in common by group members, and (2) arises from and influences their interaction and behavior.** Several aspects of this definition require explanation and can be illustrated from the case.

First, climate is not psychological—it is not an intangible belief or feeling in members' minds. Climate is a quality of the social unit itself because it arises from interaction among group members. For this reason a **climate is more than the beliefs or feelings of any single individual**. The climate of Riverdale was hostile and suspicious not because any particular member had suspicions about or disliked another, but because of how the group as a whole interacted. Members were hostile and suspicious toward each other, and these interchanges built on themselves until most group activities were premised on hostility.

This is not to say that individual members' perceptions of climate are not important. People's perceptions play an important role in the creation and maintenance of climate, because these perceptions **mediate** the effects of climate on people's actions. However, climate cannot be **reduced** to the beliefs or feelings of individual members. Various individuals in the Riverdale case had different perceptions of the hostile situation. George thought the group was hostile because Carole wanted his job and the staff resented him. Carole felt the hostility was because George cursed at her and went around her in making decisions. It is clear that neither George nor Carole had the "correct" or complete view, but they were reacting to a common situation. Their beliefs and feelings represent a particular sampling and interpretation of experiences in the group.

Members' perceptions of climate are strongly influenced by their positions in the group, as a study by Albrecht (1979) illustrates. Albrecht compared the perceptions of organizational climate by "key" communicators (active communicators who link large groups of people) with those of "non-key" communicators (those who were more isolated from the communication flow). She found that key communicators identified more with their jobs and were more satisfied with their communication with superiors than were non-key communicators. Albrecht explained these differences as a function of greater frequency of communication (greater activity leads to a more positive image of the organization) and greater amount of information obtained by the key communicators (more information creates greater involvement on the job). Numerous other studies have also shown different perceptions of organizational climate depending on the members' positions in the authority hierarchy (Schneider & Bartlett, 1970), the type of work done (Powell & Butterfield, 1978), and how long the member had belonged to the group or organization (Johnston, 1976). Clearly, different experiences and different day-to-day interaction patterns create different perceptions of climate. Hence George, as a new manager, and Carole, as his "old-hand" assistant, had somewhat different views of Riverdale's climate. These different perceptions were one reason George and Carole reacted differently in the conflict.

George's and Carole's perspectives on Riverdale's climate can be viewed as individual interpretations of the group's climate, which is "experienced in common" by group members. However, individual perceptions provide only a partial picture of the climate itself. A social unit's climate is more than any individual's perceptions and can only be identified and understood if the unit's interaction as a whole is considered (Poole, 1985). As we will see later, individual members' perceptions of climate play an important role in maintaining or changing climates, but they are **different** from climate at the most fundamental level.

A second feature of the definition is its characterization of climate as **experienced in common** by members. As the preceding paragraph suggests, since climate emerges from interaction, it is a shared experience for the interactors. This implies that there should be some common elements in members' interpretations and descriptions of the group, even though there will be differences in specific details and concerns. Thus the staff at Riverdale all agreed that the group was tense, hostile, and hard to manage. Although each person focused on different evidence—George on the furniture incident, Carole on George's cursing—and had somewhat different interpretations, a common theme emerged, and the consultant was able to construct a unified picture of the climate from the various members' stories. Common experiences do not mean identical interpretations, but they do mean a unifying theme.

Third, because climates are products of interaction, **no one person is responsible for creating a climate**. In the Riverdale case it would be easy to blame George for creating the hostile atmosphere but closer consideration shows that all the other members contributed too. The counselors rearranged the furniture without considering that George might be insecure in a new job. Carole withdrew when George confronted her, which prevented an airing of the issues and may have increased his suspicions. The hostile atmosphere at Riverdale was so pervasive because most members acted in accordance with it. Their actions reinforced each other and created an expectation of hostility in most interchanges.

Climates are also **relatively enduring;** that is, they persist for extended spans of time and do not change with every change in interaction (Tagiuri, 1968). In some social units the same climate may hold for months or years. At Riverdale, for example, the hostile climate built for ten months before a mediator was called in. Members of a community consulting group reported a consistent atmosphere of support and cooperation extending for several years; although many disagreements and controversies arose during this time, they were worked out in a constructive and cooperative manner. Furthermore, employees of some corporations have observed a consistent "tone," "flavor," or "attitude" in their work environment, which has evolved over months or years and seems likely to persist into the future (Dalton, 1959; Roy, 1959; Kanter, 1977). In other cases a group's climate has a shorter life, as in the brown-bag discussion, where a challenging, hostile climate supplanted the generally relaxed climate after only an hour.

Both long- and short-lived climates represent periods where definite themes and directions predominate in a social unit's interaction. The "life span" of a climate is determined by the relative stability of its themes, and this in turn depends on whether the themes are reinforced in day-to-day group interaction (Poole & McPhee, 1983; Poole, 1985). In some groups the climate is firmly established in fundamental assumptions of group operation and therefore changes very slowly. For example, in the community consulting group, cooperative means of decision-making were built into the group's meeting procedures, and cooperative activity was therefore reinforced whenever conflicts arose. In other groups, interaction remains more unstable; there is little consensus on basic assumptions, and the overall sense of the group shifts relatively easily. Shifts in group interaction can shift the underlying assumptions of the group rather quickly. The brown-bag discussion, which brought together a group of relative strangers, is one such case. Because climate **reinforces**

the patterns of interaction from which it arises, the longer a climate holds for a group, the more entrenched and enduring it is likely to become (Poole & McPhee, 1983). Climates are changed by changes in interaction that "break the spell" and reroute the group.

CLIMATE THEMES

But just what is the "content" of climates? What do climates tell members that helps them make specific projections? Climate can best be described as a set of general **themes** running through interaction. At Riverdale, for example, one theme was the lack of respect members had for one another. This was clearly reflected in the behaviors of Riverdale's staff: George cursed at people and worked around Carole's authority; staff members excluded George from their office improvements and talked about him behind his back. Identifying this theme permitted the consultant to understand some of the dynamics at Riverdale.

A barrier to the identification of climates is the amazing diversity of themes. If we observe a hundred social units, we will probably find a hundred different sets of themes. In some social units we might find a cooperative atmosphere based on dedication to a common task or mission and in others cooperation based on warm and supportive friendships. At Riverdale hostility and mistrust were grounded in suspicions about the possible misuse of authority, while in another group hostility might be grounded in competition for scarce rewards, such as raises or promotions. The variations are endless. However, from the many specific variations it is possible to identify general categories of concerns addressed by group themes. The four general themes we will discuss arise from "universal" features of human relationships identified by a number of previous studies (Foa, 1961; Wish & Kaplan, 1977; Bales & Cohen, 1979). These themes, shown in Table 6.1, emerge repeatedly because they relate to problems and concerns faced in every social unit. Although they certainly do not cover every theme, we believe they offer useful guideposts for the identification of climates.

One category of themes revolves around **dominance or authority relations**. These themes are concerned with a set of questions concerning how a social unit ordinarily deals with the distribution of power and respect. Is power concentrated in the hands of a few, or is it accessible to most or all members? How important is power in decisions: to what extent are power and influence used to mandate decisions or resolve disagreements, as opposed to open discussion and argument about the issues? How rigid is the power structure: can members readily shift roles and assume authority, or are the same members always in control? Related to this: Are the differences in power, status, and respect accorded to leaders greatly different from those accorded to followers? Answers to these and related questions are important in understanding how members are differentiated in the social unit and how they act together.

At Riverdale, for example, power was part of the day-to-day interaction. George used his directorship to berate staff members. His attempts to circumvent Carole and her opposition created a climate in which the use of power and opposition were taken for granted, with predictable consequences for the group's interaction. Dominance

Table 6.1   FOUR IMPORTANT CATEGORIES OF CLIMATE THEMES

Type of Theme	Examples of Issues Associated with Each Type of Theme
1. Dominance and authority relations	Is power concentrated in the hands of a few leaders or is it shared? How important is power in group decisions? How rigid is the group's power structure: do members shift roles? How are power and respect distributed among members?
2. Degree of supportiveness	Are members friendly or intimate with one another? Can members trust one another? Can members safely express emotions in the group? Does the group tolerate disagreements among members? To what degree does the group emphasize task versus socioemotional concerns?
3. Sense of group identity	Does the group have a definite identity? Do members feel ownership of group accomplishments? How great is member commitment to the group? Do members share responsibility for decisions?
4. Interdependence	Can members all gain if they cooperate, or will one's gain be another's loss? Are members pitted against one another?

themes are important determinants of conflict behavior because they enable members to draw conclusions as to how differentiation will be handled by other members and how differences will be resolved. If, for example, members perceive domination of the group by a few and they disagree with the dominant position, it is logical to assume they believe they have to use force to bring their own views into prominence. This reasoning may lead the member to avoid conflict because there is too much to lose, or to state his or her case in extremely forceful terms in an attempt to fight the dominant members. Just such an assumption about George kept Carole from confronting him about the issues that were undermining their relationship.

A second category of themes concerns the **degree of supportiveness** in the social unit. This category covers a cluster of related issues. Are members friendly toward each other? Can members trust one another? Can members safely express their emotions? Is there tolerance for disagreements and different points of view? What is the relative degree of concern with tasks and members' socioemotional needs? Answers to these and related questions give members an idea of their safety in the social unit and level of commitment members have to one another. At Riverdale there was very little emotional safety. Members distrusted one another, and there was little tolerance for disagreement. Members dug into entrenched positions and assumed they were right, that it was up to others to mend their ways. People protected themselves and showed little concern for others' feelings. Although emotions were expressed to some extent (at least by George), they were perceived as levers and not as a means for deeper understanding. Emotionality themes are important in conflict because they allow members to draw conclusions about whether needs and feelings should and will be addressed in managing the conflict. In cases where emotional expression is not safe, there will often be a tendency to conceal needs or address them indirectly. This veiling can make successful conflict management much more difficult.

Consider Case 6.2 and the impact that supportiveness (or lack thereof) can have on emotional conflicts. The organization in question is a small cooperative bakery with seven staff members. Although these workers were generally congenial with one another, they did not have sufficient intimacy or trust to air an emotional crisis, and this lack of trust made the conflict much worse than it should have been.

Case 6.2 ## The Breakup at the Bakery

A group of seven people had established and run a bakery for two years when a severe conflict emerged and threatened the store's existence. Two workers had been in a committed intimate relationship for several years but were now going through a difficult breakup. During this time, neither the man nor the woman could stand being around one another, but neither could afford to quit his or her job. The store needed both members' skills and experience to survive financially.

Over three months the climate in the workplace grew more and more unbearable. Workers had to deal with the tension between the couple while working under daily time pressures and the constraints of having a minimal staff. Many believed that they could not work effectively if the situation got much worse. Important information about bakery orders and deliveries was not being exchanged as workers talked less and less to each other. The group decided to call in a third party to help improve the situation. In discussing the problem with individual staff members, the third party realized that the workers strongly resented having to deal with the "relationship problem" at the bakery. They felt they were being forced to choose sides in the conflict or they would risk losing the friendship of both. At the same time, it was painful to see two friends endure a very difficult emotional trauma. Although the staff members were eager to share these feelings with the third party, almost nothing had been said to the man or woman about these reactions. The staff was not willing to discuss these emotional issues because they seemed highly volatile and might lead to the breakdown of the work group. The climate deterred people from expressing emotional reactions, which might have helped the couple understand how their breakup was affecting the entire staff. As a result, tension heightened, and the bakery was about to go under. The third party increased members' feelings of safety, and eventually they were able to talk about their problems. It was finally decided that the man would train his successor and leave the bakery within three months, while the woman would stay on.

A third category of themes concerns members' **sense of group identity** (Wilson, 1978). It covers questions such as the following: Does the social unit have an identity of its own or is it just a collection of individuals? Do members feel ownership of its accomplishments? How great is their commitment? Do members know about and trust in each other's commitment? Themes related to these questions give members information that allows them to project the consequences of conflict for the social unit. For example, if a group does not have a definite identity, and member commitment is low, the group may fracture into subgroups if conflict comes into the open. Members with an interest in preserving the group might try to hide conflict in order to prevent this. An important reason the staff at Riverdale was unable to manage its conflict was because members believed raising the issues again "wasn't worth the hassle" and would only worsen an already unpleasant situation. The group's cohesiveness had been so disrupted by its problems that members feared they would not be able to do their jobs if the conflict advanced any further.

A final category of themes concerns the type of **interdependence** among group members. These themes address the motivational set of the situation. Can all members gain if they cooperate, or will one member's gain be another's loss? Do members normally take a competitive attitude toward each other? The themes in this category are closely related to the climates discussed by Deutsch (1973). As we noted in Chapter 1, at least three types of interdependence can be identified—cooperative, competitive, and individualistic—and these have quite different effects on group interaction.

For example, interaction at Riverdale was premised on a competitive assumption. George and Carole were each trying to protect their own "turf" from the other. The other staff members were resistant to George and regarded him as an opponent who would try to defeat them by browbeating and by using his authority. Answers to questions revolving around motivational interdependence are important because they influence whether working habits in groups already predispose members toward destructive redefinition of conflicts into win–lose terms (see Chapter 3). A "competitive" climate can encourage this tendency, while a "cooperative" climate can discourage it.

We have advanced these four categories in order to illustrate common climate themes, and not as a complete description. Although these themes capture important aspects of climates, climates are much more complex and dynamic than the categories themselves imply. The categories represent general types of climate themes and, taken in isolation, give only a "frozen" picture of climate; they cannot mark the ways in which climate is constantly being renewed in an interaction. Moreover, the four categories omit many features of climates. To adequately understand a group's climate, it is necessary to identify the specific combinations of themes in the particular group under consideration. Even if all themes in a group happen to fall in the four categories, the specific combination will very likely be unique to the group in question. The unique combination of climate themes influences the patterns of conflict that emerge in the group.

The four categories of themes are not totally independent. The same theme can cross more than one category, as the Riverdale case shows. The suspicious and hostile relationship between George and the rest of the staff (notably Carole) had consequences related to **both** the dominance and supportiveness categories. As this also implies, not all the categories of themes will be important in every social unit. In some units one theme may dominate all others. For example, in one office, the boss was so authoritarian and angered his employees so much that they organized against him. When the boss was not around they ridiculed him and fantasized about revenge. They slowed down their work and covered for each other so the boss would not find out. The office was preoccupied with authority relations; other concerns were less of an influence over members' behavior.

CLIMATE AND CONFLICT INTERACTION

The key to understanding the impact of climates on conflict is to explore the reciprocal influence of climate and interaction. Climate affects interaction, and the interaction, in turn, defines and alters the climate in a group. Both sides of this relationship need close examination in order to understand the role climate plays in conflicts. Once we understand this better, we can posit some methods for creating productive climates and avoiding nonproductive ones. This section examines how climate constrains and channels conflict interaction. The next section will consider the other side of the coin: how interaction shapes climates.

The Effects of Climate on Conflict Interaction

In all interaction, and particularly in conflicts, one of the key problems group members face is their **uncertainty** about how to act and about what the consequences of their actions will be. Uncertainty is natural in conflict because many people are not as accustomed to conflict as they are to other sorts of interaction. Perhaps due to a cultural tendency toward avoiding or ignoring undesirable situations, many people simply do not think or learn very much about conflicts. Even for those who are accustomed to conflict, every conflict presents specific problems and choices never faced before. Even if it is a dreary rehash of a long-standing argument, each conflict holds the potential for change, for better or worse.

There are two ways in which group members can respond to this uncertainty. As noted in Chapter 1, the psychodynamic perspective posits that some members reduce their uncertainty by becoming rigid, that is, by responding to all conflicts in the same way regardless of circumstances. Rigid behavior can take many forms, but two of the most striking examples provide good illustrations. Most of us have seen people who get defensive and lash out at anyone in their way. We also see others who try to ignore or avoid all conflicts regardless of how important they are. Both forms of behavior tend to perpetuate themselves and they can be maddening for those who have to deal with them, but rigidity has definite benefits in both cases. There are numerous ways that an attacker can intimidate potential opposition into giving in or never registering a complaint (Donohue, 1981). In the same vein, the avoider can often stifle issues that are threatening to him or her. Like the working habits discussed in Chapter 3, rigid responses also have the psychological benefits of reducing internal tension and enabling the member to mount some response to a potentially paralyzing situation. However, like permanently fixed working habits, rigidity can result in destructive escalation or avoidance cycles, because it encourages stereotyped, repetitive responses. If the counterattacker cannot intimidate others or if the avoider cannot successfully stifle issues, their rigid behavior quickly accelerates negative spirals of conflict interaction.

Rubin and Brown (1975) summarize evidence suggesting that men are more likely to fall prey to this type of rigidity than are women. They believe this is because women are more responsive to others' interpersonal cues than men and therefore tend to be more flexible: they call it "interpersonally oriented." Men, on the other hand, tend to interpret conflicts in win–lose terms and therefore approach all conflicts with whatever strategies usually win for them. Although these explanations are somewhat debatable, they are certainly thought provoking.

More numerous—and also more effective—are those members who **attempt to cope with their uncertainty by diagnosing the situation and reacting in a manner appropriate to it**. Because exact prediction is impossible, members must project their actions and estimate how others will respond to them. This projection can occur consciously (as when a member plots out a strategy for the conflict), or it can be unconscious (as when a member takes a reactive stance and only looks ahead to the next act), but it always involves estimations and guesswork about the future. Climate is indispensable in this process. Members use their sense of the group's climate to gauge the appropriateness, effectiveness, or likely consequences of their behavior. **The prevailing climate of the group is projected into its future and sets a standard for behavior in the conflict**. At Riverdale, for example, the firmly entrenched climate of hostility and suspicion led Carole to expect hostile interactions with George, and therefore she came into the situation with her guard up, tended to interpret most of George's actions in an unfavorable light, and tended to act in a hostile or defensive manner toward George. Unable to predict the specifics of a conflict, members use their general impressions of a situation (in other words, of its climate) to generate specific expectations about how things should or will go. Because climate is so diffuse and generalized, it is difficult to trace the particular reasoning involved in these projections; for this reason, they are often called "intuition."

In the preceding paragraph we concentrated on members' projections of their own behaviors, but equally important is their understanding of others' behavior. Here again, climate plays a major role. Especially critical are members' attempts to deduce the intentions of other members. For example, at some point early in the conflict Carole decided George intended to undermine her authority and maybe even force her to leave Riverdale. As a result, she was uncooperative and withdrew whenever George confronted her, answering what she perceived as hostility with hostility. Carole may have been right or wrong in her conclusions about George. That she drew conclusions at all was enough to stimulate her hostile behavior.

As we discussed in Chapter 2, researchers have called the process by which people draw conclusions about others from their words or deeds **attribution** and have focused on the biases that creep into such judgments (Sillars, 1980a–c). A particularly important bias has been found in conflict situations, and climate plays a critical role in promoting it. In a thought-provoking article, Thomas and Pondy (1977) report that when people in business describe conflicts, they tend to exaggerate their own cooperativeness while at the same time exaggerating their opponent's competitiveness (in other words, his or her responsibility for the conflict). These findings imply a bias toward overestimating others' competitive tendencies (Pruitt & Rubin, 1986). This bias can have important effects on conflict interaction. Remember that Sillars (1980b) found that subjects who attributed responsibility for the conflict to the other were more likely to use avoidance and competitive strategies and less likely to use collaborative strategies than were those who did not make this attribution. However, the bias reported by Thomas and Pondy does not show up in some situations. In particular, studies of trust have found a bias toward assuming cooperativeness on the part of others once trust has been established (Zand, 1972; Deutsch, 1973).

These different outcomes can be understood in view of our discussion of climate. In the Thomas and Pondy study the business workers were asked to talk about a recent conflict, and it is likely they chose instances where there was open controversy, in line with the common conception of conflicts as fights. In such cases the climate is very likely to be competitive and at least somewhat hostile, and the participants are thus primed to see others as competitive. The studies on trust specifically tried to induce a climate of cooperation, by instructing participants to be concerned about how the outcome of a game affected their opponents. Therefore it is not surprising people perceived each other as friendly and cooperative. In both cases the direction of the bias toward attribution of either competition or cooperation was determined by the climate of the situation. Interestingly, the studies of trust also postulate that members' perceptions of others as cooperative caused them to behave more cooperatively and reinforced the trusting atmosphere. The same self-reinforcing cycle is also presumed for situations where distrust and competition prevail: perceptions of competition breed competitive behavior and reinforce hostile reactions (Sillars, 1980c). The prevailing climate of a conflict situation colors members' interpretations of one another, thereby encouraging certain types of behavior and reinforcing the situational climate.

To this point we have considered the uses of climate for individual members. But members' actions, each guided by climate, combine and build on one another to impart a momentum to the social unit. At Riverdale, for example, individual members picked up on the hostile climate and their defensive and unfriendly actions thrust the group into a tense spiral of hostile exchanges. This process can also work to the benefit of social units. Friendly and responsive actions encouraged by an open climate also tend to create a chain reaction and give the conflict a positive momentum. The influence that climate exerts on individual members' behavior translates into a more encompassing **influence on the direction of the unit as a whole**.

The Effects of Interaction on Climate

In our definition of climate, we pointed to the critical role of interaction in creating and sustaining climates. Members' immediate experience of climate comes from interaction; by observing how others act and react, a member picks up cues about others' sense of the climate. Since each member acts on an interpretation of climate based on observations of the other members (and their reactions to him or her), the prevailing climate has a "multiplier" effect in the group: it tends to reproduce itself because all members orient themselves to each other and each orients to the climate in projecting his or her own acts. For example, in a friendship, people tend to be cooperative because they assume that is "the way things should be" between friends. When one person sees the other being friendly and cooperative, this reaffirms the relational climate and probably strengthens their inclination toward cooperativeness. Because this is happening for all members, the effect multiplies itself and becomes quite strong.

However, this multiplier effect can also change the climate under some conditions. If a member deviates in a way that "breaks" the prevailing climate, and other members follow the lead, the direction of the group's interaction can be changed. If the change is profound and holds on long enough, it can result in a shift in the overall climate. Take the cooperative relationship we just mentioned. If one person selfishly starts to press his or her interests, the other may conclude that he or she must do the same. Once members begin to act only for themselves, the underlying assumptions may shift to emphasize competition and taking advantage of the others. This reflects a radical shift in the relational climate, the result of a single member's shift multiplied through the actions of the others. This is obviously a very complicated process.

To illustrate how conflict interaction both reflects and reproduces climate, we explore Case 6.3 and how a psychological evaluation unit at a large hospital responded to several controversies and disagreements surrounding an important decision.

Case 6.3   ## The Psychological Evaluation Unit

The unit is composed of three psychiatrists, a psychologist, and two social workers and is charged with diagnosing disturbed patients and with running a training program for newly graduated doctors interning at the hospital. The climate of this group can best be described as "quietly suppressed." The psychiatrist who heads the committee, Jerry, is a "take-charge" person, and the psychologist and social workers are intimidated by his forceful style. Jerry tries to be open, but, partly due to Jerry's strength, and partly due to uncertainty about their own status, the three have relatively little input in group discussions. The other two psychiatrists, John and Laura, sometimes provide a balance, but they are not as aggressive as Jerry and therefore tend to be overshadowed. John and Laura are aware of Jerry's take-charge tendencies and have tried to encourage the psychologist and social workers. However, all tend to hang back in the face of Jerry's initiatives.

Three themes set the climate of this group. The first pertains to **dominance and authority relations** and can best be described as a dilemma. On the one hand, operation of the group is premised on Jerry's dominance. He is the formal head of the unit; he chairs most meetings and represents the unit in the hospital bureaucracy. Partly as a result of his leadership, Jerry has evolved a forceful, take-charge style, and members of the group seem to expect this of him. On the other hand, full, relatively equal participation by all members is necessary for the unit to be effective. The unit was purposely designed as a multidisciplinary cross section, with competent professionals from all "helping" areas: psychiatry, psychology, and social work. Each profession must exert its influence if the unit is to function properly. However, Jerry's dominance discourages participation by the social workers and psychologist in the group decision-making process. This aspect creates a paradox. If all members insist on a strong voice in the group, the group will be less effective, because the power Jerry needs to negotiate with the bureaucracy is undercut and because Jerry may resist sharing power and disrupt the group. But if weaker members do not assert themselves the group will also be less effective, because representatives of all disciplines are not contributing. Members' behavior is colored by their responses to this dilemma.

The second theme pertains to **supportiveness** and concerns the safety of being open in the group. The unit emphasizes a high level of professionalism for its members and, because of this, presentation of oneself as a professional is very important. In some areas this code implies that members should hold back: for example, expression of anger is seen as unprofessional, as is making a "half-baked" suggestion in a decision-making discussion. In other areas this implies full openness: for example, when researchers come in to present new therapeutic ideas to the group, members are encouraged to ask questions as part of the learning process. Thus whether it is safe to be open with the group is determined by whether the specific instance of openness is regarded as "professional" or not. For most of the duration of the meeting we will examine, openness is not considered to be professional.

The third theme concerns the group's identity and can be described as the **problem of survival**. The psychological evaluation unit was created at a time of budget surplus for the hospital. The services it provides were originally provided by the staff psychiatrists, but the unit was created to consolidate diagnostic techniques in one unit and leave the staff psychiatrists free for therapy. However, a budget crunch set in the last year and the hospital board is looking for services and units to cut. Since the evaluation unit is new, it is high on the list of departments that will be scrutinized. Members are worried about the unit's survival and most decisions are made with an eye toward making the unit look good, or, at least, not look questionable to outside observers. Members are concerned with legitimizing the functions of the unit to the hospital.

These themes were identified from observation of a number of group meetings and form the backdrop for the controversy we will consider. In the meeting we will discuss (Case 6.3, Continued), the unit is evaluating a psychiatric intern who has repeatedly missed his turns of duty at evaluation clinics. In the ensuing discussion, disagreements emerge that the group must negotiate on its way to a decision.

Case 6.3 **The Psychological Evaluation Unit Continued**

Jerry, who chairs all meetings, introduces the issue. Talking for about five minutes, he gives a brief history of the intern's problems and summarizes his own attempts to talk to the intern. In particular, Jerry asked the intern what a proper attendance rate should be. The intern ventured a 10 percent absentee rate as an adequate figure. Jerry introduces this figure as a standard and then asks the others, "What do you think?" The psychologist and one social worker, Megan, ask what the intern's excuse is, and Jerry responds with a lengthy answer detailing the excuses and offering commentary on them. [One thing Jerry does here that reinforces his position of strength is to talk at length when he introduces the problem. The amount of time spent talking in a group has been shown to be both an indicator and a determinant of dominance in the group (Hayes & Meltzer, 1972; Folger, 1980; Folger & Sillars, 1980). Moreover, Jerry defines the problem based on his own perceptions and opinions, thereby keeping any conflict that might arise on his own "turf." Laura, who also knows about the problem, does not introduce it; although Jerry asks Laura if he is presenting the case accurately, he dominates the floor when the discussion is set up.]

Laura then speaks, arguing that once every two months is more than enough. Megan, one of the two social workers, jumps in, and this exchange follows:

MEGAN: You shouldn't even give him that (once every two months) . . . I mean, if an emergency comes up that's one thing. If you say you're gonna get off . . .

JERRY: (*interrupting*) This is not . . . This is not time that we expect him to take. This is how often we expect emergencies to occur.

MEGAN: But he's going to interpret it as if we're gonna give him a day or two every two months if we say it . . .

JERRY: (*nodding "no" as Megan speaks and speaking immediately on her last word*) It depends on how we want to say it, but what we had in mind was, if you look at how often he's here or not here—it's sort of a gross way to do an evaluation, but it's one possibility. And one could say, "If emergencies come up with more frequency, you need more time to attend to your emergencies and we could make an exception." How you word it might vary, but I think what we need is some kind of sense for what's tolerable.

FRANK: (*the other social worker*) What about the things he has done when he shows up—expectations as far as staying or leaving early. Which is . . . I think, one of many things. After his last patients, five or ten minutes later he's gone. And yesterday that happened and five minutes later we had a walk-in who really needed medical help, and I was the only one there and I could have used (help) . . . that was, you know, it was like 11:15 and he didn't show up. Don't we expect the interns to check to see if there are any walk-ins before they leave?

JERRY: (*interrupting*) We can talk about that as another issue . . .

FRANK: (*interrupting*) Well, it's another expectation that needs to be addressed . . .

At this point Laura clarifies her position on the intern's attendance, and the issue raised by Frank is dropped. In both cases Jerry cuts off the social workers, redefines the issues they raise, and turns the discussion back in the direction he has defined. That the other two psychiatrists tacitly support his approach reinforces the social workers' uncertainty and hesitancy. In effect, Jerry and the others are reproducing the suppressed climate of the group. This also allows Jerry to use the presumption of his dominance to "win" the argument.

Laura and Jerry then pursue a long exchange in which they try to define an acceptable level of participation for interns. Jerry's participation in this interchange is marked by his attempts to define criteria for evaluating the intern. For example:

LAURA: (*after a long speech*) . . . to vanish from sight (when patients need him), I just don 't find that acceptable. (pause)

JERRY: On the other hand, if it's 11:15, and you don't have any patients . . .
LAURA: (*interrupting*) That's a different issue.
JERRY: We don 't have to provide any options. We can say that we recognize that over a year and a half your participation has been mitigated because of unusual circumstances, and that's the end. I mean, we don't have to make a deal at all. . . .

[In this sequence Jerry attempts to help by raising another option available to the group. As group decision-making research has shown, the more options a group considers, the better its decision is likely to be. However, notice that Jerry still controls the definition of the issue. He does not respond to Laura's disagreement but shifts the discussion to another alternative, an alternative that he dismissed as a legitimate topic for discussion earlier. Since other members generally go along with these shifts, Jerry unwittingly maintains control. Moreover, since the way in which issues are defined is in line with Jerry's style of thinking and his particular concerns, other members of the group are caught off balance in discussions. They are not as prepared to work issues through to their conclusions as Jerry is, and so they come across as less competent or as having little to say. This is especially likely to be true of the social workers, who have very different backgrounds and less administrative experience than Jerry. The other two psychiatrists and, to a lesser extent, the psychologist raise their own issues, but these issues are usually redefined and commented on by Jerry. When Jerry raises an issue he has the advantage of forethought; he can think things through before the discussion because he dictates when it will begin.]

As the discussion progresses, the group tries to set an acceptable number of absences for the intern. After arguing back and forth, the group determines that setting an ideal attendance rate is impossible. Rather, members decide to talk to the intern in order to make him aware of the problem and then to reevaluate the situation in two months. Throughout this process Jerry moderates the discussion. He is responsive to concerns of the members but still sets the tone of the decision, as the following excerpts from the discussion suggest.

LAURA: I guess I agree. I want to give him time off . . . but if he's gonna be there, then he has to be there.
JERRY: But we have to come up with some kind of sense that if he exceeds we have to say "thank you, but no thank you."
LAURA: I'd say more than once in two months, or maybe twice in two months more than an hour late. Nobody else does that . . . that I know of . . . in terms of missing times.
MEGAN: (*talking over Laura's last sentences*) Rather than just specifically making a case for him maybe we should decide what's appropriate—what the expectations are for all the residents . . .
JERRY: (*interrupting*) I think we are. I think you're right that the kind of sense we're generating is not necessarily specific. . . . It turns out that he's going to be the one for whom it's an issue . . . and we also have to acknowledge that there will be individual circumstances that . . . change. We may need to face that. But I need to have some type of sense of what we expect of him and at what point we should acknowledge that he should or should not participate. And one way—it's sort of simple and artificial—is to do attendance, to say "How many

hours are you late? How many times are you late?'' That avoids in part coming to grips with, you know, an overall kind of evaluation, and maybe we don't want to use a numerical scale. I'm open to lots of different suggestions. The one that I wasn't willing to accept was that if others in the subspecialties used their own internal sets I wasn't going to ask them to change (i.e., other departments could evaluate the intern according to their own criteria) . . .

[Jerry continued to elaborate this position for another minute. Note that he interrupted Megan and gave a summary of how he sees the issues and what he is willing to accept. Note also that he spoke much longer than Megan.]

JOHN: I think there's a double-barreled threat (from the intern's absences). Dr. Jacobs (director of the hospital) is coming and casual conversation says (the intern) is OK when he's here, but he's never here, then clearly that's another, that's a threat . . .

JERRY: (*interrupting*) That's been defined. That one seems clear and has been addressed.

[In this passage, Jerry attempted to move the group on to another issue. He did so by interrupting John to tell him his first concern (of two) has been addressed. John never raised the second concern. The discussion moved on to another topic after Jerry's interruption.]

JERRY: (*summarizing the group's decision*) I'm comfortable if what the group wants to do, then, is take it back to (the intern) and say we have a set of expectations—they include your participation—your full participation—in this program. That we will reassess our impression of that participation—and we hope you will assess it—on a monthly basis or something and that if we need to—because there's some question of whether or not your participation is complete—then we'll meet and we'll need to talk about it.

[This is a fair summary of the group's decision, but it is cast in terms of what Jerry is comfortable with. He personalizes and takes charge of the group's decision.]

The inhibited climate of the group is not a result of total control over group decisions by Jerry: Jerry eventually gives in to the arguments of others and shifts his position away from setting a figure for absences. The group's climate results from the way in which the group manages its decision-making process, particularly actual or potential disagreements. Jerry's attempts to lead the group to an effective, efficient decision end up controlling the discussion. By persistently stepping in to restate, redefine, summarize, and comment, Jerry channels the discussion. The other members, with few exceptions, respond by following Jerry's lines of thought and thereby reinforce his control over the discussion and his resolutions of disagreements. The end result of this process is to create a sense that Jerry can and will jump in and redirect the discussion at any time, that he is an arbiter of opinions and suggestions in the group, and that lower-status members do not have as good a grasp of the priorities of the group as Jerry does. The social workers and the psychologist are hesitant and tense during meetings, and outside meetings they complain to each other and spend a good deal of time planning how to "get heard" in meetings.

Another striking feature of this decision is how much disagreement and frustration there are yet how little of this actually emerges in the discussion. Members, especially the weaker ones, are very restrained and try to speak in "reasoned, measured tones." Disagreements are rarely admitted, much less sharpened. Instead, Jerry (and to a lesser extent Laura) incorporates dissenting ideas into the final solution insofar as they fit. If dissenting opinions do not fit, they are cut off. Other members of the group do not seem to play an active role in changing the original proposal; they introduce ideas and passively allow them to be incorporated, relying on Jerry's willingness to cooperate. This pattern is in part due to the professionalized climate of the group, which works against strong expressions of disagreement, and in part due to members' acceptance of dominance relations in the group. But members' subdued behavior also reinforces these qualities of the group's climate: by assenting to "professionalism" and Jerry's leadership they are reproducing it.

None of these effects are necessarily intentional. Jerry makes honest attempts to be open to others' suggestions and often changes his stand in response. He asks others for their ideas and uses a lot of open questions (e.g., "What should we do here?") in an attempt to elicit their participation. However, Jerry's style—even when he is seeking only to clarify—translates ideas into his own terms and tends to stifle different points of view. His interruptions and lengthy answers prevent others from taking the initiative: they "disenfranchise" members with less forcefulness or less skill at managing interaction. Members' reactions to Jerry do little to counteract these tendencies and, in some cases, even reinforce them. Although the excerpts do not show it, when members speak, they direct most of their comments to Jerry. As we have noted, they also pick up on Jerry's comments and defer to him when he interrupts. Members are generally unaware (or only marginally aware) of these tendencies. They see themselves as trying to contribute—and perceive Jerry as trying to cut them off—without recognizing their own complicity in the process. The entire group "works together" to create and sustain the suppressed, hesitant, uncomfortable atmosphere.

In this example we have focused on how a climate is reproduced in interaction. However, interaction can also change climates. One bit of advice often given to lower-status members is simply to be more assertive, to speak up when issues concern them, and to resist interruptions. We believe this advice is sound, for the most part. To shift the climate of their group in a less suppressed direction members could, for example, make Jerry aware of his tendency to interrupt; they might also support each other when they attempt to redefine the problems facing the group. If Jerry is sincere about opening up the group, he will not resist these moves. This lack of resistance should, in turn, encourage further moves that will open up the group even more and reproduce the open climate. This opening up should not, however, be done in a fashion that threatens Jerry's authority. In the face of an openly divisive challenge Jerry is likely to strike back in order to save face and this could promote bitter, open conflict. In Chapters 4 and 5, where we discussed the dynamics of power and face-saving, there were some important qualifications of this analysis.

Moves that depart from the patterns implied in the prevailing climate function as "bids" for change in the group. If members follow up on these bids, they become institutionalized and have the potential to alter the group's climate. At least two laboratory studies have shown that clear and unambiguous changes in behavior could quickly change climates from cooperative to competitive or vice versa (Lindskold, Betz, & Walters, 1986). More often, however, bids are rejected by the group. Sometimes members simply fail to support an action that departs from accepted patterns, while in other cases dominant members actively suppress a bid for change. When members look back at successful bids for change, they often identify them as **critical incidents** (or turning points) in the life of the group. Critical incidents break up climates, either because they make members more aware of themselves or simply because they are so striking that members unconsciously pick up on them and perpetuate new patterns. Once interaction patterns are changed, they generalize to climates, and if they change for a long enough period, the prevailing climate changes. Unfortunately, we do not know enough about critical incidents to specify what allows a bid to become a turning point. In general, however, the bid must catch the attention and imagination of members, it must address some deep-seated problem in the group, and it must not move powerful members to organize against it.

The interaction–climate relationship is a complex one and works on several levels. **Climates are maintained and changed through specific actions that are relevant to particular issues and concerns.** Jerry's tendency to jump on people implicitly told members who wished to enter into the discussion that the group (specifically, Jerry) was judgmental and therefore likely to criticize or reject their contributions.

Donald Roy's famous case study of a factory work group, "Banana Time," provides another good example (Roy, 1959). In this study Roy took a job in a factory assembling plastic raincoats so that he could observe how workers dealt with boring and repetitive work. He was assigned to a work unit with three other workers who soon "taught him the ropes" and included him in their social circle. Games, jokes, and teasing provided the major escape for Roy's comrades. Usually all would participate with enthusiasm in these incidents, but Roy observed one instance when a joke backfired and disrupted the group's congenial atmosphere. When one member (Ike) teased another member with higher status (George) about his son-in-law (who was a college professor), George blew up and withdrew from Ike. George would not speak to Ike, with whom he had formerly been very close, and Ike's apologies were ignored. The normally pleasant atmosphere of the group was poisoned. The group gradually returned to normal, but George's message was clear: there were limits on teasing in the group. George's outburst defined (and perhaps narrowed) the latitude members had in their relationships, and thereafter the group was more restrained for some time.

Because climates are generalized, interaction influences climate on a second level: **changes in one theme can generalize to other related themes.** In the psychiatric unit, Jerry's controlling moves in group discussions directly maintained dominance relationships. However, they also influenced members' sense of the safety and supportiveness of the group. If one's contributions are likely to be overruled or ignored, one is unlikely to feel highly regarded or safe in a group. George's reactions to Ike pertained not only to emotional relationships in the group but indirectly to the group's sense of its own identity. Roy commented that the work group fell apart for all practical purposes when George refused to speak to Ike. The lack of supportiveness threatened the group's effectiveness and called the group's sense of itself into question.

At a third level, **interaction can create a climate that temporarily overshadows more enduring qualities of a social unit**. In the psychological evaluation unit, a meeting several weeks after the one examined above exhibited a much more relaxed atmosphere. The group discussed a schedule of in-service meetings members would present over the next year. Interaction was relatively uninhibited, and both social workers contributed freely on topics that fell in their areas of expertise. Jerry talked no more than any other member, and the other two psychiatrists facilitated the meeting in a noncontrolling manner. For this one meeting, the tensions in the group disappeared. Perhaps due to differences in topic, perhaps to a fortunate conjunction of moods, the group's interaction cast an altogether different spell. For the time being, a more spontaneous, open atmosphere prevailed, and the joking and excitement evident in the meeting reflected this more fraternal attitude. At the next meeting members were more inhibited, though not as tense as before. The previous climate, marked by quandaries about power relations and safety, had reasserted itself.

Because they are sustained by interaction, climates are vulnerable to temporary shifts due to temporary alterations of interaction patterns. These shifts can be beneficial, as in the evaluation unit, or they can present problems, for example, when a normally harmonious group is disrupted by a "no holds barred" fight between two members. The shifts, however, are also vulnerable to the reassertion of the former climate. The longer the climate has been sustained, the deeper its grooves are worn, and the more likely the traditional quality of the social unit is to reassert itself. It is only by hard work that a temporary improvement in climate can be institutionalized.

As we have shown, climates are created and maintained by particular events in interaction. However, because climates are generalized and diffuse, it is easy for members to forget this. Members are often aware of a change in the tone of the group soon after a critical incident occurs. It is hard, for example, to miss the connection between an insult and increased tension. However, if the tension persists and becomes a part of the prevailing climate, the climate tends to become second nature. Members forget that climate depends on how they interact and assume the social unit is "just that way," that the enduring qualities of the group are independent of what people do. When this happens, it becomes a **trained incapacity** like those discussed in Chapter 3. In failing to realize that they themselves hold the key to maintaining or changing the climate, members are thereby controlled by the climate. Like the social workers in the psychological evaluation unit, members may assume they have to keep acting as they do because they have no alternatives. This assumption is responsible for the tendency of climates to reproduce themselves rather than change.

In closing this section, it is necessary to introduce an important qualification: throughout this discussion we have spoken as though every social unit has a well-defined climate. This is not always the case. Climates are generalizations from interaction, and they can only emerge insofar as group interaction has at least some consistent, characteristic patterns in the social unit. Most social units exhibit such patterns, however sketchy. Even though most of the attendees at the Columnist's Brown Bag (Case 3.3) had never met, the group developed a definite atmosphere, because participants freely entered into the exploratory, question-and-answer format. The group evolved a pleasant climate that was threatened by the challenge to the speaker.

However, if a social unit's interaction patterns vary frequently and unpredictably, there is no foundation for a coherent climate. Groups of people thrown together for an "exercise" in a class or workshop are often chaotic, because members have no knowledge of each other and no commitment to future interaction. As a result, they act only for themselves and the group as a whole develops no coherent themes. Even more difficult are social units beset by a crisis, often in the form of an unexpected and bitter fight between two important members. In conflicts of this type members often feel their relationship, group, or organization is falling apart; they lose their bearings because the situation gives them no clues for predicting what will happen next. This is in part because the conflict introduces a whole new situation, one that is incompatible with the traditional climate, but not clear enough to institute a new climate.

How definite a social unit's climate is depends on its degree of structure. Social units range on a continuum from very rigid and structured to almost chaotic, and climates may range accordingly. This should not imply, however, that change in a social unit is synonymous with lack of structure. In fact, most changes use existing structures and do not require a radical break in the prevailing climate. Even fundamental alterations in climate often occur gradually and result in relatively little disruption. Only when change calls the existing basis of the social unit into question at once does it throw the unit into chaos. This does not happen often, but it is important to recognize that it can happen, and that when it does, all bets are off so far as climate is concerned.

IDENTIFYING CLIMATES

Because climates are so diffuse, yet so important, it is critical for people to be able to identify them. Unless people can detect and work on climate, it will remain a nebulous, "untamed" force, always liable to "get away" from people and impart a harmful momentum to interaction. Our discussion implies several guidelines for the diagnosis of climates.

(1)   Climate themes can only be identified by **observing the entire group for an extended period**. Although exchanges between key members—for example, George and Carole at Riverdale—may play an important role in the group, they must be generalized and influence other members' interchanges to become part of the unit's climate. To become a "relatively enduring" feature of a social unit, interchanges "with the same feel" must occur repeatedly and be recognized as characteristic of the unit by members. This implies that climate themes should permeate interaction and that those that are most enduring and significant will tend to emerge most frequently over time.

(2)   To diagnose climate it is necessary to focus on interaction. Talking with members is a critical part of diagnosis. The consultant got most of her initial ideas

about Riverdale by interviewing the staff members involved in the conflict. However, members' ideas will always be somewhat biased. One member may be angry at another and therefore attempt to cast that person in a negative light by claiming he or she causes problems. In other cases, members will bias their accounts in order to make themselves look good. Thomas and Pondy (1977) interpreted their finding that business employees reported their own conflict behavior as generally cooperative to be a tendency on the part of their subjects to perceive themselves more favorably than they perceived others. In some cases, members' reports will be biased because they are unaware of their own behavior and therefore do not see themselves as part of the problem. In the Riverdale case neither George nor Carole were aware that their own behavior contributed to the conflict; each blamed the other and believed the other had to change to resolve the conflict. Because individual oral or written accounts are thus "contaminated," they cannot be the sole source of evidence on climate. Accounts can give us initial insights, but these must be checked by **observing how members interact**. If observations based on interaction are consistent with reports, then the conclusions in the reports can be trusted, at least to some extent.

However, if interaction is inconsistent with reports, the inconsistency itself can be an important source of information about the group. One of the authors was working with a city-wide charitable group to try to resolve arguments over its budget. The secretary of the charitable group had confided that he believed the president always favored funding proposals by groups in which she had special interests. However, on observing several meetings, the consultant noted that the president was fairly objective, whereas the secretary pushed his own interests very strongly. This suggested the secretary had trouble monitoring his own behavior and had projected his personal tensions and biases onto the president, who was threatening because she stood in the way of his priorities. The consultant took the secretary aside in a confrontational manner to discuss the problem, and, for a while, the secretary was able to take his biases into account. (The group later reverted to its old bickering, however, because of problems in following the third party's advice.)

Only by **cross-checking individual's oral or written accounts, minutes of meetings, other historical records, and actual observations** can an accurate estimate of climate be made. This need for cross-checking has a particularly important implication for members trying to diagnose their own relationships or groups: they need to talk to other members (and to outside observers, if available) to get their views. Their own views represent only one perspective and may yield biased perceptions. There is no privileged vantage point; even the external observer can be subject to misperceptions: all views must be cross-checked to identify climates accurately.

(3) The four categories discussed earlier (see Table 6.1) supply some ideas of the types of themes likely to emerge in climates. Most of these themes can be interpreted as answers to questions of concern in these categories—for instance, is power evenly distributed? **Metaphors** used by group members are a particularly fertile source of themes. Often they contain unconscious associations capable of telling us more about the group's sense of itself than any member's account. For example, one college department we are acquainted with described itself with a "family" metaphor. Members repeatedly referred to the department "family," and people being interviewed for faculty positions were told the department was like a

"big family." In line with this metaphor several faculty members filled the slots reserved for father, mother, uncle, and aunt. Even the problems and conflicts in the faculty related to issues of authority and independence often associated with parent–child or parent–parent relationships. Patterns of conflict behavior in the department reflected the family metaphor to some extent: the "father" tried to take charge of the situation, and the "mother" tried to soothe those involved and sympathized with them. The "children" were rebellious but unsure of themselves and tended to knuckle under when the "father" applied pressure. Of course, the family metaphor should not be carried too far in this case, because it was not the only force affecting conflict behavior. However, it did give some insights into the workings of the department that could not have been gleaned from direct questioning of the faculty. Because the precise details of meaning are only **implicit** in a metaphor, people will often use metaphors, whereas they would not provide an explicit description carrying similar meaning. This makes them very valuable as a means of understanding a group.

In some cases a metaphor or theme will be expanded considerably, into an entire fantasy for the group. Bormann (1986) has discussed the dynamics of fantasy themes and their roles in holding a group together. In particular, he argues that fantasy themes often develop as a drama, with a definite plot, scene, and distinguishable heroes and villains. These dramas provide a deeper meaning for group life and help members understand their world and guide their actions. Building on his work, Cragan and Shields (1981) analyzed fantasy themes in a fire station in St. Paul, Minnesota. The firefighters saw themselves as heroic, courageous professionals acting in a dangerous situation. In order to do so, they needed to be dedicated, competent team players, able to get along with others and get the job done. They emphasized self-confidence and "were willing to let their actions do the talking." An integral part of the fire station's climate was also the belief that the public thought of firefighters as having a soft job, being reckless in fighting fires, and being undependable and slow. So the vision emerges of courageous, professional people performing heroic and hazardous duty, but who are misunderstood and disliked by the very people they save. This interpretation of their world is likely to promote the supportiveness necessary to carry the firefighters through their hazardous duties. It also promotes a sense of the fire company as a misunderstood and badly treated group, setting firefighters off against an ignorant and ungrateful public. Clearly this may have important effects both on how firefighters interact with each other in conflicts and how open they are to citizen complaints. Likely this perception of distance from the ungrateful public would cause firefighters to use avoidance strategies and "stonewall" any citizen complaints.

Of course, not all themes will be as well developed as those in this firehouse. Many climates are much more literal and consist of themes or ideas devoted to the particular social unit itself with little dramatization or exaggeration. Nonetheless, **metaphors and dramatic self-descriptions** are one of our best sources of clues about a climate.

(4)   Intuition (unverbalized knowledge) can and does play an important role in the diagnosis of climates. Because most of us have spent considerable time in relationships, groups, or organizations, we have experienced climates firsthand and

therefore know at least what some climates "feel" like. The problem is developing our intuitions to the point where we can verbalize and work with them. This chapter is designed to help in this process, but **practice** in becoming attuned to climates as we experience them is the real key.

CREATING CONSTRUCTIVE CLIMATES

To this point, we have studiously avoided discussing any sort of "ideal" climate because we wanted to emphasize the complexity and diversity of climates. However, several writers have described an "ideal climate" that is likely to lead to productive conflict management. The most famous description comes from an article by Jack R. Gibb titled "Defensive Communication." He addresses the problem of how to create a climate that prevents defensive behavior. In order to define this climate, Gibb contrasts two types of climates, defensive and supportive. A defensive climate is one in which parties perceive or anticipate threats. A defensive person devotes a great deal of energy to protecting himself or herself and focuses on defeating the other. Defensiveness prevents one from listening fully to others' messages. The defensive person often distorts or misinterprets these messages to confirm his or her own sense of threat and danger. Moreover, defensiveness causes the person to behave in a way that makes others defensive too. Gibb (1961, p. 141) comments that "defensive behavior, in short, engenders defensive listening, and this in turn produces postural, facial, and verbal cues which raise the defense level of the original communicator." Conversely, a supportive climate tends to produce accurate communication and to reinforce supportive behavior in others. Producing a supportive climate gives a conflict its best chance to move in a productive direction.

All this should sound pretty familiar in light of the earlier discussions. However, Gibb takes this one step further and describes how to communicate in order to produce a supportive, as opposed to a defensive, climate. He discusses six categories of behavior on which defensive and supportive climates contrast.

According to Gibb, a defensive climate is produced by communication that is **evaluative**, while a supportive climate is encouraged by **descriptive** language. For example, an evaluative statement "You are messy and inconsiderate!" might be reframed as the descriptive message, "Your things were scattered around the living room this morning." No one likes to be judged, and evaluative language implies judgment. Once a judgment is made the other cannot try to reason with it; it is final. The only option the other has is to reject the judgment, thus erecting barriers between the parties. Evaluation also implies that the communicator does not grant legitimacy to the person's arguments or position. By contrast, descriptive language leaves the field open for discussion. The other can explain that the room is not really cluttered by his or her standards. Descriptive statements tend to open up dialogue, while evaluative statements tend to close off communication, leaving resistance or avoidance as the primary options.

The wording of statements plays an important role in determining whether they are evaluative, but nonverbal communication is also important. As Gibb (1961, p. 142) puts it:

Anyone who has attempted to train professionals to use information-seeking speech with neutral affect appreciates how difficult it is to teach a person to say even the simple "Who did that?" without being seen as accusing. Speech is so frequently judgmental that there is a reality base for the defensive interpretations which are so common.

A second type of characteristic of communication that encourages defensiveness is that it is **controlling.** Speech that attempts to control the other often fosters resistance, especially in conflict situations. This can be contrasted with supportive communication, which is more **problem-oriented**. Rather than trying to get the other to do what the speaker wants, problem-oriented messages try to define a problem on which both can work. So rather than saying "Stop talking so loudly!" which attempts to tell the other what to do, we might say, "You are talking too loudly and this is making it hard to hear Jack," which designates this as a problem to be dealt with. The other can dispute the definition of the problem, or explain why he or she is talking loudly, or apologize, but the choice is left to the other person by how the statement is phrased. Of course, the history of a relationship influences whether a statement will be taken as controlling or not. Even statements phrased in a problem-oriented fashion may be perceived as controlling if one person has used them to manipulate the other in the past.

Third, defensive climates are promoted by statements that seem **strategic**. Supportive climates are promoted by **spontaneous** messages. "When the sender is perceived as engaged in a stratagem involving ambiguous and multiple motivations, the receiver becomes defensive" (Gibb, 1961, p. 145). If we believe a message that seems like a sincere request on the surface is really a tactic to get us to do something we would not otherwise want to do, we are likely to react defensively. Deception promotes reaction. On the other hand, if "what we see is what we get," if the other is sincere and open, then we are likely to respond more spontaneously as well. People are not always reluctant to give others what they want, but they may be reluctant to be forced to do so.

A fourth speech characteristic that creates defensiveness is apathy toward us by the other. If the other's speech is **neutral**, it often conveys the message that they do not care about us. On the other hand, **empathetic** speech styles, which indicate true concern for the other, promote supportive climates. To create a supportive climate it is important to acknowledge the legitimacy of the other's emotions and needs, to empathize with him or her. This does not imply agreement with the other's demands, merely acceptance of them as real, legitimate concerns.

Defensiveness may also result when the other's messages convey a sense of **superiority** in position, power, wealth, intelligence, family background, education, or physical attributes. Gibb reasons that such statements cause defensiveness because they cause the listener to "center upon the affect loading of the statement" rather than its content. "The receiver then reacts by not hearing the message, by forgetting it, by competing with the sender, or by becoming jealous of him" (Gibb, 1961, p. 147). To promote a supportive climate it is important that sender and receiver perceive common ground, a shared, problem-solving relationship. Communication should convey **equality** between the parties. Although differences may exist between sender and receiver, it is important to attach little importance to them in the situation.

Finally, defensiveness is encouraged by messages that seem **certain** and dogmatic. Statements that assert they are the final word on an issue leave the other with little control over the interaction and may provoke resistance. Anyone who has talked with a dogmatic "know-it-all" has experienced the reactions to certainty that create a defensive climate. Messages that convey the attitude that one is willing to experiment with ideas and to change one's own position are more likely to create a supportive climate. So ideal messages should have a **provisional** quality. Rather than saying "You are always late for meetings," it may be better to say something like, "It seems like you've been late quite a bit lately." A less absolute and more provisional message encourages the other to think over your comment and leaves room for a constructive response.

It is hard to ensure that our communication style avoids the six characteristics of defensive communication and fits the six characteristics conducive to supportive climates. Most of us habitually communicate in ways that provoke defensiveness. But a more supportive style can be learned. To start, you might try to write down what you said in a case when someone else became defensive and evaluate this according to the six categories. Think of how you might rephrase your comments in a more supportive fashion. There is no guarantee that adopting a supportive communication style will cause the other to be supportive as well. However, it offers the best chance for success and is well worth trying.

CONCLUSION

On sheet music, composers describe the emotional tenor of the piece they have written in a short phrase above the first measure. Phrases like "allegro agitato," "appasionato," or "tenderly" are instructions that tell the performer what mood the piece should convey to an audience. In some ways, climates are like these musical instructions. They do not specify the "notes," the specific behaviors members undertake. Instead, they give an indication of the expected tone or temper for interaction. Climates reduce members' uncertainty about how to act and about how to interpret others' actions by providing a simple, general idea—a "feel"—of the situation and of whether things are right or wrong, appropriate or out of place. This is particularly important in the uneasy uncertainty of conflict; the general temper of the situation surrounding a conflict is a critical determinant of whether it takes a productive or destructive direction. A hostile, tense climate can make escalation inevitable; a cooperative climate can turn the same situation toward problem-solving.

Climates are composed of general themes expressing members' beliefs and feelings about the social unit and its leading problems or concerns. We discussed four major categories of themes, those that (1) concern dominance and authority relations, (2) relate to the supportiveness that group members show toward one another, (3) express the group's sense of its own identity, and (4) concern the type of interdependence among group members. These general categories do not exhaust the variety of possible conflict themes, but they do represent the areas most commonly found in climate analyses.

Climates are the product of interaction. Climatic themes shape conflict interaction, and conflict interaction moves in a cyclical fashion to reproduce (and sometimes to change) climates. This cycle leaves an opening for those who would like to change the climate. Changes in interaction and critical incidents can alter climates by creating new behavioral precedents and by making members aware of undesirable ruts into which their group may have fallen. Changes in interaction set up new expectations for the future and raise new issues that may persist and change the climate if sustained by people's actions. As the "composer" of its own interaction, a social unit changes the instructions on how behaviors will be played out and interpreted. These shifts in climate come as the people hear their own changes in emotional pitch; they become a strong influence on the forms that conflict interaction takes.

Chapter
7

Doing Conflict: Styles, Strategies, and Tactics

What is the best way to handle conflicts? Should we stick to one approach or be flexible? Should we let other parties have a say or try to control the situation? Should we carefully plan how we will react or improvise? And how do we avoid getting caught up in spiraling escalation or avoidance cycles?

A common recommendation is that parties should try to plan a conscious **strategy** for the conflict. One example of strategic planning is when parties rehearse what they are going to say. Along with the well-planned strategy would come carefully selected **tactics**, actions for carrying out the strategy. While sound advice in general, this approach overemphasizes the degree to which people can plan interactions. The key to an effective strategy is the ability to control the situation. However, conflicts are the product of two or more parties' interaction, and often parties move in quite different directions. In the face of the others' moves, it is often hard to stick to plans (even if we can remember them after the other party has succeeded in flustering or upsetting us). Also, it is often hard to determine which tactics will serve a given strategy. An openly belligerent approach, for example, can serve strategies of avoidance (by scaring the other so much that he or she avoids the conflict) or integration (by convincing the other that the party is serious enough to want to fight over the issue), as well as forcing.

Rather than overemphasizing planning, it is more useful to work on mastering various **styles** of doing conflict. The notion of style **emphasizes a consistent, specific orientation** toward the conflict, an orientation that unifies specific tactics into a coherent whole, yet does not stress planning and foresight too much. As we will see, research indicates that people have characteristic conflict-handling styles, which they tend to apply regardless of differences in situations. However, you can teach old dogs new tricks. People can learn new behaviors if they are aware of alternatives. Moreover, there is evidence that people change styles as disputes develop. Therefore it is useful to consider conflict and negotiation styles as a repertoire of options that people can learn to apply.

There will always be an element of strategy in the selection of styles, but it is important to emphasize the **emergent** nature of conflict interaction. Interactions can take many directions, and about the best one can hope for is to be responsive to changes as the conflict unfolds. Of course this still leaves all the original questions intact. How do we select an appropriate style? When should we change styles? What are the long-run consequences of various styles? How do we select the proper tactics to carry out styles?

It is also important to remember that the strategies or styles are not the only things to which we have to attend. The development of conflicts is also shaped by **individual actions or tactics.** Many of us have experienced this firsthand: a conflict seems to be moving constructively, but then someone says "the wrong thing" and everything falls apart. Another example of this is when individual acts set up a cascade of escalation moves, creating the type of self-perpetuating conflict we discussed in Chapter 3. So it is also important to consider tactics and their possible influence on conflict interaction.

CONFLICT STYLES

To be able to choose conflict styles, it is important to know what they require and what their potential consequences are. This section describes various conflict styles and specifies a set of rules for selecting styles.

Describing Styles

To understand styles it is useful to consider some basic concepts that describe styles and their effects on the other party. In Chapter 1 we briefly described the five traditional conflict styles—competing, avoiding, accommodating, compromising, and problem-solving. We noted that they can be distinguished along two dimensions: **assertiveness**—the degree to which the style attempts to satisfy the party's concerns with respect to the issues—and **cooperativeness**—the degree to which the style attempts to satisfy the other party's concerns. Four additional dimensions of style can be identified. Sillars, Colleti, Parry, and Rogers (1982) defined **disclosiveness**—the degree to which a conflict style or tactic discloses information to the other party—as a basic dimension of conflict behavior. Disclosiveness is closely related to the maintenance of an open communication climate. Styles also differ in **empowerment**—the degree to which they grant the other party some control or power. Some styles hinge on the party's control of the situation, others share control between the two parties, and others give control to the other party. Hence styles can have an effect on the balance of power and its impacts on conflicts, as discussed in Chapter 4. **Activeness** (Riggs, 1983) represents the degree of involvement with conflict issues. Parties' activeness may range from very intense concern to apathy. Finally, styles may differ in **flexibility**—the degree of movement the party is willing to make in working out the conflict (Ruble & Thomas, 1976; Riggs, 1983). Some styles allow for considerable pliability in the party's position, whereas others are quite rigid in their insistence that the initial position not be changed.

Thinking in terms of these dimensions can clarify the differences among styles. The dimensions also help us link tactics to various styles, because they can be used to classify tactics. The section on tactics discusses general sets of tactics in terms of these dimensions so that they can be matched to respective styles.

Each of the five styles introduced in Chapter 1 has a unique set of values on the six dimensions, as the description of the boldfaced headings in Table 7.1 shows. So, for example, parties who adopt a competing style place a great deal of emphasis on their own concerns and little on those of the other party; they are not very disclosive or flexible; and they are highly involved in the conflict and attempt to maximize their control over the situation and to minimize that of the other party. Table 7.1 is a starting point for understanding the styles and the consequences of using them.

Table 7.1 CONFLICT STYLES AND THEIR VARIANTS RATED ON SIX DIMENSIONS

Conflict Style	Assertive	Cooperative	Disclosive	Empowerment		Active	Flexible
				Self	Other		
Competing	High	Low	Low to moderate	Yes	No	High	Low to moderate
Forcing	High	Low	Low	Yes	No	High	Low
Contending	High	Low	Moderate	Yes	No	High	Moderate
Avoiding	Low	Low	Low to moderate	Varies	No	Varies	Low to moderate
Protecting	Low	Low	Low	Yes	No	High	Low
Withdrawing	Low	Low	Low–moderate	No	No	Low	Moderate
Smoothing	Low	Low	Moderate	No	No	Moderate	Moderate
Accommodating	Low	High	Low to moderate	No	Yes	Low to moderate	Moderate to high
Yielding	Low	High	Low	No	Yes	Low	High
Conceding	Low	High	Moderate	No	Yes	Low to moderate	Moderate to high
Compromising	Moderate	Moderate	Low to moderate	Yes	Yes	Moderate to high	Moderate to high
Firm compromiser	Moderate	Moderate	Low–moderate	Yes	Yes	High	High
Flexible compromiser	Moderate	Moderate	Moderate	Yes	Yes	Moderate	Moderate
Problem-solving	High	High	High	Yes		High	High

Much research has been directed to defining and measuring conflict styles. The articles in Putnam (1988) examine five different instruments designed to measure conflict styles: Hall's (1969) Conflict Management Survey, the Thomas and Kilman (1974) Management-of-Differences (MODE) Survey, Rahim's (1983) Organizational Conflict Inventory–II, the Putnam and Wilson (1982) Organizational Communication Conflict Instrument, and the Ross and DeWine (1988) Conflict Management Message Style Instrument. Each of these instruments identifies somewhat different styles or dimensions underlying conflict, but in general their styles can be related to the five defined here. The instruments by Putnam and Wilson and Ross and DeWine are specifically focused on communication behaviors in conflicts and are therefore of special interest.

As the plethora of measurement instruments suggests, there are several different ways to conceive of conflict styles. We now attempt to sort out several different interpretations of conflict styles.

The Meaning of Conflict Styles

Some writers, like Filley (1975), define style as the **way a person usually responds to conflict**. In this view the styles identify types of people—the "tough battler," the "friendly helper," "the problem-solver"—who are predisposed to handle all conflicts in the same way. This tradition has strongly influenced how the tests that measure a person's predominant style of conflict-handling behavior have been interpreted. Although the way the tests are scored allows people to fall under more than one style (e.g., people are often classified as compromisers **and** problem-solvers), styles are interpreted as a relatively **stable** aspect of the individual's personality. Several studies have yielded evidence that people develop habitual styles of responding to conflict, which are consistent across situations (Gormly, Gormly, & Johnson, 1972; Jones & Melcher, 1982; Sternberg & Soriano, 1984).

We believe this view is somewhat misleading: while people certainly develop habitual ways of responding to conflict, they also have a capacity to change or adapt their behavior from situation to situation. There is abundant evidence (Phillips & Cheston, 1979) that people **change** their conflict behavior during the conflict process (Phillips & Cheston, 1979; Sillars, 1980; Papa & Natalle, 1989; Sambamurthy & Poole, 1991). There is also evidence that more effective people are more flexible in their responses to situations (Hill, 1974; Stogdill, 1974; Phillips & Cheston, 1979). In the larger view, an extensive body of research on personality traits has shown that they do not lead to consistent behavior in all situations (Mischel, 1968; Endler & Magnusson, 1976). Two recent studies showed very low correlations between conflict styles and personality traits such as dogmatism, deference, and Machiavellianism (manipulativeness) (Jones & Melcher, 1982). People can and do adapt and change, and denying this capacity through the assumption of fixed styles denies an important human potential.

Taught to large numbers of people this view could even be harmful. If people assume their styles are stable traits, they may not be motivated to change in order to break out of destructive patterns. If a supervisor assumes an employee is a "tough battler" and will always be one, he or she is likely to go into any disagreement with the employee with a belligerent, "they're-not-going-to-run-over-me" attitude that greatly increases the possibility of destructive escalation. Alternatively, the supervisor may just give in to avoid the employee's wrath but later resent this act of submission. Neither response is a good one; not only do both responses increase the probability of destructive conflict and bad decision-making, but they also deny the worker's ability to change. Assuming that the other person is inflexible may discourage parties from trying different approaches. The boss' anticipatory attack may make the employee respond as a "tough battler" as a defense, even though the worker would actually have preferred to discuss the issue quietly. Expectations about "how people are" too easily turn into self-fulfilling prophecies: they lead individuals to act toward others in ways that cause others to respond with the undesirable but expected behaviors. They freeze others into a mold that prevents the flexible and responsive behavior needed for effective conflict management. This problem is compounded when people believe they themselves have a characteristic personal style. "I'm a battler," they say and assume they cannot or do not have to be flexible, because "that's just the way I am." Thus conflict training programs and tests that purport to identify "characteristic styles" may worsen the very conflicts they are intended to help. People do fall into habits, but they can also change.

A second view of style turns away from personal characteristics and defines styles as specific **types of conflict behavior** (Cosier & Ruble, 1981). In this view, any behavior intended to defeat the other—for example, making a threat—is competitive, while a behavior designed to achieve a mutually acceptable solution—for example, restating the conflict in problem-oriented terms—is collaboration. The styles refer to **categories of behavior**, not types of people. This definition is an improvement over the previous one, because it neither assumes nor encourages inflexibility. However, it too has a problem: the same behavior can fall under different styles. A threat, for example, can be classed under competing, but it could also be classed under avoiding if it were intended to keep an opponent from raising a conflict ("I'll leave if you bring that up any more"). Postponing a conflict is often advocated as a problem-solving tactic because it gives both sides a "cooling off" period, but it can also be an avoiding tactic if used persistently. An offer to "split the difference" is certainly a compromise, but it can also be accommodating if what the offerer gets is of little value and he or she did it simply to avoid losing. There is a good deal of truth in the definition of styles as behaviors, but a third interpretation offers a more accurate conception of styles.

The third, and most useful, position defines styles as **behavioral orientations people can take toward conflict** (Thomas, 1975). In this view a style is a general expectation about how the conflict should be approached, an attitude about how best to deal with the other party. A competing style is oriented toward defeating the other, toward achieving one's own goals without regard for the others, and it dictates certain behavioral choices to achieve these ends. A problem-solving style reflects an orientation toward mutual benefit. It favors moves that enhance cooperation and creative thinking toward this end. The definition of styles as orientations solves the problem of classifying specific behaviors under one or the other style: the same tactics can serve different intentions and attitudes. Moreover, this definition is true to the observations showing that people exhibit definite, consistent strategies or thrusts during conflicts without denying their capacity to change. Choosing an orientation is making a decision about the principles that will guide one through the conflict; it is choosing the degree to which parties will be cooperative and/or assertive.

According to this definition, behavioral strategies and general orientations are bound up with each other, because behaviors are not meaningful outside the context of the style they represent. So the behavior of postponing the conflict can be seen in one way if it is part of a problem-solving style and in another if the party is avoiding. While Conrad (1991) usefully discusses the distinction between behavioral strategy and styles, it does not seem possible to draw a clean line, as he tries to do. In this book we have chosen to emphasize that strategy is a planned sequence of behaviors, whereas style is a general orientation that does not require explicit behavioral planning.

The ultimate problem with this definition (or with any definition of style for that matter) is its focus on the individual. Style refers to the orientation of the individual in conflict; it reflects one person's approach independent of the other person. Certainly, any action starts with an individual's behavioral choices. However, in the long run, it is inaccurate to stay at the level of the individual. We must take the interlocking actions of all parties into account. Styles represent the "mind sets" that parties have in the conflict, but what another person does often changes one's attitudes and intentions, often without the individual realizing it. Someone may go into a disagreement with a firm intention to problem-solve, but if the other person betrays, or viciously attacks, or refuses to talk about the conflict at all, it is hard to keep problem-solving. The other's reactions make one want to defend oneself, or strike back, or scream in exasperation, or withdraw completely. Whatever the response and reaction to that response, it makes no sense to talk of strategies or styles as if they were independent of the other's actions. Conrad (1991) summarizes substantial evidence that the actual behaviors people engage in during conflicts differ from how they expect to behave. He attributes this largely to the influence of the others' behavior.

In line with this concern with style as behavioral orientations that interact with others' orientations, we have used gerunds to name each style. This is because the "-ing" form indicates the active process involved in using a style. Styles are not something people simply put on and forget about, but something they must perform. In our descriptions of styles we will refer to the parties who carry out styles with the "-er" or "or" suffix: a party employing competing will be called a competer, a party using accommodating an accommodator, and so on. This is purely for ease of expression and not because we think the styles are traits of the people who use them.

Variations on Conflict Styles

Riggs (1983; see also Savage, Blair, & Sorenson, 1989) suggests that there may be variations on styles that are consistent with the general orientation but represent different ways of carrying out the style. This is illustrated in Figure 7.1 (a revised version of Figure 1.4), which shows the five styles not as single points but as regions on the graph. So, for example, a supervisor using a competing style may "pull out all

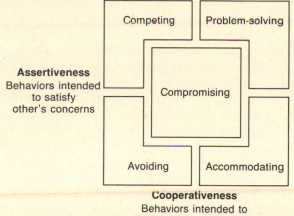

Figure 7.1 A revision of Figure 1.4, showing styles as "regions" on the graph.

the stops" and push for his own goals, showing no concern at all for his staff, or he may use his authority to gain staff members' compliance, but acknowledge their feelings and explain the necessity for his orders. These are very different ways of carrying out a competing style, and they are likely to have different consequences for the supervisor's future relationship with the staff. In general, styles take a limited range of values on each of the six dimensions, rather than a single value. As we turn now to defining styles, it is important to try to identify variations. Styles and their primary variants are shown in Table 7.1.

Competing This style is marked by a primary emphasis on satisfying the party's own concerns and disregard of others' concerns. It is a closed style, low to moderate in disclosiveness; parties make their demands apparent but often hide their true motives and any other information that might weaken their position. Competers are quite active and highly involved in the conflict. Competers aggressively pursue personal goals, taking any initiatives necessary to achieve them. Flexibility is generally low in the competing style. Competers attempt to avoid sacrificing any goals, instead using any effective means to compel others to satisfy their concerns. This requires that competers attempt to control the situation and to deny others power or control.

There are two major variants of the competing style. In **forcing**, parties exhibit very low flexibility and disclosiveness and simply try to get others to go along with them by virtue of superior power. There is no expression of concern or understanding for the other's position, nor any effort to build or to preserve a future relationship.

Contending is a "softer" form of competing. A contending style is somewhat flexible with the other, as long as flexibility does not threaten to prevent the party from attaining his or her goals. A contending style is also moderately disclosive. Contenders may try to explain why they are compelling others and they may also express understanding and sympathy for others' feelings. A contending style is concerned with future relationships.

Research indicates that utilizing authority to compel others to accept a resolution to a conflict is more effective if the superior explains why the decision was made (Phillips & Cheston, 1979). Bies, Shapiro, and Cummings (1988) add that the explanation must be based on "objective" factors, such as company norms or budget constraints, rather than on the superior's preferences. This suggests that contending may be more effective than forcing in long-term working relationships. However, forcing is less time-consuming than contending, and it does not require the effort of maintaining a good relationship with others. In some cases, this may be a low priority.

In general, competing styles tend to be selected by managers when the outcomes of conflicts are very important to them and when achieving an agreement through other means seems unlikely (Phillips & Cheston, 1979). Competing, especially forcing, is often advantageous when there is pressure to come to a resolution quickly, because competers can push their own agendas through. However, when employing a competing style it is important to bear in mind that it may create resentment that leads to resistance later on. This may be a significant problem if the cooperation of other parties is critical in implementing the decision. Moreover, as noted in Chapter 4, use of a power resource in competing may ultimately undermine one's power base.

Avoiding   Parties who avoid conflict show low levels of concern with both their own and other parties' concerns. Avoiding prevents these concerns from being aired and addressed. There is, of course, one exception: when parties use avoiding to get out of conflicts they fear they will "lose." But even in this case, issues remain unresolved and may resurface in the future. Avoiders choose a low level of activeness, sometimes bordering on apathy. They exhibit a low level of disclosiveness as well, because avoiding prevents parties from communicating about concerns or positions. An avoiding style varies in terms of the party's level of control, but it attempts to disempower others by denying them the possibility of dealing with the conflict.

The first variation of avoiding is **protecting**. The protecting style emerges when parties are determined to avoid conflict at all costs. They are so concerned that the conflict will surface that they build a shell around themselves, and in some cases they respond to attempts to raise the issue with a strong counterattack, designed to warn others off. A protecting style involves very low activeness and flexibility: protectors do not want to work with the conflict at all and will accept no attempts to surface the conflict. Protecting is also very low in disclosiveness, except for the information that the party is determined to avoid conflict. Protectors' motives for avoiding generally remain hidden. A softer version of avoiding is **withdrawing**. In withdrawing parties work to keep issues off the table, but they are somewhat more flexible than with the protecting style. Withdrawers may be apologetic, or address some aspects of the issues while avoiding others. They may find ways to change the subject or to leave the conversation, but these will not carry warnings. Withdrawing is more subtle and flexible than protecting. A third variation of avoiding is **smoothing**, in which the party plays down differences and emphasizes issues on which there are common interests. Issues that might cause hurt feelings or arouse anger are avoided. In essence smoothing tries to emphasize the positive, to keep the topic on subjects that will take up the time that could be spent on conflict.

Avoiding styles may be useful if chances of successful problem-solving or compromising are slight and if parties' needs can be met without surfacing the conflict. Avoiding may also be effective if the party has a very weak position or faces a formidable opponent. It may enable the party to save face. However, avoiding leaves the issues behind the conflict unaddressed, and they may fester, eventually surfacing with destructive consequences. Wall and Nolan (1987) report that an avoiding style led to relatively low satisfaction among students describing their conflicts. Avoiding can become destructive if parties skirt issues, "walking on eggs" by mutual agreement. Avoiding can also impede development of relationships. As noted in previous chapters, successfully dealing with a conflict can enhance parties' relationship and increase their mutual knowledge.

Protecting, in particular, may incur all the disadvantages associated with forcing. It may anger others and encourage them to compete, since it has a surface resemblance to competing. Protecting has an advantage over withdrawing in that it is not likely to make the party seem vulnerable, whereas withdrawing may. However, withdrawing and smoothing are more likely to promote a good relationship with other parties than protecting. All three variations can be frustrating for a party who sees the conflict as important.

Accommodating An accommodating style permits others to realize their concerns but gives less attention to the party's own concerns. Accommodators basically give in to others. Often this is designed to improve a bad or shaky relationship or preserve a good one, especially when the issue is less important to the party than the relationship. Accommodators are highly flexible; they are willing to accede to the other's demands and to change their own positions. Accommodators' level of activeness is low, because they are not involved in the issues per se, but rather in their relationships with the other party. Accommodating involves a low to moderate level of disclosiveness. Accommodators learn much about the other parties' positions and concerns but generally disclose little about their own. Accommodators generally empower the other party and suspend their own control. They "go with the flow" of the other parties' agendas. There are two variations of accommodating.

In **yielding** parties exhibit apathy toward the conflict. Parties show no concern with their own needs and accommodate others entirely. Yielders are very high in flexibility and very low in activeness. They allow the other to control the situation and to define the outcomes of the conflict. The passivity of yielding does not encourage others to be concerned with the relationship. Yielders disengage themselves from the situation and go along with what others want. A "firmer" version of accommodation is **conceding**. In conceding, the party still accommodates others' concerns but is more involved in the conflict. Conceders maintain contact with the issues and accommodate in order to build a better relationship with others. Conceders have a mixture of motives, including real concern for others and a tactical concern for building a relationship that may be useful in the future. Conceding generally is higher in disclosiveness than yielding, because conceders are more involved in the conflict and others become aware of their willingness to build relationships.

Accommodating is a useful strategy when the party is more concerned with future relationships with others than with the issues behind the conflict. Skillfully employed, an accommodating style can convey the party's understanding of the other's needs, improving their relationship. Withdrawing and smoothing are more effective than yielding in doing this. Accommodating is also useful when the party is weaker than the other and will lose in any competition. The other party may take accommodating as a sign of weakness. This may encourage the other to take a more competitive approach on the assumption that the party fears confrontation. The complementary relationship of dominance and submissiveness is quite common (Millar & Rogers, 1987). Once such a pattern develops, breaking it may require considerable effort.

Compromising   This style has moderate levels of assertiveness and cooperativeness, because it requires both parties to give up some of their needs in order to fulfill others. Compromising attempts to find an intermediate position or trade-off through which parties can achieve some important goals in exchange for foregoing others. Compromisers are moderate to high in activeness: in some cases a great deal of energy and involvement are required to arrive at an acceptable compromise, while in other cases parties settle for compromise because finding an optimal solution seems unlikely. Compromising is in the moderate range of flexibility, because compromisers are flexible enough to give in on some of their demands, but not so flexible that they will rework their positions to allow problem-solving or accommodating. Compromising involves moderate to moderately high disclosiveness: compromisers let other parties know what they are willing to trade and their evaluations of other positions, but they do not always explain the reasoning or needs that underlie their offers. Compromisers attempt to empower both themselves and others, because shared control is essential to the give and take necessary for compromise.

One variation is **firm compromising**, which offers trade-offs but exhibits limited flexibility of position and low to moderate disclosure. In this case, compromisers push other parties somewhat, showing a rather tough approach designed to motivate them to cooperate, hopefully on the compromiser's terms. Firm compromisers are highly involved in the conflict, working actively and taking the lead in hammering out the compromise. A somewhat more cooperative variation is **flexible compromising**. Flexible compromisers have less well-defined positions than their firm kin. They exhibit moderate to high disclosure, because sharing thoughts and positions is an important requirement for the evolution of compromises from flexible positions. And flexible compromisers may be less actively involved in the conflict, in some cases following the other parties' initiatives.

Compromising is often confused with problem-solving (Cosier & Ruble, 1981). Trade-offs and exchanges are many people's idea of integrative behavior (Putnam & Wilson, 1982). In many cases—especially those in which there are two equally strong parties who are locked in an impasse—compromises are the best that can be achieved. As Filley (1975) notes, however, compromises often attain a low level of commitment from parties, because they force parties to give up something they value. With the satisfaction of achieving some goals comes the bitterness of having to give up others. This does not happen with problem-solving, which tries to find solutions that meet all the parties' needs.

Problem-solving   This conflict style has received the most attention because its goal is to develop a solution that meets all important needs of both parties and does not lead to any significant disadvantages. This is a tall order, and it is doubtful that any actual problem-solving achieves this goal. But problem-solvers generally believe they have done so. In part this may be due to the fact that the parties redefine their goals during the integrative process, emphasizing those that are achievable. Following successful problem-solving, parties are generally pleased and often enthusiastic about the resolution. This can promote implementation of the solution. It is exhilarating to discover a creative solution through joint effort. Parties learn about themselves and new possibilities open up for the future.

Burke (1970) lists a number of characteristics of problem-solving:

1. Both people have a vested interest in the outcome.
2. A belief on the part of the people involved that they have the potential to resolve the conflict and achieve a better solution through collaboration.
3. Parties recognize that the conflict or problem is mainly in the relationship between the individuals and not in each person separately. Thus if the conflict is in the relationship, it must be defined by those who have the relationship. In addition, if solutions are to be developed, the solutions have to be generated by those who have the responsibility for seeing the solution work and making the relationship last.
4. A concern with solving the problem, not accommodating different points of view. This process identifies the causes of reservation, doubt, and misunderstanding between the people confronted with conflict and disagreement. Alternative ways of approaching conflict resolution are explored and tested.
5. Problem-minded instead of solution-minded; fluid instead of fixed positions. Both people together search out the issues that separate them. Through joint effort the problems that demand solution are identified and later solved.
6. A realization that both aspects of a controversy have potential strengths and potential weaknesses. Rarely is one position completely right and the other completely wrong.
7. Trying to understand the conflict or problem from the other person's point of view and from the standpoint of the "real" or legitimate needs that must be recognized and met before problem-solving can occur. Full acceptance of the other.
8. Importance of looking at the conflict objectively rather than in a personalized sort of way.
9. An examination of one's own attitudes (hostilities, antagonisms) before interpersonal contact on a less effective basis has a chance to occur.
10. An understanding of the less effective methods of conflict resolution (e.g., win–lose).

11. Prevent face-saving situations. Allow people to "give" so that a change in one's viewpoint does not suggest weakness or capitulation.
12. Try to minimize effects of status differences, defensiveness, and other barriers to working together.
13. An awareness of the limitations of arguing or presenting evidence in favor of own position while degrading opponent's position.

Problem-solvers are highly concerned with both their own and others' needs. They are very involved in the conflict, actively pursuing every issue to increase their understanding and probe possible integrative solutions. They are also flexible, not rigidly adhering to positions. However, this does not mean that problem-solvers give in to the other: they are firmly committed to achieving their goals and do not sacrifice them. Problem-solving works best when parties have high aspirations for the outcome of the conflict, firmly insist that their goals and needs be satisfied, but are flexible about the means by which this is done (Pruitt, 1983). Problem-solvers are also moderately to highly disclosive. Problem-solving requires a high level of information about the issues and about parties' needs, and this requires an open communication climate. Problem-solving also requires parties to share control over the emerging solution. Hence problem-solvers attempt to empower others while not sacrificing their own power bases. As we note above, this is most easily done when both parties have common power resources.

Problem-solving is not without its problems. It requires a great deal of time and energy. Creativity is not easy, and parties may have to spend a considerable amount of time exchanging offers and ideas before an acceptable solution can be hammered out. So problem-solving tends not to work well in cases where there is little time or great pressure to act immediately. Parties' enhanced aspirations may also present a problem. During the problem-solving process parties get their hopes up. If a problem-solving approach fails to deliver a timely solution, they may give up on the process and decide that only forcing or some other style may work. Indeed, parties in a stronger position may make a show of problem-solving, set things up so that it fails, and then justify their use of force with the argument that they "tried everything short of force."

Shifting Styles During Conflict Episodes

It is tempting to think of styles as more or less stable choices people make. But it is common for parties to change styles as the conflict unfolds. Several studies have documented changes in conflict styles (Sillars, 1980c; Papa & Natalle, 1989; Conrad, 1991). Case 7.1 illustrates several styles two women adopted during a protracted conflict.

Case 7.1 **College Roommates**

Jill, Rachel, Connie, and Tina decided to room together during their sophomore year at college. Jill and Rachel, best friends, decided to share one bedroom, and Connie and

Tina the other. After a couple of months Rachel noticed that Jill and Tina spent a great deal of time together, doing laundry together, fixing their hair in the same style, shopping together, going out. Rachel had little in common with Connie, and she was "a little hurt" that Jill had abandoned her.

More seeds for the conflict were sown right after Christmas break. Jill decided to try to lose some weight and went on an "oatmeal diet," in which her main food consisted of five bowls of oatmeal a day. Rachel did not think Jill needed to lose weight and teased her about her diet. Jill joined in the laughter and asked Rachel for nutrition advice. But Jill kept up her oatmeal regimen, and Rachel dropped the subject after about a week. During this time Jill and Tina continued to spend a lot of time together. Rachel reported being somewhat resentful because she had introduced Tina to Jill.

About a week later, Jill began to make sarcastic remarks whenever Rachel mentioned her diet. For example, Rachel walked into the kitchen and saw Jill standing and eating cottage cheese out of the carton. Rachel asked Jill if she was planning on eating the whole carton, and Jill replied harshly, "I will if I want to!" Rachel had meant this as a joke, but Jill's reply made her mad and she replied, "Do whatever the hell you want!" and walked out of the room.

Rachel gave Jill the silent treatment after this incident. Within earshot of Rachel, Jill complained about Rachel's behavior to the other two roommates. Rachel talked to Connie about the situation, but Connie did not offer much insight: she interpreted the whole conflict as a result of personal attacks between Jill and Rachel.

Rachel reported that she had decided to give up on her friendship with Jill. However, Jill felt differently and decided to confront the issue. Two weeks before spring term was over, Jill approached Rachel and told her that the two of them needed to talk. They went into the bedroom and closed the door. The following dialogue ensued:

JILL: What's going on between us?

RACHEL: I don't know. What do you mean?

JILL: I mean why won't you talk to me anymore? You won't even say "Good morning" to me when you walk past to go to the bathroom.

RACHEL: I didn't realize I was supposed to talk. Sorry.

JILL: Were you planning on not speaking to me for the rest of the year and leaving without ever seeing me again?

RACHEL: That was not what I meant to do . . . but I figured, why bother saying anything? Every time I open my mouth I get a sarcastic remark back. I just didn't need that anymore, so I shut up.

JILL: I'm sorry, but I was hurt and the way I handle it is by getting defensive and making sarcastic remarks. I didn't really mean to hurt you.

RACHEL: Well you did.

JILL: Well, you hurt me too and I didn't know what to do.

RACHEL: How did I hurt you?

JILL: I didn't like it when you made fun of my eating habits, like eating oatmeal five times a day. I also didn't appreciate it when you would make fun of my exercising or my big butt. How would you like it if I started teasing you about your thighs?

RACHEL: Jill, I had no idea you were so upset about those remarks. Why didn't you tell me this a long time ago? It certainly would have saved a lot of hurt feelings and resentment.

JILL: I figured you would stop making them sooner or later. I thought you would realize you were hurting my feelings.

RACHEL: Jill, how could I? You were always going along with me and even making fun of yourself. Do you think if I had known I was hurting you I would have continued? I'm not that mean.

JILL: I know you're not, and I'm sorry I made so many rude remarks when I was hurt. I really want to get things straightened out between us. Doesn't our friendship mean anything to you anymore?

RACHEL: Yes, it means something to me, but I didn't think it meant anything to you. I've been feeling really hurt lately by your behavior with Tina. I feel like you guys just run off and forget that I even exist. You are always doing everything together without including me. I figured she was just more important to you than me. Therefore, I would just finish out the year and go home and let you two have each other. I felt like I wasn't needed anymore.

JILL: I feel bad that you felt this way. I realize I have been spending a lot of time with Tina, but you've been pretty busy with your boyfriend. I didn't think you had much time for me either.

RACHEL: Yes, I have been spending a lot of time with my boyfriend, but that doesn't mean I don't need your friendship too. We have been friends for quite a while and it was hard for me to see you turn away like you did. I started spending so much time with my boyfriend because of that. Now, don't get me wrong. I realize what you and Tina have is special. However, that doesn't ease my pain at being rejected or excluded from everything you guys do.

JILL: I'm not rejecting you as a friend or picking Tina over you. It just so happened that Tina and I have a lot in common and we have fun together. This naturally leads us to spend more time together. We didn't really think you wanted to do everything with us.

RACHEL: You're right, I probably wouldn't have. But I felt like you didn't need me for a friend at all anymore.

JILL: Well, you're wrong, I still value our friendship and I hope we can keep it going.

RACHEL: I feel better for having talked it over and I'm sorry for having hurt you.

JILL: I'm sorry too—I hope you can forgive Tina and me somehow.

RACHEL: I think I can.

Jill and Rachel utilized several different styles in this conflict. Jill started with a forcing style during the kitchen incident and Rachel responded with the protecting remark, "Do whatever the hell you want." As often happens after protecting, Rachel moved into a withdrawing style, giving Jill the silent treatment. This type of withdrawing also contains elements of competing, because the silent treatment is often used to punish the other and "show them how upset I am." During this period Jill continued forcing, talking to the other roommates about how unreasonable Rachel is being. Finally, Jill shifted to a problem-solving style, telling Rachel that they have to talk. Rachel at first responded with protecting ("I didn't realize I was supposed to. Sorry.") Jill persists with problem-solving, trying to get Rachel to talk about the problem openly. Rachel went along with her and the two women had an open discussion about their problems. The discussion did not resolve the issue, however, and it ended with a compromise: both of them apologized and Rachel said that she thinks she can forgive Tina and Jill. However, this resolution was not wholly satisfactory—to Rachel, at least. She reported that she and Jill "have never been as close as they once were." In part, this was because Rachel and Jill did not work out a solution that addressed the sources of the conflict. Merely forgiving Tina and Jill was not the issue; Rachel wanted Jill to spend more time with her, and it is not clear that Jill was willing to do this.

The styles each woman adopted changed as the conflict unfolded. Shifts in styles are common when a conflict stretches over time. As the dialogue at the end of the conflict illustrates, it is also possible to shift styles within a short discussion. And if one style does not "work"—as the problem-solving style did not in the discussion between Rachel and Jill—parties will often shift to a related style—compromising in this case. Another thing to notice is how Rachel shifted between protecting and withdrawing while remaining in the same overall style—avoiding. These shifts are common in the ebb and flow of conflict, as parties bring issues to the fore and then back away from each other.

Selecting Conflict Styles

In choosing a conflict style, parties should consider several factors. First and foremost, consideration must be given to how effective the style is likely to be in the immediate situation. The effectiveness of styles will vary depending on characteristics of the situation, which will be discussed shortly.

Second, parties should consider the long-term consequences of a style. Styles may improve or worsen relationships with other parties, and this may come back to help or haunt if parties must work with each other in the future. Then too, the styles that parties adopt may change them. If a style is used often enough it becomes habitual. So a party who accommodates often may develop a reputation for so doing, and others may assume they can get what they want by competing. Repeatedly seeing themselves accommodating, parties may define themselves as relatively weak, ignoring their own unique resources and setting up a self-reinforcing cycle of accommodating behavior. Over the long term, conflict styles shape definitions of self. A final long-term consequence is that two or more parties may develop complementary styles that they fall into more or less automatically. For example, one person may engage in competing and the other in accommodating. In effect, the two people become prisoners of each other's style. Because it is rare for one style to be appropriate for all situations, this inflexible interdependence can prevent parties from meeting their needs and cause long-term problems.

Third, parties should consider the ethical implications of selecting a style. While no single set of values can be applied in all conflicts, parties should assess their own values with respect to the styles. Some people are uncomfortable with styles that do not take the other into account; this would indicate a preference for problem-solving, compromising, and accommodating and a dislike for competing and avoiding. Others may believe it is very important to be assertive, favoring competing, problem-solving, compromising, and the more active forms of accommodating and avoiding. All styles involve value choices. Although we discuss style choice from a situational standpoint, ethical imperatives may override concerns with short- and long-term effectiveness.

Fourth, it is important to bear in mind that when parties enact a style, they may provoke responses from other parties. Others still have latitude to choose how they will respond, and in many cases they are attempting to be strategic too. However, Cosier and Ruble (1981) found that there was a tendency for people to reciprocate competing, compromising, accommodating, and problem-solving styles. This is particularly important in light of the tendency noted in earlier chapters toward matching and the development of nonproductive cycles of behavior.

Evidence on the Effectiveness of Conflict Styles

Several studies have evaluated the effectiveness of styles in various situations. Cummings (reported in Filley, 1975) studied the consequences when pairs of different styles interact with each other. Among other things, he found that competitive versus competitive styles generally resulted in stalemates in bargaining and that competitive versus collaborative styles led to mutual agreement in many cases, though the competitive person still won in over 50 percent of the cases. In a related study of group decision-making, Jones and White (1985) found that groups composed of members who preferred problem-solving were more effective in terms of task accomplishment, while groups composed of accommodators were less effective. In general, the more group members differed in their preference for the problem-solving style, the less effective the group was. This was not found for either competing or accommodating styles.

Phillips and Cheston (1979) compared the effectiveness of forcing (competitiveness) and problem-solving (collaboration) strategies in 52 conflict cases reported by middle managers. Managers used forcing twice as often as they used problem-solving but also reported more "bad" solutions with forcing than with problem-solving (about half the incidents in which forcing was used had "bad" results, whereas all instances of problem-solving yielded "good" results). Phillips and Cheston concluded both methods were effective, but under different circumstances. Forcing was more successful when:

- there was one best solution to the problem
- there was a value conflict between the manager and a subordinate
- the manager was fair and could give an objective explanation of his or her reasons for forcing a solution
- the ultimate outcome benefitted the organization rather than one person or a small group

Problem-solving was more successful when:

- the parties were highly interdependent and had to work together in the future
- there was mutual awareness of the potential for conflict
- those involved were open-minded
- there was a willingness to ignore power issues
- formal procedures for problem-solving were available

- one or both people detected the conflict early and initiated problem-solving before things got bad
- attention was focused on solving a common problem rather than defeating or adopting one person's preferred solution

In a pathbreaking study of organizational effectiveness, Lawrence and Lorsch (1967) found that problem-solving was endorsed as the most effective method of conflict resolution by managers in six different types of organizations. Competing was regarded as a useful backup behavior, when problem-solving was not feasible or effective.

Burke (1970) found that engineering managers also chose problem-solving as the most effective method of conflict management, but they also believed "smoothing" was a useful style. Burke argues that it is a backup behavior to problem-solving. Forcing was rated as a poor way to manage conflict, as was withdrawing. Burke replicated the results for problem-solving and forcing with a mixed sample of about 70 managers from various companies.

Wall, Galanes, and Love (1987) found that open recognition and expression of conflict—as would occur in competing, compromising, and problem-solving—tended to increase the quality of outcome, as measured by the quality of solutions groups arrived at. Sambamurthy and Poole (in press) found the same thing when outcome was measured by the increase in consensus among group members. Canary and Spitzberg (1990) found that a subject's perceptions of his or her own competence and effectiveness in recalled conflicts were positively related to his or her use of integrative strategies and negatively related to competitive strategies. Moreover, the other party's perceptions of the subject's competence and effectiveness were also positively related to the party's use of integrative strategies and negatively related to the use of competitive strategies. Putnam and Poole (1987) summarize evidence that the earlier a conflict is brought out in the open, the more promising its outcome. However, this result must be tempered in light of the survey by Wall and Nolan (1987) showing that quality of group outcome was not associated with whether a conflict occurred in a group or not.

It should be noted that styles that surface and openly acknowledge conflicts—problem-solving, competing, compromising—are not uniformly advantageous. One exception to the findings cited here is conflict in marriages and intimate relationships. Although many satisfied couples employ problem-solving, other satisfied couples opt for an avoiding style, consisting of "topic shifts, jokes, denial of conflict, [and] abstract, ambivalent, or irrelevant comments" (Sillars & Weisberg, 1987, p.147). The satisfied problem-solving couples endorse personal values of interdependence, openness, and sharing, whereas the avoiding couples value autonomy and discretion more highly.

An interesting twist to the results on avoidance is that avoiding also seems to be an effective response when the conflict is unimportant. Baxter (1982) found that students playing a classroom game often resorted to avoiding. This may well have been because they were not very involved in the issues behind the conflict.

A limitation to all the studies cited so far is that subjects were from American or British cultures. Different styles are likely to be differentially effective in different cultures. The tendency of Japanese to favor avoiding or accommodating styles is widely known (Krauss, Rohlen, & Steinhoff, 1984). Cultures that are more group-oriented and less focused on the individual than American culture—such as Native American, Mexican, Japanese, and many African cultures—tend to favor styles such as accommodation or compromise over self-focused styles. Possible cultural differences are too numerous to trace, but it is clear that cultural context can make a difference in the effectiveness of conflict styles.

A Model for Selecting Conflict Styles

This section proposes a model for style selection based on the evidence summarized above and other discussions of strategies in conflict and negotiation (Thomas, 1975; Musser, 1982; Ebert & Wall, 1983; Savage, Blair, & Sorenson, 1989). The model takes the form of a "decision tree," a diagram that supports the selection of options based on answers to a series of questions. The diagram presents a question to the party and, based on the answer to this question, the party traces different branches of the tree, which lead to other questions and branches, and finally to a recommended style. In the conflict style decision tree shown in Figure 7.2 the party would have to answer a maximum of five questions to arrive at a style selection. The questions are arranged in logical order, prompting the party to consider the factors that studies and common sense suggest are important.

(1) **How important are the issues to the party?** An importance dimension has long been used to define conflict styles (Thomas, 1975; Pruitt & Rubin, 1986). If the issues are **important**, the decision model indicates that the party should pursue "firm" strategies that focus on realizing the party's interests, that is, forcing, contending, firm compromise, flexible compromise, and problem-solving. If the issues are **unimportant**, however, less assertive strategies (i.e., yielding, conceding, smoothing, withdrawing, and protecting) are recommended because they can be less costly in time or energy.

(2) **How important are the issues to the other?** This question reflects a second dimension in the classical conflict style diagram, **concern for other**. The decision model assumes that if the issues are important to the other, each party will benefit most by choosing strategies that take the other into account, that is, flexible compromising, firm compromising, problem-solving, yielding, or conceding. If the issues are not important to the other, then it is more efficient to choose strategies that place less emphasis on the other's needs, that is, contending, forcing, protecting, withdrawing, or smoothing.

(3) **How important is maintaining a positive relationship?** How conflicts are managed affects the long-term relationship between parties—their degree of trust and liking for each other and whether parties nurse grudges or hard feelings. In some cases it is important to maintain a good relationship with the other. This is true when people must work together in the future, or when one may control or influence the other's fate at some future time. In this case, it would be best to choose styles that build (or at least do not undermine) trust and positive feelings, that is, flexible compromising, firm compromising, problem-solving, yielding, withdrawing, smoothing, conceding, and contending. In other cases, the party may be dealing with the other only for a short period.

Alternatively, a good relationship may be impossible to maintain and the party

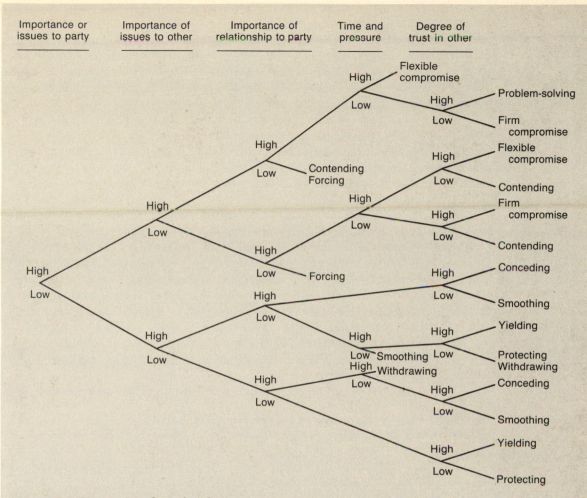

Figure 7.2 Decision tree for style selection.

may decide that the best that can be done is to maintain a formal relationship with the other, thereby keeping a protective guard up. The relationship between lawyers negotiating a divorce is an example of this. Both lawyers often try to maximize their clients' gains; there is little place for trust. Instead, they work on the basis of legal codes and professional practices that maintain decorum, foster progress on issues, and afford protection against cheating. In such cases, building or maintaining a relationship is not of concern and styles that do not show concern for the other may be adopted, that is, forcing and protecting.

(4) **How much time pressure is there?** In cases where time pressure is **great**, the best course is to adopt styles that are not time-consuming, that is, forcing, contending, flexible compromising, protecting, withdrawing, or yielding. When there is **little** time pressure, more time-consuming strategies may be better, because they can promote deeper exploration of issues. These include smoothing, conceding, firm compromising, and problem-solving.

(5) **To what extent does one party trust the other?** Trust determines the degree to which one party is willing to let the other control the situation. When trust is **high**, styles that empower the other can be used, including problem-solving, flexible compromising, firm compromising, conceding, and yielding. When trust is **low**, styles that protect one's own power are safer, that is, forcing, contending, protecting, smoothing, and withdrawing.

Answering the five questions leads the party through the diagram to recommended strategies. It is important to note that these are the optimal strategies for each case under the assumptions reflected in the choice rules. While the rules represent some of the best evidence available on conflict styles, they do not exhaust all factors one might consider. As the diagram shows, in some cases not all questions are applicable. For example, time pressure is not relevant in distinguishing some styles. Also, there are a few "twists" to the general rules, as when firm compromising is a "low trust" strategy compared to problem-solving in the very top branch of the tree. Although firm compromising is generally a trusting style, it protects the party relative to problem-solving and is recommended when trust is low and problem-solving is the other alternative.

To illustrate how the decision tree works, consider the following example:

Jack is a foreman for an industrial cleaning company. He really enjoys his work and has been with the same company, Acme Cleanzit, for 12 years. Recently his boss was replaced by a younger woman, fresh out of business school. Jack's new manager, Ms. Jorgensen, graduated at the top of her class, and while in school worked for the branch of Acme Cleanzit in her college town. Jorgensen has lots of new ideas and is quite impatient to have them tried out. She tends to lean toward using her authority to force issues. She has hinted that she expects Jack to help her implement her ideas and that she might have to replace any problem employees. Jorgensen has the complete faith of top management at Acme Cleanzit, and Jack believes she will have management's backing in whatever she does.

Jack sees a conflict on the horizon. Jorgensen wants to try new water pressure cleaning equipment to replace the air pressure equipment Acme Cleanzit has always employed. Jack has used water pressure equipment in the past and does not like it. Although it cleans faster than air pressure equipment, it breaks down easily and is somewhat dangerous to repair. He is afraid the rate of absenteeism and resignations will go up, because the workers do not like the tedious process of repairing the water pressure equipment. Still, when the water pressure equipment works it does increase productivity, so he must concede Jorgensen has a point. When he received her memo asking his input on water pressure equipment, he wrote her a memo outlining his objections clearly. After Jorgensen received it, she brushed past him on her way out of the plant, saying, "We'll talk about this in the morning." It was clear to Jack that she was angry and as he had a couple of beers with Wilma and Joe, a couple of his workers, he found himself rehearsing what he would say to her the next day.

What style should Jack choose?

In this case, the issues are important to Jack, so he should take the **High** branch of the tree. The issues are also important to Jorgensen, so again take the **High** branch. Unless Jack wants to lose his job, his relationship with Jorgensen should be highly important to him, so again, take the **High** branch. There is little time pressure, so the **Low** branch is most appropriate. Finally, it is not clear Jack can trust Jorgensen, so the **Low** branch regarding degree of trust in the other is most appropriate, leading to the **firm compromising** style. This style encourages Jack to enter the discussion with clear and well-stated positions, to demonstrate a willingness to move on views if he is truly convinced by Jorgensen, but remain committed to having some of his important needs met, whatever the outcome of the discussions. This style takes the concerns outlined in the questions into account. Of course, other styles might also work, but they would not meet the criteria in the model as well as firm compromising.

Consider a second example:

> Cindy and John have been married for three years. As with many married couples some of their worst fights seem to stem from seemingly simple issues, like how to decorate their house. They are in the process of redoing their rec room and John really wants to put in wallpaper with a hunting motif. Cindy does not like the idea of looking at ducks and pointers while she plays cards and would rather have wallpaper with a modern design of some sort. She has found that with the right furniture any kind of wallpaper can look good, and she thinks she could probably live with ducks and dogs if it is really important to John. What is important to Cindy is that their relationship and their faith in each other not be undermined by incessant arguments over "little things." As they sit together at breakfast, John once again raises the issue of the hunting paper, this time a bit testily.

What style should Cindy adopt?

The best answer in this case is **conceding**; it takes into account the importance of the issue to John, that it isn't that important to Cindy, that their relationship is a high priority to Cindy, and that Cindy trusts John.

Some observations about the decision tree need to be considered. First, the model is ambiguous in cases when some issues are important to the party, while others are not. The model confronts us with a dichotomous choice: it assumes issues are either important or they are not. In the common case where there are a number of issues, some important and some not, parties may try to switch styles when different issues are discussed, hoping to set up trade-offs. For example, if John adopts a firm compromising style when discussing his wallpaper and a conceding style when discussing furniture, Cindy may respond positively to his demands about wallpaper because she senses she can pick out furniture that will make even ducks and dogs look good. The combination of styles results in terms acceptable to both.

In applying the model it is also important to bear in mind that the answers to the questions may change over the course of the conflict. As we have emphasized throughout the book, conflict is an interactive process. As a result, earlier interactions may influence later ones. A party may begin a conflict episode with a firm conviction that her relationship with the other should be preserved, but as the conflict unfolds, she may find that she no longer wants a relationship with the other. If this happens, styles that were suitable at the outset of the conflict are no longer appropriate. It is important to monitor changing conditions to determine if conflict styles should change. It is also possible that combinations of two styles may be effective. Putnam (1990) summarizes considerable evidence that a mixture of competing and problem-solving styles is effective in inducing cooperation.

Finally, this model is useful because it is quite general and can apply to a wide range of conflicts. However, this also means the tree may be less useful in particular situations. Savage et al. (1989) and Ebert and Wall (1983) lay out decision trees for negotiation tactics specifically adapted to organizational negotiations. Musser (1982) describes a choice model for subordinate responses to conflicts with superiors. These models are tailored to specific contexts and can be highly useful in their intended settings.

CONFLICT TACTICS

Tactics are the specific moves and countermoves used to enact conflict styles. Several researchers have developed lists or typologies of conflict tactics (Sharp, 1973; Roloff, 1976; Wilmot & Wilmot, 1978). Typologies of influence or compliance-gaining messages also map tactical choices because influence and persuasion are important aspects of certain conflict styles (Marwell & Schmidt, 1967; Miller, Boster, Roloff, & Seibold, 1976; Kipnis, et al., 1980). It would be impossible to discuss the more than 100 tactics that have been distinguished. Instead, we have defined the tactics briefly in Table 7.2, indicating their characteristics in terms of the six dimensions that describe conflict styles. Also indicated in Table 7.2 are the power modes involved in carrying out each tactic. Tactics are, essentially, the **vehicles of the power processes** discussed in previous chapters; they constitute "power-in-action." How appropriate and skillful a party's moves are determines the party's effective power.

Table 7.2 groups tactics based on common ratings on the six dimensions and common principles of operation. These groupings expand on those developed by Kipnis et al. (1980) and Miller et al. (1976).

As we noted at the beginning of this chapter, the same tactic can be used to carry out several different styles. To match tactics to styles, use the values of the tactics on the six style dimensions. A careful reading of this table also shows numerous tactics that match a given style on all but one or two dimensions. These tactics can be used to create variations on the style. For example, a competing style can be pursued by threatening the other (tactic 4c) or by invoking formal authority (if the authority will side with the party)(tactic 7a). The two tactics give a very different "flavor" to the competing style.

As indicated in Chapter 3's discussion of episodes, the same tactic may have different meanings and effects depending on the context and the nature of ongoing conflict interaction. In a discussion marked by verbal aggression and hostile jokes, offering a **quid pro quo** might invoke suspicion, whereas the same offer would be taken as an attempt to compromise during a discussion full of integrative tactics. While it is useful to consider tactics in isolation, it is important to remember that they form part of more complex interaction.

Table 7.2 CONFLICT TACTICS RATED ON SEVEN DIMENSIONS

Tactic	Definition	Assertiveness	Cooperativeness	Disclosive	Empowerment		Activeness	Flexibility	Power Mode
					Self	Other			
1. Avoidance									
a. Topic shift	Change topic from conflict issue (Sillars et al., 1982)	Low	Varies	Varies	Yes	No	Low	Low	Indirect, hidden
b. Leave field	Remove self from contact with other party	Low	Low	Low	Yes	No	Low	Low	Indirect, hidden
c. Refuse to recognize conflict		Low	Low	Low	Yes	No	Low	Low	Indirect, hidden
d. Postponement	Postpone dealing with the conflict until a future time	Low	Low	Varies	Varies	Varies	Low	Varies	Indirect
2. Accommodation									
a. Give concession	Accede to other's demand	Low	High	Varies	No	Yes	Low	High	Indirect
3. Subordination									
a. Appeal, plead	Act helpless or incompetent as a way of gaining pity or support	Low	Low	Moderate to high	No	Yes	Moderate	Varies	Indirect
b. Supplication		Low	Low	Low	No	Yes	Low	Varies	Indirect
4. Assertive tactics									
a. Demand concessions		High	Low	Moderate	Yes	No	High	Low	Direct, virtual
b. Toughness	Adopt an extreme initial demand and move away from it slowly and reluctantly. Justify position logically (Bartos, 1970)	High	Low	Moderate	Yes	No	High	Moderate	Direct, virtual
c. Threat	A statement that if other does not meet party's demand, negative consequences will result	High	Low	Moderate	Yes	No	High	Low	Direct, virtual

Table 7.2 (*Continued*)

Tactic	Definition	Assertiveness	Cooperativeness	Disclosive	Empowerment		Activeness	Flexibility	Power Mode
					Self	Other			
d. Irrevocable commitment	Party makes a commitment to a course of action so that party cannot back down from it, others must go along (Pruitt & Rubin, 1986)	High	Low	Moderate	Yes	No	High	Low	Direct, virtual
5. Aggressive tactics									
a. Verbal aggression	Shouting, blaming, browbeating, etc.	High	Low	Low	Yes	No	Varies	Low	Direct
b. Hostile joke	A joke that insults or derides the other party or his or her behavior (Sillars et al., 1982)	High	Low	Low	Yes	No	Varies	Low	Indirect
c. Physical aggression		High	Low	Low	Yes	No	Varies	Low	Direct
d. Gunnysacking	Attacking the other by addressing a number of accusations or complaints to him or her at once, sometimes a group gangs up on the party (Wilmot & Wilmot, 1978)	High	Low	Low	Yes	No	Varies	Low	Direct
6. Manipulation									
a. Self-abuse	Verbal or physical abuse to self intended to make other comply	Varies	Low	Varies	Yes	No	Varies	Varies	Indirect
b. Guilt	Attempts to make other feel guilty so he or she will comply	High	Low	Varies	Yes	No	Varies	Low	Indirect
c. Mis-representation of position	Misleading other about party's true position	High	Low	Low	Yes	No	Low	Varies	Indirect

Table 7.2 (Continued)

Tactic	Definition	Assertiveness	Cooperativeness	Disclosive	Empowerment		Activeness	Flexibility	Power Mode
					Self	Other			
d. Gamesmanship	Party does things to create a "muddled fluster" in the other, to throw the other off balance and render other more likely to concede (Pruitt & Rubin, 1986)	High	Low	Varies	Yes	No	Low	Varies	Indirect
7. Authority tactics									
a. Invoke formal authority	Use authority of position to influence other	High	Varies	Low to moderate	Yes	No	High	Varies	Direct
b. Expertise	Use special knowledge or experience to influence other	High	Varies	Moderate to high	Yes	Varies	High	Varies	Indirect
c. Invoke higher authority	Ask superior to resolve conflict	High	Low	Varies	Yes	Varies	Varies	Low	Direct, virtual indirect
8. Exchange tactics									
a. Promise	A statement that if the other meets party's demand, a positive consequence will result (see text)	High	Varies	Moderate	Yes	Yes	High	Low	Direct, virtual
b. Pregiving	Reward other prior to requesting compliance (Marwell & Schmitt, 1967)	High	Varies	Low	Yes	Yes	Moderate to high	Varies	Direct
c. Call in debt	Ask other to comply because of a previous favor or concession party gave	High	Varies	Low	Yes	Yes	Moderate to high	Varies	Indirect

Table 7.2 (*Continued*)

Tactic	Definition	Assertiveness	Cooperativeness	Disclosive	Empowerment		Activeness	Flexibility	Power Mode
					Self	Other			
d. Quid pro quo	Giving "something for something." Each party gives the other something in exchange for granting something; for example, party A agrees not to shout at B, if B will listen better	High	High	Varies	Yes	Yes	Varies	Moderate to high	Indirect
e. Tit for tat	Party responds to each of other's moves with a move from the same style; for example, if A adopts a competing style, B answers with competing moves	High	Varies	Moderate	Yes	Yes	Varies	High	Direct
f. Logrolling	Propose solution to conflict that involves both parties giving something up to get something (Pruitt & Rubin, 1986)	High	High	Moderate to high	Yes	Yes	High	High	Direct
9. **Coalition tactics**									
a. Coalition formation	Two or more parties form an alliance against another member	High	Low	Varies	Yes	No	High	Low	Direct

Table 7.2 (*Continued*)

Tactic	Definition	Assertiveness	Cooperativeness	Disclosive	Empowerment Self	Empowerment Other	Activeness	Flexibility	Power Mode
10. Ingratiation									
a. Liking	Use other's liking for party to influence other	High	Varies	Varies	Yes	Yes	Varies	Varies	Indirect
b. Flattery	Exaggerate other's admirable qualities and soft-pedal other's weaknesses to influence other (Pruitt & Rubin, 1986)	High	Varies	Low	Yes	Yes	Varies	Varies	Indirect
c. Opinion conformity	Express agreement with other's opinions and values to create impression of similarity and increase other's liking (Pruitt & Rubin, 1986)	High	Varies	Low	Yes	Yes	Varies	Varies	Indirect
d. Give favors	Do nice things for other to increase other's liking of party (Pruitt & Rubin, 1986)	High	Varies	Varies	Yes	Yes	Varies	Varies	Indirect
e. Self-promotion	Present self as deserving, virtuous, self-sacrificing to build liking (Pruitt & Rubin, 1986)	High	Varies	Moderate	Yes	Yes	High	Varies	Indirect
f. Entitlement	Claim responsibility for a favorable event to gain other's esteem (Cialdini, 1984)	High	Low	Varies	Yes	Yes	Varies	Low	Indirect

207

Table 7.2 (*Continued*)

Tactic	Definition	Assertiveness	Cooperativeness	Disclosive	Empowerment Self	Empowerment Other	Activeness	Flexibility	Power Mode
g. Basking in reflected glory	Associate oneself with other successful party to gain esteem by association (Cialdini, 1984)	High	Low	Varies	Yes	Yes	Low	Low	Indirect
h. Blasting the opposition	Criticize or derogate unsuccessful or despised others to gain approval (Cialdini, 1984)	High	Low	Varies	Yes	Yes	Low	Low	Indirect
11. Issue definition a. Fractionation	Breaking a conflict down into individual issues that can then be handled separately (Fisher, 1969)	High	Varies	High	Yes	Varies	High	High	Varies
b. Umbrellas	Issues introduced to legitimize anger or grievance resulting from another less legitimate issue: for example, A may resent B because of an insult. This is not a legitimate excuse to argue. However, if B is unfair to A in some small way, A may use this as an umbrella to take out anger on B (Walton, 1969)	High	Low	Low	Yes	No	Low	Low	Indirect

Table 7.2 (Continued)

Tactic	Definition	Assertiveness	Cooperativeness	Disclosive	Empowerment Self	Empowerment Other	Activeness	Flexibility	Power Mode
c. Negative inquiry	When B raises an issue, A responds by asking for more information: for example, B charges A with "sloppy work"; A engages in negative inquiry by asking exactly what B means, what A could do differently, and so on. This often clarifies issues and, by so doing, reduces conflict (Wilmot & Wilmot, 1978)	High	Varies	Varies	Yes	Varies	High	Varies	Indirect
d. Issue control	Directly or indirectly indicating that an issue is off-limits (see Chapter 4 for explanation)	High	Low	Low	Yes	No	Low	Low	Hidden
e. Fogging	Turning aside a criticism or attack by acknowledging only part of it. If B criticizes A: "You have ruined this report. You are always so late!" A may respond: "Yes, the report wasn't as good as it could have been." A fogs by not acknowledging the lateness issue (Wilmot & Wilmot, 1978)	High	Varies	Varies	Yes	Varies	Varies	Moderate to high	Indirect

Table 7.2 (*Continued*)

Tactic	Definition	Assertiveness	Cooperativeness	Disclosive	Empowerment		Activeness	Flexibility	Power Mode
					Self	Other			
f. Two-column method	List party's needs in one column and other needs in a second column and compare, searching for commonalities	High	High	High	Yes	Yes	High	Varies	Varies
g. Issue expansion	Party purposely adds issues to a conflict to strengthen case; also called "bundling boards" by Walton (1969)	High	Low	Moderate to high	Yes	No	Moderate	Low	Direct, virtual indirect
12. **Conflict process reflection**									
a. Meta-communication	Discussing and commenting on communication patterns, particularly with the goal of improving communication processes	Varies	Varies	High	Yes	Yes	High	High	Varies
b. Labeling	Attaching a name, often unfavorable, to the other's behavior in the conflict; for example, A says to B: "You don't have to be so hostile!"	High	Varies	Varies	Yes	No	Varies	Low	Direct, virtual indirect

Table 7.2 (*Continued*)

Tactic	Definition	Assertiveness	Cooperativeness	Disclosive	Empowerment Self	Empowerment Other	Activeness	Flexibility	Power Mode
13. Indirect communication tactics									
a. Precueing	Giving information about party's reaction to the conflict prior to openly dealing with it; for example, when A nonverbally indicates disgust at B's mention of an issue	High	Low	Moderate to high	Yes	No	Varies	Low	Direct, virtual indirect
b. Tacit coordination	Choosing a position the other is likely to accept without discussing it with the other. Often, this depends on norms or social conventions; for example, A, anticipating B's objections, offers to "split the difference" with B, taking advantage of the norm of equality	High	High	Moderate	Yes	Yes	High	High	Indirect
c. Use intermediaries	Party asks an outside party to convey messages or offers to other (Pruitt & Rubin, 1986)	High	Varies	Varies	Yes	Varies	Moderate	Varies	Varies

211

Table 7.2 (*Continued*)

Tactic	Definition	Assertiveness	Cooperativeness	Disclosive	Empowerment		Activeness	Flexibility	Power Mode
					Self	Other			
14. Normative tactics									
a. Moral appeal		High	Varies	Varies	Yes	Varies	Varies	Low	Indirect
b. Altercasting	A tells B to comply with a request, because "a good" person would comply, or, alternatively, because "only a bad" person would not comply (Marwell & Schmitt, 1967)	High	Low	Low	Yes	No	Varies	Low	Indirect
15. Integrative tactics									
a. Propose novel solution		High	Varies	Moderate to high	Yes	Yes	Varies	Varies	Indirect
b. Invoke superordinate goals	Identify a common goal or end for which parties can work together: the goal should be one both value	High	High	High	Yes	Yes	High	Varies	Indirect
c. Acknowledge legitimacy of other party's position	Party does not necessarily agree with other's position but acknowledges that other has legitimate interests that should be taken into account	Varies	High	Moderate	Yes	Yes	High	High	Indirect
d. Reformed sinner	Switch to cooperation after a period of competition (see text)	High	Low	Moderate	Yes	Yes	Varies	High	Varies

212

Table 7.2 (*Continued*)

Tactic	Definition	Assertiveness	Cooperativeness	Disclosive	Empowerment Self	Empowerment Other	Activeness	Flexibility	Power Mode
e. Experimental integration	Party makes an integrative move as an experiment, to see if other will reciprocate. If other does, then party makes another integrative move and awaits reciprocation	High	Varies	Moderate	Yes	Yes	Varies	High	Varies
f. Joint fact-finding	Parties investigate the issues together in an attempt to establish a factual basis for agreement	High	High	Varies	Yes	Yes	High	High	Varies
g. Single text method	Parties work on a written draft of an agreement passing it back and forth with revisions until an agreement can be met (Fisher & Ury, 1981)	High	High	Varies	Yes	Yes	High	High	Varies
16. Joking									
a. Joking	Party jokes with other in a tangent from the issue	High	High	Low	Yes	Yes	Low	Low	Varies
17. Change forum of the conflict									
a. Move conflict into formal adjudication	Party takes the conflict into a formal procedure for judging the merits of the two cases, such as a grievance procedure or a court of law	High	Varies	Varies	Yes	Varies	Varies	Varies	Varies

Table 7.2 (*Continued*)

| | | | | | Empowerment | | | | |
Tactic	Definition	Assertiveness	Cooperativeness	Disclosive	Self	Other	Activeness	Flexibility	Power Mode
b. Use the media	Party takes issues to the media to either pressure the other or get redress; for example, party uses television "action-lines" or "blows the whistle" on illegal practices	High	Low	Varies	Yes	No	Varies	Low	Direct, virtual
c. Call in a third party	Parties agree to have a third party, such as a mediator or counselor, help them work on the conflict	High	High	Moderate to high	Yes	Yes	High	Varies	Varies

High: the tactic exhibits a high degree of this characteristic.

Moderate: the tactic exhibits some, but not a high degree, of this characteristic.

Low: the tactic exhibits a low degree of this characteristic.

Varies: the amount of this characteristic exhibited by the tactic varies, depending on how the party carries out the tactic.

Although it is impossible to discuss all the tactics in Table 7.2, several have been studied extensively and others deserve additional explanation. Not included on this list are many formal procedures for managing conflict; these will be discussed subsequently.

Threats and Promises

In one form or another, threats and promises appear in almost every conflict described in this book. Formally, we define a **threat** as an individual's expressed intention to behave in a way that appears detrimental to the interests of another, if that other does not comply with the individual's request or terms, and a **promise** as an individual's expressed intention to behave in a way that appears beneficial to another, if the other complies with the individual's request or terms. Threats and promises then are two sides of the same coin, one negative and the other positive (Kelley, 1965; Deutsch, 1973; Bowers, 1974).

Research suggests that the effectiveness of threats and promises depends on at least five factors—their **specificity**, the party's **credibility**, their **immediacy**, their **equity**, and the **climate** in which they are presented.

If threats and promises operate by constraining another's behavior, then the more **specific** the behavior requested, the more effective the threat or promise is likely to be. Because threats and promises involve the **virtual** use of power, they constrain the other's behavior only by the instructions they give, and the more specific the instructions, the tighter the constraint (Tedeschi, 1970). This line of reasoning is also supported by the finding from bargaining studies that threats generally elicit more compliance than promises because threats are usually more specific than promises (Rubin & Brown, 1975; Pruitt & Rubin, 1986). Consider the case where one party wants to get another to choose one of four possible behaviors. A promise of the form "If you do X, I will reward you," gives the other a constraint, namely, a reward if he or she does X. A threat, "If you do not do X, I will punish you," carries more constraints, because it threatens punishment for **three of four choices**. In general, the more specific the constraints, the more likely the threat or promise is to prove effective.

The **credibility** of the person making a threat or promise is strongly related to its effectiveness, although the dynamics of credibility differ for the two tactics (Rubin & Brown, 1975). In the case of **threats**, credibility is established by demonstrating the ability and willingness to carry out the threat, in other words, by a show of determination. Accounts of the Cuban Missile Crisis, for example, detail a number of specific "tough" moves the Kennedy Administration made—such as mobilizing armed forces, mounting air patrols, and stirring up public opinion—to demonstrate to the Soviets that it meant business (Allison, 1969). **Promises**, on the other hand, depend much more on the person's being perceived as trustworthy and having good intentions toward the other, as well as being able to "deliver the goods." Indeed, the very act of making a promise tends to make others feel friendlier and more trusting toward the promiser and so may set up a cycle reinforcing the person's credibility as long as promises can be delivered (Evans, 1964; Heilman, 1974; Rubin & Brown, 1975).

Burgess (1973) argues that violent threats are effective because they "collapse time"; that is, they require the other to make an immediate choice and therefore heighten the impression of constraint still further. Faced with an urgent choice, the man with a gun at his head complies because there seems to be no safe alternative (although, given time to reflect, he may find several). To the extent that threats or promises can be made **immediate**—-for example, by imposing time limits, exhibiting a sample of the reward or punishment to come, or giving a "hard sell"—they are more likely to be effective. A fourth consideration influencing the effectiveness of promises or threats is the degree to which the promise or threat is perceived as **equitable** by those being influenced. In an excellent study on compliance to threats, Kaplowitz (1973) showed that a subject's compliance depended on whether he or she perceived the threatener's request to be equitable or not. This result suggests that threats are more likely to be rejected (with an accompanying decrease in endorsement) if they are perceived as inequitable, and that effective use of threats depends on the threatener's ability to make the required behavior seem fair, reasonable, justifiable, or beneficial to the other. Given the positive value generally placed on equality and fairness in our culture (Walster, Berscheid, & Walster, 1973), it seems safe to predict that equity will also enhance the effectiveness of promises: a promise that does not cost the promiser unfairly should elicit more compliance than one that does.

Finally, the effectiveness of threats and promises depends on the **climate** surrounding the conflict. Friedland (1976) found that threats were viewed differently by subjects in a bargaining experiment, depending on whether they were cooperatively or competitively interdependent. In a **cooperative** climate, threats were seen as attempts by the person to **influence** the other for the other's own good. In a **competitive** situation, threats were seen as attempts to **coerce**. Given these different perceptions, the effectiveness of the threat depends on differences in the two climates. In the cooperative climate, compliance with the threat depended on the other's belief that the person really does know what is best for both of them. In the competitive climate, compliance depended on the other's belief in the person's willingness and ability to punish him or her. It is quite likely that other climate themes, especially supportiveness, may influence how threats are perceived. In the same vein, a **promise** given in a competitive climate is likely to be perceived quite differently than one in a cooperative climate. In general, different climates will influence what makes a threat or promise effective.

Promises and threats have another function in addition to influencing others. They also convey **information** about the person's preferences and determination and can be used strategically to communicate toughness or the willingness to compromise. If a small child defies her father at bedtime, and he threatens her with a spanking, he conveys that her going to bed is important to him and that he is unwilling to compromise. If he promises to read her a story if she'll go to bed, he is still conveying the importance of the issue (although more "softly") but he is offering a deal: she can stay up for the story if she'll sleep afterward.

Threats and promises also convey important information about the person's perceptions of the other. In our father–daughter example, a threat implies that the father thinks his daughter can be intimidated (or that nothing less than the threat of punishment will get her into bed). A promise implies a more easygoing relationship in which both are working for the same ends. Interestingly, making too small a threat can imply that the other can be easily intimidated, while making a large threat may be seen as a sign of respect for the opponent (Raven & Kruglanski, 1970).

By carefully observing another's threats and promises (especially those that are implicit or indirect) and how they are carried out, parties can learn about others' values, intentions, and determination. Conversely, of course, parties may use promises and threats to mislead. A common labor negotiation tactic is to make threatening gestures about a minor issue—say, the number of paid vacation days given employees—in order to get the employees to focus on that issue and draw their attention away from more important issues like retirement benefits. Skillful threats and promises can misdirect attention and are often as strategically important for what they do **not** say as for what they communicate.

In closing, it is important to note some problems with threats. The use of threats tends to beget threats or competition from the other party (Pruitt & Rubin, 1986). The cycle of threat and counterthreat can easily develop into uncontrolled escalation. Moreover, the successful use of threats often entraps a party into using them again and again (Tedeschi, 1983). This is because threats earn the hostility and distrust of the other and those who witness the action. As a result of this suspicion, more benign modes of influence, such as promises and reasoning, fail to induce compliance. Therefore the party must continue to rely on threats.

Toughness

Toughness has been studied extensively in experimental gaming research. A tough bargainer makes extreme opening demands, relatively few concessions, and small concessions when he or she does move (Bartos, 1970). Generally, the negotiator attempts to convey strength and determination and to discourage others sufficiently so that they will yield first. The tactic is designed to maximize the person's gains, if need be at the expense of the other. It is consistent with the competitive, compromising, and collaborative styles discussed earlier: all three orientations imply that the party asserts his or her needs, a necessary prerequisite of toughness.

The research on toughness indicates that a party can obtain a more favorable final agreement by being tough (Chertkoff & Esser, 1976). Indeed, Bartos (1970) has shown that if both bargainers are tough, other things being equal, they will achieve the optimal solution. However, there are limitations on this result. If tough bargainers are too uncompromising, their partners may respond with counterattacks or equal intransigence. When there is little pressure on the bargainers to come to an agreement or when time is short, excessive toughness can lead to impasses. In general, it seems best to convey an impression of "tough but fair" and give on less important points. Toughness encourages the other to take one seriously, but excessive toughness may seem foolish and bullheaded.

Tit for Tat

A good example of an exchange tactic is **tit for tat**, or **matching**. In this tactic one person matches the moves made by the other. If one party makes a competitive or hostile move, so does the other; if one party makes a cooperative or conciliatory move, so does the other. This strategy can be effective in persuading the other to cooperate, but it can also backfire, trapping both parties in an escalating spiral. Two explanations of this result can be offered. The first is based on Leary's (1957) conception of matching, which was discussed in Chapter 3. Briefly, Leary argues that partners in a relationship tend to reciprocate similar levels of hostility or friendliness almost unconsciously. This **interpersonal reflex** leads to perpetuation of the hostile or friendly tendencies in relationships. Hence by matching cooperativeness one partner may induce the other to unconsciously continue cooperative moves. The second explanation assumes a more conscious process of inference. By matching, the partner is demonstrating to the other that he or she is responsive and therefore could be persuaded to cooperate. This encourages the other to exercise any impulses he or she may have to cooperate, to see if the partner can be induced to respond (Apfelbaum, 1964). This interpretation is strengthened by the finding that if the first person is slow to reciprocate matching behavior (giving the impression that he or she is deliberating whether to reciprocate or not), the other is more likely to remain cooperative. Apparently, reluctant cooperation suggests conscious or deliberate intention and thereby implies a stronger commitment to cooperation.

Axelrod (1984) demonstrates that matching can generate cooperative behavior under a wide range of circumstances. Most striking, Axelrod's studies show that matching can induce even extremely competitive parties to cooperate. Axelrod cites four properties of matching tactics that tend to make the technique successful in inducing cooperation:

> avoidance of unnecessary conflict by cooperating as long as the other player does, provocability in the face of an uncalled for defection by the other, forgiveness after responding to a provocation, and clarity of behavior so that the other player can adapt to your pattern of action (Axelrod, 1984, p.20).

In a series of studies, Axelrod shows that tit for tat can create cooperation in large groups (even entire societies) provided small clusters of individuals base their cooperation on matching and interact regularly. Once established on this basis, cooperation based on matching forms a very powerful pattern that persists even if others adopt competing tactics.

Coalition Formation

Consider the following example: Ed and Janet are members of the Affirmative Action Committee of a large corporation. In the two years they have served on the committee, both have grown to dislike Brandon, the committee's chairperson. Brandon is an assistant administrator from the president's office and tends to be very careful in his recommendations on grievance cases, because he is afraid to offend his superiors. Janet and Ed have seen Brandon's caution result in the dismissal of several good cases and they are determined to try to counteract Brandon's slowdown of the committee. What should they do?

Although either Ed or Janet could try to control the group singly, it is more likely that they will form an alliance or coalition. Since both have less power than Brandon, they have a greater probability of success if they team up. There are also costs involved, because both Ed and Janet give up a certain amount of freedom when they form a coalition. Since their effectiveness depends on joint action, each must trust the other and each is vulnerable if the other decides to betray the coalition. However, in this case the benefits are likely to outweigh the costs, because a coalition greatly enhances Ed and Janet's chances of influencing their group.

These considerations suggest that the principles of game and social exchange theories would be very useful to explain coalition behavior. Game and exchange researchers have conducted numerous studies of coalition choices, and this research gives us some clues to how coalitions form.

The earliest theory of coalition formation was advanced by Caplow (1956), who argued that coalitions formed on the basis of **minimum power** necessary to defeat the opponent. Caplow assumed that parties are guided by a motivation to maximize the number of others they control (and therefore their ability to control the rewards they obtain). If this motivation holds, then relatively strong members will seek to form a coalition with the weakest member (or members) who still has enough power to defeat their opponent. For example, for three members A, B, and C whose ratio of power is 4 (A) to 3 (B) to 2 (C), the principle of minimum power would predict that coalitions between A and C, or B and C, would be more likely to form than between A and B. Caplow's theory suggests that "weakness is strength"; the weakest member of the triad is the only one who will always be included in a coalition. Evidence from several studies supports this prediction and the minimum power theory.

Gamson (1961) advanced a different theory based on the rewards received from coalitions. He theorized that rewards depended on the resources a person could contribute to the coalition: the greater a person's contribution the greater the share of rewards to which the person would be entitled. On the assumption that each person in the coalition desired to maximize his or her rewards, Gamson predicted that coalitions would form on the basis of **minimum resources**. This principle predicts that the most likely coalition would be the one capable of controlling the group that involves minimum resources contributed by the two members. In this case, members would attempt to maximize their own rewards by preferring those coalitions where their own contribution is as great as possible relative to other members. In the case of A, B, and C the most likely coalition would be the B–C alliance. Both A and B will seek to ally with C, but C will prefer B, because this alliance will maximize C's contributions relative to the other and therefore entitle C to a greater share of rewards.

The minimum power and minimum resource theories make somewhat different predictions about coalition formation. Minimum power theory argues that coalitions A–C and B–C are equally likely, while minimum resource theory predicts that B–C is much more probable than A–C. This difference permits comparison of the two principles. Generally, the evidence has favored Gamson's minimum resource theory. For example, one way of studying coalition formation is to create a political game simulating a political convention. Subjects are assigned different amounts of power by varying the number of votes they control. For example, A might control 40 votes, B 30 votes, and C 20 votes. In these studies all three possible coalitions form, but A–C and B–C form much more often than A–B, and B–C is much more likely than A–C (Gamson, 1961; Komorita & Chertkoff, 1973; Murnigham, 1978; Baker, 1981).

Hence minimum resource theory seems a more plausible explanation than minimum power theory.

Minimum resource theory assumes members of coalitions divide rewards in proportion to their contributions. If B contributes 30 votes and C only 15, then B is entitled to twice as much benefit as C. However, Komorita and Chertkoff (1973) studied the division of rewards in coalitions. They found that members bargain over the division of rewards prior to joining coalitions. This bargaining is not always open: it may be done "under the surface" without people's admission that it is occurring. The bargaining process determines what coalitions form, and it may result in distributions of rewards that differ considerably from the proportion of resources contributed. Minimum resources still seem to influence what coalitions form, but it does not necessarily **determine** the division of rewards.

Going back to Ed, Janet, and Brandon, these findings would suggest that the Ed–Janet coalition was more likely to form than the Ed–Brandon or Janet–Brandon alliances. As Ed and Janet talk about working against Brandon we would also expect them to refer to their contributions as a way of setting the division of rewards. For example, Ed might refer to his own verbal skill by saying, "I'll try to point out the flaws in his case, and you back me up." In saying this, Ed implicitly assigns to Janet the supporting role and, hence, a weaker contribution. If Janet accepts this, she may be granting Ed a greater claim to any benefits that result, such as the gratitude of other members for stopping Brandon. Of course, Ed and Janet may address the issue of division of rewards directly. Many coalitions depend on members' openly agreeing to do X in exchange for Y. However, there does not have to be an explicit agreement for minimum resource theory to apply. Unspoken agreements may hold just as strongly as spoken ones.

Minimum resource theory is not sufficient to explain all coalition behavior. There are cases where Janet or Ed would join forces with Brandon rather than with each other. In every coalition experiment, there are at least some A–B coalitions, a fact that runs counter to both Caplow's and Gamson's predictions. What accounts for this? Research by political scientists reveals that **similarities of attitudes and beliefs can also motivate coalition formation** (Gamson, 1961; Axelrod, 1970). These political theories assume that parties join coalitions not only for rewards but also because they are interested in getting certain policies or measures enacted. For example, they assume Ed and Janet form a coalition not only to obtain rewards but also because they desire to change the committee, independent of rewards. From this assumption it follows that parties will prefer coalitions with others with similar preferences: if both favor similar goals from the beginning they have a common ground for cooperation, and they are less likely to be sidetracked from their original ends.

The similarity principle implies a considerably different explanation for coalition formation than the minimum resource principle, an explanation not directly tied to rewards. Lawler and Youngs (1975) compared the two explanations with an experimental game simulating a political convention. They found that both rewards and attitude similarity determined coalition choice, but attitude similarity was "by far, the most important determinant." This finding may not hold for other situations where specific platforms are not so important, but it does show that similarity must be taken into account as well as reward.

The study of coalition formation is important, because coalitions are a primary path to power for weaker members (Janeway, 1980). Because of this fact stronger members often move to head off coalitions among weaker parties, either by forming coalitions themselves or by confusing issues and sewing seeds of discontent among their weaker counterparts. The findings discussed here underscore the importance of communicative processes in coalition formation. Members must convince others of rewards to be won and of their similarities in order to promote coalitions. In addition, they must downplay or make plans to counter any costs or problems they might face. However, these strategies cut both ways. Just as weaker members can use them to band together, so can stronger members use them to win over weaker ones or prevent their alliances. Conflict interaction is an arena for the struggle over allies.

Issue Definition

There is a tendency to assume that the issues in a conflict are the needs and interests the parties have at the outset. This view is too static. Issues may be defined and redefined throughout the conflict. Several issue definition tactics from Table 7.2 will be discussed.

Umbrellas are issues one party introduces to legitimize grievances when the original issue is one that others would not normally accept as valid. For example, David may be angry at Jim because Jim has gotten a promotion to a position David wanted. For David to express anger toward Jim because of Jim's promotion would seem petty. However, if Jim persistently comes to meetings late, David can legitimately chide him for that. David can then transfer his anger related to the promotion into an attack on Jim for always being late. The lateness issue serves as an umbrella for the anger generated by the real issue. People often do this in everyday conflicts: they are angry at someone and use the first legitimate issue that arises as an excuse to vent anger.

Bundling boards were identified by Walton (1969) because they are like the board early American families put up to guarantee the separation of courting couples sleeping in the same bed. Essentially, bundling boards are extra issues used to enhance the apparent distance between people's positions. As more and more issues are added, people see their interests as more and more incompatible. For example, assume David has lashed out at Jim for Jim's lateness. Jim could respond with a remark such as, "Well, you're not perfect yourself—your reports are always late!" David might then comment on Jim's sloppiness and Jim on David's jealousy, and so on, as the conflict develops into a real "everything but the kitchen sink" fight.

Bundling boards are useful in some ways. They allow parties to save face by shifting attention to others' shortcomings. They are one way for members to point out that others share the responsibility for the conflict as well. However, they also contribute to the tangle of issues and can accelerate the conflict.

The tactics of **negative inquiry** and **fogging** redefine issues in ways that narrow and refocus the conflict. Negative inquiry involves asking the other what he or she means by ambiguous statements in order to pin down the issues. The simple process of questioning can often encourage parties to think through vague and judgmental statements and to reduce them to more objective terms that specify their needs. For example, under questioning the statement "You are sloppy" may change to "I want you to stop leaving the car such a mess."

Fogging also focuses issues but is more manipulative than negative inquiry. On hearing another's complaint, the party acknowledges only part of it, thus narrowing the "live" issues to those one party is ready or willing to address. For example, A might say to B, "This car is a mess. You are so sloppy!" B then fogs by replying, "It is a mess. I'm so sorry," shunting the sloppiness issue aside. Fogging focuses the issues, which may be useful for problem-solving and compromising. It can also be used in an avoiding style.

Fractionation (Fisher, 1964) and the **two-column method** are two methods of issue definition that can be used to promote integration. Fractionation involves breaking a complex conflict into component issues that can be dealt with singly or in sequence. It involves setting an agenda for the conflict. In the two-column method, the two parties' interests or needs are listed side-by-side and commonalities identified.

A good way to follow the progress of a conflict is to pay attention to the shifting patterns of issues. The redefinition, expansion, and narrowing of issues determine what parties work on and, ultimately, how the conflict turns out.

Metacommunication

Metacommunication, explicit discussion about how the parties are handling the conflict, can open up channels of communication. Handled properly, metacommunication enables the correction of misunderstanding and the negotiation of norms that encourage helpful communication practices and discourage harmful ones. For example, Keith may habitually raise his voice when excited; Marla, however, may interpret Keith's loudness as an attempt to intimidate her. When Marla metacommunicates, she tells Keith how she interprets his loudness and how it affects her, and he has the opportunity to explain that it is just a habit. As a result, Marla may be able to disregard Keith's loudness or Keith may try to keep his voice down more. Metacommunication not only solves immediate problems but can also build parties' relationship. Successful metacommunication increases parties' awareness of and trust for each other. It fosters open communication.

Sillars and Weisberg (1987) register two warnings about metacommunication in relational conflicts. First, verbal metacommunication is not always effective, because people tend to trust nonverbal, analogic messages more in relationships. Keith may tell Marla that his loudness is just a bad habit and not meant to intimidate her, but if he raises his voice as he says this, she may disregard his explanation, reasoning that he is trying to intimidate her into accepting it. There is more to metacommunication than words, especially when the parties know each other well. However, this highlights a second problem with nonverbal metacommunication (Sillars & Weisberg, 1987, p. 151):

> Analogic forms of metacommunication are mostly imprecise. A particular tone of voice, for example, often admits many interpretations of the speaker's intent. Consequently, the same utterance may be variously seen as a compliment, verbal "jab," or good-natured joke.

Metacommunication must be handled carefully. Well-managed metacommunication is a useful tool for moving conflicts in productive directions.

Integrative Tactics

One of the most effective integrative tactics is to find a common goal that both parties value, commonly called a **superordinate goal**. Sherif's Robber's Cave experiment was one of the first studies of this technique (Sherif, Harvey, White, Hood, & Sherif, 1961). Sherif created two opposing groups of summer campers, the Bulldogs and the Red Devils. When the two groups had to work together on the common goal of solving several emergencies, between-group conflict was reduced. Numerous subsequent studies have supported the utility of superordinate goals (Hunger & Stern, 1976; Pruitt & Rubin, 1986). To be effective the superordinate goal must have high appeal for both parties and accomplishing it must be beyond the capabilities of any single party. In addition, competition and conflict among parties over other issues must be set aside. So a couple who often argue about how much to spend on redecorating their house may pull together when threatened by a financial crisis. The common goal of weathering the storm overcomes their perceived differences. As this example illustrates, a superordinate goal need not be something both parties want; it can also be something they want to avoid or a common enemy. Political leaders have used the perception of threats from without to unite factionalized nations from time immemorial.

Superordinate goals are one of the most reliable integrative tactics, but they do not work under all circumstances. If the parties fail to attain the superordinate goal, the goal may lose its attractiveness and competition will ensue (Hunger & Stern, 1976; Worchel, Andreoli, & Folger, 1977). Given their previous conflict, the parties are likely to blame each other for the failure. Then too, finding a superordinate goal does not resolve the preexisting conflict, as the example of our redecorating couple shows. Once the couple is in the clear again, or if they fail to get out of their financial crisis, bickering over redecorating could easily resurface.

The superordinate goal tactic will also fail if each party does not have a clear and distinct role in attaining the goal (Deschamps & Brown, 1983). They must have a clear idea of how their efforts fit together or they may lose their sense of identity. If this happens, they are less likely to be attracted to cooperating with the other. It is also worth noting that parties may have trouble discovering or recognizing superordinate goals when hostilities run high. A "cooling off" period is often necessary before the superordinate goal can be used to promote cooperation.

Experimental integration is a tactic designed to overcome lack of trust between parties. As we have seen in Chapter 3, moving a conflict in an integrative direction is often difficult because of self-reinforcing cycles of behavior and interpretation, which create and perpetuate distrust, tension, and hostility. This may result in the paradoxical situation where neither party wants to compete, but both adopt competing styles because they believe the other is competing. This cycle can create uncontrolled escalation, making it hard to break out of competing orientations. This is the stuff of which arms races are made. The key to experimental integration is to make a conciliatory or cooperative move, yet not let one's guard down so that the other can take advantage. If the other party responds in a positive fashion, then we can answer with more integrative moves and eventually move into full-fledged integration. The approach is experimental in that the conciliatory or cooperative move is an experiment: it tests how the other will respond. If it really is a false conflict the other should respond cooperatively, and the party can then signal back with another cooperative move, and so on to gradually bring about integration.

The best known method for experimental integration is Osgood's **GRIT** strategy—graduated and reciprocated initiatives in tension reduction (Osgood, 1959, 1962, 1966; Lindskold, 1979). The specific points in the GRIT strategy are as follows (after Lindskold, 1979):

1. Set the climate for conciliatory initiatives by making a general statement of intention to reduce tension through subsequent acts, indicating the advantages to the other of reciprocating.
2. Announce publicly each unilateral move prior to making it and indicate that it is part of a general strategy.
3. Each announcement should invite reciprocation from the other. Reciprocation needn't come in the form of the same move but should be a conciliatory step of some sort.
4. Each initiative must be carried out as announced without any requirement of reciprocation by the other.
5. Initiatives should be continued for some time even if the other does not reciprocate. This gives the other a chance to test the party's sincerity and also puts pressure on the other.
6. Initiatives must be unambiguous and permit verification.
7. Initiatives must be risky and vulnerable to exploitation, but they also must not expose the party to a serious and damaging attack.
8. Moves should be graded in degree of risk to match the reciprocation of the other. Once the other begins to reciprocate, the initiator should reciprocate with at least as risky or slightly more risky moves.

The first three points make the initiative clear and may enlist other parties to put pressure on the other to comply with the conciliatory gesture. Points 4 through 6 make it clear to the other that he or she has the freedom to respond or not, that this is not a trick or maneuver. Point 7 is crucial, because it gives the party the security to attempt the experiment. The party stands to lose if the other takes advantage of the move but does not expose his or her position so that the other can totally win the day. Finally, point 8 represents an attempt to gradually increase cooperation.

Etzioni (1967) shows how Kennedy and Khrushchev followed a pattern similar to GRIT to bring about the thaw in East–West relations that followed the Cuban Missile Crisis. Improvement in international relations is often launched by small "confidence building" measures set in motion during negotiations. Lindskold (1979) summarizes evidence from numerous game studies supporting the effectiveness of GRIT. This evidence suggests that what works in the international arena also works in interpersonal conflicts. There is always some risk in embarking on integration. However, experimental integration tactics can ease parties' fears of disaster and encourage them to try to move the first few steps along the road to problem-solving.

Another tactic related to experimental integration is **reformed sinner**. Unlike toughness, which simply aims to maximize the individual's outcomes, the reformed sinner attempts to induce an uncooperative partner to cooperate and thereby enhance outcomes (Pruitt & Kimmel, 1977). In this strategy, the person initially competes for a period of time and then shifts over to cooperation. The method demonstrates that the individual could compete if he or she wanted to, but that he or she chose instead to cooperate and reward the other. In most studies this strategy, or a similar one in which the individual is initially tough and then relaxes his or her demands, is unusually effective in inducing the other's cooperation. Of course, for the strategy to work, there must be an incentive for the person responding to the reformed sinner to cooperate rather than exploit the weakness. Thus the reformed sinner must maintain a "stick" and be prepared to resort to it again if the "carrot" does not work.

Why does the reformed sinner strategy work? One explanation points to the respect that such a strategy creates for the person using it. By initially competing, the person demonstrates an ability to punish the other. Voluntarily giving up this punishment and exposing oneself to the other generates respect and also a sense that the person must be sincere in his or her offer of cooperation. This explanation is illustrated in the strategy used by many elementary school teachers who want to have an "open classroom" atmosphere, yet do not want students to abuse this openness. The teachers often try to be somewhat stern at the beginning of the year and make an effort to show the students that they can punish them if need be. Only after respect for the teacher's authority is established does the teacher gradually relax and attempt to promote a more open atmosphere. The second explanation is simpler than the first and goes hand-in-hand with it: it posits that once the other has experienced the negative consequences of competition, sudden cooperation will be attractive and motivate the other to cooperate. If this explanation is valid, it implies that the person employing the strategy should take care to make the other recognize the disadvantages of competition and the advantages of cooperation.

STYLES AND TACTICS IN PRACTICE

The preceding discussion may create the somewhat misleading impression that people can simply select and use whatever styles and tactics they think will work. However, things are often more complicated than this when we consider styles and tactics in the rough-and-tumble world of "real conflict." It is one thing to sit and calmly deliberate about the choice of a style or tactic. It is quite another to have to deal with the reactions that styles and tactics provoke in others. Case 7.2 illustrates how styles interact in a conflict episode.

Case 7.2 **The Would-Be Borrower**

A roommate conflict developed between Joan and Mary over the use of Joan's new car. When Joan talked to Mary about her anticipated purchase, Joan often said things like,

"It will be wonderful when **we** have a car." Mary interpreted Joan's use of the word "we" to mean that she might be allowed to borrow the car on certain occasions. When Mary's sister had come to visit, Joan had driven Mary's sister's car, and Mary figured this was a case of "share and share alike."

Joan began to shop seriously for a car during the two weeks before Thanksgiving. When Joan was about to make her purchase, Mary saw a new opportunity open up for her. Due to scheduling problems on her job, Mary was not able to go home for Thanksgiving. This would be the first Thanksgiving Mary had not been home. Mary asked Joan if she could use Joan's car to visit her parents, who lived about 120 miles away. Mary knew Joan would not need her car that weekend, because Joan was going out of town with her parents for the holiday.

At first, Joan refused, but Mary persisted in raising the subject. Joan reported that she was "appalled that Mary had even asked." For Joan it was an issue of "invasion of personal property." As the tension over this question began to build, Joan began to use a withdrawing style: she gave Mary ambiguous, noncommittal replies and often simply did not reply at all. Mary had a more forceful, dominating communication style than Joan, and Joan saw avoidance as a way of sparing her a direct confrontation with Mary. Joan assumed that a direct denial of Mary's request would provoke an emotional outburst, which she wanted to avoid at all costs.

In response to Joan's nonresponsiveness, Mary began to apply pressure indirectly, using a contending style. She pressed Joan to loan her car. Mary also had phone conversations with her parents within earshot of Joan in which she talked about the things they could do if she could get a car from Joan. Joan interpreted this as an attempt to make her feel guilty, and it worked. Joan felt a great deal of stress and turned to her family for support, which they readily gave. The interaction of the two styles set up a competitive climate and an impasse developed: Mary saw the issue as a question of a favor one would willingly do for a friend. Joan saw it as a question of whether Mary could infringe on her personal property.

Joan bought her car on the weekend before Thanksgiving and stored it in her parents' garage until it was insured. Mary mentioned her holiday plans with the car several times during the weekend and interpreted Joan's silence as acquiescence. The blowup occurred when an insurance salesman called on Joan. Mary had been giving Joan advice on insurance and was also present at the meeting. After discussing rates, the salesman asked Joan when she wanted her coverage to begin. Joan replied, "Thursday night at midnight." Thus the car would be uninsured on Thanksgiving day and Mary could not drive it. Joan reported that this move was not premeditated: "I saw an escape hatch and I took it." The significance of Joan's shift to contending was not lost on Mary. She was shocked at "the devious way Joan had gone about it."

Mary reported that after the salesman left, Joan "just started babbling and babbling about nothing at all and getting really nervous." Joan shifted back to withdrawing after her one "trump." In the "20-minute scream-fest" that followed, styles shifted several times more. Mary asked Joan if she purposely started the insurance later to keep her from borrowing Joan's car. Joan replied "Yes" and shifted back to other topics. After listening with half an ear for a while, Mary told Joan that she was "really ticked" with her. Joan replied, "I know you are. I knew you'd be like this. I knew you'd do this." Mary said that it would have been better if Joan had just told her "straight out." Joan replied that her mother had said that Mary should not be allowed to use her car. Mary was upset that Joan had told her mother: "Now I suppose you're going to tell your whole family what a rotten, miserable roommate you have!" Joan did not reply to this. Mary kept up her challenges, charging Joan with being selfish. Joan did not respond. Mary tried a normative justification, arguing that Thanksgiving is a special occasion. Joan did not respond. Mary asked Joan if the issue was that Joan thought she was a lousy driver. Joan replied that it was just too soon for someone to borrow her car. "Oh, so you don't want me to soil it before you can use it!" Mary flashed back.

When the shouting match ended, Joan did her laundry and remained in the laundry room for an hour, crying. Mary remained in their apartment, crying. When Joan returned to the apartment, the two did not speak until Joan approached Mary to show her a magazine article Mary had been looking for. This softened the mood somewhat but did not initiate conversation. Eventually, as they prepared for bed, Mary approached Joan: "Look, we've got to end this. I'm sorry I asked for your car. It's too soon for me to be asking. I should have realized this from other things you said." Joan replied that she was sorry she didn't give Mary a straight answer at first. Mary was disappointed at Joan's answer, because she expected an apology from Joan for not letting her use her car. Both women went to bed.

The two did not have much contact over the next few days. Mary reported feeling alienated from Joan: "It was a pretty terrible couple of weeks after that." The conflict was never really resolved, but it gradually faded into the background and the two women resumed their friendship.

This conflict was not resolved because there was no successful differentiation phase to set the stage for integration. The issues and concerns each party had were never clearly defined. Mary tried to bring the issue out in the open, but Joan persisted in smoothing and withdrawing. In effect, Mary's contending style was neutralized by Joan's successful avoidance. Mary tried several times to shift her style toward compromising or problem-solving, but she was blocked when Joan persisted in avoiding the conflict. Mary could not involve both of them in a discussion unless Joan cooperated, and Joan did not. And if Joan had wanted to discuss the issues openly, she was deterred by Mary's active persistence. Joan feared that she would not be able to hold her own in any discussion, so it probably seemed easier just to avoid. Her only forceful venture was the brief foray into competing when she set the insurance date. In anticipation of Mary's pressure, Joan quickly reverted to avoiding styles. The two were trapped in their respective styles; each style reinforced the other in a destructive self-reinforcing cycle.

The effectiveness of styles and tactics is dependent on the other's actions. It is not simply a matter of selecting a tactic on one's own. The other's reaction may reinforce or neutralize a tactic, or even cause it to "backfire." And a party's ability to choose or change styles and tactics is also limited by what others do. In some cases, things get so out of hand that the parties are trapped, like Joan and Mary. Only after a concerted effort can the direction of such conflicts be changed. This case clearly illustrates the interactive nature of styles and tactics and underscores an important point we have emphasized: conflict interaction often acquires a momentum of its own.

This does not mean that selection of styles and tactics is a hopeless undertaking. People always have degrees of freedom that allow them to act in their own interests and to change situations for the better. However, there are limitations on what parties can control, and it is well to bear these in mind. The principles of conflict interaction discussed in earlier chapters offer useful resources for understanding the dynamics of styles and tactics.

CONCLUSION

This chapter has focused on the basic moves in many conflict episodes. The tactics described in this chapter are used by parties to enact styles of conflict. Styles are general orientations toward conflict and represent the overall approaches that give tactics their meaning. As the discussion of variants on styles indicates, the five styles may be carried out in different ways, each giving something of a different flavor to the interaction.

We have emphasized, however, that styles alone are not sufficient to understand conflict. The other's style influences how effective the party's style can be and whether the party can even stick with the original style. So, at a minimum, the interaction of parties' styles and how these reinforce or cancel each other must be studied. Beyond this, we must recognize that descriptions of styles are not sufficient to capture fully what happens when parties enact a conflict. The communication processes discussed in previous chapters create a field of forces driving conflicts, and styles are parties' attempts to navigate this field. Styles operate in a context set by other processes. For example, when face-saving is important, a competing style will be received differently than when parties are not attending to face. If parties are caught in a spiral of escalation, a competing style may simply increase the escalation. But during periods of integration, brief use of the same style may contribute to constructive movement by increasing pressure for conflict resolution.

The selection of a style does not tell the whole story. Style choice has a major influence on conflict processes, but conflicts are also driven by the larger interaction context and by cycles of action and response, which are beyond any individual's control. It is important not to underestimate the difference judicious style choices can make. It is also important not to overestimate it.

Chapter
8

Changing Conflict Dynamics

To this point, we have been concerned primarily with understanding what drives conflict interaction. Understanding, however, is of little value unless it can be put into practice. This chapter suggests measures parties can take to improve their chances of dealing with conflict productively. In this chapter, we are concerned with how **parties can regulate their own conflicts**. Self-regulation is the optimal method of managing conflict: people are more likely to accept necessary measures if they personally choose them, and the measures they select are often more appropriate and effective than outsiders' suggestions. Alternatively, a formal third party may facilitate or mediate the group's attempts to deal with conflict. Third parties may do many of the same things parties in conflict would, but because of their special role, their actions often have a significantly different impact. We will consider third party intervention in Chapter 9.

We attempt to go beyond the principles and explanations presented in previous chapters to develop approaches for working through conflict. These guidelines will not be pat answers, because there are simply too many variables in conflicts. Formulas would be misleading. Instead, we discuss forces that change the course conflict takes and consider problems and pitfalls that parties face in attempting to control those forces.

SELF-REGULATION OF CONFLICT

Self-regulation refers to behavior that checks destructive conflict interaction and turns it in a constructive direction. The previous discussions of the forces shaping conflict—power, styles, working habits, face, and climate—suggest actions that can counter whatever negative influence these forces may exert and turn them into positive influences. In order to work with the forces, parties must be able (1) to diagnose emerging problems and (2) to use their diagnoses to successfully alter conflict interaction patterns. Accordingly, this section presents suggestions for both diagnosis and action for each force. Before proceeding, however, two caveats:

First, it is often difficult to determine when conflict interaction has made a turn in a destructive direction. As we have seen, conflict interaction can develop in gradual and subtle steps. Parties can suddenly find themselves caught in an escalating spiral or active avoidance without suspecting it. **Members must be constantly on the alert for signs of destructive patterns and act quickly to alter them**. Because escalation or avoidance cycles can stem from trained incapacities, these interaction cycles often go undetected until irreparable damage is done. Seeing that parties are in a protracted, destructive spiral is crucial because such insight is the first step in changing destructive tendencies. People in conflict must be aware of concrete symptoms that signal the possible onset of escalation or avoidance.

Table 8.1 summarizes several symptoms that may emerge when the conflict is heading toward destructive escalation or avoidance of the issue. It should be emphasized that the mere appearance of the symptom is not an automatic cause for concern. Constructive conflict interaction can pass through periods of escalation, avoidance, constructive work, and relaxation. Cycles only become threatening when they are repetitive and prevent other forms of interaction from emerging.

Second, changing conflict interaction patterns often requires *structural* change in parties' relationships, groups, or organizations. For example, discussing a problem may prompt parties to apologize and promise to change their attitudes and feelings: "Really, it's just a matter of taking a different perspective and respecting each other's opinions." This change in attitude is admirable and represents an important first step, but more often than not it proves ineffective. **In order to alter parties' methods of dealing with conflict, it is necessary to structurally change interaction patterns by altering working habits, climate, power relations, or parties' need to save face**. Changes in attitude are important, but they are usually insufficient to sustain more productive patterns of conflict interaction. Too easily, existing structures reexert their influence on interaction and undermine resolutions made in more reflective moments. This occurred in the Riverdale Halfway House (Case 6.1). After talking with the consultant, both George and Carole attempted to put a new face on things and to have more constructive attitudes toward each other. Over the long run, however, their attempts proved fruitless, because the suspicious climate at Riverdale prevented serious work on their problems. After a while both George and Carole fell back into their old patterns of sniping and misunderstanding, which persisted until George left. Only when the **forces** moving interaction in destructive directions are eliminated or neutralized is lasting change possible. For this reason, the principles we

Table 8.1   INTERACTION SYMPTOMS OF ESCALATION OR AVOIDANCE CYCLES

Symptoms of Avoidance	Symptoms of Escalation
Marked decrease in the parties' commitment to solving the problem ("why would we care?")	An issue takes much longer to deal with than was anticipated
Quick acceptance of a suggested solution	Parties repeatedly offer the same argument in support of a position
Parties stop themselves from raising controversial aspects of an issue	Parties overinflate the consequences of not reaching agreement
People "tune out" of the interaction	Threats are used to win arguments
Unresolved issues keep emerging in the same or different form	Mounting tension is felt
Discussion centers on a safe aspect of a broader and more explosive issue	The parties get nowhere but seem to be working feverishly
Little sharing of information	Name-calling and personal arguments are used
Outspoken people are notably quiet	Immediate polarization on issues or the emergence of coalitions
No plans are made to implement a chosen solution	Hostile eye gaze or less-direct eye contact between parties
No evaluation is made of evidence that is offered in support of claims	Sarcastic laughter or humor as a form of tension release
	Heated disagreements that seem pointless or are trivial issues

discuss are oriented toward **unfreezing and changing** the structures that shape interaction.

WORKING WITH POWER

There are a number of barriers to accurate diagnosis of the role of power in conflicts. For one thing, people are often unwilling to talk about power or to provide honest and accurate assessments of their own or others' power, for several reasons. Given our culture's emphasis on democracy and equality, the open use of power is not socially sanctioned. People may be unwilling to admit that they use "force" or that a group is controlled by only a few members because they believe it makes them look bad. Furthermore, since power depends on endorsement, powerful parties often try to keep their power unobtrusive, in order not to alienate those they influence. If weaker parties cannot see the power, or if they do not understand how it "works," they can do nothing to upset the present balance. In addition, as we noted in Chapter 7, many moves (such as issue control) use power indirectly and it is hard to determine who is having influence. Finally, power and endorsement processes depend on relationships **between** parties rather than being properties of individuals, so it is often hard to determine where the source of power is. If power stems from relationships, it is misleading to try to identify a particular person who holds power. The more important question may be who assents to the use of power or who withholds endorsement.

These barriers make the assessment of power a complex process for which there can be no set formula. It is best to try several approaches. One way to assess power is to **determine the possible power resources in the situation and identify who holds them.** This involves identifying both obvious resources like status, knowledge, personal attractiveness, or formal authority and more subtle sources of power, such as confidence or the ability to predict another's behavior. A second, complementary approach is to **identify power through its effects.** Those people whose preferences consistently win out and who are accommodated by other members are generally those who control resources and use them effectively. As Frost and Wilmot (1978) note, the **ability to label the conflict** is also a sign of power. If a conflict could be interpreted either as a minor difference of opinion or as an important matter of principle, and it ends up being interpreted as a minor difference, the members who favored this view are likely to hold the high ground. A third indicator of power is **conservatism.** If power is relational, then changes in existing relationships generally alter the balance of power, while stability preserves it. People who are against changes are likely to believe they will lose by it. These are often the people who hold substantial power under the status quo.

None of these three indicators is foolproof and each can lead to mistakes. However, they provide a good starting point for thinking about power. Judgments about power ultimately rest on knowledge of relationships among parties, their particular history, and the nuances that signal dominance and subordination. Diagnoses cannot be programmed and must be continually refined.

Another important diagnostic tool in analyzing power is the ability to recognize when parties draw on unique or shared power resources as a basis for influence in conflict. Parties can attempt to influence a conflict by drawing either on the unique resources they hold or on sources of power commonly available to everyone and explicitly endorsed as a legitimate basis for influence. When people draw from their unique power sources, the conflict is likely to turn away from problem-solving and toward heightened escalation. Each move premised on unique sources of power "tells" others that an attempt may be made to resolve the issue by means not available to everyone. In effect, use of unique power resources is an attempt to exert unilateral control. This message can promote escalation by prompting other parties to use their own unique resources to counter moves they cannot reciprocate.

The Creativity Development Committee (Case 4.3) provides an illustration of people moving from the use of shared to individual resources. In the early meetings, parties' actions were contained by boundaries the group as a whole accepted. The project directors and the manager drew from a set of resources they all shared and saw as a legitimate basis for changing opinions and determining possible outcomes. When the manager indicated that **he** might make the final choice based on his position as director, the emphasis shifted to the **unique** sources of power that individual parties held. Similarly, in the Job Resignation at the Social Service Agency (Case 4.6), the conflict drew on unique power bases. The two newer staff people used their friendship and agreement on agency policy to move against Kathy. Kathy drew from her "seniority" and experience as an older worker to justify her positions in response to the challenge she faced. The three women never developed an implicit agreement about what resources could be used to influence each other. There was not, in other words, a mutually endorsed set of resources that could be used to work through the conflicts over the quality of work and the long-range objectives of the agency. Although differences of opinion on these issues may have been difficult to resolve, the staff's inaction prevented a **group** assault on the problem. In making moves based on their unique sources of power, parties worked on the problem from their own standpoints and discouraged give and take on common ground.

To safeguard against the dangers resulting from unbalanced power, parties need to forestall power moves based on unique resources. Individually held resources become less salient and are less likely to be invoked when all parties have established a mutually endorsed power base. But what conditions are conducive to the use of shared power? Although there is no cut-and-dry answer to this question, conditions for fostering the use of shared power resources in specific contexts can suggest what might be done. As one detailed illustration, we discuss conditions that foster the use of shared power in group or organizational conflicts.

Fostering Shared Power in Group and Organizational Conflicts

There are three primary conditions that encourage reliance on shared power in intra-group conflicts. First, **if all members agree on the primary goals of the group or organization, unique sources of power are less likely to be used.** A shared sense of purpose gives members a common orientation, which encourages interchange on common ground. A common goal gives the group a center that encourages members to identify with each other. When they identify, members are likely to think in similar terms about how to influence each other. They are not as likely to resort to unique resources that would underscore potential divisions among them.

Of course this is easier said than done; members must be able to articulate what the general goals of the group mean when they are applied in particular situations. An organization can easily say it intends to work for the community good. But what does this mean exactly? When members look at any given problem and examine alternative, and perhaps incompatible, proposals in light of the group's general purpose, they are engaging in behavior that promotes constructive conflict interaction. This process enables the group members to check each other and to articulate the group's purpose again, to build cohesion around that purpose, and to consistently steer itself, on a decision-by-decision basis, toward common goals.

Classroom groups that are formed to complete a group project assignment often fail to attain a common goal or purpose. Some students see the group's major aim as education; they accept the premise that going through the trials and tribulations necessary to complete the term project will be a good learning experience. For these students the general purpose of the group is to learn how to carry out assigned tasks as a team. Other students do not buy into this educational objective. Their goal is simply to complete an acceptable assignment that meets the basic requirements for the course and get a good grade without spending too much effort.

When two different goals exist in a project group, differences over how the project should be accomplished, how often the group should meet, or how much time should be spent on each task are ripe for escalation into full-blown conflict. Without an overarching goal to guide them, members are likely to feel disconnected from others and to turn to unique sources of power to influence the group's choices on these issues. In groups where all members buy into the same goal, there can still be considerable debate over how long meetings should run and so on, but the group is working toward the same conception of success as it tries to reach agreement on these issues. Members may have to spend considerable time defining what success entails, what the best means for achieving success are, and how much time is needed to reach the goal, but this discussion is constructive. It points the group toward a more well-defined conception of itself, and it allows the group to set explicit standards for what behavior is expected from members. In terms of power, it forms a basis for common effort that encourages members to operate on the same level when they try to influence each other.

In the Job Resignation case, the three women never reached agreement about what the primary goals of the agency should be. There were implicit differences that the two factions never tried to resolve or meld into one shared mission for the office. As a result, differences over an issue like what constituted "quality work" at the agency were "settled" when members turned to the unique sources of power they held. Sticking to the shared definition of their problem—should the agency expand?—might have helped the three women to identify common goals.

It is important to note that a common goal does not guarantee that shared power bases will be used. Many groups with clear goals also have strong leaders who have access to resources different from those of other members, such as formal authority. The point here is that a common goal encourages member identification, which may predispose members to use common resources.

A second condition conducive to a shared power base is **the group's or organization's willingness to make power resources accessible to all members.** A resource truly shared by the membership is an attractive alternative to unique sources. If, for example, knowledge of the past history of the organization is endorsed as an important resource for influencing decisions, settling differences about policy matters, and so on, then all members—even new people—must be given access to this knowledge. New members will, of course, be less influential than others at first, because they do not enter the group with a full history in hand. However, if the relevant information is made available on a decision-by-decision or issue-by-issue basis, newer members can draw on the same basis of influence older members use. In some groups this is done through formal channels, such as orientation sessions, training in skills valued by the group, and written histories.

Even when all information is available and "access" is given to all members in principle, certain members may consistently be more influential than others because they are more skillful. Some members may be more powerful than others because they are better able to articulate positions the group recognizes as appropriate or consistent with its direction. Ensuring access to all does not mean that all members will be **equally able** to use a resource. Some members may be able to apply the resource more quickly or insightfully as new issues arise, and thus their power, their ability to influence the direction of conflicts, will appear to be greater. The difference is, however, that the power these members exercise is legitimate because the group as a whole continues to endorse the resources regardless of who uses them.

The importance of equalizing the power resources available to all members is clear in the Job Resignation case. In their coalition, Lois and Janelle had a source of power unavailable to Kathy. If Lois and Janelle had not taken advantage of their alliance and had instead tried to deal with Kathy "one-on-one," they might have been able to work out a more constructive solution. From one-on-one conversation, Lois and Janelle might have been able to understand Kathy's needs and feelings better. They might also have seen her potential and the problems that kept her from contributing. Kathy, on the other hand, would not be intimidated by Lois and Janelle's "united front" and might herself see the merits in their case. Once each side understood the other's needs and problems, working out a solution would be easier. Moreover, once Kathy was assured that the other two would not use their superior power to force her, she might become less reactive and more willing to work on improving the agency.

A third condition underlies the first two: the group should recognize that **its members are the source of power and that they participate continually in the exercise and renewal of power.** The group must work to see through the myth of power as a possession, to the process of **endorsement** necessary for any move to be effective. It must acknowledge that this endorsement occurs in members' interaction and that therefore, as Janeway (1980) argues, all power is grounded in "community" among members. This is what democratic nations try to do in their constitutions, and this is what groups must do to build a shared power base. However, just as governments often have trouble remembering their popular roots, so too do groups have trouble remembering the roots of their power. As we noted in Chapter 4, the endorsement process operates to hide the source of power from members. **Long socialization, the mystique of power,** and **subtle interaction processes** veil members' roles in endorsement. To achieve a balance of power in the group, members must adopt structural measures to counteract these forces. Groups have done this in a variety of ways, including rotating leadership regularly, appointing "process watchers" to comment on members' moves and group interaction, setting up retreats and evaluation periods to help members discuss power-related problems, and forcing their leaders to adopt a nondirective style. Whatever the specific steps, these moves tend to be effective because (1) they make members aware of their community and their responsibilities to the group and to each other, (2) they emphasize admitting all members into discussions on an equal basis, and (3) they de-emphasize the prominence of any particular individual vis-à-vis the group.

In this section we have emphasized the need to develop shared power bases. We mean this as an ideal or goal to strive for, not as the only effective or justifiable use of power. Some groups have such deep-seated discrepancies that weaker members have no choice but to develop and use unique power bases. In such instances, the use of force or countervailing resources may be the only way to check or get the attention of the controlling members. The literature on groups and organizations is full of examples of groups with authoritarian leaders who became so oppressive that members saw no choice but to band together and to rebel. A forceful countermove was the only way these parties could get their message heard. Although we acknowledge cases where unique sources of power may be used beneficially, it is important to remember that they create unstable situations over the long run. One side may topple the other, but, in time, the other is likely to strike back. Moving to a shared power base greatly enhances the likelihood of a constructive and mutually beneficial solution.

In one sense, these suggestions are preconditions; they must be in place in a group if members can hope to develop shared power resources and use them as a basis for moves in any conflict interaction. In another sense, these suggestions offer long-term intervention strategies; they are areas that the group can work to establish as part of the general expectations for how it operates. They can govern what members consider doing when they try to sway each other's thinking about issues.

What happens, however, when these preconditions have not been established in a group or when a member uses unique resources in a conflict particularly important to them? Although no intervention is foolproof, several approaches may help prevent escalation in such instances.

First, it may be helpful if members discuss their likely reaction to the use of unique resources. For example, members might acknowledge that they will see someone who uses seniority to justify job assignments as "out for themselves." Open discussions can effectively raise the group's consciousness about power moves. It can help the group learn that certain resources will change conflict interaction dramatically. It also alerts the group to possible dangers or pitfalls that might result.

A second approach is aimed at developing structural changes in interaction when power moves are based on unique resources. One of the most effective tools for changing the influence of power in conflicts is to increase members' **awareness** of the role they play in creating and sustaining others' power. If members become aware of how their endorsement is shaped by social categorization, the mystique of power, and their own interaction, they are well on their way to "seeing through" the existing power structure. The value of "consciousness raising" is illustrated by the support groups that spring up in professions undergoing rapid change and coping with the struggles that result. These groups, which range from female executives in male-dominated corporations to nurses and medical orderlies attempting to gain more input into hospital decisions, give their members a chance to share problems and fears and to give each other advice. Members help each other understand how the dominant groups in their professions maintain their positions. They also work out ways of being more effective, and build resolve and courage to face difficult situations. They encourage members to question what was previously unquestionable, the taken-for-granted relations of authority and obedience, strength and weakness in the group. Formal support groups are not the only thing that can serve this function: a conversation over dinner or after work can generate important insights. Just realizing one is not alone and sharing experiences are often important steps.

As Janeway (1980) observes, in addition to awareness, mutual support is another way for weaker members to counterbalance stronger ones. People generally associate coalitions with open shows of strength and solidarity, as in a union vote, but such displays may be ineffective in group and organizational contexts. Raising the flag of defiance may threaten stronger members and cause them to overreact, sending the conflict into an escalating spiral. Those who have greater resources stand to lose if the current balance tips in a new direction, and they will resist such moves. A coalition is more likely to be successful in moving a conflict in a productive direction if it is unobtrusive. The pact between members should not be openly displayed, and, if possible, any coordination or support should not be obvious. In addition, a coalition is more likely to turn conflict in a productive direction if it aims for a balance of power than if it tries to win. If the powerful members' interests are not threatened, and if they do not face serious losses, they are more likely to cooperate with efforts to achieve a balance of power.

WORKING WITH TRAINED INCAPACITIES

Trained incapacities are work habits inflexibly applied in response to conflict. The key to diagnosing the effect of trained incapacities is therefore to examine "standard operating procedures" for traps. The discussion in Chapter 3 of incapacities, and the problems they imply, provides a set of starting points for this search: parties can monitor discussions for problems due to goal centeredness (such as insufficient analysis of problems underlying the conflict), dependence on objective standards, or reliance on procedural rules. This monitoring process must go on continuously, because people can slip into harmful patterns without recognizing it. Because trained incapacities are "second nature," they are subtle and hard to detect: parties know something is wrong, but they cannot put their finger on the source.

The chair of an administrative committee in one midwestern social service agency keeps a checklist of possible problems to help her overcome potential blind spots. It includes questions such as: "Is there too little dissent to have a balanced discussion?" "Are votes being used to suppress minority views?" "Are differences discussed in win–lose terms?" The chair goes over this list (or parts of it) during and after every meeting, carefully monitoring the group's process. Although the answers are negative for most meetings, the list has turned up several unexpected problems.

One dangerous symptom of trained incapacities is a high level of tension in the group. Recall from Chapter 3 that differentiation of positions in the early stages of a conflict creates tension that can lead to inflexible behavior and promote trained incapacities. Although there is not a perfect cause–effect relationship between tension level and trained incapacities, tension increases their likelihood. Situations that create tension—a serious threat from outside the group, a rapidly approaching time limit, or a severe and important disagreement—are ripe for the dangers of differentiation.

The most straightforward method of counteracting trained incapacities is for the parties to adopt **procedures** that correct for the biases they introduce (Poole, 1991). The widely used **Reflective Thinking Process** for decision-making is one such procedure (Scheidel & Crowell, 1979; Gouran, 1982). Basically, the Reflective Thinking Process is designed to avoid errors that may result from trained incapacities such as emphasizing solutions prior to analyzing problems or premature evaluation of ideas.

Reflective Thinking avoids these problems by positing a five-step problem-solving procedure and requiring parties to go through the steps in order, keeping deliberations on each step separate:

1. Definition of the Problem or Task—the parties assess the nature of the problem before them and determine if the problem is significant enough to act on.
2. Analysis of the Problem—once the problem is defined, the parties analyze its causes. Only after these are understood do the parties move on to step 3.
3. Suggestion of Possible Solutions—the parties research and develop a wide array of possible solutions. No serious evaluation or elimination of solutions occurs at this stage.
4. Solution Selection—the parties evaluate and select the best solution.
5. Implementation—the parties plan how to put the solution into effect.

This procedure closely parallels logical thought processes and is the basis for most group decision-making methods (see also Etzioni, 1968) and conflict management sequences (see also Filley, 1975). By requiring parties to analyze the problem prior to developing solutions and to develop a long list of solutions prior to evaluating them, it counteracts a tendency to focus on and evaluate solutions prematurely. By focusing attention on a well-defined pattern for thinking about a common problem, it also helps avoid destructive redefinition.

Hall and Watson (1970) present another procedural format that works against the ill effects of trained incapacities. Rather than focusing on **what** the parties talk about at particular stages of decision-making, they attempt to develop a set of ground rules for **how** parties should work on a problem. These consensus-seeking rules are designed to help parties work through differences and disagreements in a constructive fashion:

1. Avoid **arguing** for your own position. Present your position as clearly and logically as possible, but consider seriously the reactions of the group in any subsequent presentations of the same point.
2. Avoid **win–lose** stalemates in the discussion of positions. Discard the notion that someone must win and someone must lose in the discussion; when impasses occur, look for the next most acceptable alternative for both parties.
3. Avoid changing your mind **only** to avoid the conflict and to reach agreement. Withstand pressures to yield that have no objective or logically sound foundation. Strive for enlightened flexibility; avoid outright capitulation.
4. Avoid suppressing conflicts by resorting to voting, averaging, coin flipping, and the like. Treat differences of opinion as indicative of an incomplete sharing of information and viewpoints and press for additional exploration and investigation.
5. View differences of opinion as both natural and helpful rather than as a hindrance in decision-making. Generally, the more ideas expressed the greater the likelihood of conflict will be, but the richer the array of resources will be as well.

6. View initial agreement as suspect. Explore the reasons underlying apparent agreements; make sure that people have arrived at similar solutions for either the same basic reasons or for complementary reasons before incorporating such solutions in an agreement or decision.

These rules encourage parties to air and address differences rather than to come to agreement quickly. They counteract several problems of trained incapacities, including premature convergence on a single solution and reliance on objective standards where none exist. Hall and Watson tested these procedures and found that groups trained in the rules produced better answers on a problem-solving task than did untrained groups. They attributed this to a "synergy bonus" from the procedure: it allowed groups to make use of all their members' skills and knowledge. Untrained groups fell prey to difficulties that precluded effective involvement of all members.

There are literally dozens of procedures that can facilitate creativity, decision-making, and planning (Scheidel & Crowell, 1979; Nutt, 1984). Often it is best to tailor and adapt them to the particular situation rather than simply following them by rote.

Although these and other formats are invaluable in helping to avoid trained incapacities, it is important to remember that they can, themselves, become procedural incapacities. Neither of the two procedures we have mentioned is appropriate under all conditions. For example, Reflective Thinking does not work well when people have fundamental disagreements over values, because it presumes agreement on criteria used to evaluate solutions. The consensus-seeking rules would not be appropriate for intense disputes where parties have long-standing grievances. In such cases sticking to either procedure would only compound the conflict. Although the procedures protect against some possible problems, they can unintentionally introduce others.

The effectiveness of procedures is limited by the fact that they can only counteract those trained incapacities they are **explicitly** designed to aid. Reflective Thinking, for example, does nothing to control the inappropriate use of objective criteria because its rules do not take this incapacity into account. Another way to counteract trained incapacities is to give the group **critical tools for recognizing and surmounting trained incapacities**, whatever their particular form might be. Trained incapacities feed on parties' lack of self-awareness. Therefore critical methods that make people conscious of their own narrow thinking offer a powerful means of controlling destructive habits.

One approach to understanding patterns of thinking and their impact on interaction is to consider ways in which parties **frame** and **reframe** issues and episodes. In its broadest sense, the concept of **framing refers to people's ability to construct interpretations of events or actions and thus define situations they are in** (Bateson, 1972; Goffman, 1974). Just as a frame changes one's perception of the painting it surrounds, the perceptual frames people impose on events alter their understanding and reaction to those events. The idea of framing or reframing (changing or substituting frames) has been used to examine important aspects of many social phenomena. In some forms of therapy, for example, reframing is used as an approach that enables people to create change in response to difficult problems (Watzlawick, Weakland, & Fisch, 1974; Bandler & Grinder, 1982). In conflict, reframing is important to an understanding of self-regulation in two senses: conflict interaction is often redirected when parties reframe substantive issues or when parties reframe the episode of interaction that they see themselves engaged in.

Reframing Issues

There is substantial research suggesting that the way people define problems influences the choices they make in attempting to solve them (Kahneman & Tversky, 1979; Tversky & Kahneman, 1981). This known tendency in decision-making contexts has led many conflict and negotiation researchers to examine its implications for the way parties frame and reframe issues during conflict. One line of research in bargaining and negotiations has studied how differential framing of bargaining proposals can influence the evaluations and choices made about those proposals (Bazerman, 1983; Bazerman & Neale, 1983). Bargaining proposals can be worded to suggest what might be **gained** by adopting or accepting the proposal. Or the same proposal can be worded to suggest what will be **lost** by adopting or accepting the proposal.

As an illustration of these gain or loss frames, consider the following example that has been used as a basis for research on negotiations (Bazerman & Neale 1983; pp. 54–55; reprinted by permission of Sage Publications):

A large manufacturer has recently been hit with a number of economic difficulties and it appears as if three plants need to be closed and 6000 employees laid off. The vice president of production has been exploring alternative ways to avoid this crisis. She has adopted two plans:

> Plan A: This plan will save one of the three plants and 2000 jobs.

> Plan B: This plan has a 1/3 probability of saving three plants and all 6000 jobs, but has a 2/3 probability of saving no plants and no jobs.

Which plan would you select?

Both of the proposed plans (A and B) are cast in terms of gain (saving plants). Now reconsider the same problem but with the following alternative choices:

> Plan C: This plan will result in the loss of two of the three plants and 4000 jobs.

> Plan D: This plan has a 2/3 probability of resulting in the loss of all three plants and all 6000 jobs but has a 1/3 probability of losing no plants and no jobs.

Which plan would you select?

Both of these plans (C and D) are cast in terms of what people can possibly lose if they are adopted. However, these two options are objectively identical to those worded in terms of gains. That is, Plan A is the same as Plan C and Plan B is the same as Plan D. The difference is in the way in which the proposals are framed—as potential gains or losses.

The way options are framed has an important effect on people's preferences. Given the choice between Plans A and B, about 80 percent of people choose Plan A. But given the choice between Plans C and D, the choice is overwhelmingly for Plan

D. The difference in framing as potential for gain versus potential for loss is enough to shift the choices that people make. When people choose among options cast in terms of gains, they are more likely to choose the sure thing. In this instance, Plan A is chosen over Plan B because the choice is among plans that offer gain and Plan A is a sure thing, while Plan B is the riskier choice. In contrast, when people choose among options that are cast in terms of losses, they are more likely to choose the riskier option. In this instance, Plan D is chosen over Plan C because the choice is among plans that offer losses and Plan D is the riskier choice.

The difference between wording proposals as gains or losses is a difference in how the proposals are framed. The reactions to this difference have important implications for how formal negotiations unfold. When labor and management frame their proposals in terms of the losses likely to result from various options, parties may be more likely to make riskier choices, including agreeing to let an outside arbitrator decide the outcome rather than settling. On the other hand, if parties frame issues in terms of gains, they may be more likely to choose the less risky choice; they may settle for what is on the table rather than risking a stalemate and turning the choice over to an arbitrator (a riskier option) (Bazerman & Neale, 1983). Negotiators who view possible outcomes in terms of gains rather than losses are, in some cases, more likely to attain better overall outcomes (Bazerman, Magliozzi, & Neale, 1985; Neale & Northcroft, 1986).

Other studies of labor–management negotiations suggest other ways issues can be framed in negotiations (Putnam & Holmer, 1992). Negotiators can differ in how they develop an argument about an issue on the table (Putnam et al., 1986; Putnam, 1990). One side in the negotiations might approach an issue by arguing about the harms of a current situation and how a particular proposal will address those harms. The other side might approach the same issue by attacking the possible benefits of a proposal. When parties start with different argument frames, the negotiations may be more likely to head toward problem-solving rather than compromising or trade-offs. It appears that when issues are argued differently at first, the parties develop their cases more fully and tend to search for more alternatives. It is not then that one frame wins out in the negotiations, but that frames are altered and new frames are constructed by parties conjointly: frames on the issues emerge and develop in the interaction (Putnam & Holmer, 1992).

One side in negotiations can reframe an issue for themselves and thereby influence the negotiation process as well (Brown, 1983). The decision to support a strike as a tactic in a labor–management dispute is often a troublesome and potentially divisive issue for workers. How striking is framed by the workers—what it means to them to strike—can have a powerful influence over whether the tactic is supported. Striking can be seen as "getting revenge" or striking can be seen as "principled behavior" (Donnellon, Gray, & Bougon, 1986). Reframing the meaning of striking during the process can influence the degree of support for adopting the tactic.

Parties in conflicts are known to reframe issues in contexts other than formal negotiation as well. In legal arenas, disputes are sometimes broadened or narrowed to suit the forums available for addressing them (Mather & Yngvesson, 1980–81; Menkel-Meadow, 1985). Disputes are narrowed when the issues are reframed in such a way that they can more easily be addressed in available forums such as courts or mediation centers. A complex, interpersonal fight that involved relationship issues, threats, and assault, for example, may be addressed solely in monetary terms by a judge in court. Such treatment narrows the dispute: many issues go unaddressed because they are not easily handled.

Disputes may also be broadened through reframing. For example, a dispute between a doctor and patient may be broadened into a complaint of discrimination against an entire group of people. In such instances, a single conflict is used as a test case for addressing a much broader social injustice or protecting a group's rights.

Reframing of issues and problems is unavoidable as the parties discuss them. In many instances, parties frame and reframe issues without fully realizing it. Reframing may redirect conflict interaction in either constructive or destructive directions. If parties want to control conflict interaction and direct it constructively, they need to be able to reframe issues and problems so that a wide array of alternative solutions can be considered.

In response to this need, Volkema (1981, 1983) developed the **Problem-Purpose Expansion Technique** to help members recognize and transcend narrow thinking. Volkema argues that the effectiveness of any conflict management strategy depends on how people **formulate** the problems they face. Problem formulation has at least two effects on conflict. First, it channels parties' thinking and can severely limit the range of solutions considered. In the Creativity Development Committee (Case 4.3), the major problem was expressed as "selection of the best possible procedure for making decisions in the research meetings." This formulation of the problem constrained members to search for a single procedure to be used by all project teams, which eventually worsened the conflict. How this problem was formulated implicitly ruled out several solutions that would have allowed members to work on common grounds, such as adopting two procedures and testing each in half of the project teams or adopting several procedures and allowing the project directors to choose whichever they liked best. As we have seen, people tend to converge on solutions prematurely, and an overly narrow problem formulation encourages this.

Second, problem formulation also affects parties' motivations when a conflict emerges. How the research committee formulated its problem set up a win–lose situation once members became divided over the two candidate programs. Since only one program could be adopted in this approach, a win–lose fight became inevitable, with the manager ultimately forcing his preferred solution.

Volkema shows that problem formulations vary along a narrow to broad continuum. For the Creativity Development Committee, the formulation "Selection of Tom's procedure for the project teams" would be the narrowest scope possible, because it focuses on a **single** solution and specifies **what** must be done. The alternative problem formulation, "Selection of the best possible procedure for making decisions in the research meetings" is broader than the first. Note that the second formulation admits a greater number of possible solutions than the first, because it does not specify **which** procedure should be chosen and opens up a range of possibilities. The second formulation also focuses attention on a different set of actions than does the first. With the first formulation, parties are likely to focus on how they can get project teams to like Tom's procedure. With the second, they are likely to concentrate on searching for alternative procedures and choosing one. A still broader problem formulation than the second would be: "Selection of the best possible procedures that can be used by the teams." Broader still is: "To make the best possible decisions in the project teams." Both of these formulations open up a wider range of possibilities and imply different actions than do the first two (indeed, the fourth opens up the possibility of chucking the procedures altogether, if members agree it is impossible to find a good one).

Volkema argues that some levels of formulation promote better and more acceptable solutions than others. Exactly which formulations are best varies depending on the parties, the nature of the conflict, the surrounding environment, and other factors. In general, it is difficult to identify the best formulations. However, our discussion of trained incapacities suggests one way to identify which formulations are **not desirable**, namely, those that promote trained incapacities.

Identification of the problem formulations being used in a conflict is a complex process. For one thing, problems are not always explicitly stated. Sometimes, in fact, people consciously **avoid** clear problem statements in an attempt to keep conflicts suppressed. In such cases, problem definitions can be inferred by listening to discussions. Figuring out the definition is fairly easy once one is familiar with some examples of problem formulations. An additional complication is introduced by the fact that problem formulations may change as the group works on an issue. In the Creativity Development Committee (Case 4.3), the problem was initially "selection of the best possible decision-making procedure for the project teams" but over time shifted to "should we adopt the manager's preference?" which implied confrontation. Clearly, these shifts reflect significant occurrences in the conflict and changes in the relationships among members. Indeed, several researchers have proposed that decision-making is nothing more than a series of redefinitions and reconceptualizations of problems leading gradually toward narrow solution statements (Lyles & Mitroff, 1980; Poole, 1982). It is important to be sensitive to these shifts and their implications for the direction conflict takes.

Volkema has developed a technique called **Problem-Purpose Expansion** (**PPE**) to help parties generate a range of problem formulations. The method makes parties aware of their assumptions and makes it possible to recognize trained incapacities by comparing different levels of problem formulations. The **Problem-Purpose Expansion Method** has two basic parts. The first is a format for stating the problem: an infinitive + an object + a qualifier. For example, if the problem is presently thought to be "how to convince the residents of a neighborhood that a sidewalk should be installed along their block," the problem might be stated as:

> to convince neighbors that a sidewalk is needed
> Infinitive + Object + Qualifier

This statement of the problem then serves as the basis for brainstorming a set of possible solutions (see Table 8.2 for possible solutions associated with this formulation of the problem).

The second part of PPE expands the first problem statement by reformulating it. The reformulation allows for a second round of brainstorming—one that generates a set of different solutions. Reformulation is done by asking the following:

Table 8.2   A HIERARCHY OF EXPANDED PROBLEM STATEMENTS

Problem Statements	Possible Solutions
TO CONVINCE NEIGHBORS THAT A SIDEWALK IS NEEDED (What are we trying to accomplish by this?)	Gather data; hold public hearings; go door-to-door
TO GET NEIGHBORS TO PAY FOR SIDEWALK INSTALLATION (What are we trying to accomplish by this?)	Go to the Transportation Department; sue neighbors; introduce a resolution at City Hall
TO GET A SIDEWALK INSTALLED (What are we trying to accomplish by this?)	Pay for sidewalk yourself; install sidewalk yourself
TO MAKE THE AREA WHERE A SIDEWALK WOULD GO PASSABLE (What are we trying to accomplish by this?)	Level off area; build boardwalk
TO MAKE PEDESTRIAN TRAFFIC SAFE	Reroute auto traffic; partition off part of street; stop auto traffic for pedestrians; put up caution signs for autos

What are we trying to accomplish by this?

We want (most recent formulation) . . . to convince neighbors that a sidewalk is needed

In order to (reformulation) . . . get neighbors to pay for the sidewalk installation

The group might decide it wants **to convince neighbors that a sidewalk is needed** in order **get neighbors to pay for sidewalk installation**. This process is then repeated to generate a whole set of formulations and solutions (see Table 8.2). Comparison of the levels can enable parties to recognize narrowness in their thinking and trained incapacities that may be operating. By making parties aware of different formulations, PPE can disclose the values and assumptions underlying a current way of looking at a problem and suggest innovative viewpoints.

PPE can also be used when the problem in question is "about" a relationship or group itself rather than about something people might do. For example, in the Riverdale Halfway House (Case 6.1) the problem was formulated as how "to resolve the animosities between George and Carole." PPE might lead to other formulations more conducive to constructive dialogue, such as how "to clarify lines of authority at Riverdale" or how "to create a more supportive climate at Riverdale." In both cases these broader reformulations change the focus of the problem from Carole and George to the group as a whole and provide a common problem that the entire group can work on.

PPE tries to jolt people out of their well-worn, unreflective channels and encourages them to consider new ideas. As we noted in Chapter 6, a surprising or startling move can also do this. A former chair of the board of General Motors is reputed to have said during a particularly docile meeting, "Well, it appears as if we're all in agreement. Why don't we all try to work up some conflicts over the weekend so when we come back on Monday we'll be able to think this proposal through thoroughly?" The chair's statement was designed to surprise the other members and jolt them out of their premature agreement. When members return to their task they may well do so with greater concentration and renewed vigor.

Reframing Interaction

The third property of conflict interaction we discussed in Chapter 3 emphasized that conflict interaction unfolds in phases and episodes and that parties see themselves doing certain episodes at various points in a conflict. What parties see themselves doing is often crucial in shaping conflict interaction. When people change their perception of what they are doing, it can have a powerful influence over the interaction. When done strategically, this can promote effective self-regulation. Through reframing interaction, parties can move conflict in new and more productive directions.

At times, the momentum and force of conflict interaction itself cause parties to reframe interaction. At the outset, parties may attempt to launch certain types of episodes that they feel will help them reach their goals. However, once an interaction has started to unfold, the individual's goals are not the only, or even the primary, influence on how the conflict develops. The series of actions, reactions, and responses create a force of their own, which shapes perceptions of what is being done and, in turn, changes parties' goals (Putnam, 1990). In other words, the types of interaction episodes the parties perceive themselves engaged in are influenced by the emerging interaction itself. Interaction often gets reframed based on what the parties find themselves doing (rather than what they may have planned to do).

Axelrod's (1984) research on concession making (discussed in Chapter 1) illustrates how interaction is reframed by the moves and responses of the parties. The tit-for-tat interaction sequences that parties engaged in—exchanging small concessions over a series of moves—led to further cooperative action as parties reassessed possible outcomes and revised goals. What parties saw as in their interests was influenced by the experiences they had in the tit-for-tat sequences. The experience of the tit-for-tat sequences produced a framing of the interaction as a cooperative endeavor and induced further cooperative moves.

Analyses of labor–management contract negotiations also illustrate how interaction is reframed by the actions and reactions of unfolding negotiations. Putnam (1990) describes a pivotal interaction sequence in a contract negotiation between teachers and school administrators where the framing of interaction was key in determining how the bargaining developed. After considerable negotiating, the bargaining representatives for the teachers made several comments about an offer on the table that were somewhat ambiguous. Some administrators in the negotiations felt that the comments meant the teachers might renege on an earlier concession. Interpreting the comments as reneging was one possible frame on how the interaction was about to unfold. If the teachers' signals were framed as reneging, the interaction might produce face threats, accusations, and destructive escalation. However, some of the administrators framed the teachers' comments differently. They heard the same comments but thought they were an inadvertent error or oversight on the teachers' part. Ultimately, the spokesperson for the administrators cast the moves as an error rather than strategic reneging. This allowed the teachers to correct the problem gracefully. (From all indications, the teachers had made an inadvertent error.) The teachers' move was framed in such a way that it encouraged the negotiations to proceed in a sequence of cooperative rather than competitive, escalating moves.

WORKING WITH FACE-SAVING ISSUES

The key to diagnosing face-saving issues successfully lies in parties' ability to recognize two major symptoms in interaction. First, when face-saving is occurring, the **interaction becomes centered on a secondary issue rather than on the substance of the conflict.** The substantive problems that parties must resolve are buried by statements and reactions indicating resentment or by arguments that defend individual positions but do little to advance parties' understanding of the problem. Since the face-saving issues are related to the more substantive problems, they can come to dominate the interaction before parties realize it.

For example, people may defend alternative positions in what appears to be a heated debate. But they may do so only because they feel that if they back away from their positions, they will not have credibility in future discussions or decisions. In this case, the most pressing issue, the one that has greatest influence over the interaction, is "how will other parties treat someone who changes his or her minds?" However, the content of the discussion remains focused on a substantive point, disguising the face issue. If parties fail to realize that a secondary issue is driving the interaction, face-saving can produce destructive escalation and seriously threaten relationships.

Establishing climates that prevent face-saving concerns from emerging is probably the most effective means of eliminating their destructive influence. The climate of a group, organization, or relationship plays a critical role in determining whether face-saving concerns will emerge and become problematic. People have shared expectations about whether it is safe to move away from a stated position, whether conflict issues can be raised without threatening the relationships, and whether someone's feelings of unjust treatment can be discussed openly. While establishing a "healthy" climate is something people can work toward using methods discussed in Chapter 6, the difficult interventions are those that are needed **when a preventive climate has not been established or when some event calls the climate into question**. For example, when something happens that makes parties unsure about whether they can step back from a position and still be seen as credible, even the most comfortable atmosphere may begin to disintegrate.

Interventions that attempt to stop the destructive effects of face-saving must recognize that face-saving centers around the **negotiation** of one's image. As we demonstrated in Chapter 5, the alignment actions that people use to prevent loss of face serve as flags or markers to the other party that attention to face wants is desired. When one hears an alignment action, bells and whistles should go off. These devices signal that the hearer is experiencing or anticipating a threat to face. Further challenge will result in a face-saving strategy. At this point, the use of protective strategies to align the other party's actions may help to prevent their face-saving measures.

Several forms of face-saving we have discussed threaten to impose an undesirable image on the speaker. Consider the following "statements," which various forms of face-saving behavior make:

> Resisting Unjust Intimidation: "Don't see me as someone who accepts unfair treatment or intimidation."

> Stepping Back from a Position: "Don't see me as someone who is indecisive" (easily beat, weak, etc.).

> Raising Unacknowledged Conflict Issues: "Don't see me as someone who is willing to **cause** problems by raising conflict issues."

Each of these statements reflects a guess the party has made about others' likely reactions, and each indicates that the person feels threatened by the image he or she assumes others will assign. However, each statement is founded on an **assumption** about others' interpretations and reactions, and these assumptions can either be confirmed or refuted by subsequent events. The interaction that occurs when face is an issue is always a negotiation; it is an attempt to settle what image others can assign to the speaker.

Interventions that treat face-saving as a negotiation process may have the greatest chance for success. We see three steps that can be taken to help facilitate this process. First, the negotiations can occur with less chance of continued escalation if defensiveness is reduced. A person trying to save face always perceives a threat—the threat of having an undesirable image assigned to him or her by others. Defensiveness is a likely reaction to perceived threat (Gibb, 1961). People feel they must be on guard because a mistaken move on their part can result in some undesirable consequence. Research by Rapaport (1960) suggests that defensiveness may be reduced by having an opponent indicate an understanding of another's position and recognizing some area of validity in the other's position. Parties can show that they understand why another feels unfairly treated or worried about appearing weak or indecisive. They can also recognize ways in which the belief may actually be legitimate. If the parties have handled similar incidents poorly in the past, acknowledging these can show a sympathetic understanding for the person's concern. Acknowledging another's position as legitimate and indicating an understanding of it do not ensure that the issue can be settled easily, but they do allow for the possibility of an open discussion as the negotiation unfolds.

Second, the negotiation of a face-saving concern can be facilitated if the **parties open the door for an exchange of concessions on the issue.** Pruitt (1971) has demonstrated the importance of letting both parties in a negotiation tell each other (either implicitly or explicitly) that an exchange of concessions is possible and safe. The parties need to know that there will be some reciprocity if one side begins making offers. Although face-saving issues are not the same as formal bargaining situations where offers can be made in increments, it is useful to think of the negotiation of a face-saving issue in the same general terms. Take as an example the face-saving situation where someone is hesitant to step back from a position. The person who is concerned about losing face needs some assurance that moving away from a position is a safe move. A person who is afraid of losing face if he or she backs away from a stand needs some assurance that shifting positions will not reduce his or her credibility. Comments or reactions that give parties a "way out" of these fears are likely to reduce the concern for face that may be keeping parties from conceding a position they themselves no longer want to defend.

In Case 8.1, a supervisor in a large record-keeping office at a corporation recently dealt with a difficult face-saving issue by trying to reassure an employee that it was safe to move away from a position.

Case 8.1   The Productivity/Performance Report

Ron, an office worker, was assigned the task of putting together an extensive report that described the productivity and performance of people in various divisions of a corporation. When the report was printed, a copy was sent to each division head for his or her inspection before the book was distributed generally in the corporation. One division head called the research office after reading the report and was irate about an error that he found in the description of his department. He saw the mistake as a significant problem that could cause considerable damage to his division's reputation and future.

The complaint was discussed by several supervisors in the research office before it reached Ron. When Ron was told about the error, he became very defensive and argued that the information that appeared in the book was accurate. It was clear to his supervisors that the information was in error and that the employee was trying to save face. Ron was defending his position, not because he firmly believed that it was correct, but because acknowledging that he had made a mistake could mean that he would be seen as incompetent.

The approach Ron's supervisor took in handling this situation was to point out that compiling the report was an immense and difficult task because the information had to be drawn from so many different sources. Often it had to be inferred from sketchy notes or letters that various people in the departments submitted to the records office. She congratulated Ron for putting together a catalogue that had 10,000 pieces of **correct** information. These comments allowed Ron to admit the error because they reduced the threat of being seen as incompetent. More importantly, they allowed Ron and his supervisor to begin discussing possible ways that the error could be handled so that the irate division head would be satisfied and accurate information would be disseminated about the unit.

Signaling that an exchange of concessions is possible is important in other face-saving situations we have discussed, although the way this signaling occurs would, of course, be different. The person trying to save face because of perceived unfair treatment is often preoccupied with making this known. Broadcasting perceived slights can take precedence over any desire to discuss issues per se. To address this, others must provide some assurance that the issue of mistreatment will not be lost or forgotten, if the party stops emphasizing it. This is often more difficult than it may appear at first glance. If a person feels that he or she has been treated unfairly in the past, it may be difficult for him or her to believe that others actually want to address the issue. But until such assurance is given, the face-saving issue may continue to escalate as the party criticizes others without allowing for a productive discussion of the issue.

A party who raises a conflict in a situation where parties typically avoid potentially divisive issues, or actually believe that none occur, may also show a concern for face. This party can believe that others see him or her as the cause of the problems rather than as someone who raised an issue that needed to be addressed. At least one other party must step forward and say that he or she believes it is important that the issue be addressed. If such a signal is not sent, the person who raised the conflict may become defensive, assuming others hold him or her responsible for the conflict. Other parties have to offer some signal that they are beginning to **own** the conflict.

If defensiveness cannot be reduced, or if parties cannot facilitate negotiations through an exchange of concessions, a third step may be taken to help stop the possible destructive effects of face-saving interaction. One or more parties can **stress the consequences of not settling the substantive issue**. This tactic is frequently advocated as a way to sharpen conflict so that members will become more motivated to deal with the issue (Walton, 1969). When face-saving is an issue, increasing tension by pointing to the consequences of an unresolved conflict can encourage a party who is concerned about face to care more about the substantive issue than the potential threat to image. It can, in other words, help direct the interaction away from a personal focus and toward a substantive focus.

WORKING WITH CLIMATE

We discussed possible approaches to diagnosing climates in Chapter 6. This section advances three measures for changing climate to influence conflict interaction. Our earlier analysis of climate clearly implies a first principle: **small, cumulative changes in interaction can eventually result in major changes in climate.** For example, in groups or organizational contexts, many members report that their first feeling of belonging to their group occurred when members began using "we" when talking about group activities. This subtle difference signals a change in identification from "individual" to "member"; it promotes a more relaxed climate in the group by indicating to members that others are well-disposed toward them and that they are on common ground. In the Psychological Evaluation Unit (Case 6.3), Jerry maintained his dominant position as well as the group's authoritarian climate through a series of moves that enabled him to control the issues on which the group worked. In this case, members could have changed the group's climate by being more assertive and making "bids" to have a say in controlling the group. Jerry might not have noticed these changes, but they would gradually alter the group's climate to encourage more equal participation by members.

A second tactic for working on climates is to **discuss openly themes that trouble**

parties. Much of the climate's influence on interaction depends on parties' inability to recognize it. If they can bring its effects out in the open and consciously move to counteract them, climate can be used to channel conflict interaction in constructive directions. Often this "consciousness raising" is done by one insightful member (see Case 8.2).

Case 8.2   **The Consulting Agency**

In a small, 12-person consulting agency, two important members, the program coordinator (Joe) and the publications manager (Juanita), were having serious problems getting along together because their five-year marriage was failing. Joe and Juanita decided not to bring up their problems in front of the group, because they believed it could only disrupt the operations of the ordinarily harmonious group. Their suppression of the problems certainly kept their antagonism from becoming an open issue in the group, but it did not prevent their tensions from influencing the group's climate. The agency's weekly meetings were marked by uncomfortable pauses and evasions of pressing issues. Relationships in the group became cautious and artificial; authority relations were also ambiguous because two important members were reluctant to talk to each other and fought over small issues. Finally, at one tension-filled meeting another member, Karen, openly stated that she felt uncomfortable and that she wanted to talk about Joe and Juanita's problems and their effect on the group. In the ensuing discussion many issues and feelings emerged. Members were relieved to talk openly, and both Joe and Juanita were able to unburden themselves and get support from the group. The tension between Joe and Juanita did not subside as a result of Karen's intervention (in fact, it continued until Joe left the agency), but the group's climate improved markedly and members were better able to cope with their co-workers' relationship problems.

There are also formal procedures for evaluating a group's climate and functioning (Auvine, Densmore, Extrom, Poole, & Shanklin, 1977). Self-evaluation questionnaires on which members of groups or organizations rate their own and others' performance and weaknesses are often used (see Johnson & Johnson, 1975, for several good forms). The questionnaire provides a structured and legitimate way to raise criticisms of the group and open them up for discussion. This "survey-feedback" process can be used to set goals for changing the group's interaction and, ultimately, its climate (see Case 8.3).

Case 8.3   **The Expanding Printing Company**

A small but prosperous printing company had been experiencing tremendous growth in a relatively short period of time. New equipment, expanded services, new employees, and expansions in sales territories and clients were just some of the changes that accompanied this growth. Older employees noticed a gradual change in the working climate in the company. What had once been a playful, relaxing atmosphere, had quickly become somber and tense, at least in the eyes of several outspoken critics of the change. Open conflicts became more frequent. For the first time, employees began to hold informal gripe sessions. Verbally aggressive behavior among employees was no longer kept behind closed doors. Perplexed, the president of the company turned to a team of communication consultants to assess the situation and recommend strategies for improving the climate.

The consultants conducted in-depth interviews with the president and a select number of employees to discern their perceptions of the company. This interview process was guided by a series of questions geared toward understanding the company's working climate. For example: (1) What kind of people work here? (2) Do people respect each other? (3) How do they show respect or disrespect? (4) Describe the leadership in this organization. (5) How are decisions made in the company? (6) What types of conflict surface with regularity? (7) How does information travel through the company? (8) What role does the grapevine play in disseminating information?

After reviewing the information obtained through these interviews, the consulting team elected to survey the entire organization with a self-report instrument measuring 16 dimensions thought to be important to the working climate. Dimensions such as work space, performance standards, managerial structure, job pressure, and employee morale were assessed through this instrument. Within days of administering the measure, the consultants led a "town meeting" to report the results.

The meeting allowed employees to share openly opinions about the change and to compare perceptions. Key issues uncovered through the interviews and the climate measure were raised and discussed. Although the president of the company resisted competing views at first, she soon began to listen and inquire about the employee feedback. With the help of the employees, the consulting team had identified three issues central to the climate of the company.

First, employees believed that the expectations and standards for performance were too low, especially for new recruits. The president was flabbergasted. The employees wanted higher performance standards for everyone—something she thought would never occur without a fight. Second, the group perceived a threat to the physical surroundings. They were worried that new equipment and expansion in the same physical space would create poor working conditions. Third, many employees felt that the opportunity to participate in decisions was reduced as more employees were added. This resulted in frustration and struggle over many of the new decisions passed along during the recent changes. The consultants, the president, and the employees drafted a set of policy and procedural changes that addressed these and other issues. A follow-up survey of the organization a few months later reflected a much healthier organization, a company with a working climate described in one report as "robust."

A third tactic for altering climate was mentioned in Chapter 6—a party can create a **critical incident** that shifts the entire direction of the climate. Recall the example in Chapter 3 of the faculty brown-bag discussion where the student suddenly challenged the speaker: the climate shifted from congenial to tense. In the same vein, parties can attempt to create critical incidents to alter unfavorable climates. Several considerations must be taken into account in order to do this effectively. For one thing, **timing** is critical. Members must be able to recognize propitious moments for acting on the group's climate. Bormann (1972) gives a good example of the importance of timing. In the groups he studied he found a certain point in discussion at which one member would venture a favorable comment or joke about the group. In cases where the other members responded with other favorable comments or followed up on the joke, the group generally developed an open, inclusive climate. When members let the favorable comment drop, the group usually took a much **longer** time to develop cohesion, if it did so at all. Timing is vital in these cases; if the critical moment passes it is gone and members may not get another chance.

Along with timing, **salience** is also important. The move must hold the parties' attention if it is to serve as a watershed. The student's attack on the brown-bag lunch speaker captured the attention of other people; thereafter, they were reacting to the student's move, and their reactions reinforced the tension his statement originally interjected. There are many ways of enhancing the salience of a move—including raising the volume of one's voice, using colorful or symbolic language, being dramatic, or saying something surprising. Used properly, these tactics increase the probability that the move will prove effective. Finally, a party who aspires to create a critical incident should have credibility and **respect** in the eyes of other people. The actions of a respected group member, for example, are likely to receive attention from other members and therefore have a good chance to influence the group's interaction. In addition, making an effort to change the group's climate can be interpreted as manipulation; moves of a respected and trusted member are unlikely to be rejected as self-serving.

Of the three approaches, creating a critical incident is the most uncertain. It is hard to do, and it has the potential to backfire: other people may reject the person who attempts to maneuver the group. When effective, however, it gets results quickly and it can be initiated by a single member. Small, cumulative changes and open discussion are more certain but also have problems. Small changes operate piecemeal through day-to-day interaction; therefore it is easy to lapse back into old patterns. To use this technique successfully requires a clear sense of purpose and patience. It does not work quickly and is of limited utility in situations where climate is causing an immediate crisis in a group. Open discussion works much more quickly than cumulative change, but it may add fuel to a conflict by introducing a new issue: members satisfied with the present climate may side against those who are dissatisfied. The emotions associated with discussions of power relations or supportiveness may generalize to the conflict and intensify disagreements on other issues. In using any of the approaches it is important to be aware of possible problems and take measures to circumvent them.

RELATIONS AMONG THE FORCES

It should be clear that the forces are often interrelated and that work on one can be counteracted by the effect of others. Climate pervades everything that happens in conflict interaction, so an unfavorable climate can undermine work on other forces.

A competitive situation with great differences in parties' influence and little supportiveness will have great difficulty avoiding destructive redefinition and problems related to face-saving. At the same time, forces that shape immediate interaction can prohibit changes in climate, because climates depend on interaction. The use of unique sources of power may reinforce an authoritarian and suspicious climate, despite the best efforts of parties to relax the climate. Premature evaluation may anger parties and introduce a competitive atmosphere as well as face-saving concerns. In the same way all four forces may intersect and reinforce one another under certain circumstances. It is important to take this possibility into account when attempting to turn conflict in productive directions.

CONCLUSION

In one sense, parties involved in a conflict are always intervening in their own interaction. Each move or response directs the interaction, at least for the moment. Not all moves are self-regulating, however. Self-regulation requires an attempt to diagnose the forces that are pushing the conflict in a destructive direction and the ability to act in a way that mitigates those forces. Self-regulation is difficult because parties may not see the destructive turn interaction has taken until repetitive patterns are firmly in place. Moreover, when someone who is involved in a conflict attempts to alter interaction with the interests of all in mind, their motives can be questioned and their moves misinterpreted.

Despite formidable obstacles, there are a number of ways that parties can diagnose their own conflicts and act to redirect them. Parties can expand the definition of a problem or reframe issues so that a broader array of alternative solutions can be considered. They can change a group's climate by a series of small changes in interaction, a discussion of climate themes, or the use of some critical incident. They can assess power differentials in the group and develop ways to deal with power imbalances. They can view face-saving interaction as a negotiation process and then facilitate this negotiation by reducing defensiveness, allowing for an exchange of concessions, or stressing the consequences of not reaching a resolution of the face-saving problem.

Chapter
9
Third Party Intervention

*I*n Chapter 3 we noted that conflict interaction tends to be self-perpetuating. This characteristic of conflict has important implications for understanding how patterns of interaction develop, how escalation cycles gain momentum, and how constructive or destructive climates are sustained. This property is also important in understanding why people who are not parties in a conflict have—since biblical times—intervened in ongoing disputes. The self-perpetuating nature of moves and countermoves, actions and reactions, can stifle attempts at self-regulation, even when we try assiduously to track or alter these patterns. Moreover, trained incapacities can prevent parties from recognizing the problems in their interaction patterns. An outsider has some distance and can often see persistent cycles and ways of altering them. By necessity, the mere entry of a third party alters conflict interaction, if for no other reason than the intervenor's moves become part of the sequence.

The term **third party intervention** connotes a wide range of activities that span diverse conflict contexts, from the spontaneous attempts of parents to settle conflicts between siblings, to the carefully planned attempts to mediate the release of hostages across international borders. Third party intervenors may be fact-finders, process consultants, go-betweens, ombudsmen, clergy, managers, conciliators, mediators, group facilitators, attorneys, friends of the court, or arbitrators. As this list suggests, third parties enact different roles and have different responsibilities in different conflict settings.

Over the past 15 years, there has been increasing interest in using a variety of third party roles in diverse conflict settings. For example, over four hundred community dispute resolution programs have been established in the United States in recent years. These programs often use trained volunteers to intervene in neighbor, small claims, or landlord–tenant disputes. In the past, if these cases were severe enough they might end up in court. In many cases, these conflicts simply festered because the parties had no recourse outside the courts to help resolve them (Merry, 1979; Marks, Johnson, & Szanton, 1984; Folger, 1991). In divorce cases, mediators are now used in many states to try to settle issues related to custody or property, rather than having a judge impose a decision about such matters (Riskin, 1985).

In business environments, a market has developed for dispute resolution services that can provide out-of-court settlements for a wide range of conflicts (Singer, 1990). In addition, changes in employer–employee relationships have brought changes in third party roles within organizations. Businesses, medical facilities, and educational institutions have developed intervention roles such as hearing officers, ombudsmen, and client representatives to address conflicts "in-house." Middle managers have increasingly been viewed as dispute resolvers who intervene in conflicts among subordinates or between department members.

In this chapter we examine **how third parties influence conflict interaction.** No matter what intervention third parties perform, the moves they make can be examined in light of their impact on conflict interaction. This chapter provides a framework for thinking about and analyzing conflict interaction as influenced by third party intervenors.

Our analysis of third party intervention is organized around the five properties of conflict interaction introduced in Chapter 3. Although conflict interaction is often quite different when a third party is involved, it is still shaped by these properties—by moves and countermoves, exertion of power, self-perpetuating momentum, episodic structure, predictable themes, and relational influences. Each of the properties points to important and unique features of third party intervention and its impact on communication. In this chapter, we examine how these five properties help describe and explain the effects of third party involvement on conflict interaction.

PROPERTY 1   *Conflict Interaction Is Sustained by the Moves and Countermoves of Participants; Moves and Countermoves Are Based on the Power Parties Exert.*

When third parties intervene in conflicts, they become active participants in the interaction sequences. Third parties make **moves**—initiatives that spark reactions and launch sequences of interaction. They also respond with **countermoves**—reactions to disputants' moves. In this sense, the third party is as vulnerable to the moment-to-moment influences of action and reaction as the disputing parties themselves. Although the conflict issues may be of more (or different) consequence for the parties than the intervenor, the conflict **interaction** is consequential for both: the interaction emerges as the product of the third party's and disputants' actions, it has moment-to-moment effects on the third party's moves, it shapes the third party's interpretations of unfolding events, and it has relational consequences for the intervenor.

The moves a third party makes clearly influence the conflict interaction. What gives third parties the ability to shape conflict? What powers are available to any particular intervenor? Given a third party's available power, what influences the moves he or she actually makes? To understand how third party influence occurs on a move-by-move basis, it is important to understand that the potential for third party moves stems from two primary sources: the third party's **mandate**—the ascribed source of power the intervenor holds—and the third party's moment-to-moment **responsiveness** to emergent characteristics of the unfolding conflict interaction. We consider each of these influences on third party moves.

Third Party Mandate

Any move a third party makes is rooted in the power he or she is able or willing to exert. In this sense, the basis of third party moves is identical to that of the disputing parties. However, the sources of third party power are often quite different from those held by the disputants. This is because the type of **interdependence** between third parties and disputants is very different from that which defines the conflicting parties' relationships. Disputants are dependent on intervenors for such functions as structuring the interaction, reducing hostilities, and providing expertise on specific substantive or legal issues. These sources of dependency stem from the power or **mandate** given to the third party by the disputants (Delbecq et al., 1975; Auvine et al., 1977; Shubert & Folger, 1986; Kaufman & Duncan, 1989). Like the forms of power we discussed in Chapter 4, the third party's mandate is fundamentally relational: it is power that is endorsed by the disputing parties and thereby gives the intervenor certain resources that can be drawn from on a move-by-move basis to control the interaction and substantive issues. If endorsement of the mandate is withdrawn or questioned, the ability of the third party to act is altered or curtailed (Merry & Silbey, 1984). Of course, some third party mandates, like those given to judges, stem from broadly based endorsements that societies or large groups of people provide. Disputing parties are under strong pressures to endorse third party mandates when they are so widely accepted.

A third party's mandate—as an endorsed basis of power—can stem from **formal** or **informal** sources (Kaufman & Duncan, 1989). Many third party roles carry **formal** endorsements, which authorize certain types of interventions in specific conflict arenas. Such roles are typically established by law, societal traditions, or rules of an organization. The adjudicative role that judges play in legal contexts and the ombudsman role employed to settle disputes within organizations are examples of formally defined third party mandates (Kolb, 1987, 1989; Rowe, 1987).

Other third party mandates are granted **informally**, usually via the implicit expectations people have about who can appropriately intervene in conflicts. These informal mandates are often the results of resources the third party holds, such as specialized knowledge or skill in intervening, or of the third party's relationship to the disputants. Informal mandates are given to a wide range of individuals including managers in organizations, parents or older siblings in families, group members who are skillful at framing problems and facilitating productive interaction, community leaders, and clergy. When third party mandates are informal and hence less clearly specified, questions may arise about the appropriateness of or limits on intervention. In such cases, the nature of the third party's mandate may require explicit negotiation in order for the intervention to proceed.

Third party mandates can carry a range of possible powers to conflict interaction. Specifically, three forms of third party control can be distinguished: process control, content control, and motivational control (Sheppard, 1984).

Process control refers to the third party's ability to organize or structure the procedures that the disputants follow during the interaction. This would include such diverse activities as arranging when and where the parties should meet, setting time limits on speaking turns or intervention sessions, establishing how decisions will be made, and setting rules for decorum. Third parties whose mandates are formally established often impose clearly specified forms of process control; these controls may be stated explicitly to the parties at the outset. Process control is often less clearly specified when a third party's mandate emerges informally. Frequently, less forethought is given to the procedural rules; these rules are more likely to emerge during the intervention rather than to be stated initially. For example, a group member who is trying to intervene in a conflict among other members may ask that each person speak in turn rather than allowing a free-for-all to escalate.

Third parties also vary in the amount of control they have over the **content** of the dispute. This form of control refers to the third party's influence over the arguments and substantive positions taken by the parties or over the terms parties accept as a final agreement. Third parties differ in their ability or willingness to refute or attack specific points made by the parties; interpret, frame, or add issues; present additional information relevant to the topics under discussion; or suggest or impose the terms that the parties adopt as an agreement or solution.

For some third party mandates, the last item in this list, the amount of control over the terms of settlement, is the most important defining feature of the intervention. We now consider three forms of intervention that differ in numerous ways but whose character stems primarily from the degree of control the third party has over the terms of settlement.

(1) **Arbitrators** have clear control over the terms of a final agreement. An arbitrator is given authority to hear all sides of a case, discuss it with each party, and then make a final decision on how the dispute will be settled, much like the judge in a legal case. In most cases, the parties are compelled by law or prior agreement to enact the terms the arbitrator imposes. One less widely used form of arbitration is called **nonbinding arbitration**. In this form of arbitration, the third party follows the same general process, but the arbitrator's decision is not one the parties are bound by law or prior agreement to accept. Rather, the arbitrator's decision is a neutral opinion that the parties can consider.

An arbitrator often has special background knowledge that enables him or her to grapple with the specific issues underlying the conflict. For example, arbitrators are often used for highly technical disputes such as labor contracts, which require knowledge of both economics and labor law. Arbitrators can also be used for "hopeless" cases, where a decision must be made, but repeated attempts to settle have proved impossible.

(2)   Less authority over settlement terms is given to **mediators**. Mediators are third parties who facilitate negotiations. They may or may not have special knowledge about the issues. The key characteristic of mediation is that final resolution rests with the parties themselves. The process of reaching a settlement is essential to winning the parties' commitment to reaching a solution. Mediators intervene mostly through structuring the negotiation process, raising issues for consideration and clarifying parties' positions.

For example, mediators frequently intervene in environmental disputes (Wehr, 1979; Lake, 1980; Mernitz, 1980; Riesel, 1985; Singer, 1990). In these disputes there are a number of parties involved such as government representatives, citizens, and industry spokespeople. The objective is to help these diverse parties negotiate an acceptable resolution to issues such as land use, watershed preservation, or highway construction.

Although mediators have traditionally been used in environmental and labor disputes, over the last two decades they have been employed in a wider array of contexts. Volunteer or professionally trained mediators now attempt to assist parties in reaching agreements in community and neighborhood disputes, landlord–tenant conflicts, small claims, consumer and business disputes, and divorce and child custody cases (Haynes, 1981; Folberg & Taylor, 1984; Lemmon, 1985; Beer, 1986; Stulberg, 1987; Haynes & Haynes, 1989; Singer, 1990; Duffy, Grosch, & Olczak, 1991).

Although there are a range of mediator styles and differences in how willing mediators are to risk influencing a settlement (discussed further below), the important point to note here is that mediators have no explicit mandate to make or implement choices for the parties. They do, however, have a mandate to inform the choices the parties consider and discuss during an intervention (Kaufman & Duncan, 1989). It is not uncommon, for example, for divorce mediators to offer suggestions or solutions that the parties have not thought of, based on solutions the mediator has seen work for other couples (Lemmon, 1985).

Occasionally, mediators consciously or inadvertently promote certain choices (Folger & Bernard, 1985; Greatbatch & Dingwall, 1989). For example, a divorce mediator may push for an agreement that gives one spouse greater financial autonomy once the marriage is dissolved. Such a move is often controversial because it may overstep the bounds of a mediator's mandate or be seen as a potential breach of neutrality (Bernard, Folger, Weingarten, & Zumeta, 1984). Pushing for financial autonomy for one spouse may cause the other spouse to view the mediator as biased. The mediator, on the other hand, may believe the spouse's autonomy will contribute to a more workable settlement.

(3)   Even less involvement with settlement terms is enacted by third party **facilitators** or **conciliators**. Facilitators and conciliators are process experts who have neither extensive expertise related to the issues under discussion nor the power to make a final decision (Auvine et al., 1977). They are often brought in when the

parties believe they can reach a resolution through direct negotiations but need help managing the process.

Although the two roles are quite similar, the labels "facilitator" and "conciliator" are used to describe third parties who intervene in somewhat different settings. The facilitator label is used most often to describe a third party who intervenes in ongoing decision-making groups such as management teams, boards of directors, or department staff. The conciliator label is used to describe third parties who intervene in multiparty disputes among recognizable adversaries such as those involved in public policy disputes, environmental conflicts, or race-related issues.

Facilitators or conciliators offer process expertise but are not at the "center" of the interaction. They can, nonetheless, be an active force directing the conflict. However, all the impetus for substantive movement—proposals, compromises, changes in position—arise from the parties themselves. Facilitation and conciliation differ from arbitration or mediation not because they are more passive forms of intervention, but because they carry a narrower range of possible involvement with substantive issues. The third party called into the Riverdale Halfway House (Case 6.1) was a facilitator. He chaired several meetings at which members tried to talk out their problems and offered assistance in clarifying needs and proposals, but he did not try to direct the discussion in any forceful or intrusive way.

An important consideration in determining the degree of process and content control to exert is how fair parties perceive the intervention to be. Thibaut and Walker (1975) argued that perceived fairness of intervention styles varies according to the nature of the dispute. In disputes involving highly intense conflict, and high degrees of interdependence among parties, arbitration (high process and content control) is perceived as the fairest approach (Sheppard, Saunders, & Minton, 1988). On the other hand, for conflicts that are less intense, mediation, with its lower degree of control, is perceived as fairer. Arbitration was also found to be preferred in disputes for which a settlement seemed very difficult to attain, whereas mediation was preferred for cases where a settlement seemed possible (Heuer & Penrod, 1986). Finally, other things being equal, participants who have some say in the selection of the third party role generally seem to perceive the intervention to be fairer than those who do not (Sheppard et al., 1988).

Besides process and content control, third party mandates also differ in the **motivational control** they grant to the intervenor. Third parties have lesser or greater ability to move parties to perform desired actions. Some informal third party intervenors, like parents or managers, control incentives that can influence the parties and ultimately the outcomes of a dispute. Managers, for example, can indicate that they might reallocate or demote a recalcitrant employee if he or she does not address an ongoing dispute with a co-worker. In an attempt to encourage movement, a labor mediator may indicate that he or she is going to tell the press that one side in a dispute is making unreasonable demands (Sheppard, 1984). Many third parties, including parents, clergy, and teachers, have a significant motivational influence over disputants. Other intervenors may have very little direct motivational power. Of course, the arguments all third parties make—to continue negotiating, to move from a position, to accept a compromise, and so on—are another source of potential motivational influence.

Responsiveness to Emerging Interaction

The third party's mandate provides the broad framework of endorsed powers, the possible bases third parties can draw on in making moves. Like all characterizations of behavior in terms of roles, however, a third party mandate only delimits the range of possible moves that are perceived to be appropriate or expected. It does not entirely account for the moves a third party actually makes in the interaction or the timing of those moves. Even though a third party is involved, the conflict interaction still unfolds turn-by-turn and is subject to all the momentary forces—such as defensiveness cycles, episodic structure, immediate face threats—that are at play in any emergent interaction. Third party moves may start from some formally or informally defined sense of what the nature of the intervention will be and what role the third party will adopt, but on a move-by-move basis, any given act is inevitably responsive: it is part of the stream of interaction and is, in a fundamental sense, a product of it.

In many recent discussions of third party intervention and dispute processing, there has been an increasing recognition of the emergent nature of conflict intervention processes (Felstiner et al., 1980-81; Mather & Yngvesson, 1980–81; Sarat, 1988). Theorists and critics have attempted to debunk what they see as a static image of disputes, dispute processing, and third party intervention. This static image depicts disputes as fixed entities that are brought to third parties and are then acted on by intervenors to achieve some goal, like reaching a settlement or handing down a decision. The conflict that the parties bring to the table is seen as relatively unchanged as the dispute moves through the intervention process. This image also implies that third parties and the intervention process remain unaffected by the dispute being addressed.

The critics of this image say that it is misleading. It fails to capture all the dynamics, the elements of change and influence, in third party interventions. They would replace this image with a less static conception—one that casts disputes and third party processes as much more fluid and malleable activities. It has been argued, for example, that "disputes, even after they emerge and are articulated, are indeterminate. They do not exist in fixed form prior to the application of particular dispute processing techniques; they are instead constituted and transformed as they are processed" (Sarat, 1988, p. 708). In this view, the very act of presenting a dispute to a third party can reframe the conflict.

Several researchers have demonstrated how disputes are presented to intervenors in ways that "fit" the third parties' modes of intervention (Mather & Yngvesson, 1980-81; Merry & Silbey, 1984; Conley & O'Barr, 1990). Courtroom disputants might, for instance, narrow the issues in a conflict, simplifying a very complex history of events, injuries, and relationship struggles so that a judge can impose or suggest readily available settlement terms, such as monetary awards. In the organizational context, employees sometimes select issues and define disputes in ways that will increase the likelihood that they will be addressed by their managers (Kolb, 1986). Other research suggests that mediators in several conflict contexts influence the parties' views of the issues and may even take a strong hand in shaping attitudes toward possible settlement terms (Folger & Bernard, 1985; Greatbatch & Dingwall, 1989; Lam, Rifkin, & Townley, 1989). In such cases, key elements of the dispute—

how parties view the issues, what they think is reasonable or worth fighting for, what they are willing to agree to—are transformed as the intervention occurs.

Just as disputes are influenced by the third party and the intervention process, so too are third parties influenced by the disputes, the parties, and the context of intervention. In this more dynamic view of intervention, third parties are not unresponsive either. Because they are part and parcel of interaction, they are constantly adapting to contingencies that arise as interventions unfold.

To understand how third parties and intervention forums adapt to cases and disputing parties, third party mandates must be seen in a dynamic perspective. For many third party roles—even those for which the mandate is relatively clear—there is considerable leeway in the amount of process, content, or motivational control that is exerted in any given intervention. In practice, third parties acting as arbitrators, mediators, facilitators, or ombudsmen engage in a wide range of moves that often blur their mandates and can erode any hard and fast distinctions among these forms of intervention. Parties who have clear arbitrative powers, like judges or labor arbitrators, sometimes act in mediative capacities (Wall & Rude, 1989; Phillips, 1990). Judges in divorce and custody cases, for example, often attempt to construct settlements rather than impose them. They may try to assess what terms are acceptable for both parties, encourage compromise, and involve parties in creating viable options. There are also forms of arbitration that build in a certain degree of disputant control over the final settlement. In "last-offer–best-offer" arbitration the arbitrator decides a settlement for a dispute by having each party submit their last best offer and then choosing from among these options (Feuille, 1979). The decision of the arbitrator is limited to one of the settlement terms suggested by the parties. In this form of arbitration, the parties have somewhat more control over the substantive outcomes of a final settlement than they would in "stricter" forms of arbitration because the options for settlement are determined by what the parties put forth.

In the same vein, mediators' actual behaviors during interventions have been found to vary considerably. Several different studies of mediators in diverse contexts paint a very diverse picture of what mediators actually do in practice; at times, this picture blurs the line between mediators and arbitrators. Descriptive studies of labor mediation suggest that mediators adopt quite different styles of intervention (Kolb, 1983; Shapiro, Drieghe, & Brett, 1985). Some labor mediators have been characterized as **dealmakers** because they take an active role in shaping the substantive issues, put pressures on parties to move, and spend considerable time caucusing with each side in an active attempt to forge a deal (Kolb, 1983). **Orchestrators** take a different approach to mediation. This is a less impositional style, in which mediators orchestrate the negotiations among the parties, setting up processes that allow the parties to keep talking and leaving substantive issues more directly under the disputants' control.

Differences have been found in intervention styles in other arenas of mediation as well. Studies of mediators who intervene in community, neighborhood, and small claims disputes suggest that mediators adopt **bargaining and therapeutic** styles of intervention (Silbey & Merry, 1986). In the **bargaining style**, mediators place great emphasis on reaching settlements through control over the interaction and encouraging less direct discussion among the disputants. Caucuses—private discussions between the mediator and one of the parties—are more frequent in this style, as are explicit attempts to narrow issues, to push for compromise, and to synthesize arguments and positions. In the **therapeutic style**, mediators emphasize increasing understanding among the disputants and overcoming relationship problems. Face-to-face contact between the parties is maximized during the intervention, as are attempts to uncover underlying issues and veiled interests. The goal is not simply to reach agreements but to use the intervention as an opportunity to improve communication and to develop a foundation for addressing problems in general.

As might be expected, in informally mandated third party roles, there is as much or more leeway in how the third party intervenes. Studies of managers in organizations suggest, for example, that they also take on a range of roles (Kolb, 1986). In some instances, they adopt an **advisory** role, consulting with one or more of the parties in the dispute and suggesting moves parties might make to help direct a conflict. At other times, the same manager may become more of an **investigator**, collecting facts and assessing the source and nature of the problem. In other conflicts, the manager can become a **restructurer**, dealing with the conflict by moving personnel or reorganizing subunits or chains of command. In still other situations, the manager steps into a **mediative** role, guiding communication among the disputing parties and attempting creative problem-solving.

Given the range of third party options in both formally and informally mandated third party interventions, what influences the intervention style and thus the specific moves that third parties make? This is a difficult question to answer because of the range of factors that can influence the third party's moves—from habits individual third parties fall into to specific characteristics and demands of the case and disputing parties.

Third parties adapt to the conflict cases at hand in important ways. Consider Cases 9.1 and 9.2, which illustrate how third parties with informal mandates developed styles that they felt were appropriate for the circumstances and conflict as it unfolded.

Case 9.1 **The Food Distribution Company**

A third party was called in to mediate a conflict between two managers of a food distribution company. The conflict began as a quarrel over bookkeeping procedures and soon developed into a fight over lines of authority between two managers. In the midst of a stalemate where neither manager would talk to the other, the other managers decided to call in a third party. The third party, Richard, was a distinguished-looking man in his late forties. He held a Ph.D. in economics, had written several books, and had a local reputation as a knowledgeable and impartial intervenor. Richard first interviewed each party separately. From these interviews he discovered that the roots of the conflict lay in one manager's emotional needs. The more blustery combatant, Thad, had a great need for warmth and support from his co-workers, a need he traced to bad experiences with his family and his first wife. Thad was not getting the support he needed and believed the others were purposely freezing him out (although Richard found no evidence that this was the case). Thad's anger was channeled toward Marlena, the other manager and the second party. The jurisdictional dispute had rapidly escalated into a bitter, brutal fight that fed on itself. Thad and Marlena could not even work in the same room without harassing each other.

In determining his strategy, Richard took the following facts into account. (1) A serious emotional problem, which might take years to untangle, underlay the conflict. Other members probably were not aware of this problem, and it was uncertain whether they would be sympathetic if they knew of it. (2) The conflict was long-standing and sides were clearly drawn. It was going to be difficult for parties to move from their entrenched positions. (3) The conflict was very damaging for the company. It had been going on for four months and was beginning to hurt the business financially. Something definite had to be done. (4) The managers of the company were all young; they tended to look to Richard for help and accorded him considerable respect.

These considerations led Richard to adopt what he termed a "paternalistic style." He took on a role very close to that of arbitrator and in a caring, yet somewhat domineering, way told the managers what they should do. He took the managers aside and told them, "Thad is in pain; he needs support." The managers tended to scoff at this initially, but Richard did notice that they were more supportive in later meetings. Richard also wrote a formal report with definite recommendations and urged the company to adopt the recommendations and enforce them "from the top down." By taking this tack, Richard hoped to break the conflict by catching the participants "off balance" and pushing them to change before they could draw back into their well-worn positions. Quick action would mean a quick remedy for the company's problems. The paternalistic approach also protected Richard's position as a third party; the paternal role is characteristically slightly distant and kept Richard one step removed from the "action" of the conflict.

Case 9.2 The Radio Station

In another intervention, two private consultants, Louis and Sue, were called in by a radio station with administrative problems. Lines of authority among the programming, advertising, and engineering departments were unclear. As a result, conflicts often arose over the scheduling of commercials and the purchase of air time. Workers at the station concluded that a reorganization was needed to clarify which departments were responsible for decisions and to establish procedures for making decisions in an orderly fashion. One of the managers in the advertising department knew Louis and Sue and obtained permission to invite them to a meeting.

Through observation of the meeting and interviews with several members, Louis and Sue discovered that the station was operating effectively and was in no immediate financial trouble. Workers felt a strong need to do something about their problems, because the constant friction over decisions was beginning to create personal animosities. Their decision to act had been crystallized by a shouting match between the director of advertising and two disc jockeys. This incident had disturbed several workers, who brought the problem out during a station-wide staff meeting. After kicking it around for a while, the staff had then decided to try a reorganization. The staff held a goal-setting meeting during which workers raised problems and then drew up a list of possible changes. Because the changes were rather complex and members were not sure they could manage the change process themselves, they called in the third parties.

Faced with this situation, Louis and Sue decided to adopt a facilitative style. The group obviously recognized a need for change and had a sense of direction. Members were able to talk out their differences and saw the importance of good working relationships. Even during tense discussions workers attempted to offer emotional support to each other. It was clear that the staff had the skills and sensitivity needed for constructive work. The third party's role was to help the staff channel its own efforts and initiatives. Moreover, there was ample time for the staff to work through the conflict at its own pace. The station was in no immediate danger; a relatively slow, measured process of discussion and consensus-building was feasible. The third parties recognized the value of facilitating the group's efforts to develop its own unique solution "from the inside" because it would greatly increase members' commitment to the reorganization plan.

The facilitative style also had three additional advantages. As facilitators, Louis and Sue took a neutral stand toward any particular proposal for restructuring; they managed the negotiations and let the members work out proposals on their own. This enabled them to avoid being perceived as favoring the member who invited them in; as "process managers" they were able to distance themselves from partisan proposals and help the workers come to mutually acceptable conclusions. Louis and Sue also found facilitation a more comfortable style than those requiring a higher degree of control, such as arbitration. Both Sue and Louis believed strongly in participatory management. As facilitators, they were in a position to maximize member participation. Because the facilitative style was consistent with their values, Sue and Louis were able to fit into the restructuring process in a way that felt natural and appropriate to them. This allowed them to relax, and they believe it contributed greatly to the ultimate effectiveness of the intervention.

Finally, the facilitative role was more in line with the staff's expectations than a more authoritative style would have been. The staff had actively worked with its problems and had considerable knowledge about communication and group process. Members had a definite idea of the part they wanted the third party to play: they wanted someone to guide their decision-making processes, but they wanted control over the form and content of the solutions. An outsider—even an expert—who tried to take over the restructuring process would likely have been perceived as overly controlling and condescending. By adopting a facilitative style, Louis and Sue achieved legitimacy almost immediately, because they filled the staff's needs. Moreover, having demonstrated they were in tune with the staff, the third parties were later able to criticize the group's ideas without creating resentment. They took advantage of what Hollander and Julian (1969) have termed "idiosyncrasy credit." By conforming in their early relations with the group, the intervenors established "credits" that gave them greater leeway as the intervention progressed.

These cases suggest that there are contingencies that influence the general approach and specific intervening moves third parties make. Although all possible contingencies have not been systematically studied, some attempts have been made to examine third party adaptation.

In one line of research, four general approaches to intervention have been studied (Carnevale & Pegnetter, 1985; Carnevale, 1986; Carnevale, Conlon, Hanisch & Harris, 1989; Carnevale, Putnam, Conlon, & O'Connor, 1991). In establishing a general orientation to intervention, third parties can (1) **integrate**: attempt to solve a conflict through encouraging negotiations and reaching a mutually acceptable agreement (a problem-solving approach); (2) **compensate**: persuade one or more of the parties to move or reach settlement by some reward or incentive offered by the third party (e.g., a manager acting as a intervenor offering a "perk" in exchange for accepting some outcome in a conflict with a co-worker; (3) **be inactive**: allow the disputants to handle the conflict themselves; and (4) **press**: pressure disputants to change their goals or willingness to settle (e.g., persuading a party to move from a currently held position, giving information that shapes perceptions of fairness). These four approaches were originally developed to apply to mediators, but we believe they apply more broadly to any third party with some leeway in his or her general intervention mandate.

Research suggests that third party selection of approaches depends on two primary factors (Carnevale et al., 1989). First, the choice seems to be contingent on how much value the third party attaches to the achievement of disputants' goals. The importance the intervenor places on this outcome may stem from a concern about the parties' welfare or it may come from some vested interest of the intervenor (e.g., a manager whose unit's performance is being influenced by the conflict). Second, the choice may also hinge on the third party's perception of whether there is sufficient common ground to reach a mutually acceptable solution. This factor suggests that third parties' approaches are influenced by an assessment of how likely it is that the disputants can reach an agreement.

Figure 9.1 summarizes the choices third parties are likely to make among the four approaches, given their concern for parties' aspirations and their perceptions of common ground. Third parties attempt integration when concern for the goals of the parties is great and the intervenor feels that there is sufficient chance that the parties can reach an agreement. The third party is most likely to be inactive when there is a good chance of reaching agreement and the third party is concerned about reaching an agreement. In this situation, the third party may believe that parties will reach an agreement on their own and thus third party involvement is unnecessary. Third parties are likely to compensate when they are highly concerned about the parties' reaching an agreement but the chances of agreement occurring appear slight. In this case, the third party has significant motivation to use available resources as incentives to promote agreements. Finally, the third party is most likely to press when the

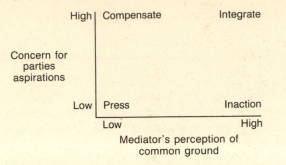

Figure 9.1 Third party intervention approaches. Adapted from Carnevale, Conlon, Hanisch, and Harris (1989, p. 346).

intervenor is not highly concerned about having the parties reach settlement and there appears to be little common ground on which to build the intervention. In this case the third party may feel there is nothing to lose in pressuring parties since the outcome is not seen as greatly significant. It has also been found that third parties may be more likely to use pressing tactics at later stages of the intervention because intervenors may become increasingly pessimistic about the amount of common ground as the intervention proceeds.

Of the four intervention approaches in this model, the press stance has received the most attention in other studies of third party adaptation. There are several other factors that appear to influence whether third parties adopt a pressing strategy (Kressel & Pruitt, 1989). There is a tendency for intervenors to become more directive when the intervenors' own values or interests clash with the parties'. One study of labor arbitrators found, for example, that arbitrators often settled labor grievances in ways consistent with the interests and rights of management rather than workers (Gross & Greenfield, 1986). Pressure tactics also appear to be more likely when disputing parties are very hostile toward each other. For instance, mediators have been found to press for concessions, mention costs of failing to settle, and attempt to change bargaining expectations when parties are hostile (Kochan & Jick, 1978; Hiltrop, 1985, 1989). Similarly, divorce and family mediators have been found to impose more procedural structure and control when parties became defensive (Donohue, 1991). Third parties may also be more directive under the pressures of a deadline or when they have well-defined formal mandates (Kressel & Pruitt, 1989).

In addition to studies that bear on the general approaches to intervention like those discussed in the Carnevale et al. model, other more specific moves that third parties make are contingent on emerging factors as well. When bargainers bring too many issues to the table in negotiations, mediators often attempt to reduce the agenda, develop an overarching framework, or prioritize issues (Carnevale & Pegnetter, 1985). When bargainers lack experience, mediators also simplify agendas and try to educate parties in impasse processes. When issues have a potential impact on absent parties (i.e., children in a custody mediation) and absent parties' interests are not well represented by the disputants, third parties may be more likely to reject parties' suggestions and terms for settlement (Folger & Bernard, 1985).

It is clear from this discussion that intervenors are, in a real sense, interactors in the ongoing conflict. Their moves shape and define interaction in ways similar to the disputing parties' moves: third parties' moves are possible because of endorsed power, they are adaptive to moment-to-moment influences in the unfolding conflict, and they are influential in shaping conflict as it emerges during an intervention. When a third party is involved in conflict, conflict interaction is, in important ways, constituted by the moves and countermoves of the third party as well as the disputants. We now turn to the second property of conflict interaction and examine how it helps to describe and explain third party involvement in conflict interaction.

PROPERTY 2 *Patterns of behavior in conflict tend to perpetuate themselves.*

We noted at the beginning of this chapter that the self-perpetuating nature of conflict interaction is often a rationale for bringing a third party into a conflict. If interaction is self-perpetuating, if momentum becomes difficult for disputing parties to control or direct, or if cycles of interaction are difficult to recognize because parties contribute to them, then a third party may have the best chance to alter these self-sustaining tendencies. But in the discussion of how the first property of conflict interaction applies to intervention, we have seen that third parties do not stand apart from the conflict interaction; they are interactors themselves. Does this mean that third parties' moves are vulnerable to the self-perpetuating tendencies of conflict interaction? Or that interaction involving third parties is itself self-perpetuating? We will see in the discussion of this second property that certain forms of third party intervention are capable of controlling or redirecting patterns of conflict interaction. Third parties can alter cycles and patterns of conflict interaction. But we will also see how conflict interaction involving third parties is itself susceptible to self-perpetuation.

Although there are a wide range of third party mandates, most intervention roles put third parties in a position to alter repetitive patterns in conflict interaction. Many intervention moves are aimed specifically at the interaction itself and hence may counteract self-perpetuating tendencies. Restructuring of conflict interaction occurs in diverse and often subtle ways. It occurs any time the third party sets time limits, organizes the agenda, controls when parties talk, focuses the interaction on the problem before considering solutions, encourages the parties to make statements in a clearer, less hostile, or more productive way, fosters an exchange of small concessions, or sets a climate that allows the parties to provide information that previously went unstated. These are just a few examples of the type of third party moves that direct the process and thereby influence conflict interaction.

Parties are immersed in the conflict and often cannot easily monitor or control aspects of the interaction that third party moves influence. As a result, disputing parties rarely address these issues themselves. In the midst of an unfolding conflict, people typically have all they can do to track issues, deal with emotions, and plan responses. It is difficult for parties to channel or control the interaction as a whole. Partly because disputants cannot easily make these moves, these interventions are central to a third party's ability to alter well-grooved patterns and cycles of interaction.

There are some forms of intervention, such as arbitration or court hearings, where the process is highly structured and the parties are prohibited from carrying on the interaction patterns that characterized the conflict before the intervention. The third party takes almost total control of the process and thereby ensures a radically different sequence of moves and countermoves, actions and reactions. Under some process rules, the parties may not even speak for themselves; for example, in a courtroom an attorney may speak for them. In these interventions, cycles of interaction are almost inevitably broken. There are potential downsides to these interventions as well, however. Because existing patterns are altered by the strong hand of an intervenor, the process does little to foster new patterns that could be sustained by the parties themselves after the intervention ends. The parties have not initiated new, sustainable interaction among themselves due to the intervention. Moreover, these forms of intervention can, in some instances, exacerbate destructive cycles. Arbitration or other adjudicative procedures can encourage blaming or can dwell heavily on the history of the conflict, thereby reinforcing destructive tendencies.

Other forms of intervention attempt to strike a balance between controlling the process and allowing the parties to control their interaction. In these cases, third parties try to structure the interaction by setting ground rules and intervening in ways that redirect the parties' moves. At the same time, the intervenor wants to encourage the parties to interact freely with each other so they have a strong hand in shaping the outcome and new patterns of interaction are initiated. Most forms of mediation and facilitation are premised on this attempt to balance process control with free-form interaction. Particular mediators or facilitators may give more emphasis to either objective, but the intervention as a whole attempts to achieve a balance.

In interventions that attempt to balance control of the process and spontaneous interaction, there is variation in the success third parties have in altering the self-perpetuating cycles of interaction. If the intervenor leaves too much room for un-controlled interaction, the parties' own patterns of interaction can prevail. Surprisingly, third parties can themselves contribute to and become part of these patterns. Several researchers have examined the consequences of not sustaining a balance between process control and disputants' interaction. Close studies of the move-by-move interactions of disputants and mediators suggest that third parties who break disputants' cycles of interaction actively resist the momentum these cycles exert. They actively avoid being pulled into the patterns already established by the disputants.

The interaction that occurs in child custody mediations where the parties reach agreement has been compared with the interaction that occurs in mediation where the parties fail to reach agreement (Jones, 1988, 1989; Donohue, 1989, 1991). These comparisons suggest that in **no-agreement** mediations, disputants engage in competitive exchanges characterized by indictments of the others' motives and negative attributions about the others' behavior, followed by defensive comments by the person under attack. The third party does not intervene with process moves to break or control these sequences. Instead, the mediators' comments are more likely to sustain these attacking cycles. Sometimes mediators clarify the bases of the comments, ask for further details, or paraphrase comments in less threatening ways, but they do not fundamentally alter these patterns.

In the mediations where parties successfully **reached agreements**, the third party took more active intervention steps to break cycles and to control the interaction. Instead of attack/defend cycles, the interaction started with information exchange, then turned to a consideration of possible solutions, and finally shaped the final terms of a settlement. Achieving this progression depends on a mediator's ability to break the momentum of the parties' own interaction. This is most frequently accomplished by summarizing, pointing to common ground, redirecting the substantive focus of the interaction, and, in general, placing a high premium on controlling the process.

The major implication of this research for our purposes is that it demonstrates how third parties can alter or thwart the self-perpetuating tendencies in parties' conflict interaction. This usually requires a concerted attempt to control process. Without well-timed and appropriate moves that influence the conflict process, third party moves can actually contribute to the sequences that drive the original conflict. In a real sense, the self-perpetuating tendencies can overwhelm the intervention moves.

Becoming trapped in the disputants' destructive cycles is not the only problem the self-perpetuating nature of conflict interaction can cause in third party interventions. The intervention itself is vulnerable to repetitive tendencies, much like other forms of conflict interaction. Two brief examples will show how self-perpetuating tendencies establish themselves in third party interventions.

Studies of mediation in labor and business contexts suggest that third parties set up similar patterns of intervention across different cases (Shapiro et al., 1985; Kolb, 1986). Early in a case, mediators tend to assess and classify the dispute before them. In essence, they ask themselves: "What is possible in this case? How can this case develop? What outcomes are possible?" After answering these questions, they tend to draw from a small repertoire of favored approaches and choose one based on previous cases they have handled (Shapiro et al., 1985). The interaction following from this approach then becomes quite predictable and similar across cases. The third party may, for instance, pressure one of the parties to make concessions. Or the intervenor may encourage negotiation. Or the approach could be to separate the parties and shuttle back and forth between them in individual caucuses. The type of approach the mediator thinks will work for the dispute at hand shapes the mode of intervention and consequent interaction among the parties.

This work suggests that, just like disputing parties, intervenors find it useful to "know what to expect." Predictability is helpful in anticipating the way the parties will react and in planning future moves. In attempting to attain the security that comes with predictability, third party approaches to intervention thus become self-perpetuating. A limited number of solutions or intervention moves are applied across a wide range of cases. The danger is, of course, that the "canned" solutions favored by the intervenor may not work in new and different circumstances and that intervenors' well-defined scenarios will blind them to the need for different approaches.

Third party interventions may become vulnerable to self-perpetuation in a second sense as well. The form of intervention applied in a case can shape future interventions. This tendency has been found in analyses of informal third-party-ship—where the third party's mandate is an informal one such as those typically held by parents, managers, or even friends. In these settings, the same third party often becomes involved in a series of conflicts with the same parties over some length of time. Once a style of intervention is adopted with disputants, it may be reapplied in future conflicts. Although there is only anecdotal evidence to support this claim, several reasons have been advanced to expect such repetition (Sheppard, Blumen-feld-Jones, & Roth, 1989).

First, the type of resolution produced by an initial intervention is likely to shape the future direction of what may develop into an ongoing conflict. For example, a manager may intervene in a dispute between two employees over how vacation time will be scheduled. The manager may decide to talk to each worker separately and then assign the vacation time in a way that he or she feels is fair. When the same issue comes up a year later, the workers may have learned little about how to interact with each other. Seeing that the employees are unable to deal with the second conflict, the manager may believe that he or she has no choice but to take the same approach—hand down a decision on how the issue should be settled.

Moreover, in interacting with an intervenor, the parties learn something about how the third party is likely to deal with the conflict. As a result, future conflicts with the same party may be shaped in ways that the intervenor is likely to address. For example, a parent might intervene in a sibling conflict by having each sibling state his or her case and then judging who was in the right. In future conflicts, the children are likely to get better at stating a defensible case, because they know that is how the parent will decide things. So whereas they may have directly fought in the past, the children may instead turn to the parents with a prepared complaint.

Finally, the third party may be likely to approach future conflicts with the same parties similarly because the approach may be salient in memory or may be seen as "the" most effective way to respond to these parties. Interventions can be influenced by force of habit.

PROPERTY 3   *Conflict moves are embedded in larger interaction sequences.*

Like other forms of conflict interaction, third party interventions can be viewed as a series of episodes and phases unfolding over time and shaping parties' understandings of what is going on at any point along the way. To the extent that third parties take a hand in establishing the unfolding interaction, they can significantly influence how parties view their own conflict activity during the intervention. This third principle of conflict interaction points to important ways in which third parties (1) steer broad phases of interaction by structuring the process and (2) shape specific conflict episodes by framing issues.

Considerable effort has been spent describing the way interaction develops over time during third party interventions. This work suggests that third party interventions are characterized by broad, but recognizable, phases of interaction. Based on descriptions provided by eight researchers, Sheppard (1984), for example, posits that four generic stages of interaction emerge in third party interventions. In many forms of intervention, interaction first proceeds through a **definition** phase in which parties select a procedure, get a sense of each other and the intervenor, and determine what is in dispute, what relevant information is available, and what alternatives for settlement seem possible. In the second phase, **discussion**, parties present relevant information and argue for alternatives. Then the intervention moves through **alternative selection** in which the parties and/or intervenor determines the validity of information, weighs arguments, and selects an alternative. Finally, there is a stage of **reconciliation** when parties accept and enact the agreement. The reconciliation phase also includes enforcement of the decision and possible discussion of problems with the agreement once the parties have attempted to enact it.

Similarly, a recent analysis of seven different phase discussions of mediation suggests that four generic phases emerge during this specific form of intervention (Donohue, 1991). During a period of **orientation** parties reach an understanding of what the process of mediation entails, what the ground rules of interaction are (e.g., who will talk first, the possibility of caucusing, confidentiality), and what role the mediator plays. The **background information** stage describes that period when the parties share information about the dispute; the parties tell their stories and often state their settlement objectives (i.e., what they want out of the intervention). **Issue processing** refers to the phase in which parties address points of difference, clarify why they favor or disfavor certain options, and address underlying issues that may not have surfaced in earlier phases. Finally, parties engage in **proposal development,** when the disputants and mediator attempt to reach a final agreement by negotiating, compromising, accommodating, or dropping issues.

It is important to note that not all mediations actually pass through these phases (Jones, 1988). At best these are the phases of interaction that are likely to occur if the parties actually reach agreement. They are actually derived from recommendations about the course mediations should take (Donohue, 1991). In this sense, the four phases are based more on prescriptions about what interaction should look like rather than on documented descriptions of what does occur. Nonetheless, the four phases capture a widely held sense of how mediation develops, especially when the intervention moves toward agreement.

This last point suggests an important difference between phasic development in third party interventions and other self-regulated forms of conflict. In interventions, third parties often make a conscious attempt to move interaction through a set of preconceived phases like those described by either Sheppard or Donohue. Intervenors are often taught a prescribed series of phases as part of their training (Haynes, 1981; Folberg & Taylor, 1984; Moore, 1986; Stulberg, 1987). They employ process rules that promote the emergence of the phases in sequence. They also make specific moves such as summaries, questions, or paraphrases that help keep the interaction within a phase or move it from one phase to another. Moreover, intervenors may track the progress of the interaction through the phases as the intervention occurs and make the parties aware of the need to remain in, or move into, a particular phase.

When third parties are not present, there is rarely such a conscious attempt to envision and enact a sequence of phases.

In using phases to steer interaction, intervenors frame interaction for the disputing parties. Through the explicit labeling and control of stages that third parties exert, disputants come to have a clear sense of what they are doing as the intervention process unfolds. Not only does this establish boundaries for what moves seem appropriate or inappropriate, it also creates a redefining force much like that covered in our discussion of reframing interaction in Chapter 8. Part of the power of third party intervention is its ability to transform disputants' goals. As parties enter various phases of intervention, their involvement in that interaction shapes their goals; it influences what they think can or should be done. The type of interaction the parties see themselves engaged in is influenced by the emerging interaction itself. Interaction is framed by what the parties see themselves doing rather than by what they may have planned to do. This effect reveals how the process itself holds the potential for creating significant change. The conscious use of phases in intervention—structuring interaction around sets of broad interactive goals that change over time—plays a key role in reframing conflicts.

In adjudicative forms of intervention where third parties impose final agreements, the interaction flows inevitably through phases like those Sheppard has summarized. Even if a judge, hearing panel, or manager (acting adjudicatively) downplays discussion of issues, he or she must know enough about the issues to make a decision. Thus the process progresses toward an imposed agreement. However, in intervention formats where third parties do not have the power to impose settlements, disputants may or may not progress through the phases. Some interventions only reach a discussion of issues and then head "back" toward more information exchange, or even further orientation (Jones, 1988).

What propels movement through the phases in nonadjudicative forms of intervention? How is it that some interventions lead to settlement or proposal development and others do not? There is no single, easy answer to these questions. How interventions develop depends on a broad range of factors, including the issues in dispute, the extent of common ground among the parties, the third party's talent, and the conditions under which the disputants enter the intervention, to name just a few. What is clear is that all forms of nonadjudicative intervention attempt to move parties through the two broadest phases of conflict we examined in detail in Chapter 3—differentiation and integration. Moving from definition and discussion to alternative selection and reconciliation in the Sheppard model, or moving from orientation and background information to issue processing and proposal development, is essentially a move from differentiation to integration. Thus movement through the intervention phases hinges critically on the third party's ability to lead disputants through successful differentiation and effective integration (Walton, 1969).

A third party's skill in performing certain functions is critical in propelling movement through the various phases of interaction described above. Some of these functions are linked to differentiation in that they help sharpen conflicts without fostering spiraling escalation. Other functions are linked to integration in that they help induce consensus and support for mutual agreements. These functions are related to several tactics discussed in Chapter 7, but they take on a different cast in third party applications.

Third Parties, Differentiation, and Integration

Sharpening Conflicts   In many nonadjudicative contexts, an intervenor's most important and difficult task is to "sharpen" the conflict (Van de Vliert, 1985). A sharpened conflict results from a successful differentiation phase: when a conflict is sharpened, parties have an accurate (and often painful) understanding of the issues, they see the consequences of not resolving the problem, and they have some understanding of what a solution must do in order to reach the needs of all involved. The success or failure of an intervention ultimately rests on whether the third party can guide parties through differentiation without developing inflexible avoidance or spiraling escalation.

An effective third party will structure interaction in differentiation so that a clear definition of the problem can emerge without locking parties into solutions that have stifled creative thinking, produced inflexibility, or promoted escalation. Although the specific techniques that the third party must employ to achieve this general goal depend on the specific conflict, three intervention functions facilitate sharpening of conflicts.

Unearthing the historical roots of the problem. By the time a third party is called in to help work through a conflict, the parties may have lost sight of important facts or events that played a significant role in shaping the problem. As the parties argue for preferred solutions and "fight things out" at this level, some of the dimensions of the problem itself may be lost. Having parties review the conflict chronologically may seem pointless to the members at first but it often provides important breakthroughs. It encourages parties to write a more careful definition of their own problems.

Encouraging a statement of needs rather than a fight over solutions. Successful differentiation depends on a clarification of parties needs. Any solution a party advocates meets some set of **needs** that the party has. A problem exists not because people are pressing for different solutions or positions but because none of the solutions being considered or advocated meet all parties' needs (Fisher & Ury, 1981). Conflicts, in other words, stem from the apparent inability of the parties' to meet diverse needs on some issue. The continual fight over solutions is a symptom that all parties' needs will not be met if any of the solutions being considered is adopted.

Third parties can take an active role in confronting parties with the incompatibility of needs. This often requires that the intervenor (1) make people clarify what their needs are, (2) discourage individuals from regarding each other as the cause of the problem, and (3) prevent people from suggesting solutions before all members' needs are clarified. The process of clarifying needs in a conflict can be straightforward and explicit. The third party can turn to each person and ask: "What needs of yours must any solution fulfill?" or "You have suggested that X be done. Why do you want to see this solution adopted? What needs of yours would it meet?" Third parties often find it beneficial to put people's "need" statements on paper or a blackboard in front of the whole group. This method can allow for greater depersonalization of the conflict because specific needs become less associated with the parties who stated them. People can begin to "see," almost in a literal sense, that the problem they need to address lies above the needs of any one individual and rests in the incompatibility of positions. There is a problem "out there" that the parties as a whole can attack.

Research has shown that parties with high aspirations for meeting their needs attain better settlements than those with low aspirations (Pruitt & Rubin, 1986). This even holds true if both sides have high aspirations. Negotiations proceed best if parties set reasonable goals and have high commitment to attaining them. Third parties can help in this respect by pushing parties to be realistic and encouraging them to strive hard for their goals. In the case of weak parties, the intervenor may have to provide especially strong encouragement. Of course, high aspirations can be carried so far as to create inflexibility, thus preventing parties from finding solutions.

Cutting through multiple issues. For the differentiation phase of conflict to be successful, issues must be clarified. Often parties are unable to work through their own conflicts because the issues seem overwhelmingly complex. Multiple layers of problems may never be discussed separately. Issues may appear confused or ambiguous because parties' aggression is displaced and frustrations and anxiety from other unaddressed problems drive the interaction.

A third party is sometimes in a better position to see the multiple layers of problems than the parties themselves. An outsider can break the problem down into smaller, more manageable parts and separate areas on which parties already agree from areas that still remain unsettled (Guetzkow & Gyr, 1954; Avery, Auvine, Streibel, & Weiss, 1981; Folberg & Taylor, 1984). To cut through multiple issues, the third party must watch for cues indicating that aggression or frustration is displaced. Heated discussions that seem to go nowhere or comments that imply a relational or face-saving problem (such as, "I'm sorry I can't answer that question because I feel like you're talking to me like a three-year-old") may be cues that aggression is displaced. The third party can talk to people individually to determine whether problems that have not surfaced are influencing the interaction. If these problems are critical to a successful resolution of the conflict, the third party can raise them and explain why the parties were hesitant to address them. Careful introduction of the problem enables discussion to start cautiously. The third party can place constraints on the interaction to help control issues that may be volatile or to enable people to vent frustrations and emotions in a safe climate.

Inducing Integration   When a conflict has been successfully sharpened, the parties move through a productive differentiation phase. People have a clear understanding of the differences among them, the needs of each person, and the likely consequences of not attaining a resolution. Moving the parties from this phase to integration and the acceptance of a solution that meets all parties' needs is often a difficult task for a third party. We consider three methods that third parties employ to induce integration: suggesting common goals, defining the integration process, and inducing cooperation.

Suggesting common goals. In many conflict situations, there is often more agreement than parties realize. Parties become heavily focused on points of disagreement and lose sight of the commonalities. A third party can stay attuned to points of agreement and remind parties of these points at crucial times (Avery et al., 1981). Parties often share a common goal but differ over the means to achieve this goal. If the third party focuses attention on shared goals when conflicts become escalated, the tension of the moment can be relieved and members may reexamine their commitments to specific solutions. Comments that point to shared goals allow parties to discover commonalities and may offer significant encouragement to members who feel discouraged, exhausted, or frustrated. Of course, there are limitations to this tactic, as noted in the discussion of superordinate goals in Chapter 7.

Defining the integrative process. In suggesting common goals the third party attempts to integrate the two sides around a shared issue. The second approach assumes that the parties must define issues and move toward integrative solutions themselves, but attempts to control the *process* by which they do so. In essence, the third party sets up an agenda for the areas the two parties will discuss and ground rules for discussion. By controlling the process, the third party tries to get the sides to talk without letting the conflict escalate or de-escalate.

There are a number of procedures for integrative conflict management. Probably the best known is Filley's (1975) Integrative Decision Making (IDM) technique. This technique is premised on several assumptions. First, it assumes people must untangle the substantive and emotional issues surrounding the conflict before they can develop a solution. Second, it assumes that people must have certain attitudes in order to successfully manage conflicts—including a belief in the possibility of a mutually acceptable solution, a belief that the other's position is legitimate (if not acceptable), trust of the other, and a commitment to work for an integrative outcome. Finally, in line with our earlier discussions, the IDM model assumes that problem definition should be separated from solution generation. Based on these assumptions, Filley (1975) outlines a six-step technique for finding integrative solutions:

1. **Review and adjustment of relational conditions**. In this step conditions conducive to a cooperative climate are set up. These conditions are discussed in Chapter 6.
2. **Review and adjustment of perceptions**. Here the parties use procedures outlined by Filley to clarify the factual basis of the conflict to establish the beliefs held by each member.
3. **Review and adjustment of attitudes**. Parties clarify their feelings and attitudes. Here parties state and clarify emotional issues in the conflict and how they feel about each other.
4. **Problem definition**. The mutual determination of the depersonalized problem. Techniques discussed earlier, such as Volkema's Problem-Purpose Expansion, could be employed at this point.
5. **Search for solution**. The nonjudgmental generation of possible solutions to the problem.
6. **Consensus decision**. The evaluation of alternative solutions and the agreement on a single solution.

The first steps of IDM are designed to untangle conflict issues. Attitudes consistent with IDM are fostered throughout, but especially by steps 1–3. Finally, problem definition is separated from solution generation in steps 4–6.

Third parties impose ground rules like the IDM method in order to regulate interaction between the parties. Regulation is useful for several reasons. First, it makes parties discuss areas that must be clarified to attain an integrative solution. Often parties are simply unaware of the issues that have to be worked out to resolve a conflict; this agenda lets them know what they have to cover. Second, the agenda constrains parties to limited areas of discussion at any one time. This eliminates chaotic, "kitchen-sink" fights where both sides toss in any comments or issues they think are to their advantage. Finally, ground rules offer tangible evidence of the third party's activity and willingness to intervene in the conflict. This can reassure the parties that they are not at each other's mercy and that there is an impartial mediator to regulate the interaction.

Inducing cooperation. In the third approach the third party enlists one side as an ally in moves designed to get both sides to cooperate. A lack of trust and willingness to cooperate often prevents people from endorsing some solution that "on paper" seems to meet everyone's needs. Solutions may not be endorsed because parties do not trust that everyone will carry through on the commitments the solution requires. There is no assurance, in other words, that people are willing to cooperate even if they give their assent to a proposed solution or agreement. This lack of trust may prevent parties from moving past differentiation and toward integration; moreover, it often is a catalyst for competitive escalation.

Osgood's GRIT proposal (discussed in Chapter 7) can be used by a third party when disputants are "locked in a bond of mutual distrust" and "any innocent-seeming action is perceived as manipulative and threatening" (Lindskold, 1978, p. 777). The steps in the GRIT proposal may be most useful in cases where one of the conflicting parties wants to initiate concessions but is afraid to do so or is not being clear about his or her willingness to make concessions without a promise of reciprocity. In this instance, the third party can make sure that others recognize that a promise of concessions is being made, and that the concession is not linked to a demand for similar moves by others. The third party can also note when the promised concessions have been carried out and thereby point to the willingness of some parties to make a sincere effort to settle the conflict.

The third party's active involvement in clarifying the implicit steps in a GRIT-like offer can help establish a climate of mutual trust. The third party is a witness to the disputants' willingness to respond appropriately once a sincere conciliatory move has been made. If others fail to respond with reciprocal concessions or moves, it can be read by the third party as a sign of poor faith. There is some pressure on the responding parties to make reciprocal concessions or risk losing the third party's involvement in the process.

Thus far, in examining the third principle of conflict interaction, we have seen that third party interventions can be viewed as developmental sequences and that intervenors play an active role in defining and controlling the unfolding conflict interaction. In addition to influencing broad phasic development by conceiving of and enacting interventions in stages, third parties also influence sequences of conflict interaction by the way in which they **frame conflict issues**. In discussing self-regulation in Chapter 8, we noted that the way in which issues are framed by parties influences perceptions of the conflict and, in turn, may direct or redirect the interaction. Third parties may have as great an influence over the framing of issues as the disputants themselves. As in self-regulation, the framing of issues directs the interaction. The way issues are framed may encourage initiation of episodes parties believe they need to engage in to address the problem.

When third parties first become involved with a conflict, their knowledge of the issues, events, and parties' relationship may be quite limited. This information is not always easily attainable. Conflicts are not isolated events that can be removed, unchanged, from the stream of interaction in which they have unfolded (Beer, 1986; Kolb, 1986). As we have seen in our discussion of third party responsiveness to the conflict interaction, disputes are not fixed entities. The very act of presenting a case to a third party may alter the issues and mask or mute dimensions of the conflict that previously were pressing or important. How a third party comes to understand and represent the issues in a conflict may or may not reflect the way the conflict was understood or represented by the parties before the intervention process began. How a third party eventually frames issues in the conflict depends on a number of factors, including how the parties present the issues to the intervenor, the third party's own interpretive assumptions about what the issues are or which issues need to be addressed, the third party's repertoire of intervention strategies (i.e., which issues the intervenors feel capable of addressing), and the third party's willingness to cast issues in ways that promote agreements consistent with their values or interests.

These factors suggest that, as a third party becomes involved, issues are likely to be reframed: the way the parties view the conflict can be changed dramatically or subtly (Lam et al., 1989). Moreover, the ensuing conflict interaction follows from the third party's casting of the issues. Unfolding episodes of interaction are, in direct ways, linked to the third party's framing of the issues (Putnam & Holmer, 1992).

As an illustration of the link between framing and interaction in third party interventions, consider the options available to third parties in informal settings, such as when a parent intervenes in a dispute among siblings, or when a supervisor intervenes in a conflict among office workers. In these contexts, third parties try to get a sense of what the conflict is about. As they make sense of the situation, the problem is framed. Some research on framing suggests that third parties in informal settings draw from four broad **framing strategies** (Sheppard et al., 1989).

First, the third party can cast the conflict within a **right–wrong** frame. In this frame the conflict issue is seen as one that stems from a violation of some rule or expectation. The problem requires identifying one party as right and the other as wrong. Second, the conflict can be cast within a **negotiation** frame. Here the problem is seen as one that requires compromise; it necessitates asking both parties to consider their interests and the interests of other parties simultaneously. Third, the problem can be cast within an **underlying conflict** frame. In this case, the third party views the stated issue as a symptom of other issues not explicitly discussed. The conflict is complicated because issues are not all aboveboard. Parties may be avoiding issues because the issues are riven with a history of painful or frightening experiences or because the status quo protects someone's interests. Once an issue is framed as an underlying conflict, the third party tends to believe that no satisfactory solution can be found until the buried concerns are unearthed. Finally, third parties can view a problem from a **stop** frame. From this standpoint, the third party views the conflict as one that must be made to stop at almost any cost. When a conflict is cast in this frame, the issues themselves are downplayed. The third party has less concern for resolving issues than for making the conflict interaction cease. This occurs, for example, when a parent simply insists that two siblings stop fighting and makes no attempt to assess what problem instigated the ruckus.

Whatever framing a third party chooses, it is enacted through the sequence of moves as the intervention develops. The third party's framing of an issue is thus integrally tied to the way the conflict interaction is likely to unfold. For example, if a third party adopts a right–wrong frame, then the interaction is likely to unfold as a series of question and response episodes regarding what the facts are, who actually did what, and what the understanding of the rule or expectation was. If the issue is perceived as one that requires negotiation, the third party is more likely to engage the parties in interaction sequences that seek possible compromises. Tit-for-tat exchanges and other forms of concession exchanges are likely. If the issue is cast within an underlying conflict frame, the third party is more likely to encourage a series of interaction episodes to foster diagnosis of deeper issues. The intervenor might, for example, prompt a series of self-disclosing exchanges followed by attempts at clarification and confirmation from the parties on what the intervenor thinks may be the "real" issues. In these interactions, intervenors often paraphrase a comment that a party has just made and, in the paraphrase, suggest an unspoken concern (Lemmon, 1985; Donohue, 1991).

There are other subtler ways that third parties frame issues and thereby influence conflict interaction. If an intervenor places an issue in a negotiation, right–wrong, or underlying conflict frame, other more specific framings are made as the interaction unfolds within this broader frame. Within a negotiation frame, for example, intervenors interpret parties' statements, restate interests, synthesize positions, and suggest and word agreements. These moves may influence how parties see the issues before them and thus can influence the parties' interaction.

In sum, understanding the framing of issues by third parties is important in understanding the influence they have on conflict interaction. Framing is sometimes done strategically by a third party to move interaction in a particular direction. In formal contexts such as mediation, framing allows only certain forms of interaction to occur. Framing may also be inadvertent or unconscious, perhaps occurring with almost every substantive comment an intervenor makes. In these less strategic framings, third parties may exert influence over settlement terms by shaping values or preferences and by pursuing or dropping subissues. Here again, influence is exerted through interaction. The questions that the intervenor asks and the reactions the intervenor gives to parties' comments create episodes of interaction that ultimately determine which issues get pursued, which values supported, or which preferences are challenged.

PROPERTY 4   *As senseless and chaotic as conflict interaction may appear, it has a general direction that can be understood.*

This property of conflict interaction indicates the way in which climate sets expectations for behavior and, as a result, guides interaction. Despite an onslaught of ostensibly unpredictable moves and responses, conflict interaction usually develops around, and is bounded by, recognizable themes. These themes "tell" parties how conflict is likely to be handled. When third parties intervene in conflicts, shifts in climate are likely for several reasons. At the most basic level, third parties are "new" interactors in the conflict. They contribute to establishing a climate that reflects at least one additional interactor's moves and responses.

Second, intervenors are more than just additional interactors in the conflict; they are interactors with mandates to control process or outcomes to a lesser or greater extent. The third party's mandate carries, in this sense, the power to enforce new expectations for behavior—to establish a new climate. Many of the process controls that third parties impose are aimed at managing the parties' interaction. These controls may limit when and how long parties talk; they may stifle personal attacks or they may arrange agenda items so that more explosive issues are surrounded by innocuous or mundane topics. As we have seen in our discussions of climate, conflicts may not be well defined because parties may believe it is not safe to state their positions or express their emotions. The parties may believe that if they are honest, "things will get out of hand" or irreconcilable personal animosities will develop. Third party controls over interaction can establish a safe climate where conflicts can be sharpened without risk of spiraling escalation.

Third, because intervenors are initially "outsiders" to the dispute, the mere presence of a third party can change conditions considerably. When the third party first becomes involved, there is often a sense that parties need to "perform well" for the intervenor, to be on their best behavior. Although this performance may seem inauthentic at first (and can fade fast once the parties start interacting), it often encourages people to be more careful about their word choice and style of presentation. Parties may be more descriptive than evaluative and less likely to blame others as they define the issues. Disputants begin to recognize that more care is being taken in how people are stating their positions and making evaluations. This becomes a sign that people are trying to work on the problem without destructive escalation. Even though parties may suspect that others are on their best behavior because the third party is present, this period can allow for a greater clarification of issues than has ever been achieved previously. Moreover, climates change as interaction patterns change. Stepping through constructive exchanges, even under the guiding hand of a third party, creates the realization that such exchanges are possible.

Fourth, third parties acting in mediative or other nonadjudicative capacities often bring a sense of optimism that the parties may have lost in their failed attempts to resolve the conflict on their own (Walton, 1969). When interventions start there can often be a sense that something new is being tried, that the intervenor may have approaches, insights, techniques (even mirrors or legerdemain) that will ease tensions and settle issues. Third parties often begin an intervention by explicitly stating that they believe a constructive outcome is possible or that they have seen parties in more fractious disputes come to mutually satisfying agreements.

Finally, third party interventions are often conducted in places conducive to changes in climate (Walton, 1969; Folberg & Taylor, 1984; Stulberg, 1987). Intervenors often choose sites where threatening behavior is less likely because it seems inappropriate, such as a church or library. Any change in physical location may influence expectations about what behaviors are appropriate during the intervention.

Although all these factors contribute to third party influence on climate, there is no guarantee that new climates will be sustained during an intervention. As we have discussed earlier, the self-perpetuating nature of conflict interaction can overwhelm attempts at intervention. The parties' well-worn interaction patterns can re-create previous climates.

There is a second sense in which this fourth principle of conflict interaction helps to understand third party interventions. Our discussion of third party mandates suggests that there is usually considerable leeway within any mandate for third parties to select a variety of roles. In part, the approach a third party adopts may be explainable if the overarching climate is taken into account. The climate carries expectations for third party behavior that influence the style or approach adopted.

For example, we have described how managers in organizations may adopt a range of roles in handling conflict among subordinates. These approaches range from advisory, adjudicative, or restructurer roles, on the one hand, to less interventionist roles such as investigator, mediator, and problem-solver. Although quite a range of intervention roles is available, managers tend to prefer the more controlling advisory and adjudicative styles (Sheppard et al., 1989). They tend to impose outcomes rather than guide parties to construct their own solution. The explanation for this tendency is tied to established expectations for how managers act in their working environment (Kolb and Sheppard, 1985; Kolb, 1986; Karambayya & Brett, 1989).

Unlike third parties who intervene in legal settings, managers often have no prescribed guidelines for acting as an intervenor. As a result, managers tend to fall back on the authoritative stance they take in everyday supervisory activities such as planning, delegating work, conducting performance appraisals, and the like. Subordinates come to expect managers to take an authoritative stance when they act as third parties, and they sometimes misinterpret less authoritative intervention moves a manager may try to make. For instance, when managers offer mild suggestions in an attempt to encourage parties to settle their own dispute, subordinates sometimes take these suggestions as binding directives (Kolb, 1986).

Besides the influence of their generally authoritative role, managers' adjudicative stance in intervention may be explained by a second reason. Managers are often "insiders" who hold vested interest in the outcomes of conflicts in which they intervene. The productivity or morale of their entire unit may ride on how an internal dispute turns out. Their concern for outcomes may predispose them to take a stronger adjudicative role when conflicts arise in their work units.

In sum, it is the general set of expectations established for managerial behavior in the workplace—how managers see themselves acting and how subordinates expect them to act—that fosters the tendency to rely on more adjudicative styles of intervention. Managers' third party moves are understandable given the climates typically established in the workplace.

Intervenors in other settings may choose certain intervention roles because of established climates as well. In some divorce or community mediation programs, climates that place a heavy emphasis on reaching high rates of agreement are established. At base, this emphasis may stem from financial concerns. Funding for mediation programs may be contingent on rates of reaching agreements in cases. But, like all climates, these expectations are established and embedded in interaction. Mediators in the programs talk to each other about their agreement rates, obstacles they have to overcome in attaining settlements, or intervention techniques that work for them. Mediators who work in climates where there is pressure to reach agreements may be more likely to adopt "strong arm" styles, shaping agreements in ways that other mediators might view as inconsistent with the goals of mediation (Pearson & Thoennes, 1989).

In other mediation programs, the climate may emphasize that mediators reserve judgment about substantive issues and not press for settlements (Harrington & Merry, 1988). In these programs, an expectation is set through interaction among mediators and program directors that the disputants should be allowed to construct their own solutions, even if it means that agreements are not reached. In this climate, intervenors are more likely to adopt a nonimpositional style of mediation, one in which mediators allow parties to exchange information and remain focused on the issues, these mediators are unlikely to promote settlement terms.

PROPERTY 5 *Conflict interaction affects relationships between participants.*

Throughout this book we have seen how the negotiation of relationships is an integral and inevitable part of conflict interaction. Relationships are defined and altered during any exchange of messages. In an attempt to be strategic, people often try to manage their own images, to define the image of the other, and to establish particular types of relationships. Sometimes these attempts at controlling relational issues are in parties' self-interest and sometimes they are in the mutual interests of all sides. Regardless of strategic intent, the way in which relationships are defined and managed is as much a part of the "settlement" or "solution" as the substantive decisions. When people work through conflicts, they work through relationships as well.

When third parties intervene in a conflict, they establish relationships with the disputants through the messages they send. Third parties make conscious attempts to present certain images of themselves. These images differ depending on the third party's intervention role, but there are important commonalities as well. Foremost is the need for third parties to establish a credible image in the eyes of the disputants (Walton, 1969; Folberg & Taylor, 1984).

For adjudicators, credibility may rest on establishing that they have substantive **expertise** related to the issues; for example, labor arbitrators may try to show that they understand contract law, pension funds, fair labor practices, and so on. For adjudicators, mediators, facilitators, and many informal third party intervenors, credibility rests on the parties' perception that the intervenor is **neutral** (i.e., has no personal preference about the outcome of the dispute) and **impartial** (i.e., treats all parties in comparable ways substantively and procedurally) (Stulberg, 1987). For many third party roles, credibility may also rest on a sense that the third party is **objective**—that the intervenor has sufficient detachment to keep a clear head about the issues and unfolding interaction. Objectivity is linked to disputants' perceptions that third parties can maintain process control and establish safe climates while simultaneously tracking and fostering substantive movement on issues.

Like all images, those fostered by third parties are under continuous negotiation in the interaction. Third parties make bids for an image and these bids may be accepted or rejected by the disputants. If the expertise, neutrality, impartiality, or objectivity of the third party is challenged, it can have significant consequences for the intervention (Bernard et al., 1984). In such cases, the relationships between the third party and the disputants shift: the disputants may gain greater control over the interaction process and revert to patterns of interaction that existed prior to the intervention. Studies of mediation, for example, suggest that disputants are more likely to deadlock in sessions where a mediator loses objectivity and becomes emotionally involved in the process (Donohue, 1989). Alternatively, if impartiality or neutrality is lost, one party may think the intervention is slanted against him or her and withdraw from the process.

Third parties not only establish relationships with the disputants during the intervention, they alter relationships between the parties themselves. In particular, third parties have a significant impact on face-saving concerns between the parties. As we discussed in Chapter 5, disputants are frequently concerned about appearing weak. They can suffer "image loss" if other parties in the dispute think they will make concessions or crumble easily under pressure (Pruitt, 1971). Parties may act tough and refuse to move from positions they are actually willing to concede, because they are afraid that giving an inch will mean conceding a mile. Third parties alter this dynamic in an interesting way. They allow movement, without altering the relational image the parties want to preserve.

When disputants move from an intransigent position, they can claim that it was the third party who suggested the idea, or persuaded them to make the concession (Shapiro et al., 1985). As a result, parties can move without suffering damage to their images: they are not weak; they are simply acting under the guidance or pressure of the third party. Significant strides in breaking impasses can occur because third parties shoulder the responsibility for concessions or unpopular options (Carnevale, 1986; Hiltrop, 1989). Without the third party's presence, options that the parties are actually willing to accept may not even be explored.

Third parties alter relational dynamics in a second sense as well. Primarily through a controlling process, third parties alter the emotional tenor of the dispute and thereby change how parties see each other. We have noted that the presence of an intervenor may put parties, at least for a time, on their best behavior. This has important consequences. The presence of third parties has been found, for example, to dampen parties' desire for retribution (Peachey, 1989). It may be that simply having an outsider hear their cases makes parties feel they have already "gotten even" in some sense. Also, once parties know that someone else has heard about their mistreatment or grievances, it may be less important to take tough stands on substantive issues. Similarly, third parties reduce defensiveness by encouraging disputants to talk about themselves rather than for the other party (Jones, 1989).

Third parties also alter the emotional tenor of a conflict by controlling how and when hostility is expressed. In the caucus, a separate and confidential meeting between each party and the intervenor, third parties have a powerful tool for channeling the expression of hostility. In caucuses, disputants express a great deal of hostility toward the other party. Much of this hostility is personalized attacks in the form of character assassination and venting (Pruitt, McGillicuddy, Welton, & Fry 1989; McGillicuddy, Pruitt, Welton, Zubek, & Peirce, 1991). Movement and creative solutions appear to come on the heels of releasing hostility. Third parties can use caucuses to facilitate private release of hostility, which can foster creative movement without further damaging relationships (Beer, 1986).

Finally, intervenors can influence parties' relationships by controlling or altering the distribution of power between disputants (Lemmon, 1985; Welton, 1991). In many intervention settings, third parties influence power by controlling process. Parties who have difficulty getting the floor or expressing their arguments (and thus are in a less powerful position vis-à-vis the interaction) may have a "level playing field" during the intervention. This redistribution of power comes through interaction ground rules established by the intervenor.

Third parties also influence the power balance by controlling the exchange or provision of information. It is common in many types of disputes for some parties to have more information than others about the issues, legal options, or long-term consequences of possible settlement terms. In divorce, for example, one spouse may have more information about employment pensions, real estate laws, or financial investment programs. It has become general practice in private sector divorce mediation for mediators to require each spouse to obtain legal and financial counseling before negotiating on these issues during the intervention. Mediators are reluctant to provide such information themselves because it may undermine their impartial stance. However, by encouraging parties to each have comparable information, they alter the power distribution during the negotiations.

Third parties also equalize power by not allowing either party to lose ground when concessions are exchanged. As the rationale for the GRIT proposal suggests, parties are often reluctant to make the first move because, if no concession is returned, the initiator may not be able to easily back away from the offer. The party "loses" because he or she moved first. When third parties act as go-betweens and caucus with each side, they often "test the waters," propose hypothetical concession exchanges and arrange for simultaneous moves. This prevents either side from suffering what Pruitt (1971) calls "position loss"—the loss of bargaining ground during the negotiations. Many third parties maintain equality of power by counterbalancing concessions and movement as the negotiations unfold.

All of the above examples illustrate how third parties influence power during the intervention itself. There is good reason to believe that most third party influence over power is limited to the time the intervenor is interacting with the parties. More long-term and fundamental influence over relationships is less likely to occur (Kressel & Pruitt, 1989). There is a tendency for intervenors not to probe too deeply into underlying issues, or to have the parties rethink or change how they are dependent on each other (Kolb & Sheppard, 1985; Donohue, 1991). Given the concerns of neutrality, impartiality, and objectivity for most intervenors, this restraint is not surprising. Most nonadjudicative forms of intervention are not aimed at producing the type of social change that necessitates shifts in power among disputing parties.

CONCLUSION

Any intervention in conflict is difficult and risky. Third parties always walk a slippery slope. The principles of conflict interaction examined in this chapter suggest why. An intervention is never completely under the third party's control. Although intervenors may have mandates to control aspects of the process or influence the outcome, the spontaneous nature of conflict interaction may lead third parties down a variety of intervention paths. As interactors themselves, third parties respond contingently to the issues on the table and the unfolding sequence of actions and reactions.

Although intervenors can break parties' destructive, repetitive cycles, they can just as easily contribute to existing cycles or become part of new ones. The momentum of parties' destructive patterns can overtake third parties' attempts to direct or redirect the interaction or to create collaborative, less hostile climates. If intervenors take unwarranted measures to control interaction or issues, they run the risk of losing credibility and, ultimately, their effectiveness.

Although the issues in a conflict may appear straightforward, they are often complex and malleable. They change as the parties present them to an intervenor and as the intervenor re-presents them to the parties during the intervention. The way third parties frame issues can influence the approach they take to intervention. If intervenors frame issues in ways that the parties themselves cannot understand or fully accept, any agreement will be difficult for the parties to enact. In this case, the third party runs the risk of addressing his or her own version of the dispute, rather than the parties'.

Although third parties have useful techniques for altering the way parties relate to each other during the intervention, they often have little chance to create long-term, stable changes in ongoing relationships. Intervention is difficult when it seeks more than short-term gains.

POSTSCRIPT: THE TECHNOLOGICAL FUTURE

Computers play an increasing role in our everyday interactions. Electronic mail, faxes, computer conferencing, and computer support systems to manage group meetings are all creating new possibilities for human interaction. The influence of computers also extends to conflict management, as Case 9.3 shows.

Case 9.3 **The Negotiation Support System**

Tony and Caitlin are two project managers from an international food distribution company, FoodCo. They have become embroiled in a conflict over personnel assignments. Each project manager at FoodCo has to build his or her own team by having qualified persons assigned to him or her; project managers become "internal recruiters" and try to find talented personnel so their projects will succeed. Caitlin and Tony both have their eyes on the same two employees and cannot agree on who should have them. After several discussions that led nowhere, Caitlin and Tony had an extended argument during their division's "staffing" meeting, a monthly session to determine personnel assignments. The argument ended in a stalemate and their supervisor recommended that Caitlin and Tony participate in a computer-assisted negotiation session.

Caitlin and Tony contacted Michelle, a staff member in charge of the Negotiation Support Room. Michelle set up a meeting and explained to them how their session would go. She also met with Caitlin and Tony separately prior to the session to help them clarify their needs and positions.

Tony and Caitlin met at the Negotiation Support Room. They walked into a comfortable setting dominated by a U-shaped table with computer stations at each of the eight seats, as shown in Figure 9.2. These were the input devices for the computerized Negotiation Support System (NSS) they would use to help them work on their conflict. At the front of the U was a large screen for the display of information. Michelle had Tony and Caitlin sit at stations at the two lower corners of the U and took a seat between them. She then instructed them to work silently at their computers for an hour, responding to the prompts on the computer screens. They worked through a series of questions asked by the computer, including: "What are the main issues in this conflict?" "What does the other party think the main issues are?" "What are your needs or requirements for a successful resolution of this conflict?" "What are the other party's needs and requirements for a successful resolution of this conflict?" "What are some possible solutions that would meet your needs?" "What solutions would meet both of your needs?" "How do you feel about this conflict?"

Michelle assured Tony and Caitlin that the system would keep their information confidential. They could choose what to divulge later on. Caitlin was struck by how much better she understood what she wanted as a result of this exercise. She had not

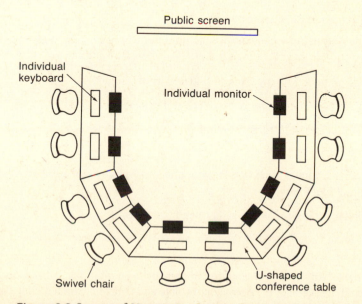

Figure 9.2 Layout of Negotiation Support Room.

really thought through the issues in the conflict. Tony had never reflected on how this conflict was making him feel or how his feelings might have contributed to the problem. He had some sobering insights during the silent work period.

After about an hour, Michelle had Tony and Caitlin turn their attention to each other. Michelle started the discussion: "Tony and Caitlin, we are going to try to find a solution to this conflict that will meet or exceed your expectations. I know you have been locked into this situation for a while, but experience has shown that our Negotiation Support System can help break through this deadlock. It is designed to focus your discussion on defining your needs and finding creative solutions to this conflict. The various procedures you will use today have been shown to be effective in resolving conflicts countless times.

"You have spent the past hour reflecting on your own point of view and analyzing your position. Hopefully this led to some insights for you. Now we will work together for a couple of hours to try to find a solution to this conflict. In the first stage of our work, we will compare positions to look for common ground. Following this, we will generate some solutions that meet both your needs. Remember several important things as we work through this conflict. Make sure the solutions we come up with meet your needs. But also, don't become wedded to a particular solution. There are usually several different solutions to any problem and at least one will meet everyone's needs. A mistake people commonly make is to cling to a single solution when a different one would really be better. Don't be afraid to experiment. Do you have any questions? If not, then let's begin."

Michelle directed Tony and Caitlin to enter their own lists of important issues into the Negotiation Support System (NSS). If they wished, they could simply copy the lists they had generated during the silent period. However, they could also omit items from their private lists that they did not wish to divulge. After they had finished, Michelle displayed the two lists of ideas side-by-side on the public screen. These lists were somewhat different. Caitlin's list was:

1. Tony has tried to prevent me from obtaining the services of employees I need for my project.

2. Tony has gone behind my back and talked to our supervisor.

3. My project cannot succeed without the right personnel.

4. Tony insulted me at our last meeting.

Tony's list was:

1. Caitlin is stubborn and demands what she needs, even if it hurts my project. We should pull together.

2. Caitlin wants the same employees I need for my project.

3. Caitlin embarrassed me at the staffing session by claiming her project was more important.

First, Michelle had Tony and Caitlin compare their "definitions" of the conflict. She pointed out that several of the points on the lists were not really issues. She also pointed out that there were clearly some bad feelings between the two. Tony apologized to Caitlin for insulting her, stating that he did not know he had done so. She accepted his apology and reassured him that she did want them to all pull together to make FoodCo successful.

Tony and Caitlin also found several common issues on their lists, and a few differences. Tony found that Caitlin regarded his project as less important than hers. He explained to Caitlin how the success of her project depended on the success of his. She was skeptical at first but began to see connections. After some discussion Tony and Caitlin began to think of their projects as interdependent. Caitlin commented, "Our two projects depend so much on each other that we should coordinate our efforts better." This caused Tony to suggest a new issue: "How to coordinate our efforts given the shortage of personnel." Michelle entered this new issue into the display. The NSS allowed almost instantaneous editing of comments, so Tony and Caitlin could see the list of common issues emerging. After about an hour of discussion a common list of issues was displayed on the screen:

1. Shortage of qualified personnel for projects A and B, and desire to assign the same people to both projects.

2. How to coordinate our efforts, given the shortage of personnel.

3. History of attempts by Tony and Caitlin to block each other's efforts.

Michelle commented that the common list of issues was much more "team-oriented" than the original lists. Then she said: "OK, let's find out if we really agree with this list. I want each of you to enter your degree of agreement with the list on the screen on a five-point scale with 5 indicating Strongly Agree and 1 Strongly Disagree. Make your ratings according to how you really feel about this issue. I also want you to enter your degree of agreement on the same scale with the following statement: 'We should go on to consider some solutions now.'"

Tony and Caitlin entered their ratings and the display on the screen showed ratings of 5 and 4 for the list, indicating strong agreement. Both also agreed that they should go on to the next step.

Michelle then led them into the next phase, solution generation. "First, we are going to brainstorm solutions to this conflict. I want you to enter ideas for how this conflict could be resolved into the NSS. Enter as many as possible and don't worry about how good they are right now. We will evaluate them later. Right now we just want to think creatively. You never know what idea will turn out to be a winner, no matter how weird it seems at first."

Caitlin and Tony silently entered their ideas into the NSS and then they displayed the list on the public screen. A list of 13 solutions appeared. Michelle, Caitlin, and Tony discussed each item on the list, eliminating duplicates and combining similar ideas. This reduced the list to six solutions.

The next step was to have Caitlin and Tony rate the six solutions on two scales: desirability and feasibility. They used a ten-point scale for each dimension, with a higher value corresponding to greater desirability and feasibility. After Caitlin and Tony had entered their ratings, the six solutions were displayed on a two-dimensional diagram on

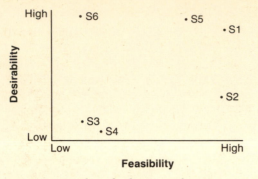

Figure 9.3 Display of solution evaluations.

the public screen, as shown in Figure 9.3. (In the interest of simplifying this figure we simply label these as S1 to S6.)

Michelle commented: "It looks like S3 and S4 won't work at all. S6 is desirable but not feasible, and S2 is feasible but not so desirable. I'd suggest we focus on solutions S1, 'Meet to coordinate the two projects,' and S5, 'Share the two employees.' Do you agree?" Caitlin and Tony agreed and began to discuss these two solutions. The two agreed to have regular coordinating meetings and to work together to get resources for their two projects. They also agreed to do a study to determine the proportion of time the two employees would need to spend in each project for them to be successful. An additional advantage of sharing the two employees, they concluded, is that their employees would be aware of the two projects and therefore able to make sure they coordinated well. They also agreed that they would look into combining their two projects to take advantage of synergies. Michelle asked Caitlin and Tony if they wanted to use the NSS to rate their agreement with the solution, but they both said that they knew they were in agreement.

The last step was to write a contract, detailing the solution and their respective rights and obligations. The NSS provided a form for this purpose and Michelle helped Tony and Caitlin fill it out. At the end of the meeting, Michelle printed out records of their issue definition, solutions, and the contract, giving a copy to each. She told Tony and Caitlin that they should feel free to use the Negotiation Support Room at any time. She also set up a follow-up meeting one month later to evaluate how well the solution was working out.

Caitlin and Tony were very pleased with this session. Both admitted they had been skeptical at first but were very satisfied with the resolution. Tony said: "Being able to see things on the screen gave them an objective quality. We had some distance from our ideas and were not as stubborn as a result." Caitlin commented: "I'll tell others about this system."

Computerized systems like NSS that support conflict management are being developed and adopted. They cannot replace third parties, but they will be an important tool in supporting third party interventions.

A careful reading of the case will show that Michelle used many strategies that contribute to third party effectiveness. But the Negotiation Support System also contributed. Research suggests that computerized systems to support communication and conflict management have several beneficial effects on interaction (Poole, Shannon, & DeSanctis, 1992). First, entering positions and solutions into a computer and displaying them objectify parties' stances. This helps depersonalize issues and focuses attention on issues, not people. Second, computer support systems provide procedures to structure the negotiations. Evidence suggests that groups perform better when they use systematic procedures, but many people resist procedures because they require preparation and are often difficult to carry out (Poole, 1991). Computerizing procedures makes them much easier to use and reduces preparation time, because they are already set up on the system. Moreover, these procedures are made available with no cost in efficiency; indeed, there is evidence that computerized systems make discussions much more efficient (Dennis, George, Jessup, Nunamaker, & Vogel, 1988). Members can enter lists of ideas much faster than they can list them verbally, and systems with word processing capabilities permit fast manipulation of information, including editing and rewriting of issues, solutions, and positions. The end result is that parties are free to concentrate on the content of the negotiations and have to spend less energy on secretarial and recording functions. In addition, computerized systems provide a memory for the parties. The system stores all lists and entries and can call them up if the parties want to go back or choose to adjourn and meet again later.

Studies suggest that groups using computerized support systems address conflicts more often than nonsupported groups (Poole et al., 1991). There are at least two reasons for this. First, the system often calls on parties to rate, rank, or vote on items, as Caitlin and Tony did. This is particularly useful in multiparty negotiations. A display of ratings or votes clarifies where differences lie, and once disagreement is out in the open parties are more likely to pursue the conflict. Nonsupported groups, on the other hand, generally deal with issues verbally and do not have readily available mechanisms for clarifying differences or summarizing them precisely. They may avoid or smooth over conflicts. Second, parties' entries into computerized support systems can be kept anonymous; the system asks people to enter ideas and then displays them without revealing who made particular contributions. This has been shown to encourage frankness, even from parties with little power. As a result, conflict issues are more likely to be stated outright. The larger the group using the system, the stronger this effect, because anonymity is a greater protection in larger groups than in small ones where people may guess who entered something. As we noted in the discussion of styles, addressing conflict may be beneficial under some conditions and harmful under others. This should be taken into account in employing computerized negotiation support.

There are also some possible drawbacks to computerized negotiation support.

For instance, the computer system may depersonalize some conflicts too much, causing parties to act without regard for others' feelings. This could result in uncontrolled escalation. The various positive and negative impacts of computer support for conflict management are just beginning to be studied. Future research will clarify how to design computer support systems so that they will facilitate constructive conflict management.

References

Adler, A. (1927). *The practice and theory of individual psychology*. New York: Harcourt, Brace and World.

Albrecht, T. L. (1979). The role of communication in perceptions of organizational climate. In D. Nimmo (Ed.), *Communication yearbook 3* (pp. 343–357). New Brunswick, NJ: Transaction Press.

Allison, G. T. (1969). Conceptual models and the Cuban Missile Crisis. *American Political Science Review, 63,* 689–718.

Allport, G. W. (1954). *The nature of prejudice*. New York: Anchor.

Apfelbaum, E. (1974). On conflicts and bargaining. In L. Berkowitz (Ed.), *Advances in experimental social psychology*, Vol. 7 (pp. 103–156). New York: Academic Press.

Apfelbaum, E. (1979). Relations of dominance and movements for liberation: An analysis of power between groups. In W. G. Austin & S. Worchel (Eds.), *The social psychology of intergroup relations* (pp. 108–204). Monterey, CA: Brooks/Cole.

Applegate, J. L., & Delia, J. G. (1980). Person-centered speech, psychological development, and contexts of language use. In R. N. St. Clair & H. Giles (Eds.), *The social and psychological contexts of language* (pp. 245–314). Hillsdale, NJ: Lawrence Erlbaum.

Arendt, H. (1969). *On violence*. New York: Harcourt Brace Jovanovich.

Auvine, B., Densmore, B., Extrom, M., Poole, S., & Shanklin, M. (1977). *A manual for group facilitators*. Madison, WI: The Center for Conflict Resolution.

Avery, M., Auvine, B., Streibel, B., & Weiss, L. (1981). *Building united judgment*. Madison, WI: The Center for Conflict Resolution.

Axelrod, R. (1970). *Conflict of interest: A theory of divergent goals with applications to politics*. Chicago: Markham.

Axelrod, R. (1984). *The evolution of cooperation*. New York: Basic Books.

Bachrach, P., & Baratz, M. S. (1962). Two faces of power. *American Political Science Review, 56,* 947–952.

Bachrach, P., & Baratz, M. S. (1970). *Power and poverty*. New York: Oxford University Press.

Baker, P. (1981). Social coalitions. *American Behavioral Scientist, 24,* 633–647.

Bales, R. F., & Cohen, S. (1979). *SYMLOG: A system for multiple level observation of groups*. New York: Free Press.

Bandler, R., & Grinder, J. (1982). *Reframing*. Moab, UT: Real People Press.

Bartos, O. J. (1970). Determinants and consequences of toughness. In P. Swingle (Ed.), *The structure of conflict* (pp. 45–68). New York: Academic Press.

Bateson, G. (1958). *Naven* (2nd ed.). Stanford: Stanford University Press.

Bateson, G. (1972). *Steps to an ecology of mind*. New York: Ballentine Books.

Baxter, L. A. (1982). Conflict management: An episodic approach. *Small Group Behavior, 13,* 23–42.

Bazerman, M. H. (1982). *The framing of organizational behavior*. Paper presented at the annual meeting of the Academy of Management.

Bazerman, M. H. (1983). A critical look at the rationality of negotiator judgement. *American Behavioral Scientist, 27,* 211–228.

Bazerman, M. H., Magliozzi, T., & Neale, M. A. (1985). Integrative bargaining in a competitive market. *Organizational Behavior and Human Decision Processes, 35,* 294–313.

Bazerman, M. H., & Neale, M. A. (1983). Heuristics in negotiation: Limitations to dispute resolution effectiveness. In M. H. Bazerman and R. Lewicki (Eds.), *Negotiating in organizations* (pp. 51–67). Beverly Hills, CA: Sage.

Beckman, L. J. (1970). Effects of students' performance on teachers' and observers' attributions of causality. *Journal of Educational Psychology, 61,* 76–82.

Beer, J. E. (1986). *Peacemaking in your neighborhood*. Philadelphia: New Society Publishers.

Beier, E. G. (1951). The effect of induced anxiety on flexibility of intellectual functioning. *Psychological Monographs, 65,* 3–26.

Bernard, S., Folger, J. P., Weingarten, H. R., & Zumeta, Z. (1984). The neutral mediator: Value dilemmas in divorce mediation. *Mediation Quarterly, 4,* 61–74.

Bies, R. J., Shapiro, D. L., & Cummings, L. L. (1988). Casual accounts and the management of organizational conflict. *Communication Research, 15,* 381–399.

Billig, M. (1976). *The social psychology of intergroup relations*. New York: Academic Press.

Blake, R. R., & Mouton, J. S. (1964). *The managerial grid*. Houston: Gulf Publishing.

Blake, R. R., Shepard, H., & Mouton, J. S. (1964). *Managing intergroup conflict in industry*. Houston: Gulf Publishing.

Blau, P. (1964). *Exchange and power in social life*. New York: Wiley.

Bormann, E. G. (1972). Fantasy and rhetorical vision: The rhetorical criticism of social reality. *Quarterly Journal of Speech, 58,* 396–407.

Bormann, E. G. (1986). Symbolic convergence theory and communication in group decision-making. In R. Y. Hirokawa & M. S. Poole (Eds.), *Communication and group decision-making* (pp. 219–236). Beverly Hills, CA: Sage.

Bowers, J. W. (1974). Beyond threats and promises. *Communication Monographs, 41,* ix–xi.

Bradley, G. W. (1978). Self-serving biases in the attribution process: A reexamination of the fact or fiction question. *Journal of Personality and Social Psychology, 36,* 56–71.

Brown, B. R. (1977). Face-saving and face-restoration in negotiation. In D. Druckman (Ed.), *Negotiations* (pp. 275–299). Beverly Hills, CA: Sage.

Brown, L. D. (1983). *Managing conflict at organizational interfaces.* Reading, MA: Addison-Wesley.

Brown, P., & Levinson, S. (1978). Universals in language usage: Politeness phenomena. In E. N. Goody (Ed.), *Questions and politeness: Strategies in social interaction* (pp. 56–310). Cambridge: Cambridge University Press.

Brown, P., & Levinson, S. (1987). *Universals in language usage: Politeness phenomena.* Cambridge: Cambridge University Press.

Burgess, P. G. (1973). Crisis rhetoric: Coercion vs. force. *Quarterly Journal of Speech, 59,* 61–73.

Burgoon, J. K., Dillman, L., & Stern, L. A. (1991). *Reciprocity and compensation patterns in dyadic interaction: I. Definitions, operationalizations, and statistical analysis.* Paper presented at the International Communication Association Convention, Chicago.

Burgoon, J. K., & Saine, T. J. (1978). *The unspoken dialogue: An introduction to nonverbal communication.* Boston: Houghton Mifflin.

Burke, K. (1935). *Permanence and change.* Berkeley: University of California Press.

Burke, R. J. (1970). Methods of resolving superior–subordinate conflict: The constructive use of subordinate differences and disagreements. *Organizational Behavior and Human Performance, 5,* 393–411.

Canary, D. J., & Spitzberg, B. H. (1990). Attribution biases and associations between conflict strategies and competence outcomes. *Communication Monographs, 57,* 139–151.

Caplow, T. (1956). A theory of coalitions in the triad. *American Sociological Review, 21,* 489–493.

Carnevale, P. J. (1986). Strategic choice in mediation. *Negotiation Journal, 2,* 41–56.

Carnevale, P. J., Conlon, D. E., Hanisch, K. A., & Harris, K. L. (1989). Experimental research on the strategic-choice model of mediation. In K. Kressel, D. G. Pruitt, & Associates (Eds.), *Mediation research: The process and effectiveness of third party intervention* (pp. 344–367). San Francisco: Jossey-Bass.

Carnevale, P. J., & Pegnetter, R. (1985). The selection of mediation tactics in public sector disputes: A contingency analysis. *Journal of Social Issues, 41*(5), 65–81.

Carnevale, P. J., Putnam, L., Conlon, D. E., & O'Connor, K. M. (1991). Mediator behavior and effectiveness in community mediation. In K. Grover Duffy, J. W. Grosch, & P. V. Olczak (Eds.), *Community mediation: A handbook for practitioners and researchers* (pp. 119–136). New York: Guilford Press.

Chertkoff, J. M., & Esser, J. K. (1976). A review of experiments in explicit bargaining. *Journal of Experimental Social Psychology, 12,* 464–486.

Chertkoff, J. M., & Esser, J. K. (1977). A test of three theories of coalition formation when agreements can be short-term or long-term. *Journal of Personality and Social Psychology, 35,* 237–249.

Cialdini, R. B. (1984). *Influence: How and why people agree to things.* New York: William Morrow & Co.

Conley, J. M., & O'Barr, W. M. (1990). Rules versus relationships in small claims disputes. In A. D. Grimshaw (Ed.), *Conflict talk* (pp. 178–196). Cambridge: Cambridge University Press.

Conrad, C. (1991). Communication in conflict: Style–strategy relationships. *Communication Monographs, 58,* 135–155.

Cooper, J., & Fazio, R. (1979). The formation and persistence of attitudes that support intergroup conflict. In W. G. Austin & S. Worchel (Eds.), *The social psychology of intergroup relations* (pp. 149–159). Monterey, CA: Brooks/Cole.

Coser, L. (1956). *The functions of social conflict.* New York: Free Press.

Coser, L. (1961). The termination of conflict. *Journal of Conflict Resolution, 5,* 347–353.

Cosier, R. A., & Ruble, T. L. (1981). Research on conflict handling behavior: An experimental approach. *Academy of Management Journal, 24,* 816–831.

Cragan, J. F., & Shields, D. C. (1981). *Applied communication research: A dramatistic approach.* Prospect Heights, IL: Waveland.

Craig, R. T., Tracy, K., & Spisak, F. (1986). The discourse of requests: Assessment of a politeness approach. *Human Communication Research, 12,* 437–468.

Crenson, M. A. (1971). *The un-politics of air pollution: A study of nondecision-making in the cities.* Baltimore: Johns Hopkins Press.

Cronen, V., Pearce, B., & Snavely, L. (1980). A theory of rule-structure and types of episodes and a study of perceived enmeshment in undesired repetitive patterns (URPs). In D. Nimmo (Ed.), *Communication yearbook 3* (pp. 225–240). New Brunswick, NJ: Transaction Books.

Dalton, M. (1959). *Men who manage.* New York: Wiley.

Deetz, S., & Mumby, D. (1985). Metaphors, information and power. In B. Ruben (Ed.), *Information and behavior, Volume One* (pp. 369–386). New Brunswick, NJ: Transaction Books.

Delbecq, A., Van de Ven, A., & Gustafsen, D. (1975). *Group techniques for program planning.* Glenview, IL: Scott, Foresman.

Dennis, A. R., George, J., Jessup, L., Nunamaker, J. F. Jr., & Vogel, D. (1988). Information technology to support electronic meetings. *MIS Quarterly, 12,* 591–624.

Deschamps, J. C., & Brown, R. (1983). Superordinate goals and intergroup conflict. *British Journal of Social Psychology, 22,* 189–195.

Deutsch, M. (1973). *The resolution of conflict.* New Haven: Yale University Press.

Deutsch, M., & Krauss, R. M. (1960). The effect of threat upon interpersonal bargaining. *Journal of Abnormal and Social Psychology, 61,* 181–189.

Deutsch, M., & Krauss, R. M. (1962). Studies of interpersonal bargaining. *Journal of Conflict Resolution, 6,* 52–76.

Deutsch, M., & Krauss, R. M. (1965). *Theories in social psychology.* New York: Basic Books.

Dill, W. R. (1965). Business organizations. In J. G. March (Ed.), *Handbook of organizations* (pp. 1071–1141). Chicago: Rand McNally.

Doise, W. (1978). *Groups and individuals*. Cambridge: Cambridge University Press.

Donnellon, A., Gray, B., & Bougon, M. G. (1986). Communication, meaning and organized action. *Administrative Science Quarterly, 31*, 43–55.

Donohue, W. A. (1981). Development of a model of rule use in negotiation interaction. *Communication Monographs, 48*, 106–120.

Donohue, W. A. (1989). Criteria for developing communication theory in mediation. In M. Rahim (Ed.), *Managing conflict: An interdisciplinary approach* (pp. 71–82). New York: Praeger.

Donohue, W. A. (1991). *Communication, marital dispute and divorce mediation*. Hillsdale, NJ: Lawrence Erlbaum.

Donohue, W. A., Diez, M. E., & Hamilton, M. (1984). Coding naturalistic negotiation interaction. *Human Communication Research, 10*, 403–425.

Donohue, W. A., Diez, M. E., & Stahle, R. B. (1983). New directions in negotiation research. In R. W. Bostrom (Ed.), *Communication yearbook 7* (pp. 249–279). Beverly Hills, CA: Sage.

Douglas, A. (1962). *Industrial peacemaking*. New York: Columbia University Press.

Downs, C. W., Smeyak, G. P., & Martin, E. (1980). *Professional interviewing*. New York: Harper & Row.

Duffy, K., Grosch, J. W., & Olczak, P. V. (Eds.) (1991). *Community mediation: A handbook for practitioners and researchers*. New York: Guilford Press.

Ebert, R. J., & Wall, J. A. (1983). Voluntary adoption of negotiation processes. In M. Bazerman & R. Lewicki (Eds.), *Negotiating in organizations* (pp. 91–113). Beverly Hills, CA: Sage.

Edmondson, W. J. (1981). On saying you're sorry. In F. Coulmas (Ed.), *Conversational routine* (pp. 273–288). New York: Moulton Publishers.

Eisenberg, A. R., & Garvey, C. (1981). Children's use of verbal strategies in resolving conflicts. *Discourse Processes, 4*, 149–170.

Ellis, D., & Fisher, B. A. (1975). Phases of conflict in small group development. *Human Communication Research, 1*, 195–212.

Emerson, R. M. (1962). Power-dependence relations. *American Sociological Review, 24*, 31–41.

Endler, N. S., & Magnusson, D. (1976). Toward an interactional psychology of personality. *Psychological Bulletin, 83*, 956–974.

Epstein, S. (1962) The measurement of drive and conflict in humans: Theory and Experiment. In M. R. Jones (Ed.), *Nebraska Symposium on motivation* (pp. 127–209). Lincoln: University of Nebraska Press.

Erikson, E. H. (1950). *Childhood and society*. New York: Norton.

Etzioni, A. (1967). The Kennedy experiment. *Western Political Quarterly, 20*, 361–380.

Etzioni, A. (1968). *The active society*. New York: Macmillan.

Evans, G. (1964). Effect of unilateral promise and value of rewards upon cooperation and trust. *Journal of Abnormal and Social Psychology, 69*, 587–590.

Felstiner, W. L., Abel, R. L., & Sarat, A. (1980–81). The emergence and transformation of disputes: Naming, blaming, claiming. *Law and Society Review, 15*(3–4), 631–654.

Feuille, P. (1979). Selected benefits and costs of compulsory arbitration. *Industrial and Labor Relations Review, 33*(1), 64–76.

Filley, A. (1975). *Interpersonal conflict resolution*. Glenview, IL: Scott, Foresman.

Fink, C. F. (1968). Some conceptual difficulties in the theory of social conflict. *Journal of Conflict Resolution, 12,* 412–460.

Fisher, R. (1964). Fractionating conflict. In R. Fisher (Ed.), *International conflict and behavioral science: The Craigville papers* (pp. 91–109). New York: Basic Books.

Fisher, R. (1969). *International conflict resolution for beginners.* New York: Harper & Row.

Fisher, R., & Ury, W. (1981). *Getting to yes: Negotiating agreement without giving in.* Boston: Houghton Mifflin.

Foa, U. G. (1961). Convergences in the analysis of the structure of interpersonal behavior. *Psychological Review, 6*(8), 341–363.

Folberg, J., & Taylor, A. (1984). *Mediation: A comprehensive guide to resolving conflicts without litigation.* San Francisco: Jossey-Bass.

Folger, J. P. (1980). The effects of vocal participant questioning behavior on perceptions of dominance. *Social Behavior and Personality, 8,* 203–207.

Folger, J. P. (1991). Assessing community dispute resolution needs. In K. Grover Duffy, J. W. Grosch, & P. V. Olczak (Eds.), *Community mediation: A handbook for practitioners and researchers* (pp. 53–69). New York: Guilford Press.

Folger, J. P., & Bernard, S. E. (1985). Divorce mediation: When mediators challenge the divorcing parties. *Mediation Quarterly, 10,* 5–23.

Folger, J. P., & Sillars, A. (1980). Relational coding and perceptions of dominance. In B. Morse & L. Phelps (Eds.), *Interpersonal communication: A relational perspective* (pp. 332–333). Minneapolis: Burgess.

Fraser, B. (1981). On apologizing. In F. Coulmas (Ed.), *Conversational routine* (pp. 259–271). New York: Moulton Publishers.

French, R. P., & Raven, B. (1959). The bases of social power. In D. Cartwright (Ed.), *Studies in social power* (pp. 150–167). Ann Arbor: University of Michigan Press.

Freud, S. (1925). *The unconscious* (J. Riviere, Trans.). London: Hogarth Press.

Freud, S. (1947). *The ego and the id* (J. Stracyey, Trans.). London: Hogarth Press. (Original work published 1923)

Freud, S. (1949). *An outline of psychoanalysis* (J. Stracyey, Trans.). New York: Norton.

Freud, S. (1953). *The interpretation of dreams* (J. Stracyey, Trans.). London: Hogarth Press. (Original work published 1900)

Friedland, N. (1976). Social influence via threats. *Journal of Social Psychology, 88,* 552–563.

Frost, J., & Wilmot, W. (1978). *Interpersonal conflict.* Dubuque, IA: Wm. C. Brown.

Gaelick, L., Bodenhausen, G. V., & Wyer, R. (1985). Emotional communication in close relationships. *Journal of Personality and Social Psychology, 49*(5), 1246–1265.

Gamson, W. A. (1961). A theory of coalition formation. *American Sociological Review, 26,* 373–282.

Gibb, J. (1961). Defensive communication. *Journal of Communication, 2,* 141–148.

Gibbard, G. S., Hartman, J. J., and Mann, R. D. (1974). *Analysis of groups.* San Francisco: Jossey-Bass.

Giles, H., & Powesland, P. F. (1975). *Speech style and social evaluation.* London: Academic Press.

Giles, D., & Wiemann, J. (1987). Language, social comparison and power. In C. R. Berger & S. H. Chaffee (Eds.), *The handbook of communication science* (pp. 350–389). Beverly Hills, CA: Sage.

Goffman, E. (1955). On facework: An analysis of ritual elements in social interaction. *Psychiatry, 18,* 213–231.

Goffman, E. (1957). *Presentation of self in everyday life.* New York: Doubleday.

Goffman, E. (1967). *Interaction ritual: Essays on face-to-face behavior.* Garden City, NY: Doubleday.

Goffman, E. (1974). *Frame analysis: An essay on the organization of experience.* New York: Harper & Row.

Goodwin, M. H. (1982). Processes of dispute resolution among urban black children. *American Ethologist, 9,* 76–96.

Gormly, J., Gormly, A., & Johnson, C. (1972). Consistency of sociobehavioral responses to interpersonal disagreement. *Journal of Personality and Social Psychology, 24,* 221–224.

Gottman, J. M. (1979). *Marital interaction: Experimental investigation.* New York: Academic Press.

Gouldner, A. (1954). *Wildcat strike.* Yellow Springs, OH: Antioch Press.

Gouldner, A. W. (1960). The norm of reciprocity: A preliminary statement. *American Sociological Review, 25,* 161–178.

Gouran, D. S. (1982). *Making decisions in groups.* Glenview, IL: Scott, Foresman.

Greatbatch, D., & Dingwall, R. (1989). Selective facilitation: Some preliminary observations on a strategy used by divorce mediators. *Law and Society Review, 23*(4), 613–641.

Grice, H. P. (1975). Logic and conversation. In P. Cole & J. L. Morgan (Eds.), *Syntax and Semantics,* Vol. 3 (pp. 41–58). New York: Academic Press.

Grimshaw, A. D. (Ed.) (1990). *Conflict talk: Sociolinguistic investigations of arguments in conversations.* Cambridge: Cambridge University Press.

Gross, J. A., & Greenfield, P. A. (1986). Arbitral value judgements in health and safety disputes: Management rights over worker's rights. *Buffalo Law Review, 34,* 645–691.

Guetzkow, H., & Gyr, J. (1954). An analysis of conflict in decision-making groups. *Human Relations, 7,* 367–381.

Gulliver, P. H. (1979). *Disputes and negotiations.* New York: Academic Press.

Hall, C. S. (1979). *A primer of Freudian psychology* (2nd ed.). New York: World.

Hall, C. S., & Lindzey, G. (1970). *Theories of personality.* New York: Wiley.

Hall, J. (1969). *Conflict management survey: A survey on one's characteristic reaction to and handling of conflicts between himself and others.* Monroe, TX: Teleometrics International.

Hall, J., & Watson, W. H. (1970). The effects of a normative intervention on group decision-making performance. *Human Relations, 23,* 299–317.

Hall, R. H. (1972). *Organizations: Structure and process.* Englewood Cliffs, NJ: Prentice-Hall.

Harre, H., & Secord, P. F. (1972). *The explanation of social behavior.* Totowa, NJ: Littlefield Adams.

Harrington, C., & Merry, S. E. (1988). Ideological production: The making of community mediation. *Law and Society Review, 22,* 709–737.

Hawes, L., & Smith, D. H. (1973). A critique of assumptions underlying the study of communication in conflict. *Quarterly Journal of Speech, 59,* 423–435.

Hayes, D. P., & Meltzer, L. (1972). Interpersonal judgments based on talkativeness 1: Fact or artifact? *Sociometry, 35,* 538–561.

Haynes, J. M. (1981). *Divorce mediation: A practical guide for therapists and counselors.* New York: Springer.

Haynes, J. M., & Haynes, G. L. (1989). *Mediating divorce.* San Francisco: Jossey-Bass.

Heider, F. (1958). *The psychology of interpersonal relations.* New York: Wiley.

Heilman, M. E. (1974). Threats and promises: Reputational consequences and the transfer of credibility. *Journal of Experimental Social Psychology, 10,* 310–324.

Heuer, L. B., & Penrod, S. (1986). Procedural preferences as a function of conflict intensity. *Journal of Personality and Social Psychology, 51,* 700–710.

Hewitt, J. P., & Stokes, R. (1975). Disclaimers. *American Sociological Review, 40,* 1–11.

Hilgard, E., & Bower, G. (1966). *Theories of learning.* New York: Appleton-Century-Crofts.

Hill, W. A. (1973). Leadership style: Rigid or flexible? *Organizational Behavior and Human Performance, 9,* 35–47.

Hiltrop, J. M. (1985). Mediator behavior and the settlement of collective bargaining disputes in Britain. *Journal of Social Issues, 41,* 83–99.

Hiltrop, J. M. (1989). Factors associated with successful labor mediation. In K. Kressel, D. G. Pruitt, & Associates (Eds.), *Mediation research: The process and effectiveness of third party intervention* (pp. 241–262). San Francisco: Jossey-Bass.

Hocker, J. L., & Wilmot, W. W. (1985). *Interpersonal conflict.* Dubuque, IA: Wm. C. Brown.

Hollander, E. P., & Julian, J. W. (1969). Contemporary trends in the analysis of leadership processes. *Psychological Bulletin, 71,* 387–397.

Holmes, M. (1992). Phase models of negotiation. In L. Putnam & M. Roloff (Eds.), *Communication perspectives on negotiations* (pp. 83–108). Beverly Hills, CA: Sage.

Holsti, O. R. (1971). Crisis, stress and decision-making. *International Social Science Journal, 23,* 53–67.

Homans, G. C. (1961). *Social behavior: Its elementary forms.* New York: Harcourt, Brace & Jovanovich.

Hu, H. C. (1944). The Chinese concept of "face." *American Anthropologist, 46,* 45–64.

Hunger, J. D., & Stern, L. W. (1976). An assessment of the functionality of the superordinate goal in reducing conflict. *Academy of Management Journal, 19,* 591–605.

Infante, D. A. (1987). Aggressiveness. In J. C. McCroskey & J. A. Daly (Eds.), *Personality and interpersonal communication* (pp. 157–192). Beverly Hills, CA: Sage.

Infante, D. A., & Gorden, W. I. (1985). Superiors' argumentativeness and verbal aggressiveness as predictors of subordinates' satisfaction. *Human Communication Research, 12,* 117–125.

Infante, D. A., & Wigley, C. J. (1986). Verbal aggressiveness: An interpersonal model and measure. *Communication Monographs, 53,* 61–69.

James, L. R., & Jones, A. P. (1974). Organizational climate: A review of theory and research. *Psychological Bulletin, 81,* 1086–1112.

Janeway, E. (1980). *Powers of the weak.* New York: Morrow–Quill.

Janis, I. (1972). *Victims of groupthink*. Boston: Houghton Mifflin.

Janis, I., & Mann, L. (1977). *Decision-making*. New York: Free Press.

Jewell, L. N., & Reitz, H. J. (1981). *Group effectiveness in organizations*. Glenview, IL: Scott, Foresman.

Johnson, D. W., & Johnson, F. P. (1975). *Joining together*. Englewood Cliffs, NJ: Prentice-Hall.

Johnston, H. R. (1976). A new conceptualization of source of organizational climate. *Administrative Science Quarterly, 21*, 95–103.

Jones, E. E., Gergen, K. J., & Jones, R. G. (1963). Tactics of ingratiation among leaders and subordinates in a status hierarchy. *Psychological Monographs, 77*, 120.

Jones, E. E., & Nisbett, R. E. (1971). The actor and the observer: Divergent perceptions of the causes of behavior. In E. E. Jones, E. Kanouse, H. H. Kelley, R. E. Nisbett, S. Valins, & B. Weiner (Eds.), *Attribution: Perceiving the causes of behavior* (pp. 79–94). Morristown, NJ: General Learning Press.

Jones, R. E., & Melcher, B. H. (1982). Personality and preference for modes of conflict resolution. *Human Relations, 35*, 649–658.

Jones, R. E., & White, C. S. (1985). Relationships among personality, conflict resolution styles, and task effectiveness. *Group and Organization Studies, 10*, 152–167.

Jones, T. S. (1988). An analysis of phase structures in successful and unsuccessful divorce mediation. *Communication Research, 15*, 470–495.

Jones, T. S. (1989). Lag sequential analyses of mediator–spouse and husband–wife interaction in successful and unsuccessful divorce mediation. In M. Rahim (Ed.), *Managing conflict: An interdisciplinary approach* (pp. 93–108). New York: Praeger.

Kahneman, D., & Tversky, A. (1979). Prospect theory: An analysis of decision under risk. *Econometrica, 47*, 263–291.

Kanter, R. M. (1977). *Men and women of the corporation*. New York: Basic Books.

Kaplowitz, S. A. (1973). An experimental test of a rationalistic theory of deterrence. *Journal of Conflict Resolution, 17*, 535–572.

Karambayya, R., & Brett, J. M. (1989). Managers handling disputes: Third-party roles and perceptions of fairness. *Academy of Management Journal, 32*(4), 687–704.

Karrass, C. L. (1970). *The negotiating game*. New York: Thomas Crowell.

Katz, R. (1979). Time and work: Toward an integrative perspective. *Research in Organizational Behavior, 2*, 81–127.

Kaufman, S., & Duncan, G. T. (1989). Third party intervention: A theoretical framework. In M. A. Rahim (Ed.), *Managing conflict: An interdisciplinary approach* (pp. 273–289). New York: Praeger.

Kelley, H. H. (1965). Experimental studies of threats in interpersonal negotiations. *Journal of Conflict Resolution, 9*, 79–105.

Kelley, H. H. (1979). *Personal relationships: Their structure and processes*. Hillsdale, NJ: Lawrence Erlbaum.

Kelley, H. H., & Thibaut, J. (1978). *Interpersonal relations: A theory of interdependence*. New York: Wiley.

Kerr, C. A., Schreisheim, C. A., Murphy, C. J., & Stogdill, R. M. (1974). Toward a contingency theory of leadership based upon the consideration and initiating structure literature. *Organizational Behavior and Human Performance, 12*, 62–82.

Kiesler, C. (1971). *The psychology of commitment*. New York: Academic Press.

Kipnis, D. (1990). *Technology and power*. New York: Springer-Verlag.

Kipnis, D., Schmidt, S., & Wilkerson, I. (1980). Intraorganizational influence tactics: Explorations in getting one's way. *Journal of Applied Psychology, 65,* 440–452.

Kochan, T. A., & Jick, T. A. (1978). The public sector mediation process: A theory and empirical examination. *Journal of Conflict Resolution, 22,* 209–241.

Kochman, T. (1981). *Black and white styles in conflict*. Chicago: The University of Chicago Press.

Kolb, D. (1983). *The mediators*. Cambridge, MA: MIT Press.

Kolb, D. (1986). Who are organizational third parties and what do they do? In R. J. Lewicki, B. H. Sheppard, & M. H. Bazerman (Eds.), *Research on negotiation in organizations* (pp. 207–227). Greenwich, CT: JAI Press.

Kolb, D. (1987). Corporate ombudsman and organizational conflict. *Journal of Conflict Resolution, 31,* 763–692.

Kolb, D. (1989). Labor mediators, managers and ombudsmen: Roles mediators play in different contexts. In K. Kressel, D. G. Pruitt, & Associates (Eds.), *Mediation research: The process and effectiveness of third party intervention* (pp. 91–114). San Francisco: Jossey-Bass.

Kolb, D., & Sheppard, B. H. (1985). Do managers mediate or even arbitrate? *Negotiation Journal, 1,* 379–388.

Komorita, S. S. (1977). Negotiating from strength and the concept of bargaining strength. *Journal of the Theory of Social Behavior, 7*(1), 65–79.

Komorita, S., & Chertkoff, J. (1973). A bargaining theory of coalition formation. *Psychological Review, 80,* 149–162.

Krauss, E. S., Rohlen, T. P., & Steinhoff, P. G. (Eds.) (1984). *Conflict in Japan*. Honolulu: University of Hawaii Press.

Kressel, K., Pruitt, D. G., & Associates (Eds) (1989). *Mediation research: The process and effectiveness of third-party intervention*. San Francisco: Jossey-Bass.

Kriesberg, L. (1973). *The sociology of social conflicts*. Englewood Cliffs, NJ: Prentice-Hall.

Lake, L. (1980). *Environmental mediation: The search for consensus*. Boulder, CO: Westview Press.

Lam, J. A., Rifkin, J., & Townley, A. (1989). Reframing conflict: Implications for fairness in parent–adolescent mediation. *Mediation Quarterly, 7*(1), 15–31.

Lawler, E. J., & Youngs, G. A. (1975). Coalition formation: An integrative model. *Sociometry, 38,* 1–17.

Lawrence, P. R., & Lorsch, J. W. (1967). *Organization and environment*. Boston: Division of Research, Harvard Business School.

Leary, T. (1957). *Interpersonal diagnosis of personality*. New York: Ronald Press.

Lemmon, J. A. (1985). *Family mediation practice*. New York: Free Press.

Levinger, G. (1979). A social psychological perspective on marital dissolution. In G. Levinger and O. Moles (Eds.), *Divorce and separation* (pp. 37–60). New York: Basic Books.

Lewin, K. (1951). *Field theory in social science*. New York: Harper Brothers.

Lim, T., & Bowers, J. W. (1991). Face-work: Solidarity, approbation, and tact. *Human Communication Research, 17,* 415–450.

Lindskold, S. (1978). Trust development, the GRIT proposal, and the effects of conciliatory acts on conflict and cooperation. *Psychological Bulletin, 85,* 772–793.

Lindskold, S. (1979). Managing conflict through announced conciliatory initiative backed by retaliatory capacity. In W. G. Austin & S. Worchel (Eds.), *The social psychology of intergroup relations* (pp. 274–287). Belmont, CA: Wadsworth.

Lindskold, S., Betz, B., & Walters, P. S. (1986). Transforming competitive or cooperative climates. *Journal of Conflict Resolution, 30,* 99–114.

Luchins, A., & Luchins, E. (1959). *Rigidity of behavior.* Eugene: University of Oregon Books.

Lukes, S. (1974). *Power: A radical view.* London: MacMillan.

Lyles, M. A., & Mitroff, I. I. (1980). Organizational problem formulation: An empirical study. *Administrative Science Quarterly, 25,* 102–119.

Maier, N. (1967). Assets and liabilities in group problem solving. The need for an integrative function. *Psychological Review, 74,* 239–249.

Marks, J., Johnson, E., & Szanton, P. L. (1984). *Dispute resolution processes in America: Processes in evolution.* Washington, DC: National Institute for Dispute Resolution.

Marwell, G., & Schmitt, D. R. (1967). Dimensions of compliance-gaining behavior: An empirical analysis. *Sociometry, 30,* 350–364.

Mather, L., & Yngvesson, B. (1980–81). Language, audience and the transformation of disputes. *Law and Society Review, 15*(3–4), 775–821.

McGillicuddy, N. B., Pruitt, D. G., Welton, G. L., Zubek, J. M., & Peirce, R. S. (1991). Factors affecting the outcome of mediation: Third-party and disputant behavior. In K. Grover Duffy, J. W. Grosch, & P. V. Olczak (Eds.), *Community mediation: A handbook for practitioners and researchers* (pp. 137–149). New York: Guilford Press.

McLaughlin, M. L. (1984). *Conversation: How talk is organized.* Beverly Hills, CA: Sage.

McLaughlin, M. L., Cody, M. J., & Rosenstein, N. E. (1983). Account sequences in conversations between strangers. *Communication Monographs, 50,* 102–125.

Menkel-Meadow, C. (1985). The transformation of disputes by lawyers: What the dispute paradigm does and does not tell us. *Journal of Dispute Resolution, 2,* 25–44.

Mernitz, S. (1980). *Mediation of environmental disputes.* New York: Praeger.

Merry, S. E. (1979). Going to court: Strategies of dispute resolution in an American urban neighborhood. *Law and Society Review, 13,* 891–925.

Merry, S. E., & Silbey, S. S. (1984). What do plaintiffs want? Reexamining the concept of dispute. *Justice System Journal, 9*(2), 151–178.

Meyer, H. H., Kay, E., & French, J. R. P. Jr. (1965). Split roles in performance appraisal. *Harvard Business Review, 43,* 123–129.

Millar, F. E., & Rogers, L. E. (1987). Relational dimensions of interpersonal dynamics. In M. E. Roloff & G. R. Miller (Eds.), *Interpersonal process: New directions in communication research* (pp. 117–139). Beverly Hills, CA: Sage.

Miller, A. (1976). Constraint and target effects in the attribution of attitudes. *Journal of Experimental Social Psychology, 12,* 325–339.

Miller, G., Galanter, E., & Pribram, K. (1960). *Plans and the structure of behavior.* New York: Holt, Rinehart & Winston.

Miller, G. R., Boster, F., Roloff, M., & Seibold, D. (1976). Compliance-gaining message strategies: A typology and some findings concerning effects of situational differences. *Communication Monographs, 44,* 37–51.

Mischel, W. (1968). *Personality and assessment*. New York: Wiley.

Mishler, E. (1979). Meaning in context: Is there any other kind? *Harvard Educational Review, 19*, 1–19.

Moore, C. W. (1986). *The mediation process*. San Francisco: Jossey-Bass.

Moore, J. C. (1968). Status and influence in small group interaction. *Sociometry, 31*, 47–63.

Morley, I. E., & Stephenson, G. M. (1977). *The social psychology of bargaining*. London: Allen & Unwin.

Moscovici, S. (1976). *Social influence and social change*. New York: Academic Press.

Mura, S. S. (1983). Licensing violations: Legitimate violations of Grice's conversation principle. In R. T. Craig & K. Tracy (Eds.), *Conversational coherence: Form, structure and strategy* (pp. 101–115). Beverly Hills, CA: Sage.

Murnigham, J. K. (1978). Models of coalition behavior: Game theoretic, social psychological, and political perspective. *Psychological Bulletin, 85*, 1130–1153.

Musser, S. J. (1982). A model for predicting the choice of conflict management strategies by subordinates in high-stakes conflicts. *Organizational Behavior and Human Performance, 29*, 257–269.

Neale, M. A., & Northcroft, G. B. (1986). Experts, amateurs, and refrigerators: Comparing expert and amateur decision making on a novel task. *Organizational Behavior and Human Decision Processes, 38*, 305–317.

Neel, A. F. (1977). *Theories of psychology*. New York: Shenkman.

Newell, S. E., & Stutman, R. K. (1988). The social confrontation episode. *Communication Monographs, 55*, 266–285.

Newell, S. E., & Stutman, R. K. (1991). The episodic nature of social confrontation. In A. Andersen (Ed.), *Communication yearbook 14* (pp. 359–392). Beverly Hills, CA: Sage.

North, R. C., Brody, R. A., & Holsti, O. (1963). Some empirical data on the conflict spiral. *Peace Research Society; Papers I*. Chicago Conference, pp. 1–14.

Nutt, P. C. (1984). *Planning methods for health and related organizations*. New York: Wiley.

Osgood, C. E. (1959). Suggestions for winning the real war with communism. *Journal of Conflict Resolution, 3*, 295–325.

Osgood, C. E. (1962). *An alternative to war or surrender*. Urbana: University of Illinois Press.

Osgood, C. E. (1966). *Perspectives on foreign policy* (2nd ed). Palo Alto, CA: Pacific Books.

Papa, M. J., & Natalle, E. J. (1989). Gender, strategy selection, and satisfaction in interpersonal conflict. *Western Journal of Speech Communication, 53*, 260–272.

Peachey, D. E. (1989). What people want from mediation. In K. Kressel, D. G. Pruitt, & Associates (Eds.), *Mediation research: The process and effectiveness of third-party intervention* (pp. 300–321). San Francisco: Jossey-Bass.

Pearce, W. B. (1976). The coordinated management of meaning: A rules-based theory of interpersonal communication. In G. R. Miller (Ed.), *Explorations in interpersonal communication* (pp. 17–35). Beverly Hills, CA: Sage.

Pearce, W. B., & Cronen, V. E. (1980). *Communication, action and meaning*. New York: Praeger.

Pearson, J., & Thoennes, N. (1989). Divorce mediation: Reflections on a decade of research. In K. Kressel, D. G. Pruitt, & Associates (Eds.), *Mediation research: The process and effectiveness of third-party intervention* (pp. 9–30). San Francisco: Jossey-Bass.

Pelz, D. C. (1952). Influence: A key to effective leadership in the first-line supervisor. *Personnel, 29*, 209–217.

Perrow, C. (1986). *Complex organizations: A critical essay.* New York: Random House.

Pfeffer, J. (1978). *Organizational design.* Arlington Heights, IL: AHM Publishing.

Phillips, E., & Cheston, R. (1979). Conflict resolution: What works? *California Management Review, 21*, 76–83.

Phillips, S. U. (1990). The judge as third party in American trial-court conflict talk. In A. D. Grimshaw (Ed.), *Conflict talk* (pp. 197–209). Cambridge: Cambridge University Press.

Pondy, L. R. (1967). Organizational conflict: concepts and models. *Administrative Science Quarterly, 12*, 296–320.

Poole, M. S. (1981). Decision development in small groups I: A comparison of two models. *Communication Monographs, 48*, 1–25.

Poole, M. S. (1982). *A multiple sequence theory of decision development.* Paper presented at Conference on Small Group Communication Research, Pennsylvania State University, April.

Poole, M. S. (1985). Communication and organizational climates. In R. D. McPhee & P. Tompkins (Eds.), *Organizational communication: Traditional themes and new directions* (pp. 79–108). Beverly Hills, CA: Sage.

Poole, M. S. (1991). Procedures for managing meetings: Social and technological innovation. In R. S. Swanson & B. O. Knapp (Eds.), *Innovative meeting management* (pp. 53–110). Austin, TX: 3M Meeting Management Institute.

Poole, M. S., Holmes, M., & DeSanctis, G. (1991). Conflict management in a computer-supported meeting environment. *Management Science, 37*, 926–953.

Poole, M. S., & McPhee, R. D. (1983). Bring intersubjectivity in: A structurational analysis of climate. In L. Putnam & M. Pacanowsky (Eds.), *Communication and organizations: An interpretive approach* (pp. 195–220). Beverly Hills, CA: Sage.

Poole, M. S., & Roth, J. (1989). Decision development in small groups IV: A typology of decision paths. *Human Communication Research, 15*, 323–356.

Poole, M. S., Shannon, D., & DeSanctis, G. (1992). Electronic modes of negotiation. In L. Putnam & M. Roloff (Eds), *Communication and Negotiation* (pp. 46–66). Beverly Hills, CA: Sage.

Powell, G. N., & Butterfield, D. A. (1978). The case for subsystem climate in organizations. *Academy of Management Review, 3*, 151–157.

Pruitt, D. (1971). Indirect communication and the search for agreement in negotiation. *Journal of Applied Social Psychology, 1*, 205–239.

Pruitt, D. G. (1983). Achieving integrative agreements. In M. Bazerman & R. Lewicki (Eds.), *Negotiating in organizations* (pp. 35–50). Beverly Hills, CA: Sage.

Pruitt, D. G., & Johnson, D. F. (1970). Mediation as an aid to face saving in negotiation. *Journal of Applied Social Psychology, 14*, 239–246.

Pruitt, D. G., & Kimmel, M. J. (1977). Twenty years of experimental gaming: Critique, synthesis, and suggestions for the future. *Annual Review of Psychology, 28*, 363–392.

Pruitt, D. G., & Lewis, S. (1977). The psychology of integrative bargaining. In D. Druckman (Ed.), *Negotiations* (pp. 161–192). Beverly Hills, CA: Sage.

Pruitt, D. G., McGillicuddy, N. B., Welton, G. L., & Fry, W. R. (1989). Process of mediation in dispute settlement centers. In K. Kressel, D. G. Pruitt, & Associates (Eds.), *Mediation research: The process and effectiveness of third-party intervention* (pp. 368–393). San Francisco: Jossey-Bass.

Pruitt, D. G., & Rubin, J. (1986). *Social conflict: Escalation, stalemate and settlement.* New York: Random House.

Putnam, L. (Ed.) (1988). Communication and conflict styles in organizations [Special issue]. *Management Communication Quarterly, 1*(3).

Putnam, L. (1990). Reframing integrative and distributive bargaining: A process perspective. In R. J. Lewicki, B. H. Sheppard, & M. H. Bazerman, (Eds.), *Research on negotiation in organizations,* Vol. 2 (pp. 3–30). Greenwich, CT: JAI Press.

Putnam, L., & Folger, J. P. (1988). Communication, conflict and dispute resolution: The study of interaction and the development of conflict theory. *Communication Research, 15,* 349–359.

Putnam, L., & Holmer, M. (1992). Framing, reframing and issue development. In L. L. Putnam and M. E. Roloff (Eds.), *Communication perspectives on negotiations* (pp. 128–155). Beverly Hills, CA: Sage.

Putnam, L., & Jones, T. (1982a). The role of communication in bargaining. *Human Communication Research, 8*(3), 262–280.

Putnam, L., & Jones, T. (1982b). Reciprocity in negotiations: An analysis of bargaining interaction. *Communication Monographs, 49,* 171–191.

Putnam, L., & Poole, M. S. (1987). Conflict and negotiation. In F. Jablin, L. Putnam, K. Roberts, & L. Porter (Eds.), *Handbook of organizational communication* (pp. 549–599). Beverly Hills, CA: Sage.

Putnam, L., & Wilson, C. E. (1982). Communicative strategies in organizational conflicts: Reliability and validity of a measurement scale. In M. Burgoon (Ed.), *Communication yearbook 6* (pp. 629–652). Beverly Hills, CA: Sage.

Putnam, L., Wilson, S., Waltman, M. S., & Turner, D. (1986). The evolution of case arguments in teachers' bargaining. *Journal of the American Forensic Association, 23,* 63–81.

Rahim, M. A. (1983). A measure of styles of handling interpersonal conflict. *Academy of Management Journal, 26,* 369–376.

Rapaport, A. (1960). *Fights, games and debates.* Ann Arbor: University of Michigan Press.

Rapaport, D. (1951). *Organization and pathology of thought.* New York: Columbia University Press.

Raven, B., & Kruglanski, A. (1970). Conflict and power. In Paul Swingle (Ed.), *The structure of conflict* (pp. 69–109). New York: Academic Press.

Reading, S. G., & Ng, M. (1982). The role of face in the organizational perceptions of Chinese managers. *Organization Studies, 3,* 210–229.

Richardson, L. F. (1960). *Arms and insecurity.* Pittsburgh: The Boxwood Press.

Riesel, D. (1985). Negotiation and mediation of environmental disputes. *Ohio State Journal on Dispute Resolution, 1,* 99–111.

Riggs, C. J. (1983). Communication dimensions of conflict tactics in organizational settings: A functional analysis. In R. W. Bostrom (Ed.), *Communication yearbook 7* (pp. 517–533). Beverly Hills, CA: Sage.

Riskin, L. (Ed.) (1985). *Divorce mediation: Readings.* Washington, DC: American Bar Association.

Rogers, S. J. (1987). The dynamics of conflict behavior in a mediated dispute. *Mediation Quarterly, 18*, 61–71.

Roloff, M. E. (1976). Communication strategies, relationships, and relational changes. In G. R. Miller (Ed.), *Explorations in interpersonal communication* (pp. 173–195). Beverly Hills, CA: Sage.

Roloff, M. E. (1981). *Interpersonal communication: The social exchange approach*. Beverly Hills, CA: Sage.

Roloff, M. E. (1987a). Communication and conflict. In C. Berger and S. H. Chaffee (Eds.), *Handbook of communication science* (pp. 484–534). Beverly Hills, CA: Sage.

Roloff, M. E. (1987b). Communication and reciprocity within intimate relationships. In R. E. Roloff & G. R. Miller (Eds.), *Interpersonal processes: New directions in communication research* (pp. 11–38). Beverly Hills, CA: Sage.

Roloff, M. E., & Campion, D. E. (1985). Conversational profit-seeking: Interaction as social exchange. In R. L. Street, Jr., & J. N. Cappella (Eds.), *Sequence and pattern in communicative behavior* (pp. 161–189). London: Edward Arnold.

Roloff, M., & Cloven, D. (1990). The chilling effect in interpersonal relationships: The reluctance to speak one's mind. In D. D. Cahn (Ed.), *Intimates in conflict: A communication perspective* (pp. 49–76). Hillsdale, NJ: Lawrence Erlbaum.

Ross, L. (1977). The intuitive psychologist and his shortcomings: Distortions in the attribution process. In L. Berkowitz (Ed.), *Advances in experimental social psychology, Volume Ten* (pp. 173–220). New York: Academic Press.

Ross, R. G., & DeWine, S. (1988). Communication messages in conflict: A message-focused instrument to assess conflict management styles. *Management Communication Quarterly, 1*, 389–413.

Rowe, M. (1987). The corporate ombudsman. *Negotiation Journal, 3*, 127–141.

Roy, D. F. (1959). "Banana time": Job satisfaction and informal interaction. *Human Organization, 18*, 158–168.

Rubin, J. Z., & Brown, B. (1975). *The social psychology of bargaining and negotiation*. New York: Academic Press.

Rubin, L. (1983). *Intimate strangers*. New York: Harper & Row.

Ruble, T. L., & Thomas, K. W. (1976). Support for a two-dimensional model of conflict behavior. *Organizational Behavior and Human Performance, 16*, 143–155.

Rummel, R. J. (1976). *Understanding conflict and war (Volume Two)*. Beverly Hills, CA: Sage.

Sambamurthy, V., & Poole, M. S. (in press). The effects of level of sophistication of computer support on conflict management in groups. Information Systems Research.

Sarat, A. (1988). The "new formalism" in disputing and dispute processing. *Law and Society Review, 21*(3), 695–715.

Savage, G. T., Blair, J. D., & Sorenson, R. L. (1989). Consider both relationships and substance when negotiating strategically. *The Academy of Management Executive, III*, 37–48.

Scarf, M. (1987). *Intimate partners: Patterns in love and marriage*. New York: Ballantine Books.

Scheff, T. J. (1967). Toward a sociological model of consensus. *American Sociological Review, 32*, 32–46.

Scheidel, T., & Crowell, L. (1979). *Discussing and deciding*. New York: Macmillan.

Schneider, B., & Bartlett, C. J. (1970). Individual differences and organizational climate II:

Measurement of organizational climate by the multi-trait, multi-rater matrix. *Personnel Psychology, 23,* 493–512.

Shapiro, D., Drieghe, R., & Brett, J. (1985). Mediator behavior and the outcome of mediation. *Journal of Social Issues, 41*(2), 101–114.

Sharkey, W. F. (1988). *Embarrassment: A review of literature.* Paper presented the International Communication Association conference, New Orleans, LA.

Sharp, G. (1973). *The politics of nonviolent action.* Boston: Porter-Sargent.

Shenkar, O., & Ronen, S. (1987). The cultural context of negotiations: The implication of Chinese interpersonal norms. *Journal of Applied Behavioral Science, 23,* 263–275.

Sheppard, B. H. (1984). Third party conflict intervention: A procedural framework. In B. Staw & L. L. Cummings (Eds.), *Research in organizational behavior, Volume Six* (pp. 141–190). Greenwich, CT: JAI Press.

Sheppard, B. H., Blumenfeld-Jones, K., & Roth, J. (1989). Informal third partyship: Studies of everyday conflict intervention. In K. Kressel, D. G. Pruitt, & Associates (Eds.), *Mediation research: The process and effectiveness of third-party intervention* (pp. 166–189). San Francisco: Jossey-Bass.

Sheppard, B. H., Saunders, D. M., & Minton, J. W. (1988). Procedural justice from the third-party perspective. *Journal of Personality and Social Psychology, 54,* 629–637.

Sherif, M., Harvey, O. J., White, B. J., Hood, W. R., & Sherif, C. W. (1961). *Intergroup conflict and cooperation: The robber's cave experiment.* Norman, OK: University Book Exchange.

Shubert, J., & Folger, J. P. (1986). Learning from higher education. *Negotiation Journal, 2*(4), 395–406.

Shubik, M. (1987). *Game theory in the social sciences: Concepts and solutions.* Cambridge, MA: MIT Press.

Silbey, S. S., & Merry, S. E. (1986). Mediator settlement strategies. *Law and Policy, 8*(1), 7–32.

Sillars, A. L. (1980a). Stranger and spouse as target persons for compliance gaining strategies. *Human Communication Research, 6,* 265–279.

Sillars, A. L. (1980b). Attributions and communication in roommate conflicts. *Communication Monographs, 47,* 180–200.

Sillars, A. L. (1980c). The sequential and distributional structure of conflict interactions as a function of attributions concerning the locus of responsibility and stability of conflicts. In D. Nimmo (Ed.), *Communication yearbook 4* (pp. 217–235). New Brunswick, NJ: Transaction Press.

Sillars, A. L., Coletti, S. F., Parry, D., & Rogers, M. A. (1982). Coding verbal conflict tactics: Nonverbal and perceptual correlates of the "avoidance–distributive–integrative" distinction. *Human Communication Research, 9,* 83–95.

Sillars, A. L., & Parry, D. (1982). Stress, cognition and communication in interpersonal conflicts. *Communication Research, 9,* 201–226.

Sillars, A. L., & Weisberg, J. (1987). Conflict as a social skill. In M. E. Roloff & G. R. Miller (Eds.), *Interpersonal processes: New directions in communication research* (pp. 140–171). Beverly Hills, CA: Sage.

Simmel, C. (1955). *Conflict.* New York: Free Press.

Simon, H. A. (1955). A behavioral model of rational choice. *Quarterly Journal of Economics, 69,* 99–118.

Singer, L. R. (1990). *Settling disputes*. Boulder, CO: Westview Press.

Skidmore, W. (1979). *Theoretical thinking in sociology* (2nd ed). Cambridge: Cambridge University Press.

Smart, C., & Vertinsky, I. (1977). Designs for crisis decision units. *Administrative Science Quarterly, 22*, 640–657.

Smith, K. I. (1989). The movement of conflict in organizations: The joint dynamics of splitting and triangulation. *Administrative Science Quarterly, 34*, 1–20.

Snyder, M., & Jones, E. E. (1974). Attitude attribution when behavior is constrained. *Journal of Experimental Social Psychology, 10*, 585–600.

Sternberg, R. J., & Soriano, L. J. (1984). Styles of conflict resolution. *Journal of Personality and Social Psychology, 47*, 115–126.

Stevens, C. M. (1963). *Strategy and collective bargaining negotiation*. New York: McGraw-Hill.

Stogdill, R. (1974). *Handbook of leadership*. New York: Free Press.

Stokes, R., & Hewitt, J. P. (1976). Aligning actions. *American Sociological Review, 41*, 838–849.

Street, R. L. Jr., & Cappella, J. N. (1985). Sequence and pattern in communication behavior: A model and commentary. In R. L. Street & J. N. Cappella (Eds.), *Sequence and pattern in communicative behavior* (pp. 243–276). London: Edward Arnold.

Stulberg, J. B. (1987). *Taking charge/managing conflict*. Lexington, MA: Lexington Books.

Stutman, R. K. (1988). *Denying persuasive intent: Transparently false disavowals of intention to influence*. Paper presented at the Western Speech Communication Association Convention, San Diego, CA.

Sullivan, H. S. (1953). *The interpersonal theory of psychiatry*. New York: Norton.

Swensen, C. (1973). *Introduction to interpersonal relations*. Glenview, IL: Scott, Foresman.

Tagiuri, R. (1968). The concept of organizational climate. In R. Tagiuri & G. Litwin (Eds.), *Organizational climate: Explorations of a concept* (pp. 11–32). Boston: Harvard University Press.

Tajfel, H. (1978). *Differentiation between social groups: Studies in the social psychology of intergroup relations*. London: Academic Press.

Tajfel, H., & Turner, J. (1979). An integrative theory of intergroup conflict. In W. G. Austin & S. Worchel (Eds.), *The social psychology of intergroup relations* (pp. 33–48). Monterey, CA: Brooks/Cole.

Tannen, D. (1986). *That's not what I meant*. New York: William Morrow.

Tedeschi, J. T. (1970). Threats and promises. In P. Swingle (Ed.), *The structure of conflict*. (pp. 155–191). New York: Academic Press.

Tedeschi, J. T. (1983). Social influence theory and aggression. In R. G. Geen & E. I. Donnerstein (Eds.), *Aggression: Theoretical and empirical reviews* (pp. 135–162). New York: Academic Press.

Tedeschi, J. T., & Riess, M. (1981). Identities, the phenomenal self, and laboratory research. In J. T. Tedeschi (Ed.), *Impression management theory and social psychological research* (pp. 272–309). New York: Academic Press.

Tedeschi, J. T., Schlenker, B., & Bonoma, T. F. (1973). *Conflict, power, and games*. Chicago: Aldine.

Tedeschi, J. T., Smith, R. B. III, & Brown, R. C. Jr. (1974). A reinterpretation of research on aggression. *Psychological Bulletin, 81,* 540–563.

Thibaut, J., & Kelley, H. H. (1959). *The social psychology of groups.* New York: Wiley.

Thibaut, J., & Walker, L. (1975). *Procedural justice: A psychological analysis.* Hillsdale, NJ: Lawrence Erlbaum.

Thomas, K. W. (1975). Conflict and conflict management. In M. Dunnette (Ed.), *Handbook of industrial psychology.* (pp. 889–935). Chicago: Rand McNally.

Thomas, K. W., & Kilmann, R. H. (1974). *Thomas–Kilmann conflict MODE instrument.* Tuxedo, NY: Xicom.

Thomas, K. W., & Pondy, L. R. (1977). Toward an "intent" model of conflict management among principle parties. *Human Relations, 30,* 1089–1102.

Ting-Toomey, S. (1983). An analysis of verbal communication patterns in high and low marital adjustment groups. *Human Communication Research, 9*(4), 306–319.

Tjosvold, D., & Huston, T. L. (1978). Social face and resistance to compromise in bargaining. *Journal of Social Psychology, 104,* 57–68.

Tracy, K. (1991). The many faces of facework. In H. Giles & R. Robinson (Eds.), *The handbook of language and social psychology* (pp. 209–226). Chichester: Wiley.

Tversky, A., & Kahneman, D. (1981). The framing of decisions and the psychology of choice. *Science, 211,* 453–458.

Van de Vliert, E. (1985). Escalation intervention in small group conflicts. *Journal of Applied Behavioral Science, 21,* 19–36.

Volkema, R. J. (1981). *An empirical investigation of problem formulation and problem-purpose expansion.* Unpublished Ph.D. Thesis, University of Wisconsin, Madison.

Volkema, R. J. (1983). Problem formulation in planning and design. *Management Science, 29*(6), 639–652.

Von Neumann, J., & Morgenstern, O. (1947). *Theory of games and economic behavior.* Princeton, NJ: Princeton University Press.

Vuchinich, S. (1984). Sequencing and social structure in family conflict. *Social Psychology Quarterly, 47*(3), 217–234.

Vuchinich, S. (1986). On attenuation in verbal family conflict. *Social Psychology Quarterly, 49*(4), 281–293.

Vuchinich, S. (1990). The sequential organization of closing in verbal family conflict. In A. D. Grimshaw (Ed.), *Conflict talk* (pp. 118–138). Cambridge: Cambridge University Press.

Wall, J. A., & Rude, D. E. (1989). Judicial mediation of settlement negotiations. In K. Kressel, D. G. Pruitt, & Associates (Eds.), *Mediation research: The process and effectiveness of third-party intervention* (pp. 190–212). San Francisco: Jossey-Bass.

Wall, V. D., Galanes, G. J., & Love, S. B. (1987). Small, task-oriented groups, conflict, conflict management, satisfaction, and decision quality. *Small Group Behavior, 18,* 31–55.

Wall, V. D., & Nolan, L. L. (1987). Small group conflict: A look at equity, satisfaction, and styles of conflict management. *Small Group Behavior, 18,* 188–211.

Walster, E., Berscheid, E., & Walster, G. W. (1973). New directions in equity research. *Journal of Personality and Social Psychology, 25,* 151–176.

Walster, E., Walster, G. W., & Berscheid, E. (1978). *Equity theory and research.* Boston: Allyn & Bacon.

Walton, R. (1969). *Interpersonal peacemaking: Confrontations and third party consultation.* Reading, MA: Addison-Wesley.

Watzlawick, P., Beavin, J., & Jackson, D. (1967). *The pragmatics of human communication.* New York: Norton.

Watzlawick, P., Weakland, J. H., & Fisch, R. (1974). *Change.* New York: Norton.

Wehr, P. (1979). *Conflict regulation.* Boulder, CO: Westview Press.

Welton, G. L. (1991). Parties in conflict: Their characteristics and perceptions. In K. G. Duffy, J. W. Grosch, & P. V. Olczak (Eds.), *Community mediation: A handbook for practitioners and researchers* (pp. 105–118). New York: Guilford Press.

White, R., & Lippitt, R. (1968). Leader behavior and member reaction in three "social climates." In D. Cartwright & A. Zander (Eds.), *Group Dynamics* (3rd ed.) (pp. 318–335). New York: Harper & Row.

Wilmot, J. H., & Wilmot, W. W. (1978). *Interpersonal conflict.* Dubuque, IA: Wm. C. Brown.

Wilson, S. (1978). *Informal groups.* Englewood Cliffs, NJ: Prentice-Hall.

Wish, M., & Kaplan, S. (1977). Toward an implicit theory of interpersonal communication. *Sociometry, 40,* 234–246.

Worchel, S., Anderoli, V. A., & Folger, R. (1977). Intergroup cooperation and intergroup attraction: The effect of previous interaction and outcome of combined effort. *Journal of Experimental Social Psychology, 13,* 131–140.

Zand, D. E. (1972). Trust and managerial problem-solving. *Administrative Science Quarterly, 17,* 229–239.

Zillman, D. (1990). The interplay of cognition and excitation in aggravated conflict among intimates. In D. D. Cahn (Ed.), *Intimates in conflict: A communication perspective* (pp. 187–208). Hillsdale, NJ: Lawrence Erlbaum.

Zuckerman, M. (1979). Attribution success and failure revisited, or: The motivational bias is alive and well in attribution theory. *Journal of Personality, 47,* 245–287.

Credits

Page 72: From *My Dinner with André* by Wallace Shawn and André Gregory. Copyright © 1981 by Wallace Shawn and André Gregory. Reprinted by permission of Grove Press, Inc.

Table 8.1: From J. Hall and W. H. Watson. The effects of a normative intervention on group decision-making performance, *Human Relations*, 23, 299–317 (1970). Reprinted by permission of Plenum Publishing Corporation.

Pages 242–243: Reprinted by permission of R. J. Volkema, Problem formulation in planning and design, *Management Science*, 29(6), June 1983. Copyright © 1983, The Institute of Management Sciences, 290 Westminster Street, Providence, Rhode Island 02903 USA.

Index

Abel, R. L., 295
Accommodating, 32, 183, 189–190, 203
Accounts, 81, 149
Activeness, 183
Adler, A., 13, 85, 291
Affective conflict, 84
Aggression, 15, 54–55
Albrecht, T. L., 157, 291
Alignment actions, 149–150
Allison, G. T., 215, 291
Allport, G., 34, 291
Altercasting, 212
Andreoli, V. A., 223, 309
Anxiety, 16–17, 86
Apfelbaum, E., 84, 101–102, 218, 291
Apologizing, 81, 149
Appeasement, 32
Applegate, J. L., 151, 291
Arbitrator, 257–258, 261
Arendt, H., 99, 291
Argumentativeness, 50
Assertiveness, 31–32, 182, 187, 203
Attribution theory, 52–54, 164–165
Auvine, B., 250, 256, 258, 274, 292
Avery, M., 274, 292
Avoidance, 32, 53, 84–85, 103, 188–189, 203, 231
Axelrod, R., 218, 220, 245, 292

Bachrach, P., 99, 115, 116, 119, 120, 124, 292
Baker, P., 219, 292
Balance of power, 70, 86, 117–125, 183
Balance theory, 83
Bales, R. F., 159, 292
Bandler, R., 239, 292
Baratz, M. S., 99, 115, 116, 119, 120, 124, 292
Bargaining, 8, 146
Bargaining style of intervention, 261–262
Bartlett, C. J., 157, 305
Bartos, O. J., 203, 217, 292

Bateson, G., 92, 239, 292
Baxter, L. A., 197, 292
Bay of Pigs, 116
Bazerman, M. H., 240, 241, 292
Beavin, J., 11, 309
Beckman, L. J., 52, 292
Beer, J., 258, 277, 283, 292
Beier, E. G., 74, 292
Bernard, S., 258, 260, 267, 282, 292, 296
Bersheid, E., 22, 216, 308
Betz, B., 172, 301
Bies, R. J., 188, 292
Billig, M., 18, 34, 38, 292
Blair, J. D., 186, 198, 305
Blake, R. R., 31, 32, 36, 292
Blau, P., 21, 292
Blumenfeld-Jones, K., 270, 306
Bodenhausen, G. V., 71, 296
Bonoma, T. F., 54, 307
Bormann, E., 176, 252, 293
Boster, F., 202, 301
Bougon, M. G., 241, 295
Bower, G., 17, 298
Bowers, J. W., 112, 113, 129, 215, 293, 300
Bradley, G. W., 52, 293
Breakup at the Bakery, 161
Brett, J., 261, 280, 299, 306
Brody, R. A., 11, 302
Brown, B. R., 27, 93, 112, 130, 135, 143, 145, 146, 164, 215, 293, 305
Brown, L. D., 11, 293
Brown, P., 128, 129, 293
Brown, R., 223, 294
Brown, R. C., 55, 308
Budget Cuts in Academia, 96–97
Bundling Boards, 210, 221
Burgess, P. G., 215, 293
Burgoon, J., 64, 114, 293
Burke, K., 73, 293

Burke, R. J., 191, 197, 293
Butterfield, D. A., 157, 303

Campion, D. E., 64, 305
Canary, D. J., 197, 293
Caplow, T., 219, 220, 293
Cappella, J. N., 64, 307
Carnevale, P. J., 265, 266, 267, 282, 293
Caucus, 261–262, 282–283
Chertkoff, J. M., 217, 219, 220, 293, 300
Cheston, R., 184, 188, 196, 303
Chilling effect, 125
Cialdini, R. B., 207, 208, 294
Climate
  characteristics of, 157–158
  competitive, 19–20, 162
  cooperative, 19–20, 162
  and defensiveness, 177–179
  definition, 90, 156
  diagnosis of, 174–177
  and dominance, 159–163
  effects on conflict interaction, 163–165
  and fantasy themes, 176
  and field theory, 18–21
  and group identity, 160–162
  individualistic, 20
  and interdependence, 18–21, 162
  and metaphors, 175–176
  and self-regulation, 249–252
  themes of, 159–163
  and uncertainty, 163–164
  vigilant, 20
Cloven, D., 125, 305
Coalition games, 27
Coalitions, 206, 218–221
Cody, M. J., 81
Coercion, 54–55
Cognitive perspective, 46
Cognitive theories, 48, 50–56
Cohen, S., 159, 292
Collaborating, 32
College Roommates, 192–194
Colletti, S. F., 182
Columnist's Brown Bag, 90
Commitment, 83, 204
Communication style, 5
Competing, 32, 183, 187–188, 196
Competitive climate, 216
Complementary relationship, 190
Compromising, 183, 190–191
Conceding, 189–190, 201
Conciliator, 258–259
Conflict
  arenas, 6–8
  definition, 4
  group, 6
  as interactive behavior, 10–11
  and interdependence, 5
  intergroup, 6–7
  interpersonal, 6
  latent, 86–87, 95, 97

manifest, 87
  productive vs. destructive, 8–10
  realistic vs. nonrealistic, 8
  substantive, 84
Confrontation episodes theory, 59–63
Conley, J. M., 260, 294
Conlon, D. E., 265, 266, 293
Connolly, C., 40
Conrad, C., 186, 192, 294
Consciousness of opposition, 96–97
Constitutive rules, 57
Consulting Agency, 250
Contending, 188, 199
Contrient interdependence, 19–20
Controversial Member, 133
Conversational repairs, 150
Cooperativeness, 32, 182, 187
Cooperative climate, 216
Cooper, J., 35, 36, 37, 294
Coordinated management of meaning, 56–59
Copywriters Committee, 119–120
Coser, L., 5, 8, 13, 16, 37, 294
Cosier, R. A., 32, 185, 190, 196, 294
Counterclaims, 149
Cragan, J. F., 176, 294
Craig, R., 151, 294
Creativity Development Committee, 106
Crenson, M. A., 115, 116, 294
Critical incident, 251–252
Cronen, V., 56, 58, 294, 302
Crowell, L., 237, 239, 305
Cuban missile crisis, 215, 224
Cultural backgrounds, 5, 197–198
Cultural patterns, 57
Cummings, L. L., 188, 292

Dalton, M., 37, 158, 294
Dealmakers, 261
Deetz, S., 124, 294
Defensiveness, 83–84, 177–179, 247
Degrouping, 102
Deindividuation, 102
Delbecq, A., 79, 256, 294
Delia, J., 151, 291
Dennis, A. R., 289, 294
Densmore, E., 250, 292
DeSanctis, G., 289, 303
Deschamps, J. C., 223, 294
Descriptive language, 177
Descriptive theories, 48
Deutsch, M., 9, 14, 18, 19, 20, 21, 64, 70, 82, 99,
  112, 143, 165, 215, 154, 162, 294
DeWine, S., 184, 305
Diez, M. E., 71, 92, 295
Differentiation
  and avoidance, 84–85
  definition 82,
  and escalation, 83–84
  and group-centered interaction, 142
  and rigidity, 85–86
  and triggering events, 97–98

Dilemmas of strength, 118–123
Dillman, L., 64, 293
Dill, W. R., 74, 294
Dingwall, R., 258, 260, 297
Disclaimers, 149
Disclosiveness, 182
Displacement, 16
Dispositional factors, 52
Distributive bargaining, 87
Distributive strategies, 53
Doise, W., 34, 35, 295
Dominance, 159–160, 166–167, 190
Donnellon, A., 241, 295
Donohue, W. A., 71, 92, 163, 266, 268, 271, 278, 282, 283, 295
Douglas, A., 81, 87, 295
Downs, C. W., 105, 295
Drieghe, R., 261, 306
Duffy, K., 258, 295
Duncan, G. T., 256, 258, 299

Ebert, R. J., 198, 202, 295
Eccentric Professor, 103–104
Edmondson, W. J., 81, 295
Ego, 14
Ego ideal, 14
Eisenberg, A. A., 71, 295
Ellis, D., 81, 88, 295
Emerson, R., 100, 295
Empowerment, 182, 183
Endler, N. S., 184, 295
Entitlement, 207
Environmental disputes, 258
Episodes, 57, 59–63, 80–82
Epstien, S., 146, 295
Erikson, E. H., 13, 295
Escalation, 83–84, 231
Esser, J. K., 217, 293
Etzioni, A., 224, 238, 295
Evans, G., 215, 295
Excuses, 149
Expanding Printing Company, 250–251
Experimental gaming
   basic assumptions of, 23–25
   criticisms of, 28–31
   and the prisoner's dilemma, 23–27
   value for understanding conflict, 27–28
Experimental integration, 213, 223–224
Extrom, M., 250, 292

Face
   in Chinese culture, 128
   definition, 128
   dimensions of, 128–129
Face-giving, 148–152
Face-loss, 129–130
Face-saving
   and conflict interaction, 136–143
   definition, 130

forms of, 143–148
and relationships, 93
and self-regulation, 246–249
as threat to flexibility, 130–136
Face threatening act, 128–129
Facilitator, 258–259
Fantasy themes, 176
Fazio, R., 35, 36, 37, 294
Felstiner, W. L., 260, 295
Feuille, P., 261, 295
Field theory, 18–21
Filley, A., 32, 184, 190, 196, 238, 275, 296
Fink, C. F., 4, 296
Firm compromising, 190, 199, 201
Fisch, R., 239, 309
Fisher, B. A., 81, 88, 273, 295, 296
Fisher, R., 77, 208, 213, 222
Flexible compromising, 190, 199
Foa, U. G., 159, 296
Fogging, 209, 221–222
Folberg, J., 70, 117, 258, 271, 274, 279, 281, 296
Folger, J. P., 7, 135, 168, 255, 258, 260, 267, 256, 292, 296, 304, 306
Folger, R., 223, 309
Food Cooperative Newsletter, 76–77
Food Distribution Company, 262–263
Forcing, 32, 196
Fractionation, 208, 222
Fraser, B., 81, 296
French, J. R. P., 100, 105, 296, 301
Freud, S., 13, 296
Friedland, N., 216, 296
Frost, J., 232, 296
Fry, W. R., 282, 304

Gaddis, W., 118
Gaelick, L., 71, 296
Galanes, G. J., 197, 308
Galanter, E., 74, 301
Game research, 219–220
Gamesmanship, 205
Gamson, W. A., 219, 220, 296
Garvey, C., 71, 295
George, J., 289, 294
Gergen, K. J., 120, 299
Gibbard, G. S., 137, 296
Gibb, J., 83, 144, 177, 178, 247, 296
Giles, H., 35, 124, 296, 297
Goal-emphasis, 74–77
Goffman, E., 128, 129, 137, 146, 148, 151, 239, 297
Going off-record, 129
Goodwin, M. H., 71, 297
Gorden, W. I., 51, 298
Gormly, A., 184, 297
Gormly, J., 184, 297
Gottman, J., 64, 77, 297
Gouldner, A., 37, 64, 297
Gouran, D., 20, 237, 297
Gray, B., 241, 295
Greatbatch, D., 258, 260, 297

Greenfield, P. A., 266, 297
Gregory, A., 72
Grice, H. P., 150, 297
Grimshaw, A., 5, 297
Grinder, J., 239, 292
GRIT, 224, 276, 283
Grosch, J. W., 258, 295
Gross, J. A., 266, 297
Group-centered interaction, 137–143
Group differentiation, 35
Group identity, 161–162
Groupthink, 116–117
Guetzkow, H., 84, 274, 297
Gulliver, P. H., 81, 297
Gunnysacking, 204
Gustafsen, D., 79, 294
Gyr, J., 84, 274, 297

Hall, C. S., 14, 15, 297
Hall, J., 31, 80, 184, 238, 297
Hall, R. H., 78, 297
Hamilton, M., 71, 295
Hanisch, K. A., 265, 266
Harre, H. 80, 297
Harrington, C., 281, 297
Harris, K. L., 265, 266, 293
Hartman, J. J., 137, 296
Harvey, O. J., 36, 223, 306
Hawes, L., 5, 298
Hayes, D. P., 168, 298
Haynes, G. L., 258, 298
Haynes, J. M., 258, 271, 298
Heider, F., 52, 298
Heilman, M. E., 215, 298
Heuer, L. B., 259, 298
Hewett, J. P., 149, 298, 307
Hilgard, E., 17, 298
Hill, W. A., 184, 298
Hiltrop, J. M., 266, 282, 298
Hocker, J. L., 4, 298
Hollander, E. P., 264, 298
Holmer, M., 241, 277, 304
Holmes, M., 81, 298, 303
Holsti, O. R., 11, 74, 86, 298, 302
Homans, G. C., 21, 22, 298
Hood, W. R., 36, 223, 306
Hu, H. C., 128, 298
Human relations theory, 31–33
Hunger, J. D., 223, 298
Huston, T. L., 146, 308

Id, 14
Individual-centered interaction, 137–143
Infante, D. A., 50, 51, 298
Ingratiation, 120, 207
Initiation phase, 86
Integration, 82–83
Integrative decision making, 275–276
Integrative strategies, 53
Integrative style, 32
Integrative tactics, 212, 223–225

Interactional perspective, 47–48
Interactional theories, 48, 56–65
Interdependence, 19–20
Intergroup conflict, 33–38
Intergroup ideologies, 37–38
Interpersonal reflex, 83, 218
Intervention mandate, 256–260
Investigator style of intervention, 262
Issue control, 112, 115–117, 124, 209
Issue expansion, 210

Jackson, D., 11, 309
James, L. R., 154, 298
Janeway, E., 99, 102, 103, 125, 221, 235, 236, 298
Janis, I., 8, 20, 37, 74, 80, 83, 116, 117, 146, 299
Jessup, L., 289, 294
Jewell, L. N., 100, 299
Jick, T. A., 266, 300
Job Resignation at the Social Service Agency, 122–123
Johnson, C., 184, 297
Johnson, D. F., 135, 303
Johnson, D. W., 250, 299
Johnson, E., 255, 301
Johnson, F. P., 250, 299
Johnston, H. R., 157, 299
Joint fact-finding, 213
Jones, A. P., 154, 298
Jones, E. E., 52, 120, 299, 307
Jones, R. E., 184, 196, 299
Jones, R. G., 120, 299
Jones, T. S., 64, 71, 87, 268, 282, 271, 272, 299, 304
Julian, J. W., 264, 298
Justifications, 149

Kahneman, D., 240, 299, 308
Kanter, R. M., 158, 299
Kaplowitz, S. A., 216, 299
Kaplan, S., 159, 309
Karambayya, R., 280, 299
Karass, C. L., 71, 299
Katz, R., 77, 299
Kaufman, S., 256, 258, 299
Kay, E., 105, 301
Kelley, H. H., 21, 23, 26, 27, 112, 125, 215, 299, 308
Kerr, C. A., 299
Key communicators, 157
Kiesler, C., 83, 300
Kilmann, R. H., 184, 308
Kimmel, M. J., 21, 27, 225, 303
Kipnis, D., 100, 103, 109, 111, 118, 120, 125, 202, 300
Kochan, T. A., 266, 300
Kochman, T., 5, 300
Kolb, D., 260, 261, 262, 269, 277, 280, 283, 300
Komorita, S. S., 121, 219, 220, 300
Krauss, E. S., 197, 300
Krauss, R. M., 14, 18, 64, 143, 294
Kreisberg, L., 10, 71, 81, 306

Kressel, K., 266, 300
Kruglanski, A., 120, 217, 304

Labeling tactic, 210
Labor mediation, 261
Lake, L., 258, 300
Lam, J. A., 260, 277, 300
Last-offer-best-offer, 261
Latent conflict, 86–87, 95, 97
Lawler, E. J., 220, 300
Lawrence, P. R., 197, 300
Leary, T., 83, 218, 300
Lemmon, J. A., 258, 278, 283, 300
Levinger, G., 7, 300
Levinson, S., 128, 129
Lewin, K., 18, 19, 22, 300
Lewis, S., 84, 303
Lien, 128
Life-space, 18–19
Lim, T., 129, 300
Lindskold, S., 172, 224, 276, 301
Lindzey, G., 14, 297
Lippitt, R., 20, 309
Logrolling, 206
Lorsch, J. W., 197, 300
Love, S. B., 197, 308
Luchins, A., 86, 301
Luchins, E., 86, 301
Lukes, S., 116, 301
Lyles, M. A., 243, 301

McGillicuddy, N. B., 282, 301, 304
Machiavellianism, 184
McLauglin, M. L., 81, 150, 301
McPhee, R., 158, 159, 303
Magliozzi, T., 241, 292
Magnusson, D., 184, 295
Maier, N., 75, 301
Malevolent cycling, 83
Manifest conflict, 87
Mann, L., 20, 74, 83, 146, 299
Mann, R. D., 137, 296
Marks, J., 255, 301
Martin, E., 105, 295
Marwell, G., 202, 205, 212, 301
Matching, 27, 217–218
Mather, L., 241, 260, 301
Matrix games, 27
Mediator, 258
Melcher, B. H., 184, 299
Meltzer, L., 168, 298
Menkel-Meadow, C., 241, 301
Mernitz, S., 258, 301
Merry, S., 255, 260, 261, 281, 297, 301, 306
Meta-communication, 210, 222–223
Metaphors, 175–176
Meyer, H. H., 105, 301
Mien-tzu, 128
Millar, F., 190, 301
Miller, A., 52, 301
Miller, G., 74, 301

Miller, G. R., 202, 301
Mindguards, 116
Minimum power theory, 219–220
Minimum resource theory, 219–220
Minton, J. W., 259, 306
Mischel, W., 184, 302
Mishler, E., 302
Mitroff, I. I., 243, 300
Moore, C. W., 271, 302
Moore, J. C., 101, 302
Moral appeal, 212
Morgenstern, O., 23, 308
Morley, I. E., 81, 87, 302
Moscovici, S., 34, 77, 302
Motivational control, 259
Mouton, J. S., 31, 32, 36, 292
Mumby, D., 124, 294
Mura, S. S., 150, 302
Murnigham, J. K., 219, 302
Murphy, C. J., 299
Musser, S. J., 43, 198, 202, 302

Natalle, E. J., 184, 192, 302
Neale, M. A., 240, 241, 292, 302
Neel, A. F., 18, 302
Negative face, 128
Negative inquiry, 209, 221
Negotiation frame, 277–278
Negotiation games, 27
Negotiations, 8, 87, 146
Negotiation support room, 285
Negotiation support system, 284–288
Newell, S. E., 59, 60, 61, 81, 302
Ng, M., 304
Nisbett, R. E., 52, 299
Nolan, L. L., 189, 197, 308
Nominal group technique, 79
Nondecisions, 115–116
Non-key communicators, 157
Norm of reciprocity, 64
North, R. C., 11, 302
Northcroft, G. B., 241, 302
Nunamaker, J. F., 289, 294
Nutt, P. C., 239, 302

O'Barr, W. M., 260, 294
Objectivity norm, 77
O'Connor, 265, 293
Olczak, P. V., 258, 295
Orchestrators, 261
Osgood, C. E., 224, 276, 302

Papa, M., 184, 192, 302
Parking Lot Scuffle, 49–50
    and attribution theory, 53–54
    and confrontation episodes theory, 63
    and the coordinated management of meaning, 58
    and reciprocity theory, 65
    and social influence theory, 55–56
    and verbal aggressiveness theory, 51

Park, R., 34
Parry, D., 52, 53, 182, 306
Peachey, D. E., 282, 302
Pearce, W. B., 56, 58, 294, 302
Pearson, J., 281, 302
Pegnetter, R., 265, 267, 293
Peirce, R. S., 282, 301
Pelz, D. C., 113, 303
Penrod, S., 259, 298
Perrow, C., 31, 33, 303
Perspective-taking, 151
Perspectivism, 40–43
Pfeffer, J., 116, 117, 303
Phases, 81–90
Phillips, E., 184, 188, 196, 303
Phillips, S. U., 261, 303
Pleasure principle, 14
Pluralistic ignorance, 35
Politeness theory, 128–129
Pondy, L. R., 53, 81, 87, 95, 97, 164, 165, 175, 303, 308
Poole, M. S., 6, 8, 78, 81, 88, 89, 157, 158, 159, 184, 197, 237, 243, 250, 289, 292, 303, 304, 305
Position loss, 283
Positive face, 128
Powell, G. W., 157, 303
Power
    and conflict interaction, 106–111
    and conflict tactics, 111–117
    definition, 69
    and emergence of conflict, 95–99
    endorsement of, 99–106
    and moves and countermoves, 69
    mystique of, 103
    relational view of, 99–106
    and resources, 100
    and self-regulation, 231
Powesland, P. F., 35, 296
Precueing, 211
Predictive theories, 48
Pregiving, 205
Pribram, K., 74, 301
Prisoner's dilemma, 23–25
Problem purpose expansion, 242–245
Problem-solving, 32, 87, 123, 183, 190, 191–192, 196–197, 199
Productivity/Performance Report, 248
Professor's Decision, 131
Promises, 112–113, 205, 215–217
Promotive interdependence, 19–20
Protecting, 188, 199
Pruitt, D., 21, 27, 70, 84, 102, 117, 120, 135, 145, 164, 192, 198, 204, 205, 206, 207, 211, 215, 217, 223, 225, 257, 266, 274, 282, 283, 300, 301, 303, 304
Psychodynamics, 13–18
Psychological Evaluation Unit, 166–170
Punctuating conflict, 42
Putnam, L., 6, 7, 8, 43, 64, 71, 87, 197, 202, 184, 190, 241, 245, 265, 277, 293, 304

Quasi theories, 149
Quid pro quo, 202, 206

Radio Station, 263–265
Rahim, M. A., 43, 184, 304
Rapaport, A., 247, 304
Rapaport, D., 13, 304
Raven, B., 100, 120, 217, 296, 304
Raw sensory data, 57
Reading, S. G., 304
Reality principle, 15
Reciprocity theory, 63–65
Reflective thinking process, 237–239
Reitz, H. J., 100, 299
Reformed sinner, 212, 224–225
Reframing
    interaction, 245–246
    issues, 240–245
    in third party intervention, 276–278
Regulative rules, 57
Relational control, 112–115
Remedies, 150
Repetitive cycles, 63–65, 70–72, 267–270
Resisting unjust intimidation, 143–145
Restructuring, 262
Richardson, L. F., 11, 304
Riesel, D., 258, 304
Riess, M., 149, 307
Rifkin, J., 260, 300
Right-wrong frame, 277–278
Rigidity, 85–86, 163–164
Riggs, C. J., 183, 186, 304
Riskin, L., 255, 304
Riverdale Halfway House, 155–156
Robber's cave experiment, 223
Robert's rules of order, 79
Rogers, L. E., 190, 301
Rogers, M. A., 182, 306
Rogers, S. J., 305
Rohlen, T. P., 197, 300
Roloff, M. E., 6, 7, 21, 22, 23, 64, 111, 125, 202, 301, 303, 305
Romen, S., 38, 306
Rosenstein, N. E., 81
Ross, L., 52, 305
Ross, R. G., 184, 305
Roth, J., 88, 270, 306
Rowe, M., 256, 305
Roy, D. F., 158, 172, 305
Rubin, J. Z., 27, 70, 102, 112, 117, 120, 164, 198, 204, 205, 206, 207, 211, 215, 217, 223, 274, 304, 305
Rubin, L., 11, 305
Ruble, T. L., 31, 32, 183, 185, 190, 196, 294, 305
Rude, D. E., 261, 308
Rummel, R. J., 81, 86, 95, 97, 117, 305

Saine, T. J., 114, 293
Sambamurthy, V., 81, 89, 184, 197, 305
Sarat, A., 260, 295, 305
Saunders, D. M., 259, 306

Savage, G. T., 186, 198, 202, 305
Scarf, M., 11, 305
Scheff, T., 35, 305
Scheidel, T., 237, 239, 305
Schlenker, B., 54, 307
Schmidt, S., 100, 300
Schmitt, D. R., 202, 205, 212, 301
Schneider, B., 157, 305
Schreisheim, C. A., 299
Secord, P. F., 80, 297
Seibold, D., 202, 301
Self-regulation, 230–231
Shanklin, M., 250, 292
Shannon, D., 289, 303
Shapiro, D., 261, 269, 282, 292
Shapiro, D. L., 188, 306
Sharkey, W. F., 130, 306
Sharp, G., 111, 202, 306
Shawn, W., 72
Shenkar, O., 38, 306
Shepard, H., 36, 306
Sheppard, B. H., 257, 259, 270, 271, 272, 277,
     280, 283, 300
Sherif, C. W., 36, 223, 306
Sherif, M., 36, 223, 306
Shields, D. C., 176, 294
Shubert, J. J., 135, 256, 306
Shubik, M., 23, 306
Silbey, S., 260, 261, 301, 306
Sillars, A. L., 52, 53, 71, 164, 165, 168, 182, 184,
     192, 197, 203, 204, 222, 296, 306
Simmel, G., 83, 306
Simon, H. A., 29, 306
Singer, L. R., 255, 258, 307
Single text method, 213
Skidmore, W., 30, 307
Smart, C., 74, 86, 307
Smeyak, G. P., 105, 295
Smith, D., 5, 298
Smith, K. I., 16, 307
Smith, R. B., 55, 308
Smoothing, 32, 189, 199
Snavely, L., 58, 294
Snyder, M., 52, 307
Social categorization, 34–35, 101
Social exchange theory
     basic assumptions of, 22–23
     criticisms of, 28–31
     value for understanding conflict, 28
Social influence theory, 54–56
Social norms, 77
Sorenson, R. L., 186, 198, 305
Soriano, L. J., 184, 307
Speech acts, 56–57
Spisak, F., 151, 294
Spitzberg, B. H., 197, 293
Stahle, R. B., 92, 295
Steinhoff, P. G., 197, 300
Stephenson, G. M., 81, 87, 302
Stereotypes, 36–37
Sternberg, R. J., 184, 307

Stern, L. A., 64, 293
Stern, L. W., 223, 298
Stevens, C. M., 146, 307
Stogdill, R., 113, 184, 299, 307
Stokes, R., 149, 298, 307
Stop frame, 277–278
Street, R. L., 64, 307
Streibel, B., 274, 292
Structured procedures, 78
Stulberg, J. B., 258, 271, 279, 281, 307
Stutman, R. K., 59, 60, 61, 81, 149, 302,
     307
Styles of conflict
     decision tree for selecting, 199
     definition, 184–186
     and human relations theory, 31–33
     as orientation to conflict, 182
     and personality, 184
     selecting, 195–202
     shifting during episodes, 192–195
     tests of, 184
     types of, 182–184
     variations of, 186–192
Submissiveness, 190
Substantive conflict, 84
Sullivan, H. S., 13, 307
Superego, 14
Superordinate goals, 223
Supportiveness, 160–161
Suppression, 15
Swensen, C., 83, 307
Szanton, P. L., 255, 301

Tacit coordination, 211
Tactics
     definition, 202
     effects of episodic context, 202
     relationship to styles, 202–203
     ratings on descriptive dimensions, 203–214
Tagiuri, R., 158, 307
Tajfel, H., 34, 307
Tannen, D., 5, 307
Taylor, A., 70, 117, 258, 271, 274, 279, 281, 296
Tedeschi, J. T., 54, 55, 112, 149, 215, 217, 307,
     308
Testing period, 88–89
Theory
     cognitive and interactional theories compared,
          48–64
     role in conflict, 43–45
Therapeutic style of intervention, 261–262
Thibaut, J., 21, 23, 26, 27, 259, 299, 308
Third party intervention
     definition, 254
     and differentiation, 273–274
     influence on climate, 278–280
     influence on face-saving, 282–283
     influence on framing issues, 276–278
     and integration, 273–276
     and interaction sequences, 270–276
     orientations to, 265–266

Third party intervention (*Continued*)
 and responsiveness to interaction, 260–267
 and self-perpetuating interaction, 267–270
Thoennes, N., 281, 302
Thomas, K. W., 31, 32, 53, 164, 165, 175, 183,
 184, 185, 198, 305, 308
Thomas, W. I., 34
Threats, 203, 112–113, 215–217
Ting-Toomey, S., 71, 308
Tit-for-tat, 27, 206, 217–218, 245
Tjosvold, D., 146, 308
Toughness, 203, 217
Townley, A., 260, 300
Tracy, K., 151, 294, 308
Trained incapacities
 and climate, 173
 definition, 73
 and goal emphasis, 74–77
 and objective standards, 77–78
 and self-regulation, 237–246
 and structured procedures, 78–80
 and working habits, 72–73
Triggering event, 86, 88, 97
Trust, 200
Turner, D., 87, 304
Turner, J., 34, 307
Tversky, A., 240, 299, 308
Two-column method, 210, 222

Umbrella issues, 208, 221
Unbalanced Intimacy, 121
Underlying frame, 277–278
Unfreezing, 231
Unwanted repetitive patterns, 58
Ury, W., 77, 213, 273, 296
U.S. Steel, 115–117

Van de Ven, A., 79, 294
Van de Vliert, E., 273, 308
Verbal aggressiveness theory, 50–51
Vertinsky, I., 74, 86, 307
Violence, 8
Vogel, D., 289, 294
Volkema, R., 242, 243, 308
Von Neumann, J., 23, 308
Vuchinich, S., 64, 71, 72, 308

Walker, L., 259, 308
Wall, J. A., 198, 202, 295, 308
Wall, V. D., 189, 197, 308
Walster, E., 22, 216, 308
Walster, G. W., 22, 216, 308
Walters, P. S., 172, 301
Waltman, M. S., 87, 304
Walton, R., 82, 83, 97, 117, 120, 208, 210, 221,
 249, 272, 279, 281, 309
Watson, W. H., 80, 238, 297
Watzlawick, P., 11, 92, 113, 136, 239, 309
Weakland, J. H., 239, 309
Wehr, P., 117, 258, 309
Weingarten, H., 258, 292
Weisberg, J., 197, 222, 306
Weiss, L., 274, 292
Welton, G. L., 282, 283, 301, 304, 309
White, B. J., 36, 223, 306
White, C. S., 196, 299
White, R., 20, 309
Wiemann, J., 124, 297
Wigley, C. J., 50, 298
Wilkerson, I., 100, 300
Wilmot, W. W., 28, 32, 100, 111, 202, 204, 209,
 232, 296, 298, 309
Wilson, C. E., 43, 184, 190, 304
Wilson, S., 87, 101, 161, 304, 304, 309
Wish, M., 159, 309
Withdrawing, 188–189, 199
Women's Hotline, 2–3
Worchel, S., 223, 309
Working habits, 72–74, 237–240
Work Stoppage Decision, 79–80
Would-Be Borrower, 225–227
Wyer, R., 71, 296

Yielding, 189, 199
Yngvesson, B., 241, 260, 301
Youngs, G. A., 220, 300

Zand, D. E., 165, 309
Zillman, D., 74, 309
Zubek, J. M., 282, 301
Zuckerman, M., 52, 309
Zumeta, Z., 258, 292